D0074924

# KING ARTHUR

# KING ARTHUR

## MYTH-MAKING AND HISTORY

— ·◆· —

## N. J. Higham

London and New York

First published 2002
by Routledge
11 New Fetter Lane, London EC4P 4EE

Simultaneously published in the USA and Canada
by Routledge
29 West 35th Street, New York, NY 10001

*Routledge is an imprint of the Taylor & Francis Group*

© 2002 N. J. Higham

Typeset in Garamond by
Keystroke, Jacaranda Lodge, Wolverhampton
Printed and bound in Great Britain by
Biddles Ltd, Guildford and King's Lynn

*British Library Cataloguing in Publication Data*
A catalogue record for this book is available from the British Library

*Library of Congress Cataloging in Publication Data*
Higham, N.J.
King Arthur : myth-making and history / N.J. Higham.
p.   cm.
Includes bibliographical references and index.
1. Arthur, King. 2. Great Britain–History–To 1066–Historiography.
3. Britons–Kings and rulers–Folklore. 4. Mythology, Celtic–Great Britain.
5. Historiography–Great Britain. 6. Arthurian romances–Sources.
7. Britons–Historiography. 8. Mythology, British. I. Title.
DA152.5.A7 H53 2002
942.01′4–dc21        2001058586

ISBN 0–415–21305–3

FOR CHERYL

# CONTENTS

——— .•. ———

# — Contents —

# FIGURES

———— ·•· ————

# ACKNOWLEDGEMENTS

—— •◆• ——

I should like to thank the University of Manchester for the year's sabbatical leave (in 2000–01) which has enabled me to write a book which has been slowly evolving in my mind for some time. Assistance with post-Conquest medieval historiography was very kindly provided by Carole Weinberg, and Dr Paul Holder of the John Rylands University Library as ever assisted in the provision of appropriate literature. Dr Elizabeth Tyler very kindly read Chapter III in draft and commented thereon extensively. Professor Peter Schrijver and Professor Richard Coates kindly provided expert opinion on the philological history of the name 'Arthur'. Dr Andrew Breeze provided valuable advice concerning early Welsh literature and its dating. Rosa Vidal typed the first draft of the bibliography and Martin Ryan provided invaluable assistance in proof-reading as well as undertaking crucial computer-based searches. Christopher Gidlow originally suggested to me the implicit parallel between Gildas's animal metaphors and Daniel's visions. An original hand-list by Elizabeth Johnson provided the basis from which Figure 18 was developed and Figures 1, 2, and 3 were based with permission on the published work of Professor John Hines. Dr Nancy Edwards kindly advised me regarding the disputed reading of the text on the slab-cross at Llanrhaeadr-ym-Mochnant. Professor David Mattingly very kindly allowed me to reproduce Figure 8. The following generously provided plates: Professor Chris Morris and Dr Coleen Batey (9), David Higham (15, 17), Bob Sylvester and the staff of the Clwyd-Powys Archaeological Trust (21, 28, 29), Margaret Worthington (22) and Derek Seddon (25). To all go my grateful thanks. The absence of these many kindnesses would have seriously detracted from the form and fabric of the final outcome. All opinions expressed, however, and likewise all mistakes remain exclusively my own.

I owe my greatest thanks to my wife, Cheryl, and family, James, Naomi and Alex, who have had to live with the processes of research and writing, and with the resultant mood swings and self-absorption which have been a consequence. This work is dedicated in gratitude to my wife, without whom my life would be infinitely less rich.

# INTRODUCTION

——— •◆• ———

The candid historian must admit that the evidence on the subject . . .
is meagre, relatively late, and almost wholly fantastic.

(Bruce 1923: 1)

The past century, or so, has witnessed a considerable, and on occasion quite
vehement, debate concerning whether or not King Arthur actually existed.
On the one side, belief in Arthur as a real figure in real time and space has
become deeply entrenched. On the other, several scholars have urged caution
or even sought to argue the negative, that no historical Arthur ever existed.
There is obviously a great gulf between these two positions, but not even the
'real' Arthur positivists are in any sort of agreement. Some have proposed
imperial Arthurs, whose power waxed and waned over the whole island, while
others offer lesser kings of petty polities at various dates and in several
different regions of Britain. Lying behind this debate are a host of issues about
local and regional identity and Arthur as a 'Celtic' (versus 'English' or
'Germanic') icon. Beyond those, even, is the entire mercantile perspective,
within which Arthur's name, recognition and reputation are used to brand
anything from lottery tickets and hotel rooms to bells and bangles – and
books, of course. Arthur's Camelot has been used variously by Hollywood
and by novelists, and to promote a particular cult of the White House under
J. F. Kennedy. While most historical debates never impact outside of
professional circles, the issue of Arthur is distinguished by its very public
nature and wide resonance.

On the face of it, the longevity, robustness and popularity of this debate
may seem surprising. On the basis of textual evidence, Arthur was widely
considered implausible as an historical figure in the late Victorian era, when
he was most often interpreted in mythological terms as a Brittonic culture-
hero or demi-god. Even those late nineteenth-century historians who
considered Arthur potentially historical conceived of him as a figure of little
relevance to the dominant historical enterprises of the day. Their principal
interest in the early Middle Ages lay in seeking in the past the unique qualities
of the English people and their institutions, to legitimize and underline

current self-perceptions of political, colonial, cultural and economic power and identity. Such 'truths' as might be deemed capable of underpinning elevated conceptions of Victorian civilization were sought primarily in the Anglo-Saxon and Germanic past, rather than Romano-British or British ones (Frantzen 1990; for further discussion see Chapter V). This powerful, Anglo-Saxonist and imperialist enterprise necessarily had little occasion to acknowledge an Arthur who, if he existed at all, did so merely to oppose the great destiny of the Germanic peoples in Britain, and threaten the historical continuum linking the Anglo-Saxon settlement with the Victorian establishment. He seemed, therefore, an aberrant figure swimming against a tide of history which was flowing ever onwards towards English civilization, and a British Empire which its apologists claimed was promoting that civilization on a global scale.

Four factors, above all others, undermined the racially framed perceptions of the past which so characterized the Victorian and Edwardian ages: two world wars fought against Germany took a heavy toll of the entire Anglo-Saxonist/Germanist historical enterprise, driving a great wedge between the patriotic vision of what it meant to be British and its roots in a Germanic past; the loss of world empire and both political and economic leadership thereafter, combined with new immigration particularly from the new commonwealth, undermined both the myth of Anglo-Saxon racial superiority and the search for that superiority in a Teutonic prehistory, to be replaced by the new causes of multi-culturalism and racial integration; finally the gradual dismantling of social and political privilege – with universal adult suffrage, for example – required and validated a host of new historical enterprises, underpinned by a greater variety of theoretical positions, which challenged and eventually overwhelmed the centrality of national and institutional histories within the narration of the past.

The reappearance of an historical Arthur has been one by-product of these several processes (Chapter I). In some respects this might have been anticipated, since the Arthurian and *Brut* (the myth of Trojan descent) historical traditions were central to the perception of history and its writing in southern Britain (in particular) from the twelfth to the sixteenth centuries, when a new interest in the Anglo-Saxon past re-emerged. Yet this post-war rebirth occurred despite the wholesale demolition of the Arthurian historical mythology which had already been achieved, for example, by Polydore Vergil, under the early Tudors. Few have argued recently that there is anything particularly historical about Geoffrey of Monmouth's, or later medieval Arthurs. Notwithstanding this, earlier texts from the ninth, tenth and eleventh centuries have been read and reread, compared and picked over for evidence of a 'real' Arthur. The result has been the re-emergence of debate concerning a fifth/sixth-century historical reality for a figure first encountered in a ninth-century text, the *Historia Brittonum* ('History of the Britons'), a work written for highly contemporary and political motives in Gwynedd *c.* 829–30 (see

Chapter III). There are plentiful voices, of course, warning against the acceptance of ninth- and tenth-century writings on their own as adequate evidence for the fifth and sixth centuries (Dumville 1977a; Sims-Williams 1983; Yorke 1993). Yet the very vagueness of our only relevant, contemporary author (Gildas), and his admission that the Britons achieved some temporary successes in war against the Saxons, provided an opportunity in the twentieth century, much as he did in the ninth, for those who wished to construct an 'historical' Arthur in the decades around 500.

To take a seminal example which is quoted at the opening of this introduction, Professor J. D. Bruce (1923) wrote the key study of the early evolution of Arthurian literature prior to that edited by Loomis (1959). On the first page he expressed incredulity concerning the case for a 'real' Arthur in Dark Age history, but then, on the very next page, inclined himself to view Arthur as historical. Such suspensions of disbelief have continued to resurface throughout the century and even beyond: King Arthur remains an extra-ordinarily persistent presence, not just as a literary construct that transcends time but also as an historical figure who requires discussion – or at least refutation – in attempts to write the history of the fifth and sixth centuries.

The current status of the 'historical' Arthur debate is, therefore, our starting point, which the initial chapter of this book will survey across the twentieth century. Arthur's triumph came briefly in the 1960s and 1970s, when insular history was reshaped around him, but the vehemence of criticism then derailed the enterprise in academic though not in popular circles. Thereafter, the struggle over Arthur's reality and place in history continued to be fought throughout the 1980s and 1990s. This has, however, been a phoney war, with academic historians in general confining their work to journals and articles and being unwilling to acknowledge or engage with the large and enthusiastic 'real Arthur' literature, which has, therefore, tended to monopolize (alongside Morris 1973) the considerable market in historical, Arthurian writing.

The present work will, however, make no effort to judge between one 'real' Arthur and another, let alone propose another variant. Rather than continue to address questions concerning Arthur's historicity, it will be proposed that a focus instead on the *idea* of King Arthur and its shifting utility in different texts has greater potential to carry forward our discussion of the past into fruitful areas. This *idea* of Arthur has been one of the most persistent and powerful in Western culture over the last millennium, at least, and shows little sign now of abating. It has had successive transformations, each refashioned to conform to the world-picture projected by a particular author writing for a particular élite at a particular time. Each Arthurian manifestation therefore reflects the way in which a particular author and his or her audience thought to fashion their own conceptions of the past, so as to benefit their own positioning in the present. It is in this process of interaction between various presents and their pasts that Arthur has been conceived and utilized ever since the ninth century.

For what? The major constant in these successive constructions is Arthur's usefulness as a means of envisioning Dark Age history from a particular and highly contemporary standpoint, which has had some potential to empower significant figures in the present – the author and his or her audience among them. When all these visions are considered as a group, it becomes clear that questions about ethnicity, group identity and nationality are commonly at issue. To be interested in Arthur is to be interested in how 'Britishness', 'Englishness', 'Welshness', 'Cornishness', 'Scottishness', and so on, have been constructed and successively revalued, both in the present and in many pasts. We cannot divorce an examination of Arthur from the investigation of how and why he has been constructed through time.

The basic issue is worth emphasizing. We are confronted by an accumulation of opinion that the Arthurian legends, in the earliest manifestations which can be identified, contain inherent historical meaning capable of both recovering and displaying a 'real' figure of the past, in an appropriate and verifiable historical context. The principal agreed methodology is careful exploration of the origins of the extant texts, their textual histories and the histories of whatever putative underlying texts it is imagined (or even occasionally demonstrated) that their authors might have used, but barely any two authors agree on any particular reconstruction of Arthur. The least disputed message coming out of this debate is the recognition that outcomes have always been contested, and that the evidence for Arthur is so ephemeral that it needs only differences of approach or different historical agendas for the resulting narratives to be contradictory (Shichtman and Carley 1994). There is nothing particularly remarkable about this, since historical writings are often mutually combative regarding re-envisioning the past. However, in the case of Arthur every single aspect of his characterization even down to his very existence is at issue, which could not be said of disagreements regarding Napoleon, for example, or Alexander the Great. To debate Arthur is closer to discussing the historicity of Christ than arguing about most figures of the past. There is an unfathomable depth to the disagreements, therefore, and no bedrock of universally accepted dates, places or events on which all concur. Put simply, an overview of the historical literature reveals a plethora of historical Arthurs, but no one safely recoverable, historical Arthur, of whose historicity, dates and locality we can be confident and on which all will agree.

If this stance seems an abnegation of responsibility on the part of an historian whose own interests do cover this so-called 'Arthurian period', I apologize. However, the evidence to sustain this view is not hard to find. I quote numerous mutually conflicting opinions in Chapter I, and offer in Chapter V a brief survey of insular, historical treatments of Arthur from Geoffrey of Monmouth up to the Victorian period. With little exception, it must be stressed that those whose work is explored enjoyed access to the same principal texts, or, at the very least, to secondary works based on those texts. Their differences of opinion concerning the historicity of Arthur and, if historical, his dates, activities and whereabouts, cannot derive primarily from the source materials themselves. Rather, attitudes towards historicizing King Arthur depend far more on the thought world occupied by the writers, and the meaning which Arthur has for them in their several presents, than on the texts *per se*.

There is nothing very novel about this, since history has long been characterized as an engagement between the present and the past, even without getting too deeply into debates about 'pastism' and 'presentism' (Biddick 1998). Differences on either side of this temporal equation will necessarily impact on the history being conceived. All histories can be thought of as attempts to influence or persuade contemporaries, written so as to change the present, as Foucault famously recognized. In this sense, the writing of history is both a political and a cultural act. A perception of history which centres on its contemporaneity, its potency and its utility, is at least as pertinent to the more distant as the recent past, and thus to the pre-Conquest period. Within the insular early and central Middle Ages, that history was written for contemporary political and cultural purposes has been widely acknowledged, but not so widely accommodated, with texts still often quarried for 'facts' or 'events', without much attempt being made to understand the viewpoint and objectives of the author. The historical perspectives of both Gildas and Bede have been particular victims, as are the *Historia Brittonum* and *Annales Cambriae* (the 'Welsh Annals') – the works of Hanning and Dumville being the long-standing exceptions. Writers of the early Middle Ages have now, in contrast, begun to be read in very different ways, with the construction of histories and chronicles, for example, being viewed as political and ideological action, rather than the passive recording of events (e.g. McKitterick 1997; Hen and Innes 2000). The time is ripe for a reconsideration of the whole question of Arthur's treatment in (primarily Latin) texts of the central Middle Ages, what he was used for and what he was constructed against. Given the texts involved, this exploration leads inevitably into issues about the contructions of ethnicity with which the authors were familiar, and how they proposed to effect those constructs. Chapter II begins, therefore, with a review of how 'Britishness' and to a lesser extent 'Englishness' were constructed prior to the writing of the *Historia Brittonum* in the early ninth century, in ways which impacted markedly on that author's text.

Stories about Arthur have also been woven into the topographical and antiquarian perceptions of the 'British' world, from southern Scotland to Cornwall. This seems to have occurred over a very long period, which stretches up to the present, making the early stages in the process difficult to distinguish and to interpret. Whether this Arthur, the superhuman demi-god, folk-hero, giant or force of nature, or the Arthur of historical literature came first is an issue which has repeatedly been raised and on which there are diverse opinions (most recently see Padel 1994, whose excellent study leaves little to add in this area). However, this polarization of Arthur between historical figure and force of nature may ultimately be unhelpful, if the 'historical' is as much a cultural construct as the elemental. It may be more useful to view both as complementary (and to an extent contemporary) manifestations of Arthur as a multi-purpose figure capable of being used in many theatres as a means of explanation. This occurs most obviously in the landscape, where Arthur's agency is invoked as interpretation of some unnatural or awesome feature. But it is equally pertinent in terms of moral justification or repositioning within salvation history – hence the Dark Age historical figure. The distinction between historical character and folk-hero is a modern phenomenon, which would have had little relevance in the central Middle Ages.

As an historical or historicized figure, Arthur was constructed initially within the context of the *Historia Brittonum*, a redemptive narrative written in northern Wales *c.* 829–30 (the author offered 831). A fundamental part of this text was necessarily a defensive review, from a British perspective, of the moral, political and military meaning of the Anglo-Saxon settlement (see Chapter III). Writers in the central Middle Ages were aware that Britain had been a long-held part of the Roman Empire. They also knew that Anglo-Saxon kingdoms had successfully supplanted indigenous control of much of it thereafter. Indeed, Anglo-Saxon kings were still then pushing their authority ever further into British-held territories.

There was plenty of room for manoeuvre. These medieval scholars were writing history to contest and appropriate memory, to own the past and drape it in particular colours for present purposes (Geary 1994). The *Historia Brittonum* is all too often treated as a rather poor attempt to *record* the past, badly flawed, yes, but an attempt nonetheless. Rather, it should be seen as more polemical than historical reconstruction in any modern sense, and as constructed for recoverable, contemporary political, cultural and ideological purposes. The anonymous author has set about ordering the past for the sake of contemporary authority (and therefore power). Like Bede's *Historia Ecclesiastica* (commonly termed the 'History of the English Church and People'), to which it is in part a reaction, this work offers a grandiose historical framework, couched in moral and providential terms. It is an explanatory narrative, or what postmodernists call a 'metanarrative', written from within a very specific ethnicity and in part at least against 'Others'. It offers an historical plot capable of joining together the past and the future into a seamless robe, which is continuous and purposive in relation to issues in the present. It uses historical figures, certainly, but its author's objective was to make a political case and the past is reformed in that image, with characters and their deeds treated as highly malleable in the process. How Arthur was used within this text was crucial to the author's binary division of current society between 'British' and 'Saxon'. However, the great 'truth' which the author was seeking to address through this text was not so much the historicity or otherwise of Arthur but the particular place of his own, 'British' people in salvation history, in the past, the present and the future.

Arthur has been one of the most deeply contested historical ideas thrown up by insular history. One aspect of that contest is the delay before his historicity became embedded, even in a Welsh context and even despite the political triumph of the second dynasty of Gwynedd, for whom this icon was initially developed. He is, for example, omitted from the early to mid-tenth-century British polemic *Armes Prydein* (Williams 1972b), which offers two other early British champions famed in poetry and legend as exemplars of military leadership in the great enterprise of ejecting the English (see pp. 191–2). Nor was Arthur included in many of the royal genealogies as those developed during the ninth and tenth centuries – that of Dyfed is the only one to use the name and had arguably done so already long before the *Historia* was written. Perhaps Arthur's mythological and topographical connections and his lack of any known claim to royalty at an early date rendered him unattractive in this regard (Padel 1994). He does feature, however, in the *Annales Cambriae*, written in tenth-century Dyfed, and in several works of Latin hagiography written in or shortly after the eleventh century (for the texts, see Wade-Evans 1944; the dating issues were addressed first by Tatlock 1939). The author of the *Annales* arguably based his Arthur on that of the *Historia* (see Chapter IV) but made subtle alterations, again for particular political purposes relevant to the time of composition. In the later hagiographical texts, Arthur's role has little of the moral authority invested in his characterization by the author of the *Historia Brittonum*, for the purposes of these authors were very different, being to glorify the individual saint and so reinforce a local authority and history particular to the cult at a time when that was in question. Other characters were necessarily diminished morally in consequence, and Arthur seems to have been utilized as a type of secular figure of power (hence a king), so necessarily quite local in context, against which to pit the saint (Loomis 1933). He does have a martial role in, for example, the *Life of St. Cadog*, wherein his protection is highly rated, but this Arthur is a lascivious figure reined in from satisfying his lust only by the protests of his followers. He is, however, a king in these works, for the first time in the literary record.

The very diversity of evidence, and the lack of consensus in the central Middle Ages as now, are important features in the modern perception of Arthur's role in history. It is this very fuzziness which has, in turn, provided space and opportunity for numerous reformations of the central stories. We have profited enormously from such works and it is largely these which will carry an interest in, and hunger for, Arthurian stories into the future. T. H. White's *Once and Future King* and *The Book of Merlyn*, for example, combined to construct what was ultimately a great tragedy, but one of great wit and warm humanity, which was founded primarily on Malory's late fifteenth-century *Mort d'Arthur*. The author's perception of the warfare of his own time, which overshadowed and charged his authorship, makes this again a highly contemporary reworking of the legend. It may well be its later, Disney cartoon version, however, that will be, for most of this generation of undergraduates, their initial introductory text to Arthurian literature. For others it will be films such as *Excalibur* or *First Knight*. Had Arthur's position in history been clearer, the suspension of disbelief necessary to accommodate each different story line would have been more difficult. It is far harder to construct attractive, imaginative stories which are capable of capturing the imagination around Alexander the Great, for example, or Edward I, than Arthur, since periodically all which is obviously fanciful is cut away by the historian. That said, there are signs that the plasticity of Arthurian ideas had begun to fail by the later sixteenth century, when Spencer and others were attempting once more to rework the legend for current political effect, bringing a distinct lull in the literary exploration across several generations.

The key question addressed is not, therefore, 'Was Arthur an historical figure?', to which a wide range of answers are on offer, although I shall return to this issue very briefly in the epilogue. There is far more to be said in the context of the contemporary cultural and political utility of Arthur as portrayed in early insular sources, and that is the focus of the current work. The central issues are: 'What role was Arthur intended to perform, why was he utilized in texts of the central Middle Ages, and what did he mean to both authors and their audiences?' Within the confines of this present work, this exploration replaces the historicity of Arthur as the central matter of debate. Discussion focuses instead on the textual evidence reflecting political and cultural worlds in which allusions to Arthur were perceived as valuable. By this means we have an opportunity to explore the genesis of the *idea* of Arthur and his meanings as projected by different authors for themselves within their own time frames.

It is only fair to state at this point what this volume will not seek to achieve. During the later Middle Ages (*c*.1150–1480), the idea of Arthur was a major focus of stories which were told, written, listened to and read from Iceland to the Mediterranean (e.g. Loomis 1959, but see Dean 1987 for a minimal picture). Clearly this theme attracted some extremely talented writers and story-tellers and the excellence of much of their output added new layers to Arthur's popularity in several languages. Additionally, Arthurian stories were sufficiently flexible to adapt to the changing cultural and social needs of Western Europe post-1100 – and the very absence of a powerful historical framework arguably aided and abetted this process considerably, in contrast to the stories surrounding, for example, Charlemagne. The Arthurs of Geoffrey of Monmouth and Chrétien de Troyes, for example, are in many respects twelfth-century figures, exemplars of kingship for the new and much romanticized realm of knighthood, inhabiting a world opened up by crusading and by the carriage of Frankish culture into Britain, Sicily and the Holy Land by (*inter alia*) Norman adventurers. His court, which eventually went by the French name of Camelot, played already by the eleventh century an important part in capturing stories which may earlier have been independent (see, for example, *Culhwch and Olwen*). The congregation at Arthur's court of droves of characters was clearly a useful mechanism by which to position particular stories within the wider repertoire. This work will not stray far into the world of Arthurian culture and medieval literature (post-1000) and its criticism (see, for example, Barron 1989, 1999; Patterson 1987; Bromwich *et al.* 1991; Warren 2000, and their bibliographies). This is a vast subject, which cannot be covered effectively in this short volume. It will, therefore, (somewhat regretfully) be passed over at great speed (in Chapter V) or omitted altogether, with no more than a very basic sketch of the development of the political cult in England. The reasons are simple: this work focuses on pre-Galfridian Latin 'historical' works and the ways in which they characterized Arthur for their own purposes. Once Geoffrey's *Historia Regum Britanniae* and its numerous spin-offs in several languages had become accepted as the central, authoritative texts on early British history, the pre-Galfridian, British histories were rarely consulted until the Renaissance, so they had little direct impact on the historicization of Arthur during the Middle Ages. Furthermore, the discussion of post-Galfridian Arthurian literature is a highly specialized area of study which this author cannot hope to engage with effectively.

This book has been written, therefore, primarily as an investigation of the nature, role and purposes of Arthur in the pre-Galfridian Latin texts, and the way that different generations of historians, both then and thereafter, have chosen to portray their Arthurs within the intellectual and political perceptions which conditioned their purposes in re-envisioning the sub-Roman past in Britain. Within this framework, it will be suggested that Arthur was initially developed in a 'Dark Age' context as a martial and Christian leader to contest visions of a cowardly and immoral British people, and a race excluded from salvation history. The strategy was empowered by the fact that such concepts, inherited by the author of the *Historia Brittonum* from Gildas and Bede, respectively, were inimical to the self-perceptions of his audience – that is of King Merfyn of Gwynedd and his supporters. The author sought to develop and then privilege a particular nationalist, 'British' identity to the advantage of this political faction. This was necessarily in opposition to the 'Englishness' of Bede's work and was intended to contest the centrality of Anglo-centric visions of providential history within Britain. Investment in 'British' identity was a fundamental part of political and cultural resistance to English conquest and Anglicization, and marks the commitment of this élite to such resistance. The separate existence of Wales is a lasting testimony to their achievement.

This work is written from a fundamentally sceptical viewpoint, and thus outside of any assumption *ab initio* of an historical Arthur during the fifth or sixth centuries. However, it is far more an exploration than a negation. It seeks, most of all, to offer new theories about how we should read the two particular texts which are fundamental to each and every argument about Arthur – the *Historia Brittonum* and *Annales Cambriae*.

CHAPTER I

# A KING OUT OF TIME

## King Arthur in the twentieth century

——— •◆• ———

It is difficult to say anything precise about the Arthur of history.

(T. Jones 1964: 3)

The historicity of Arthur has been deeply contested across the twentieth century. The roots of that debate lie, inevitably, in the previous epoch, which will be explored in Chapter V, but the discussion is of such significance to this work that the past 100 years or so are surveyed at this point, so that they can act as an introduction to the issues discussed in greater detail in Chapters II, III and IV.

The dominant voices in late Victorian perceptions of the insular early Middle Ages – Freeman, Stubbs, Green, and so on – focused on Anglo-Saxon England, and sought to demonstrate that their own, present community, its institutions and its very bloodlines, descended directly and predominately from the English settlement. It was initially Welsh and Scottish scholars who began to contest what they interpreted as glib and racially motivated, Anglo-centric dismissals of such issues as Dark Age British resistance to the Anglo-Saxons, which they in turn wished to own. The historicity of Vortigern and Arthur was inevitably involved. During the nineteenth century, Welsh medieval literature was gradually being made available in new editions and translations, which offered a considerable opportunity for the historian and literary scholar. William Skene's massive work of translation was published in 1868, containing numerous texts which could be viewed as Arthurian, and he offered a sketch of the historical framework in which he believed they should be contextualized. Skene provided a discussion in some detail of Gildas (the fifth- or sixth-century British author of *De Excidio Britanniae* – 'Concerning the Ruin of Britain'), whose historical sequence he challenged, and the ninth-century *Historia Brittonum* ('History of the Britons', which was until recently believed to have been written by Nennius). He proposed a Saxon conquest as early as 441, on the basis of the 'Gallic Chronicle of 452', against which the Britons then appealed to Aëtius, the imperial general active in Gaul from *c.* 430 to 454. Unlike Robertson, who had already published on Scotland's history in 1862, Skene gave considerable credit to the *Historia*

*Brittonum*, and therefore to the historical Arthur, whom he thought of as a quasi-Roman military commander of cavalry. His argument has a ring made familiar by later reiterations:

> There is always some substratum of truth on which the wildest legends are based, though it may be so disguised and perverted as hardly to be recognised; and I do not hesitate to receive the Arthur of Nennius as the historic Arthur, the events recorded of him being not only consistent with the history of the period, but connected with localities which can be identified, and with most of which his name is still associated. That the events here recorded of him are not mentioned in the Saxon Chronicle and other Saxon authorities, is capable of explanation. These authorities record the struggle between the Britons and the Saxons south of the Humber; but there were settlements of Saxons in the north even at that early period, and it is with these settlements that the war narrated in the *Historia Brittonum* apparently took place.
>
> (Skene 1868: 50–1)

Writing in Scotland, Skene had his own reasons for preferring a northern – even a Scottish – context for Arthur. He was not alone in this endeavour, for this was also being suggested by J. H. Burton (1873), the Historiographer-Royal for Scotland, and, in 1869, Stuart-Glennie in turn claimed to be the first to have made the connection between southern Scotland and Arthur on topographical grounds. Skene's interpretation of the names of Arthur's battle list in the *Historia Brittonum* was heavily influenced by this northern preference. Indeed, he offered a vision of Arthur's wars, complete with lines of attack, which took him far beyond the sources. For all that, his critical evaluation of the historical evidence to be found in Old Welsh poetry was the first for two generations and offered a new beginning, particularly for non-Welsh-speaking scholars. This approach was to have a profound impact over the next two generations, as various different visions of Arthur began to spread outwards from Celtic studies to be embraced by a much wider scholarly community.

This was also an era of enthusiastic folklorists (see Dorson 1968), and this proved a second and rich source of Arthur stories to be considered in any discussion of the historicity of Arthur. Sir John Rhŷs (1891) recognized the problems of reconciling the widespread but generally localized Arthurian legends with the scanty pre-Galfridian texts (the so-called 'historical', Latin texts which predate Geoffrey of Monmouth's *Historia Regum Britanniae* in the twelfth century) and suggested that we need to think in terms of two Arthurs. One was the by now commonplace Brittonic divinity who was a 'Culture Hero' or 'Celtic Zeus'. Rhŷs's was the academically respectable end of a growing literature on Arthur and many other Celtic hero-figures – the entire round table catalogue of knights were included on occasion – which argued that their proper place lay within a mythological perspective. But Rhŷs's alternative Arthur was envisaged (much like Skene's) as a military leader of the Britons in the fifth century, who might have been a late Roman-type *Comes Britanniarum* in charge of the island's field forces.

The folkloric model of Arthur has since proved a very influential, if much contested, one. Perhaps the strongest case for the 'mythological Arthur' from the first half of the twentieth century was that of Malone (1924), who approached the issue from the perspective of a philologist and argued that Arthur and Uther were not only both mythological culture heroes but identical ones at that. He was, however, also prepared to speculate regarding an early historical origin (Malone 1925), suggesting the officer Lucius Artorius Castus, a Dalmatian career soldier who commanded *VI Victrix* at York and is known to have led a force from Britain to Armorica (Brittany) in a thoroughly Roman, punitive context, in the second half of the second century (pp. 75–6). This Artorius offered, Malone suggested, remarkably close parallels to the Arthur of later legend. An origin for King Arthur in the second century also circumvented the obvious difficulty that no historical writer between 400 and 820 actually names Arthur.

Malone, therefore, followed Rhŷs in constructing a dual Arthur – a popular device at this date which was also used of both Gildas and St Patrick, to quote just two parallels. In many respects, the twentieth-century debate was to be characterized by the contest between the historical Arthur as Roman-type commander and the mythological Arthur, with the advantage going to the historical model within a few years of Malone's contributions.

Speculation that an historical reality might well lie behind the legendary Arthur marks a very different approach from the Anglo-Saxonist vision developing across the nineteenth century. This hypothesis was to become the central dictum of Dickinson's review of Arthur (1900), which opened with the words: '*Ex nihilo nihil fit*' ('From nothing nothing comes'). Dickinson argued forcefully that the later legends pertaining to Arthur *must* have some foundation in an historical figure, and he sought this prototype in several localities. He preferred a northern Arthur for the battle-list of the *Historia Brittonum* (after Skene) while focusing otherwise very largely on the south-west peninsula, on the basis of later legendary material local to Cornwall. Dickinson was unusual, at that date, in giving considerable space to topographical and archaeological evidence, so offering discussions of Tintagel, Dameliock Castle and Castle Killibury, for example, as possible 'Arthurian' sites.

In two respects this work lays down important markers for the development of Arthur as an historical figure during the course of the twentieth century. First, Arthur was most commonly to be a figure who emerged at the ragged interface of history and archaeology, rather than specifically from one discipline or another. Second, this revival was characterized by a growing interest in, and willingness to rely on, much later, folkloric, Arthurian stories.

That development could not flourish, however, until the racial constructs and theories in which English history had been enmeshed throughout the nineteenth century had begun to dispel, and this was to prove a long and fitful process, stretching into the second half of the twentieth century and beyond.

The great *History of Wales* published in two volumes by John Edward Lloyd in 1911 represented a highly scholarly approach to Welsh texts, which both encapsulated historical thought to that date and made an enormous contribution in its own right. Lloyd could, for example, review a total of seven editions, publications and/or translations of Gildas's *De Excidio Britanniae*, culminating in the authoritative work of Theodore Mommsen in 1894, which was reprinted with an English translation by Hugh Williams in 1899. Lloyd was as patriotic as other contemporary historians, but he was a Welsh patriot, writing against the dominant portrayal of the Welsh as the marginalized losers of insular history, and demanding that a higher value be attached to those whom he perceived as his own ancestors. So Lloyd resoundingly rejected the Gildas-originating vision of feeble Britons incapable of contesting the loss of Britain:

> The facts are that the Picts and the Scots were kept almost entirely
> out of the province and that the Saxons only effected a lodgment in
> it after a long struggle; obscure as is the history of the period, it may
> be regarded as certain that the place of the Roman legions was taken
> by a fairly efficient fighting organization.
>
> (Lloyd 1911: 99)

Lloyd would have found it harder to reach this conclusion had he not assumed, along with the generation before (e.g. Skene 1868: 44) that the place-name and inscriptional evidence for Irish influence in (largely) western Wales reflected an indigenous occupation left over by an early westerly wave of Celtic migrations. In practice, of course, this evidence needs to be viewed in the context of new interconnections with Ireland in the late Roman and post-Roman periods, but his position otherwise presages that of several later scholars. He was highly dubious about the relevance of Arthur to Wales, but looked favourably on the suggestion that he might have been a successor to the late Roman Count of Britain. With some provisos, he placed an historical Arthur, and Vortigern, in the south-east, and argued that the comparative lack of residual information in Wales about his contest with the Saxons was consequent upon a division of the military command of the Britons into two. For Lloyd, Wales lay in the northern and western half of the diocese, where the principal business of British generals was successful warfare against the Picts and Scots. As part of this, he envisaged that the period witnessed a war which 'secured a lasting [British] supremacy throughout Wales' (p. 111). For westward migration from the lowland zone he argued persuasively that 'there is no evidence whatever', so contesting one of the principal paradigms of contemporary English visions of the Dark Ages and threatening long-cherished and highly valued visions of Germanic racial purity in England. The only option left to those requiring a 'pure blood' style of English settlement was wholesale slaughter on the improbable scale envisaged by J. R. Green in the 1870s and 1980s (p. 261).

Lloyd's historical perception differed dramatically, therefore, from those of English contemporaries. He rejected the English vision of universal British political and moral collapse, which was necessary to the 'clean slate' vision of English origins. This he replaced with a regional narrative of conquest and achievement supportive of Wales-centric history, beyond which England – and with it Arthur – could for the time being be largely ignored.

Lloyd's strategy had little attraction for the mainstream of Anglo-centric writers, of course, who, even despite the massive shock administered by the Great War (1914–18) to their Germanist vision of insular history, continued for the moment to reiterate their collective acceptance of a wholesale British military collapse in the face of Anglo-Saxon warriors penetrating deep into western Britain in the great raid 'from sea to sea', which had been referred to by Gildas, with or without 'their half-mythical King Arthur' (as summed up by the great Whig historian, Trevelyan 1926: 37).

The most incisive, and complete, single contribution to the debate about Arthur of this period was Chambers's book-length work in 1927. This might fairly be described as the first modern study of the place of Arthur in British history. Chambers's approach was to explore Arthur as a cultural and literary phenomenon and he tried to avoid committing himself in any particular direction within the historical debate. He exploited instead Arthur's special place in 'the historical imagination', and acknowledged that Arthur was widely perceived as:

> the legend-hung champion of a dying order, through whom we reach back, beyond the advent of the chill barbarians from the north, to the slow spread of Mediterranean civilization by the shores of the Atlantic, and to that *pax Romana*, of which this island was the ultimate outpost.
>
> (Chambers 1927: 1)

It is important to recognize the extent to which Chambers attempted a critical analysis. He retained a degree of scepticism as to the reliability of ninth-century writings when putatively describing the fifth and sixth centuries, and an even more pronounced atheism regarding later accretions to the legend. Chambers attempted an historical discussion of the textual sources available for the fifth and sixth centuries in some detail, which recognized (p. 181) the complete absence of any reference to Arthur in Gildas's *De Excidio Britanniae*. He was, however, inclined towards an exceptionally early date for a prototype of the *Historia Brittonum*, imagining that such might even have been the work of St Paulinus in the early seventh century, and so credits that text with greater historicity than scholars would now accept. He also commented on the difficulties posed by archaeological dating to the notion of British control of the southern lowlands of the diocese in the mid-fifth century, but was insufficiently confident of the evidence to make as much of this issue as one can today.

Chambers was very aware of the difficulties he faced when postulating an historical Arthur, remarking that:

> Beyond the bare notice of Badon, the reports lack confirmation. The most that history can say is that they are not inconsistent with what we do know of the period to which they relate. I hope to show that it can say that. But it amounts to little, in view of the obscurity which envelopes the fortunes of the island during the greater part of the fifth and sixth centuries.
>
> (Chambers 1927: 169)

For all his caution, Chambers was inclined to accept the historicity of an Arthur figure, imagining him opposing Saxon conquests from the Thames valley, operating perhaps from the legend-enshrined South Cadbury. He surveyed in addition the widespread occurrence of Arthur-names in the countryside of Celtic Britain, in an attempt to identify from that evidence some hint as to where Arthurian legend had originated, but found it too widespread to offer any solution. Indeed, he could do little more than express bewilderment as to the occurrence of localized stories in Scotland, where he felt (p. 196) that there was a distinct lack of literary connection of Arthur even with British Strathclyde. He surveyed, as well, the battle names, in particular exploring the numerous suggestions so far made concerning the locality of Badon, in search of a southern theatre for Arthur's activities, but could offer no firm conclusions in most cases. He also noted the several occurrences of the name Arthur in insular dynasties (pp. 169–70) at around 600, without passing judgement on what light (if any) these might shed on an earlier Arthur figure.

At the same time, Chambers took issue (pp. 206ff.) with the mythological interpretation of Arthur, and with current attempts to parallel him with such figures as the Irish Fionn (attempts which would be reinforced by Van Hamel 1934). This is not to say that he disputed that there might be mythological elements in the various late stories circulating around Arthur, merely that he did not accept that Arthur's origins lay in this sphere.

Chambers's work was produced just before a new edition of the primary text (Harley 3859) of the *Historia Brittonum* was published as part of his great study of Arthurian materials by Edmond Faral in 1929, with a commentary which outlined, *inter alia*, the relationship between Gildas's description of Ambrosius Aurelianus and the subsequent wars with the Saxons and the *Historia's* construction of Vortimer's wars. Like Skene, Faral postulated a northern theatre for Arthur's battles.

It is difficult to offer a consensus within this debate at the end of the 1920s, but, on the whole, establishment historians remained unimpressed by the historicity of a great King Arthur figure and of any serious opposition to the foundations of England. However, students of late Roman Britain were increasingly prepared, on the evidence primarily of the *Historia Brittonum*, to accept the existence of some sort of 'chieftain of mixed Roman and British parentage who had learned the art of war from the Romans and successfully led the forces of the British kings against the Saxon invaders' (*Encyclopedia Britannia*, 14th edn, 1929: II, 461). Otherwise, Arthur was, in the same text and despite Chambers's recent efforts, considered the stuff of 'prehistoric myth, a hero of romance, and a fairy king', so a figure primarily for literary critics and mythologists rather than the historian. The dual Arthur was established, therefore, and a platform constructed on which an historical Arthur could begin to take shape.

The debate was to shift dramatically in favour of an historical Arthur during the late inter-war years, with the publication of three seminal works by distinguished scholars of the new, more critical school of history and textual study. The first out was volume one of a three-volume work by Hector Munro Chadwick and Nora Kershaw Chadwick titled *The Growth of Literature* (1932), the principal focus of which was comparative literature. In important respects, their offering should be viewed as seminal in the development of textual deconstruction as applied to medieval texts. The Chadwicks made no attempt to disguise their own historical concerns and they discussed the problems posed by texts such as the *Historia Brittonum* as historical sources. They particularly highlighted many of the weaknesses of the approaches then widely used by historians, which can best be described as synthesizing or reconciling. This practice involved (and still involves) different texts being ransacked for individual facts and dates, all of which could then be combined in a new narrative without explicit notice of the ultimate purposes of these snippets of information within the narratives from which they derived. They noted, for example, the significant discrepancies existing between 'Arthurian' material in the *Historia Brittonum* and the *Annales Cambriae* ('Welsh Annals'), both in the MS Harleian 3859 text, and they highlighted the 'complicated literary history' which apparently underlay the *Historia Brittonum* (pp. 146–57). It was the Chadwicks who first suggested that a Welsh catalogue-poem might have been used in compiling *Historia Brittonum* 56 – the list of Arthur's putative battles – and suggested that this was unlikely to be trustworthy as an indicator of Arthur's locality. In addition, they remarked:

> For Arthur we have not been able to find any contemporary, or indeed any very early direct evidence. The *Historia Brittonum* shows that he was famous in the first half of the ninth century. The entries in the *Annales Cambriae* (517, 538) are independent of this, but their

antiquity cannot be proved; and the same may be said of certain references in the poems.

(Chadwick and Chadwick 1932: 161)

That said, they were impressed by the appearance of the name Arthur within several royal dynasties, and argued (p. 162) that 'its wide currency towards the end of the sixth century must have been due to some famous person of that name in the near past'. For the Chadwicks, the name was certainly the Roman *Artorius*, and they felt that the pattern of Roman naming only comparatively early in surviving British genealogies (now see Bartrum 1966, 1983) should favour a date for Arthur in the first half of the fifth century. They clearly favoured an historical Arthur, therefore, but the greatest achievement of the Chadwicks was to offer a real advance in textual criticism, which historians thereafter ignored at their peril.

By far the best-known work of the 1930s, however, is *Roman Britain and the English Settlements*, written primarily by R. G. Collingwood, but with an addendum on the Anglo-Saxon Settlement (book V) by J. N. L. Myres, published in 1936 as the first volume of the newly conceived and highly ambitious Oxford History of England. The structure of this great work reflects precisely the very different conceptions and moral values of Dark Age history, with its fault line dividing the Roman and British-centric major part of the work from the very different research styles and world of knowledge of Myres's contribution on the English settlements.

Collingwood was the most erudite figure ever to have tackled the subject of Roman Britain, writing at a time when it was still possible to be master not just of its history but also its historical archaeology, all alongside his role as a leading academic philosopher. He made every effort to make sense of the fifth century, adopting a profoundly reconstructionist approach. For Collingwood, part of the puzzle lay in the archaeological record, which had to date revealed (Collingwood and Myres 1936: 318) a wholesale but peaceful evacuation of settlements. Where did the population go? The notion of a mass migration westwards was as implausible to Collingwood as it had been to Lloyd. Apart from some departing for Brittany, he postulated that 'the greater part of them were absorbed by degrees into the population of the English settlements', while those of the highland zone simply stayed put. He was comparatively sanguine about the historicity of Gildas's account, proposing Ambrosius Aurelianus as a war-leader about 470–80 and suggesting that such monuments as the Wansdyke should be viewed in the context of this era.

Collingwood was prepared to treat Arthur as historical on the basis of an only slightly more cautious reworking of Dickinson's reasoning, on the basis of what has since come (after Dumville 1977a: 187) to be called the 'no smoke without fire' school of history. He concluded that an early version of the *Historia Brittonum* had been used by Bede, and so must be comparatively close in date to Arthur's putative lifetime, and argued for the independence from it of the *Annales Cambriae*, so supposing that references in these texts to Arthur's role in the battle or siege of Mount Badon confirmed one another:

> That there was such a battle, and that it resulted in a British victory of so crushing a nature that for at least forty-four years afterwards the Saxons never took up arms again, is beyond question: Gildas, a contemporary witness, is our evidence.
>
> (Collingwood and Myres 1936: 320)

Although Collingwood was unimpressed by the argument that 'the bear' and 'the bear's stronghold' (in *De Excidio Britanniae* xxxii, 1) alluded to Arthur (his name means 'bear-man' in Welsh), if only because his association with Mount Badon stretched the chronology too far, he preferred to leave open the issue of whether or not Gildas referred to Arthur. However, even without that important testimony: 'the historicity of the man can hardly be called in question'. For Collingwood, the sheer quantity of material (which he never actually discussed but treated as if impressive enough for this conclusion *en masse*, without comment) later accruing to the literary character implied that Arthur was as real as, for example, Alexander or Aristotle: 'The place which the name of Arthur occupies in the Celtic legend is easiest to explain on the hypothesis that he really lived, and was a great champion of the British people.' Again, like the Chadwicks, he saw this fifth–sixth century figure as Roman-named, so likeliest from 'a good family in one of the *civitates* of the lowland zone'. Collingwood concurred (albeit without reference to previous adherents, such as Zimmer 1896) with the developing vision of Arthur as a *Comes Britanniarum* of the fifth century, commanding mobile troops – primarily heavy cavalry – whom he brought to the aid of British kings in their struggles against the Saxons. This persona, he felt, helped explain the apparent ubiquity of his fame within the British community. Since so many of his reputed battles – as listed in the *Historia Brittonum* – are obscure and difficult to place, he argued that they were probably factual. Indeed, he followed Skene (1868) and Crawford (1935), in treating the battle-list as historical and argued that Arthur's last battle at Camlann (unnamed in *HB*, see *AC* 537) should be interpreted as *Camboglanna* (Birdoswald). The Chadwicks' doubts concerning their historicity passed unmentioned.

In the last resort, Collingwood recognized the hypothetical nature of his case but he does seem to have been convinced himself:

> Through the mist of legend that has surrounded the name of Arthur, it is thus possible to descry something which at least may have happened: a country sinking into barbarism, where Roman ideas had almost vanished; and the emergence of a single man intelligent enough to understand them, and vigorous enough to put them into practice

by gathering round him a group of friends and followers, armed according to the tradition of civilized warfare and proving their invincibility in a dozen campaigns. There are other elements in the tradition which may have a foundation of truth. After the final victory, Arthur's occupation as champion of the Britons was gone. Twenty-one years later was fought the battle of Camlann . . . dissension had broken out in the band itself, and finally it was destroyed in a battle of one party against the other . . . For Arthur, I have suggested, was the last of the Romans: the last to understand Roman ideas and use them for the good of the British people. The heritage of Rome lived on in many shapes; but of the men who created that heritage Arthur was the last, and the story of Roman Britain ends with him.

(Collingwood and Myres 1936: 324)

And so, indeed, did Collingwood bring book four of his great eulogy to Roman Britain to an end, in an atmosphere of tragic pathos which contrasts dramatically with the bulk of the work, which celebrates Rome's furthest outpost, leaving Myres to refocus on the Anglo-Saxons. The latter declared himself (pp. 327–30) to be generally unimpressed by the literary evidence coming from either Anglo-Saxon or British sources as a basis for reconstructing the past. However, he was likewise prepared to imagine that the *Historia Brittonum* contained much early material virtually unchanged in the early ninth century, acknowledging the force of the highly uncomplimentary preface found in the 'Nennian' recension: 'I have made a heap of all that I have found.' To Myres:

It is precisely his ignorance and his stupidity which caused him to jumble together good and bad materials without amalgamating them into a single whole, and each successive commentary on the evolution of his curious book makes it more possible to sort out the different elements of which it is composed.

Even so, he did not feel that there was an historical framework for the fifth and sixth centuries to be had here. Despite this agnosticism, however, that was, to all intents and purposes, what he then constructed, weaving names and events derived from this and other texts into an account which was otherwise conceived on the basis of his own interpretations of the archaeological evidence.

Despite such frailties, it is difficult to overemphasize the influence of this two-part work on the world of history and archaeology over the next few generations, remaining a central plank in undergraduate studies well into the 1980s. While it was Collingwood's last major contribution to the study of the past, the much younger Myres went on to develop further the ideas which he had laid out. A series of works through the early post-war era culminated in a major treatise on Anglo-Saxon pottery and its historical context (Myres

1969). It is fair to suggest that his work had a greater influence on the study of pagan Anglo-Saxon cemeteries and their cremation pottery than any other of the twentieth century. He was invited at the very end of his both wide and varied academic career to rewrite his contribution to the original work (of 1936). This new, single volume was published in 1986, but the reworking was quite limited: Myres did not take account of the textual criticism, as well as artefactual and settlement archaeology, which had by then been achieved. The result was a reiteration of his earlier reconstruction, now somewhat detached from the intellectual environment in which it had been conceived fifty years earlier.

To finish with this group of studies published in the late inter-war years, what is now the least known work of the three was in fact earlier than Collingwood and Myres's by a year, being, of course, R. H. Hodgkin's two-volume *A History of the Anglo-Saxons* (1935). Hodgkin recognized the problems inherent in reconstructing the text of the *Historia Brittonum* and using it as a basis for historical writing but, despite the strictures of the Chadwicks, he was also attracted, at least, by Arthur's battle-list (I, p. 80), which he felt had 'on it some stamp of popular tradition'. In later editions (1940, 1952), Hodgkin acknowledged the authority and expertise of Collingwood in treating of Welsh Latin texts and adopted (pp. 122–3) his vision of Arthur as a cavalry general. This *comes* he imagined leading heavily armoured and armed troopers like that of the late Roman cataphracts, and fighting battles all over what had been Roman Britain. At the end of the day, Hodgkin adhered to traditional English values in considering that British resistance to the Anglo-Saxons was inadequate and undermined by its own moral failings. Of these he lists (p. 181) culpable blindness (which derives from a literal reading of Gildas), failure to understand their own political geography (the *Historia Brittonum*), lack of foresight and chronic disunity (Gildas again). Only in imagination did the Britons excel, and he particularly remarked (p. 182) 'the gorgeous web of fiction' woven around 'the sordid realities of the long struggle and their ultimate defeat' which rendered 'Artorius, the harassed leader of a rough war-band, living in a low state of civilization . . . a wonder-working national champion who [following the *Historia Brittonum*] "in all his battles was the victor", who felled 960 men by his own onslaught at Mount Badon, and whose dog, Cavall, left a magical footprint on a stone in Buelt'.

On the very eve of renewed war, a more focused work by Brodeur (1939), took issue with several recent visions of the period (including the historicity of the Gallic Chronicle of 452 and Mommsen's reading of the dating clause in *De Excidio Britanniae*, xxvi, 1). He insisted that Arthur was a matter of legend rather than mythology (*contra* Malone 1924), and argued, like Collingwood, for a *locus* for Arthur and his battles in the south, against the Jutes and in the context of Hengist's son Oisc, in the early sixth century. Like the Chadwicks, however, Brodeur was unimpressed by the authenticity of the battle list in the *Historia Brittonum* as specifically Arthur's.

In the late 1930s Frank Stenton (later Sir Frank) was working on the second volume in the Oxford History of England, which came out in 1943. This massive and authoritative work was to be the central tome of Anglo-Saxon historiography throughout the remainder of the twentieth century, and the position which Stenton adopted was central to the perception of the British Dark Ages by early medievalists for generations. In what he described (p. 2) 'either as an epilogue to the history of Roman Britain or as a prologue to the history of Anglo-Saxon England', he summarized Gildas's framework of post-Roman insular history up to Badon. He attempted to date that event *c.* 500, and discussed the Britain in which Gildas himself lived. Stenton's reading of Gildas was comparatively literal, but his observations were typically acute:

> It is remarkable that Gildas ignores the British leader whose legendary fame was to carry the struggle between Saxons and Britons into the current of European literature. Gildas has nothing to say of Arthur ... The silence of Gildas may suggest that the Arthur of history was a less imposing figure than the Arthur of legend. But it should not be allowed to remove him from the sphere of history, for Gildas was curiously reluctant to introduce personal names into his writing.
>
> (Stenton 1943: 3–4)

An historical Arthur survived, therefore, Stenton's Germanist approach and close focus on Anglo-Saxon England, but only just. He did not survive into the vision of early Anglo-Saxon England proffered by Stenton's disciple, Dorothy Whitelock, whose widely read *The Beginnings of English Society* (1952) rested on a platform of (pp. 14–18) 'great stretches of continuous woodland', 'upland villages' abandoned by the Britons, the old Roman administration broken down into 'petty rulers of native race' and 'valley sites which the English cleared and worked with their own heavy plough'. She envisaged a negligible debt on the part of the Anglo-Saxons to British material culture, language or population, all of which were entirely marginalized in her account.

Whitelock's new study aside, however, the Second World War had a considerable impact on insular history. I propose to highlight only two issues. Revulsion at Nazi genocide and the racially constructed vision of German superiority encouraged a reappraisal of the racial constructs which had, either implicitly or explicitly, been central to the way British history had been constructed for centuries. Put simply, newly raised anti-German sentiment put into perspective older tensions in British historiography and led ultimately to an appreciation that English history had previously been constructed against other peoples. More recently the primary 'Others' had been both indigenous societies within the British Empire and European (and other) competitors for world power. Before that the French had been the foil for English history for much of a millennium, plus the Jews (despite their expulsion in the Middle Ages), the Irish and the other insular communities (primarily Welsh and Scots). Pre-Conquest historiography particularly identified the Britons, thus the Welsh – the *wealas* – as unvalued and excluded foreigners, against whom ethnic values and racial identity could be constructed (Wormald 1983, 1995; Foot 1996, 1999; Smyth 1998; see generally Hutchinson and Smith 1996; Jenkins 1996, 1997; S. Jones 1997).

Secondly, the war over-extended the British Empire both politically and economically. Exhaustion within the imperial enterprise, as much as external pressures from the US and local demands for independence, led to the British retreat from Empire. In a world in which the ex-colonial race had perforce to deal as equals with ex-subjects as rulers, diplomats, religious leaders, shippers and manufacturers, Anglo-British-centric historical values and perceptions were increasingly exposed as indefensible, and were gradually both undermined and overturned.

One result was the final overthrow of the old certainties provided by a belief in the inherent superiority of English social and political institutions and Germanic ancestry, by which the British establishment had been sustained for generations. This provided opportunities for the revival or construction of alternative visions of the past. Historically, insular Germanism was rooted in the enterprise of legitimizing the early and unique rise of the English Parliament to supremacy in the seventeenth and eighteenth centuries, but its fragility was now revealed (MacDougall 1982). Despite the Germanist perceptions of the mature work of Edward Leeds (1945) and the popularist, Anglo-centred vision of history offered by Sir Winston Churchill (1956–8), even the assumption of a general Teutonic descent of the English was to be challenged repeatedly in the post-war period, with Nora Chadwick (1963) initially reviving Hector Munro's earlier vision (published in 1905) of a large British genetic contribution to the English nation. The presumption of a significant genetic continuity from Roman Britain to Anglo-Saxon England has since been mooted by a wide spectrum of authors (see particularly Taylor 1983; Arnold 1984; Hodges 1989; Higham 1992a) and from a variety of premisses. It has now become well established in the broader historical literature of Anglo-Saxon England (e.g. J. Campbell 1982: 29), if less well in the archaeological – where intellectual Germanism and an insistence that migration should remain central to our understanding of the formation of Anglo-Saxon ethnicity are both now facing their 'High Noon'. It also has support from geneticists (although that has so far made little impact on the literature). Martin Evison, for example, has suggested to me that the demographic impact of the Vikings in Britain may have been greater than the Anglo-Saxons, and Professor Brian Sykes has confirmed that his initial findings suggest that no more than 30 per cent of the insular gene pool derives from Germanic immigration of all sorts (for a general introduction to the subject, see Cavalli-Sforza 2000).

Alongside this debate about genetic continuity, which still remains without final resolution, several other planks of the Germanist position, as postulated by Whitelock, have since been irretrievably destroyed. For example, the island diocese into which Germanic warriors and their families came was far from being densely wooded. Rather, it was characteristically open farmland with managed woodlands and rather few great wilderness areas (see, for example, M. Jones 1986; S. P. Dark 1996, 2000; and a host of detailed, regional studies), much as landscape archaeologists had predicted for a generation (Taylor 1983). Significant reforestation has only so far been observed in a few areas in the fifth century, particularly in the vicinity of Hadrian's Wall and in County Durham, but pollen diagrams remain too few in the south and east of England to establish overall patterns there beyond ultimate challenge. There may, however, have been important changes. In East Anglia, for example, significant shifts in the pattern of crop cultivation took place, which may imply that large-scale agricultural enterprise was giving way to peasant farming, but neither full-scale abandonment nor large-scale replacement of either crops or livestock seem to have occurred (P. Murphy 1994). This continuity of habitat and rural activity is a crucial component in our revised perception of the Romano-British/Saxon interface and is entirely incompatible with the notion of wholesale depopulation on the eve of, or in the course of, Anglo-Saxon settlement.

Nor did Germanic immigrants bring with them ready for use the ideas of living in a nucleated village or cultivating open fields, as had been assumed by Collingwood, *inter alia*, prior to the war, and Whitelock shortly thereafter. The excavation of deserted medieval villages slowly revealed from the 1950s onwards that the process of settlement nucleation by which they came into existence was, at earliest, a late Anglo-Saxon phenomenon. Many instances post-dated the Norman Conquest, but many areas retained scattered settlement patterns throughout the Middle Ages (for example, Beresford and Hurst 1971; Lewis, Mitchell-Fox and Dyer 1997). Similarly, open fields are now recognized as a late Anglo-Saxon or Anglo-Norman phenomenon, with very different reasons for their inception than Germanic racial imperatives (see particularly Thirsk 1964; Dahlman 1980; Dodgshon 1980; Rowley 1981; Brown and Foard 1998).

With Germanist myths in disarray, therefore, and losing both credibility and relevance to changing historical perspectives, interest in insular alternatives to Anglo-centric history and its value systems revived and, for the first time in many generations, made significant inroads into the academic establishment. There had been a serious and academically highly respectable community of Celticists for a century or more, of which Sir John Rhŷs and then Sir Ifor Williams were prominent members. The leading figure of the early post-war era was Professor Kenneth Hurlstone Jackson. His *magnum opus, Language and History in Early Britain* was published in 1953 and laid down the foundations of Old Welsh philology for the first time. The British–English interface was a particular interest of Jackson, who rehearsed in great detail the evidence for contact between the two, and for the absorption of British speakers into Anglo-Saxon society. This he considered to be demonstrable from the evidence of language and place-names, and his pioneering work in providing a framework of British language history and place-name (particularly river-name) survival underpins all later discussions.

Although he was prepared to accept the evidence offered by the *Historia Brittonum* for the existence of such figures as Cunedda at an even earlier date, Jackson was not overly impressed by the historicity of Arthur:

> Somewhat later the struggle [of Ambrosius Aurelianus] with the Saxons seems to have been carried on by the shadowy figure of Arthur, but whether he too was a leader of the official Roman kind [like Cunedda in this interpretation], as some think, or whether he was only another 'tyrant' like Vortigern, we cannot really know; and nothing useful can be said about him here.
>
> (Jackson 1953: 116)

Jackson was happy to accept Badon as historical, placing it around 500 and in the south (Badbury Hill or Badbury near Swindon were the options that he offered). Like Chambers and Collingwood, he imagined the enemy to be the Saxons of the South East, but 'the British leader may or may not have been the King Arthur of later tradition' (p. 199).

Jackson retreated only a short distance from this comparative scepticism when he returned to the question of Arthur's historicity in 1959 (p. 1), with a response in the affirmative but very cautiously so: 'The only honest answer is, "We do not know, but he may well have existed." The nature of the evidence is such that proof is impossible.' Jackson then proceeded to discuss the earliest stratum of literary evidence in some detail, concluding again that we should be thinking tentatively of a southern British hero figure of the late fifth century who was vividly remembered in the late sixth. Thomas Jones posed the same question just one year earlier, although his essay is best known in the English translation which appeared in 1964. His response was very similar, very mildly affirmative but even more cautious (p. 237), as quoted at the start of this chapter: 'It is difficult to say anything precise about the Arthur of history'. He similarly conceded the possibility of an historical figure, but this time one operative in northern Britain in the years around 500, whose reputation later grew for no very obvious reason (and this process clearly puzzled Jones) within the heroic tradition.

In a paper offered in support of Jones's earlier views, and in his honour, Rachel Bromwich (1975–6) shared his puzzlement concerning the widespread and rapid development of Arthurian literature in the Middle Ages, as well as his preference for a northern origin for the Arthurian material in the *Historia Brittonum*. Like Jones, therein she saw the *Historia*'s Arthur as an integral part of the so-called 'Northern Chronicle' materials of chapters 57 onwards. Bromwich ended by offering her own more specific but still tentative vision of an historical Arthur. She speculated (pp. 180–1) that he might best be associated with the south-eastern corner of the 'Old North', i.e. the East Riding of Yorkshire or York, before being relocated along with other northern heroes to Strathclyde and only thence to Wales. This was, perhaps, in part at least to explain Arthur's putative early interaction with the Germanic invader, since Anglo-Saxon archaeological remains are only present in significant quantities in this period in the north in eastern Yorkshire. Equally, she mooted that such a construct might explain the lack of a genealogy for Arthur, if his dynasty were overwhelmed thereafter at an early stage of the English seizure of the north and the construction, in the seventh century, of the kingdom of Northumbria.

There were, at the same time, other developments in the understanding of the Arthurian texts. Following a lengthy gestation and even the death of the author, Tatlock's *The Legendary History of Britain* was finally published in 1950, providing at last a lengthy, critical and detailed exploration of Geoffrey of Monmouth's Arthur and its origins, which was both sceptical of this text's historicity and highly scholarly. Thereafter, Robert Hanning (1966) set himself (p. viii) not to reconstruct historical events from the 'fall of Britain' texts which he chose to consider, but instead to deconstruct the historical motivations and imaginations of his authors, their traditions of expression and analysis, and the themes which dominate and organize their work. The result was a groundbreaking and insightful review of the construction and organization of Gildas's *De Excidio Britanniae*, Bede's *Historia Ecclesiastica*, the *Historia Brittonum* and Geoffrey of Monmouth's *Historia Regum Britanniae*. This was, perhaps, most effective in the present context in discussing the impact of Gildas on the *Historia Brittonum*, and the broader discussion of the latter's underlying theories of history, for example (p. 108), as a national history with its own internal value system in opposition to Gildas's earlier acknowledgement of Rome's legitimacy as a political and imperial power. Such attention to underlying structure led Hanning to observe:

> Arthur performs great feats of valor in defeating the Saxons twelve times, and his appearance in the *Historia Brittonum* at this point provides an *exemplum* of the combination of social heroism and piety which, in sharp contrast to the turpitude of Guorthigirn, will save Britain. The inclusion of Patrick and Arthur in the narrative following Guorthigirn supports the impression that clerical authors-compilers were attempting to reassert in ninth-century Britain the efficacy of the Christian theology of history as a moral approach to national history.
>
> The *Historia Brittonum* is a dangerous text from which to draw conclusions about actual happenings of British history. It is also, because of its composite nature, treacherous ground for the student of early medieval historiography.
>
> (Hanning 1966: 120)

Hanning's deconstruction of the *Historia* was much hampered by his assumption – along with contemporaries – that it was a collection of works by numerous authors, which deflected him from effective analysis of its authorship. It was not until his approach was further developed by David Dumville that Hanning's exploration of changing theories of history during the period *c.* 500 to *c.* 1100 really began to impact on historical consideration of the period.

If we were to attempt to sum up the debate about an historical Arthur in the late 1960s, Sheppard Frere's recycling of Collingwood's views would arguably have been as widely accepted as any (1967):

> In the later fifth century the leadership [of Vortigern] had passed to Ambrosius Aurelianus and after him to Arthur. Little is known of either. Ambrosius appears in the pages of Gildas, but Arthur does not, and his activities and personality are almost impenetrably overlaid by medieval romance. The evidence is sufficient to allow belief that he had a real existence and that he was probably the victor of Mount Badon. . . . Using mounted forces, these leaders were able to strike back at the Saxons, who had little body armour and inferior weapons.
> (Frere 1967: 1987 edn, p. 374)

A rather vague but probably historical Arthur, then, canters through the early post-war period, leading heavily armed cavalry in a quintessentially late-Roman style of warfare, to contest the Anglo-Saxon settlement and give protection to the sub-Roman Britons.

## ARTHUR COMES OF AGE

It was in this intellectual environment that interest in an historical King Arthur developed and gained academic respectability. A new generation of (primarily) archaeologists raised on a diet in which Collingwood's study of Roman Britain was a fundamental influence now set about breaking down the barriers of historicity to turn the existing hypotheses into a real Arthurian past. The 1960s witnessed challenges to prevalent establishment views on numerous issues, stretching from sexual and religious mores to fashion and design (e.g. Marwick 1998). Received images of the insular past were not immune from this wind of change. The Germanist vision of the past seemed increasingly out of touch with a contemporary, multi-ethnic and multi-cultural society and the 'Celtic' element in Arthurian studies connected with various other strands of cultural and spiritual change, which were now come to the fore as institutional Christianity declined. It was during this era that the slide of Anglo-Saxon Studies into obscurity began to be detectable (Shippey 2000), and it was Arthurianism which rose in its place.

The great Iron Age hill-fort of South Cadbury had been rumoured to be Arthur's Camelot since at least the sixteenth century, when John Leland took the association for granted:

> At the very south ende of the chirch of South-Cadbyri standith Camallate, sumtyme a famose toun or castelle, apon a very torre or hille, wunderfully enstrengtheid of nature . . . The people can tell nothing ther but that they have hard say that Arture much resortid to Camalat.
>
> (Leyland 1542: 1964 edn, p. 151)

The Camelot Research Committee was formed in 1965, largely through the energies of Ralegh Radford, the archaeologist who had excavated Tintagel and Castle Dore, to support and drive forward a new campaign of archaeological excavations. It brought together the Arthurian enthusiast Geoffrey Ashe (1957, 1960) with Leslie Alcock, then at University College, Cardiff, Lady Fox (University of Exeter), John Hurst (Ministry of Works) and Philip Rahtz, at the University of Birmingham, all under the presidency of Sir Mortimer Wheeler. Excavations began tentatively in 1966 and continued for four years, producing a series of dramatic discoveries including a sub-Roman rampart of massive scale, the putative layout of a cruciform church and an aisled hall associated with imported Mediterranean pottery (Alcock 1972, but see also the reinterpretation of Alcock 1982).

There was clearly mutual advantage in this alliance between popular Arthurianism and academe: the wide appeal brought numerous reprints of published works (particularly Alcock's *Arthur's Britain*), interest from the BBC and a flow of the necessary funds from learned societies and institutions. It had an immediate outcome in the multi-authored volume, *The Quest for Arthur's Britain*, which Geoffrey Ashe edited in 1968. Alcock's Arthur was a military leader rather than a king (after the *Historia Brittonum* as read by Collingwood, who was by now thought of as having originated the notion of the sub-Roman army commander), and he was prepared to accept the accuracy of the dating offered by the *Annales Cambriae* to establish his hero's *floruit*. Alcock revived the argument (already noted in the nineteenth century) that entries in the *Annales* for 615 and 665 were capable of identifying Bath as *Badon*, encouraging him to make firm connections between Arthur and the south-western region in which lay South Cadbury, and he was also prepared to accept the late twelfth-century Glastonbury 'discovery' of Arthur's body as genuine (see p. 230).

The idea of a glorious Arthurian age of British achievement against the Saxons passed from the world of literature to that of history, therefore, during the 1960s and had become both extremely popular and widely accepted by the early 1970s. Its removal with extraordinary rapidity from the very edges of history to centre stage implies that it conformed particularly well with the intellectual and cultural context of the period. Within Britain, the rise of the historical Arthur should be associated with the defeat of Germany and consequent bankruptcy of Germanism (for history as context, see H. White 1978). Arthur offered an icon for the post-war British state uncontaminated by Teutonism and, indeed, victorious in his opposition to Germanic conquest. Academically, a 'real' fifth/sixth-century Arthur gained adherence primarily within the archaeological community, but that community necessarily looked to textual evidence because it was itself hampered within its own discipline by the very anonymity inherent in material evidence.

The culmination of this process was John Morris's *The Age of Arthur*, published in 1973 and never since out of print, which offers a primarily text-based review of the history of the British Isles from the mid-fourth to the mid-seventh centuries. Morris was a well established and highly respected historian with a Welsh pedigree, who had co-founded the prestigious journal *Past and Present* in 1952, worked on Pelagian writings of the fifth century and began the *Prosopography of the Later Roman Empire* (with A. H. M. Jones). Thereafter he initiated the Phillimore editions of *Domesday Book*, county by county, and other early insular texts. For the task of writing late Roman and sub-Roman insular history, therefore, Morris was in several respects well qualified.

*The Age of Arthur* is a massive work, totalling 665 pages of tightly constructed text. It heralded a new and very laudable commitment to breaking down the great divide between ancient and medieval – thus between Romanists and Anglo-Saxonists – which had been so powerful a feature of nineteenth- and twentieth-century historiography to that point. Indeed, by laying claim to an 'Age of Arthur', it proposed a complete restructuring of insular history. Another of its undoubted strengths was the vast industry and textual research on which it was based. Morris peopled his world with an array of figures, to whom he proceeded to attribute a range of deeds, dates and relationships. Although he acknowledged his preference for historical methodology, Morris attempted to incorporate archaeological knowledge and interpretation, providing schematic maps of (particularly) cemetery evidence as far as that was understood at that date. Archaeologists had long sought a chronological framework in history but historians had been less ready to reciprocate (excepting, perhaps, Hodgkin 1935).

Morris freely acknowledged the problems he saw confronting him in reading early texts:

> Most of these texts are full of half-truths, seen out of focus. They cannot be interpreted until the date and purpose of each has been determined, the original separated from the additions, the contemporary report distinguished from the recollections of the next century, when living memory was still green, and both from the imagination of later ages. Even then, a single statement in a single text

carries little weight; confidence comes only when independent texts from different peoples and different standpoints combine to record the same event or to outline the same situation.

(Morris 1973: 35)

As a methodology, this has its strengths. Morris did not always succeed, however, in pursuing his own agenda. He seems to have been simply overwhelmed by the quantity and diversity of literature which he explored and was ultimately outfaced by the complexity of the textual histories each involved, many of which were, and are, insoluble. Owing to his terminal illness (he was in the process of editing and translating the *Historia Brittonum* when he died in June 1977), the project was also, perhaps, completed in haste. He ended up mixing his own readings of the small amounts of text written in the fifth or sixth centuries with the far larger quantity of non-contemporary literature purporting to be about that period but written in the central Middle Ages and for contemporary reasons. Morris argued, or often implied, that the late material was an accurate copy of much earlier, but now lost, sources and so contained reliable historical information. Let one passage stand for many (pp. 35–6):

> About 540, the priest Gildas published a forthright attack on the princes and bishops of his day, and began with a historical preface, tracing the origins of the evils he denounced. One statement, first set down within his own lifetime, and copied by a much later writer, reports that he was born beyond the Roman frontier, in the kingdom of the Clyde; but he was brought south in childhood, to be schooled in a fully Roman educational tradition by the shores of the Severn Sea.

This confident and apparently uncontentious passage begs a number of issues by refusing to acknowledge the limitations of the evidence on which it is based. In the first place is the date of authorship, which is a matter of speculation, even though something close to an academic consensus existed when Morris wrote (thereafter, see O'Sullivan 1978; Sims-Williams 1983; Dumville 1984a and b; Higham 1994). Second is the confident designation of Gildas as a priest. He was a Christian, most certainly, and well read in the Bible, but his particular rank is unclear. Although there can be no doubt that his text favours the monastic ideal, he does not seem to have been either a monk or a priest at the time of writing and is perhaps best seen as a deacon. This may be a quibbling point, but it illustrates the failure to insert such words as 'perhaps' and 'possibly' into his text. Third is the assertion concerning Gildas's origins, which depends on the implicit assumption that the *vita* of Gildas, written sometime around 1000 in the Breton monastery of St Gildas de Rhus (H. Williams 1899), was copied from a text contemporary with

Gildas's life. On this bold assumption depends either or both a birthplace in Strathclyde and an education at the feet of St Illtud in southern Wales – which is what I assume is meant by the 'Severn Sea'. Neither claim is easily reconciled with the level and nature of Latin learning which the text reveals (Lapidge 1984), which derives from a Roman-style education, rather than an early medieval, monastic one (but see now Howlett 1998).

Morris's narrative remains a widely read description of the period, but it is less a reconstructive history than an insular pseudo-history covering the Dark Ages, to stand comparison with such literary giants as Tolkien's *Lord of the Rings* trilogy (1954–5). Tolkien adopted the Anglo-Saxons wholesale as the Rohirrim of the Mark and even, to some extent, the Hobbits themselves. John Masefield's *Badon Parchments* (1947) draws its character list from early literature referring to the fifth and sixth centuries and seeks to reconstruct the context of Badon, but his work, like the later and in some respects comparable books of Nikolai Tolstoy, is explicitly a novel.

Another message is also at times discernible in Morris's text (as in Masefield's and Tolstoy's), which is his palpable rejection of all things German. His refocusing of British Dark Age history away from the Anglo-Saxon immigrants and onto the indigenous population and their legendary history offers a metaphor for the attitudes of his own generation to the two world wars. Morris's rhetoric transcends the historical context:

> Badon was the 'final victory of the fatherland' [Gildas, of course]. It ended a war whose issue had already been decided. The British had beaten back the barbarians. They stood alone in Europe, the only remaining corner of the western Roman Empire where a native power withstood the all-conquering Germans. Yet the price of victory was the loss of almost everything the victors had taken arms to defend.
>
> (Morris 1973: 114)

He returned later to this same theme (p. 141): 'There is . . . just enough to show that in Britain he [Arthur] subdued the Germans who elsewhere mastered Europe'. This representation of Dark Age history was also, therefore, an extended metaphor which reflected the lifetime of its author and the European conflicts which had framed his world. Morris's vision was conditioned by his own need to symbolize the struggles of the present by reference to the past, and this too may have encouraged his full-blown re-imagining of the early Middle Ages. His own experiences of war in Yugoslavia and his later involvement in C.N.D. seem powerful influences.

Morris's representation of Arthur has been an influential one and his reconstruction of Dark Age history has conditioned much which has been written since, his continuing popularity assured by the power of the literary form which he used and the meanings his Dark Age Britain acquired for modern audiences (White 1973). His Arthur was the supreme commander of the

Britons who led primarily cavalry (as Collingwood) to their defining victory at the siege of *Mons Badonicus* (which he identified tentatively as Solsbury Hill, near Bath), and so halted English expansion across southern England. Morris accepted the *Historia Brittonum*'s battle list as essentially historical (p. 111). However, he reinterpreted those conflicts which seemed to lie in the north or west as later Arthurian battles against British opponents, so as to preserve his underlying thesis of an Arthur in command first and foremost of the British lowlands. With the Saxons defeated, Arthur was:

> a just and powerful ruler who long maintained in years of peace the empire of Britain, that his arms had recovered and restored. Contemporary and later writers honour and respect the government he headed. A few notices describe events and incidents that happened while he ruled. None describe the man himself, his character or his policy, his aims or his personal achievement. He remains a mighty shadow, a figure looming large behind every record of his time, yet never clearly seen.
>
> (Morris 1973: 116)

This, of course, assumes that contemporary writers demonstrably knew of Arthur's role in any such governance, and that is far from clear. As Morris recognized, only Gildas certainly offers the prospect of an author whose own life overlapped with that of the commander at Badon, and he failed to name Arthur. That he explained (following Lloyd 1911, Stenton 1943 and Jackson 1959a) by reference to Gildas's notorious unwillingness to name names over the preceding eighty years, but there are other solutions to this conundrum which would be fatal to Morris's case.

## ARTHUR IN THE SPOTLIGHT

Morris's undoubted learning did not, however, soften the criticism of reviewers, and in particular those drawn from the ranks of early medieval history. James Campbell was characteristically kindly in his condemnation (1975), describing it as 'brave, comprehensive and imaginative', even while pointing out that Morris's 'historical imagination is inadequately controlled and waxes dogmatic, and over-specific', and that his judgement erred in many details. Others were more acerbic in their rebuttals. Kirby and Williams (1975–6) admitted the book's appearance of majesty. However, they pointed out (in a thirty-two-page refutation) that the appearance conceals 'a seemingly total inability to construct a thesis which unfolds logically and by appropriate stages, together with an indifference to the views and conclusions of other scholars bordering on the absolute' (p. 454). They dismissed it, therefore, as a 'tangled tissue of fact and fantasy which is both misleading and misguided', disputing detail after detail and pointing up whole areas of methodological inadequacy, which included (p. 460), with unusual understatement, a 'certain laxity in respect of linguistic methods'.

David Dumville also wrote an impassioned response to the works of both Alcock and Morris, published in 1977, in which he set out in considerable detail the weaknesses of their treatment of Celtic literature as a source appropriate to fifth- and sixth-century history, and this has since become the bedrock of modern historiography on the subject. Dumville attempted to banish the spectre of Arthur completely:

> Arthur [is] a man without position or ancestry in pre-Geoffrey Welsh sources. I think we can dispose of him quite briefly. He owes his place in our history books to a 'no smoke without fire' school of thought.
>
> (Dumville 1977a: 187)

In the aftermath, it seemed very possible that Arthur would entirely lose the place he had so recently acquired in the history of Britain. Peter Salway published the new volume on *Roman Britain* in the Oxford History of England in 1981, effectively replacing Collingwood and Myres's volume of 1936 (although that remained in print). His treatment of the fifth century accommodated recent critical treatment of Arthurian history and archaeology:

> Over recent years there has been a growing movement to believe in the historicity of Arthur, and to go much further, identifying him with actual places, even to the extent of recognizing in the Dark Age refortification of the hill-fort at South Cadbury in Somerset the site of 'Camelot'. It should be said that the archaeology is extremely interesting but very difficult to interpret. But so much doubt has now been thrown on the state of knowledge about the Celtic written sources for Arthur that both his connection with the archaeology and his very existence are matters that need to be held in abeyance by historians till the value of the texts is re-examined by those specialists qualified to do so.
>
> (Salway 1981: 485)

Similar scepticism was evinced implicitly by Wendy Davies (1982) and the present author (Higham 1986), both of whom wrote works covering areas of Britain (Wales and the north of England respectively) in the early Middle Ages but without reference to King Arthur. Michael Wood's 'In Search of the Dark Ages', broadcast for the BBC in 1980, adopted the same minimalist approach, only to be inundated by indignant letters from Arthurian enthusiasts (Wood 1999: 27). It seemed quite possible in the 1980s, therefore, that Arthur had been consigned to the margins of academic history once and for all, albeit his credibility remained high outside academic circles.

It is, however, virtually impossible to prove a negative, particularly when strong and emotive cultural pressures work in opposition in a contemporary context. A review of the issue by Professor Thomas Charles-Edwards (1991: 29) concluded that: 'one can only say that there may well have been an historical Arthur; that the historian can as yet say nothing of value about him'. This carefully conditioned positivism mirrors the conclusion of Professor Kenneth Jackson (1959a: 1), whose article his effectively replaced: 'We do not know, but he [Arthur] may well have existed.'

These cautious remarks seemed to open the door for others to explore more openly positivist interpretations of Arthur, in a particular role and in a specific historical context. Even for those who consider it premature to postulate any particular Arthur, it still opens a window of opportunity through which to continue the hunt for the historical Arthur. The gauntlet has recently been thrown down in defence of such pursuits by Christopher Snyder, cast very consciously in Dumville's own metaphor:

> there has been an awful lot of smoke blowing around the Arthurian tradition. So much similar evidence, circumstantial though it may be, must have some cause, and it is hard to see the 'fire' as the tale of one creative medieval bard.
>
> (Snyder 1998: 254)

Again, it is difficult to disagree, although one might legitimately object that Dumville's vision does not require that *King* Arthur sprang fully formed from the imagination of a single creative muse. After all, there is a gulf between the Arthur *miles* of the *Historia Brittonum* and the King Arthur who appears for the first time in eleventh- and twelfth-century literature. Snyder went on, however, to quote (at somewhat greater length than above) from Charles-Edwards to reinforce the legitimacy of his position, then added:

> Admitting this to ourselves [i.e. the possibility of their existence] will perhaps allow the quests for Arthur and Merlin to continue without the constant griping of academics and, more important, will allow the growth of the legend to continue without the constraints of historical fact. What the historian can contribute, however, is a better understanding of the period and place in which Arthur and Merlin *may have lived* for those who wish to pin down these legendary figures to time and space.
>
> (Snyder 1988: 255)

Snyder's love affair with Arthurian legend has since been made manifest in a delightful volume, *Exploring the World of King Arthur* (2000), which covers many aspects of the history of its evolution. Regarding the issue of an historical, Dark Age king, Snyder is comfortable with the notion of a composite (thus unreal) figure, but among these strands he suggests (p. 8) 'an historical Arthur, or, if you prefer, a folklorist or mythological Arthur who came to be mistaken for a living person'. His reuse of Morris's book title as a chapter heading, for his survey of the fifth and sixth centuries, is justified on the grounds that (p. 35) 'for many people this period will always be the Age of Arthur'.

A far more critical position has been adopted by Oliver Padel (1994, 1995, 2000), the present author (Higham 1994: 203–12) and Thomas Green (1998). Padel has refocused attention on the mythological option regarding Arthur's origins, suggesting that Arthur's two appearances in the *mirabilia* of the *Historia Brittonum* should be taken to indicate the likeliest source of his historicization in chapter 56 of the same work as a British warrior figure. In this case, a 'real' King Arthur becomes improbable and his origin lies in the realm of mythology. My own re-examination of Gildas's *De Excidio Britanniae* led me to conclude that the so-called 'Age of Arthur' – of a half-century or so of British success against the Saxons – was without foundation in the key text which had hitherto served as the cornerstone of this position. If there was no such period of British domination, then twentieth-century attempts to construct a 'real' King Arthur are much weakened. Green has gone further, even, putting forward the argument that the negative can be pretty well concluded and that Arthur can be said to have *not* existed on the basis of the evidence available. Obviously, these arguments will be re-opened in detail during the course of this work, but it is important to recognize their connections with the criticisms of historical Arthurianism in the 1970s, by Dumville *et al.*, on which all three have built.

However, these contributions aside, there has been a marked unwillingness to close the box which Morris opened. Alongside the scepticism of the scholars who would prefer a mythological, unhistorical Arthur, are a plethora of arguments for various 'real' Arthurs. So, there have been numerous recent reconstructions of an historical Arthur in a particular locality (Dunning 1988; Phillips and Keatman 1993; Gilbert, Wilson and Blackett 1998; Doel, Doel and Lloyd 1998; Moffat 1999; Castleden 2000), in most instances for reasons which apparently revolve around a search for local identity and validation in the present. Additionally there have been attempts to write specialist Arthurian histories, including his portrayal as a leader of marines (Bachrach 1991), and as a military strategist, which necessarily rest in detail on the texts of the central Middle Ages and their interpretation. Each of these essays uses broadly the same body of information (with particular topographical detail added in) but interprets it very differently. So Gilbert and his collaborators favour an Arthur in south-east Wales, Phillips and Keatman locate theirs at Wroxeter, Moffat in southern Scotland and both Dunning and Castleden opt for the south-west. Over against these, Ashe (1981) has argued that Geoffrey of Monmouth's vision of Arthur's Gallic activities should be given greater credence. This is largely on the basis of the lost Breton *Life of St. Goeznovius*, written no earlier than the early eleventh century, which refers to Arthur's victories in both Britain and Gaul (see extract, Chambers 1927: 241–3), which leads Ashe to argue for an identification of Arthur with the British warlord with whom Sidonius corresponded in the Loire region, named Riothamus (d. *c.* 470: see p. 76). Then there is the theory of Littleton and Malcor (1994), developed from ideas first put forward by Nickel (1975) but since taken up by Howard Reid (2001), which proposes that the medieval Arthur derived from the folklore of the Sarmatians or Alans, ultimately from the Steppes or northern Iran but via service in the Roman army (a group was certainly stationed at Ribchester in the third century). Failing that, Reid suggests an origin in Japan.

A study of a rather different order is Mike Baillie's (1999) which focuses on the increasingly emphatic dendrochronological evidence of an environmental catastrophe occurring in the time frame 536–45, most probably as a consequence of a large comet striking earth. Baillie notes the apparent synchronism of this event and traditional death dates for King Arthur and explores Arthurian legend as a potential source for connections with that event.

There are a host of positivist histories of Arthur in publication, therefore, most of which (Littleton and Malcor excepted) offer a particular vision of a 'real' historical figure. These are pretty well all (with the same exception) works which fall outside of the 'academic' net, so are either not offered for review to appropriate academic journals or, if offered, not accepted. The standard stance adopted by academic historians is to ignore this literature, engagement with which has, perhaps, some potential to damage academic reputations. By so doing, however, the academic community fails to recognize the vitality of the debate and the robustness of the 'historical' Arthur lobby. In consequence, hardly a single work has been written by a university historian on Arthur since the 1970s, Snyder's and Padel's new studies alone excepted. With the world wide web, bookshop shelves and book club catalogues full of 'real' Arthurs, it is not surprising that belief in an historical Arthur remains high, albeit there is some confusion as to which 'real' Arthur should be privileged over others. This is a powerful lobby, which has considerable influence over a wide and public debate, operating with the active encouragement of publishers, confident that subject recognition remains high enough to sell almost any number of works on Arthur.

Arthur's place in history also remains an issue at the level of synthetic and 'national' (or even 'global') histories, as it has been for a millennium. I offer two very different visions, drawn from contrasting ends of the spectrum of contemporary historical writing. First, the following comes from Professor Norman Davies's highly lauded new history of the British Isles, published in 1999 (p. 166): 'Historians mostly now agree that an Arthur-like British warlord really did exist'. Davies notes David Dumville's work but this seems to run counter to his caution against just such remarks. Efforts have already been made to challenge Davies's vision of the insular early Middle Ages and the terminology he on occasion uses (as Campbell 2000: ix–xi), but his assumptions concerning the weight of scholarly opinion regarding an historical Arthur remain to be tested.

My second quotation is from Terry Deary's *The Smashing Saxons* (2000), a tongue-in-cheek work which is aimed at a similarly wide, but much younger audience:

> The Saxons were battering the Brits, but some Brits started fighting back. They wanted a Britain the way it was in the old Roman days of eighty years before. One leader managed to win forty years of peace. He was called 'the last Roman' and his name was Arthur.
>
> Five hundred years after Arthur died his name was remembered and storytellers came up with some great tales of Arthur's deeds. In a word they were bosh. In four words they were total and utter bosh. Any historian will tell you . . .
>
> (Deary 2000: 35)

A witty encapsulation of the Arthurian debate, therefore, and one which engages magnificently with the central medieval texts, but the underlying historicity of Deary's fifth- or sixth-century Arthur is as palpable as Davies's.

## CONCLUSION

The twentieth century has, therefore, witnessed a lengthy debate about the historicity of Arthur. Before 1940, identification as a figure of mythology had already been challenged by Arthur's re-admittance to history as a military leader in sub-Roman Britain, largely on the basis of the *Historia Brittonum*. After the Second World War, the British King Arthur who had famously triumphed over Germanic invaders in the Dark Ages was widely, but not always consciously, reconstructed as an historical icon for post-war British society, threatening to displace King Alfred and the Anglo-Saxon past in this respect. Archaeology held out the possibility of a new mechanism for exploring the fact-starved history of Britain before 600, and briefly offered the possibility that Arthur's topographical context was capable of location. That enterprise has continued into the twenty-first century, with a host of hypotheses regarding 'real' Arthurs, coupled with a wide variety of manifestations in other media.

The reactions of most academic historians have been either sceptical or hostile to this process, even while making remarkably few public statements on the subject. While some have offered the bare possibility that there was an historical Arthur, others have sought to return him to the world of mythology and deny his historicity outright. In academic circles, it is Alfred who has retained a central position and Arthur who has generally been marginal, in contrast to popular perspectives. In practice, most, if not all, of the academic community prefer to explore the so-called 'Arthurian' texts of the central Middle Ages within a contemporary intellectual, political and cultural context, rather than as a quarry for 'Dark Age facts'. It is our developing knowledge and understandings of these texts as expressions of the worlds in which they were written which offer the most attractive route forward. That route has important implications for the 'real' Arthur debate, but it is being driven less by the need to understand the fifth and sixth centuries than to explore how those distant periods of the past were being constructed in the central Middle Ages, for contemporary purposes. It is to these issues that we now turn, in the following three chapters.

# CHAPTER II

# THE GENESIS OF ARTHUR

— •◦• —

It became a mocking proverb far and wide that the Britons are cowardly in war and faithless in peace.

(Gildas, *DEB* vi, 2)

This chapter seeks to address two basic questions which underlie the emergence of an 'historical' Arthur in the ninth and tenth centuries. The first should be framed something like: 'What were the main characteristics of "British" national identity prior to 800, to which the author of the *Historia Brittonum* responded, in part at least via the figure of Arthur?' The second is: 'Where did the historicized Arthur of that same ninth-century text originate?' or, if you prefer, 'Where did the author responsible find the prototype and name "Arthur" which he then dressed in such exciting new clothes?'

These questions are rarely asked in precisely these terms. Instead, historians and archaeologists have tended to offer broad-based but reconstructionist discussions of Roman Britain and the insular Dark Ages (basically the fifth and sixth centuries) as if explanation enough on their own for the later emergence of Arthur. This, it has been assumed (see, for example, Snyder 2000), is the proper space in which to discover an 'historical' prototype-Arthur, who is expected to have been doing in reality pretty much the same sorts of things that, in the ninth and tenth centuries, he was alleged to have done. Put at its most basic, this Arthur is still expected to have been an historical British warlord fighting against the Germanic immigrants to Britain. It is, therefore, poor evidence about the period which stops us today identifying the Dark Age Arthur more clearly, not any problem of historicity. On this reading, the authors of the *Historia Brittonum* and *Annales Cambriae* had information of good quality regarding the much earlier period, which has since been lost, and included Arthur on good authority.

However, the poor quality and small quantity of our literary evidence for the fifth and sixth centuries are a fact of life, and it is arguably more helpful to recognize that fact and examine our ninth- and tenth-century works in the context of the known texts that their authors used, and the intellectual climate in which they were constructed, than to speculate on earlier but lost texts which they do not name and which may in any case have been highly fictitious and far from contemporary, or even illusory. If we are to approach an understanding of Arthur in the central Middle Ages, therefore, it is incumbent on us to explore how the world picture and ideological positioning of the Britons developed against an appropriate, and changing, political backdrop, and how that was then accessed and given meaning in the ninth and tenth centuries. This question takes us inexorably into issues about nationalism and ethnicity.

The second question has been explored rather more fully than the first, albeit most often we come back again to the assumption that a 'real' Arthur of the fifth/sixth centuries 'certainly' or 'probably' lay behind the later construct (see Chapter I). This has led to a wide trawl for possible candidates, from the second century through to the end of the sixth. These issues will be reviewed in the second part of this chapter.

## BEING 'BRITISH': THE POLITICAL AND IDEOLOGICAL CONTEXT

'Britain' and 'the Britons' are fundamental concepts within the thought-world of the author of the *Historia Brittonum*, which contextualize his Arthur figure, since his role as a specifically 'British' champion is fundamental to his characterization in the earliest 'historical' references. This section will survey the early literature which conveys an understanding of British constructions of ethnicity and national identity, which, in turn, conditioned the agenda pursued by Welsh authors in the central Middle Ages.

There is today an inescapable tension between the two ways of envisaging national identity. Most modern scholars are to some degree 'instrumentalists', in that they privilege the sense in which nations are 'invented', often by the self-conscious manipulation by élites who find the reinforcement of the group helpful in securing their own power. Most are also, to some degree, however, 'primordialists', emphasizing continuities between communities and their antecedents and the resistance to change of such social features as kinship and language (the issues are laid out helpfully in Calhoun 1997). These tensions have a significance for any discussion of 'Britishness' (and 'Englishness', etc.) which clearly meant different things at different times and to different constituencies. It will become clear that this tension was less apparent in the early Middle Ages, when a 'primordial' approach to identity was apparently taken for granted, largely on the basis of analogy with Old Testament assumptions about race as both biological and theological fact. There is, therefore, an additional tension between the ways in which identity was constructed in early Britain and how such issues are now deconstructed (see, for parallels, Geary 1983; Pohl with Reimitz 1998).

## Britain and the 'Britons'

As terms, both 'Britain' and 'British' derive ultimately from a pre-colonial, classical context, when both terms were used by Greek authors writing about geography and ethnography. The idea of a single 'British' people was constructed outside Britain, therefore, and may well have had little if any insular meaning outside of the geographical locale prior to the Roman conquest. From Greek, these terms were Latinized and adopted in political and ultimately in imperial circles, and rapidly came into use in the context of histories of conquest (Rivet and Smith 1979). *Britannia* was invaded by Caesar, therefore, and his opponents there were labelled *Britanni, hostes* ('the enemy', his standard term for 'Others'), or by various tribal names, whom he defeated and subdued. The geographical name was retained for the conquered province and ultimately the diocese, and *Britanni* remained the normal term for the provincial population under Roman rule, with more local, tribal identities reserved for *civitates*.

These visions of an insular ethnicity and geographical identity were then maintained beneath the over-arching fabric of the imperial Roman empire and the social and political identities which it privileged. The Roman system was in many respects multi-ethnic, but not all terms were equally valued. So, for example, the *Brittunculi* writing tablet from Vindolanda implies that other groups within the Empire assumed that 'nasty little Britons' should be regularly flogged by Roman (or Batavian) officers (Bowman and Thomas 1994: 343; Birley 2001). Likewise, 'Britain' was on occasion used within the rhetoric of the imperial court to signify 'the ends of the earth', where civilization was in doubt. The late imperial establishment removed troops from Britain on the assumption that the needs of other parts of the Empire were paramount (see e.g. Claudian, *De Bello Gothico* 416–18), and the island was for long periods left to its own devices. It would then be reintegrated to the Empire by punitive expedition and, one must presume, political pogrom.

The Empire acted as a vehicle for a single, over-arching vision of group identity, characterized by subordination to the central political structures, its officers and tax regimes, but also in the West by Latin Romanity, common élite cultural practices, urbanism, villa-building, legal processes, and so on. These factors obviously impacted on how 'Britishness' was perceived by the local élite. The interface between Roman imperialism and local identities has been much explored in recent years (for Britain, see Millett 1990; Higham 1992a; for the wider Roman world, Mattingly 1997). Earlier, simpler models of Romanization (Haverfield 1912) as a one-way, top-down process capable of enforcing a single model of Romanity have been modified or even abandoned in favour of the concept of a dialogue, in which both sides contributed substantially, with the local response to colonial processes perhaps the single most important factor. Local ethnicity and the sense of group remained, therefore, powerful forces within an imperial 'tribe' of provincial and sub-provincial identities. Consequently the experience of Romanization was very different in different parts of the Empire. 'Roman' arguably had very many different shades of meaning, some owned to varying degrees and by differing social groups in any one region, dioceses or province, and others not.

In very general terms, it is probably fair to see the British provincial community as comparatively poorly integrated to core notions of Roman group identity and culture, both as regards local views on the subject and outside opinion. Urban and villa-dwelling sectors of society, who constituted the political classes in control of local civil government, organized religion and the law, are archaeologically identifiable in only approximately half the diocese, and Latin-speaking and educated families arguably made up a smaller part of the total population than in Gaul or Spain, for example. The local vernacular language survived the process of Latin colonization. This did not occur on the continent, where provincial Latin eventually became the *lingua franca* of even the peasantry, although this may have occurred only comparatively late in the Roman period. Much of the British diocese retained its military and frontier characteristics throughout, with the exceptionally shallow settlement and social hierarchies, and low levels of economic specialization, which that involved. The wide frontier zones of Roman Britain perhaps coloured core perceptions of Britain throughout its history, since the security of the province and later diocese was the major responsibility of the establishment. Despite several emperors launching bids for power from Britain, none were of British birth and no great British families emerged to place 'Britishness' at the centre of the imperial enterprise, as occurred in the context of numerous other provincial identities (such as African, Syrian and Dalmatian) throughout the Roman period. The Empire may always have tended to be something which the Britons thought of as 'done' to themselves, which advantaged and privileged other regional communities but never them.

Beyond recognition of the institutions of diocese, province and *civitas*, élite habits and living styles and local religious cults, the sense of group identity of the diocesan population between AD 200 and 400 is irrecoverable. However, following the collapse of the Roman administration of Britain, the testimonies of two of the Latin-educated élite have survived, each of which offers a sense of how that individual viewed himself as a group member. To take the earlier example first (Hood 1978; for recent comment, see Dumville 1993), St Patrick set out to identify himself in the opening lines of his (undated but arguably early to mid-fifth-century) *Confessio* ('Confession'): 'I, Patrick . . . had as my father the deacon Calpornius, son of the late Potitus, a priest, who belonged to *vicus Bannavem Taburniae*; he had a small estate nearby, and it was there that I was taken captive. I was then about sixteen years old'. Patrick offered, therefore, membership of a family, the names of whom he seems to have expected his audience to recognize, or at least respect. He appended their clerical offices across two generations, so an indication of status and position within the local élite, their locality by settlement name (although the identity is now contested and is best considered lost), their status as property owners, and an indication of his generation and personal history. He was writing for a (presumably) mainly British, élite and class-conscious audience, whose language of discourse was Latin, albeit one largely within Ireland (*Confessio* 47, 48).

This small community was arguably already familiar with Patrick, as he was a leading figure within this émigré group, but may not have known his background. It was perhaps unnecessary to add either province or *civitas* to these details, any more than it would now be necessary to establish, for a group of ex-pats, that residing in Macclesfield (for example) necessarily implies living within north-west England. However, Patrick noted elsewhere in the same text (23, 43) that his parents resided in the 'Britains', i.e. the several British provinces making up a single diocese, and he considered these same *Britanniae* collectively his *patria* – his 'fatherland'. This implies that the diocese, which had long been a single province, retained a far stronger identity than the rather artificial, late Roman provinces into which it had been successively subdivided (see e.g. Salway 1981; G. D. B. Jones and D. Mattingly 1990; Millett 1990: illus. 1). The latter had occurred in deference to arbitrary, external decision-making, albeit arguably on the basis of pre-existing *civitas* boundaries.

One thing which is noticeable about Patrick's self-positioning is his disinclination to think of himself as being Roman (a point made by M. E. Jones 1996). Rather, as he made plain in his *epistola* ('letter': 2), he thought of his own (British) 'fellow-citizens' as quite distinct from, and capable of contrast with, the *cives sanctorum Romanorum* ('citizens of the saintly Romans'). He was not hostile to the Romans (as Jones imagined): rather he had a high regard for them, as is clear from this comment. However, he did differentiate them from himself and his own sense of group identity, and this is the earliest date at which this important separation becomes apparent.

This positioning is despite the very obvious Romanity which suffuses pretty well all aspects of Patrick's discourse, hence his style, language and cultural positioning. It should probably be understood both in terms of long-running tensions between insular and imperial identities during the Roman period and as something which will have been encouraged by political change over several decades (or longer) and the need to develop ideologies and group identities capable of accommodating that process. Imperial control over Britain had been no more than episodic during the late fourth century and collapsed very early in the fifth, in a welter of usurpation and civil wars. Thereafter, and presumably also in the several intermissions, Britain was, famously and from a continental perspective, ruled by 'tyrants' (hence rulers whose authority went unrecognized by the Empire). After Magnus Maximus (383–8) and, lastly, Constantine III (406–10), these were figures without any known pretensions to power outside of the insular context – although it would be foolhardy to assume that they necessarily held or even voiced no such ambitions. By contrast with Britain, the imperial system retained a degree of authority and legitimacy across Gaul well into the second half of the fifth century, and this region had long been central to Roman authority and cultural identity in the West. The Roman conquest there had also occurred a century earlier than in Britain, and even earlier in the south. Fifth-century Spanish and Gaulish writers, such as Orosius and Salvian, still identified themselves and their fellows as 'Roman' at a date when Britons seem to have shed over-arching membership of the Empire at large as no longer part of their own identity. This separate 'Britishness' was equally a product of imperialist ideology but was now freed from subservience to a sense of belonging within the Roman state to convey meaning and value in the circumstances of the political fragmentation of the fifth century, alongside and of equal value with Romanity.

The *Brittani* were rediscovering themselves, therefore, as a sub-Roman people defined by a common colonial history, common occupation of space, élite secular and clerical networks which spanned much at least of the old diocese, and some degree of common, Christian, culture and language – be it bilingual in Latin and British. This sense of ethnicity was presumably inclusive of many resident in Britain whose antecedents were from elsewhere (as Gildas perhaps suggested of Ambrosius Aurelianus) and so it should be thought of as situationally constructed (see Geary 1983 for parallels and discussion). This new *patria* of fellow *cives* of a Christian people offered a sense of community as a distinct, British people occupying what had been Roman Britain, and served to distinguish them in Patrick's eyes both from neighbouring barbarian peoples (he specifically names the Picts and Scots as separate peoples), to whom they were inherently superior by virtue of Christianity, and from the Romans, whose poly-ethnic, Christian empire still retained cultural and ideological value across the Channel. It seems likely, however, that this 'Britishness' was an élite phenomenon, with meaning and value primarily for the privileged Latin-speaking classes in control of estates, the Church and the law courts. Their value-systems and construction of group identity, as expressed through surviving Latin texts, privileged their class and its hold on power across the wider community (for parallels and theory, see Femia 1981; Hobsbawm and Ranger 1983; Martin 1998; A. D. Smith 1999).

Whatever else bound them together, this British people was clearly understood by Patrick in providential terms, as being a people of the Lord, whose history and salvation depended on God's protection in a way which was peculiar to themselves. That protection depended in turn on their obedience, with an implicit contract between God and people. In this respect, Patrick was entirely in accord with the prevailing currents of Christian thought in Late Antiquity (as explored in a British context by Hanning 1966; see now Trompf 2000). His exemplar was, of course, the Israelites of the Old Testament and their relationship with the Lord. Where he had disasters to report, his remarks suggest that he looked particularly to the fall of Jerusalem to the Babylonians and Chaldeans, and the captivity of the Israelites, as appropriate analogy. Going back to the opening lines of his *Confessio*, it is clear that it was problems within this morally conceived relationship between God and his people which he believed had conditioned his own well-being within his own experience, and provided the causal framework for his own personal history:

> I did not know the true God and I was taken into captivity in Ireland with so many thousands; and we deserved it, because we drew away from God and did not keep His commandments and did not obey our priests who kept reminding us of our salvation; and the Lord brought on us the fury of His anger and scattered us among many peoples even to the ends of the earth, where now I in my insignificance find myself among strangers.

The analogy with Jeremiah's Lamentation on the fall of Jerusalem and captivity of the Israelites in Babylon is compelling. For himself, Patrick then went on to claim the moral high ground, for he (13), not the 'wealthy rhetoricians' who ran the British church, had been raised up by the Lord (like Christ in contradiction to the Sanhedrin) to spread the gospel among the heathen. This anti-rhetorical stance – the *sermo humilis* – was characteristic of Late Antique clerical writings (associated most famously with St Jerome) but was far from being democratic in impulse. It was Patrick also who claimed that he had (33) 'sought Him earnestly and I found Him there, and He protected me from all evils, as I believe, because of His Spirit dwelling in me, which has been at work within me up to the present day'.

Patrick's claim was, therefore, that he was a chosen one of the Lord, doing God's will. Since he was writing in the context of a dispute with the British church hierarchy and was contesting judgements made against him, his claim to election was necessarily at their expense. Patrick's *Confessio* does not, therefore, portray the British people as a whole as obedient to God and protected by Him, but the author and his immediate circle alone.

Patrick's *Epistola* went much further. In response to an attack launched by the British warriors of one Coroticus against his Irish converts, Patrick addressed them as (2, 4, 5): 'fellow-citizens of demons' who, 'like the enemy live in death, as allies of Irish and Picts and apostates' and 'blood-thirsty men', 'whom Satan has sorely ensnared'. Coroticus is 'a patricide' and 'a fratricide', while his men are 'ravening wolves, devouring God's people like so much bread'.

Patrick's polemic was directed, therefore, at different points in his career, at the leadership of the British church and at a British war leader, who may or may not have been a king, and his war-band. The means he adopted were highly rhetorical: Patrick positioned himself as the beloved of God, a prophet and apostle or Christ-figure, and portrayed his opponents as acting against divine will, i.e. as unrepentant sinners, heretics, barbarians and 'Others'. Although his development of this theme was far more vigorous in the *Epistola* than in the *Confessio*, both his general stance and the strategy adopted were remarkably consistent.

Had Patrick's writings been the sole surviving texts from the period, then the manner of his argumentation might have been considered eccentric in a British context. It is the survival of Gildas's *De Excidio Britanniae* (Winterbottom 1978), with its similarly providential mind-set and assumptions about a specifically British group identity, which suggests that Patrick's political theology was commonplace within the ranks of the Christian, British, land-owning classes of the sub-Roman period. Although Patrick was well known among the Britons centuries later, there is little evidence that his writings were directly accessible in Britain. Rather, they seem to have remained in Ireland, with only secondary writings crossing the Irish Sea. By contrast, Gildas's work became the linchpin of each and every insular history of the sub-Roman period thereafter, from Bede to the *Historia Brittonum* and beyond. It was, therefore, Gildas who had by far the greater impact on thinking about the position of the Britons as regards both ethnicity and political ideology over succeeding centuries, among the Britons as well as among their neighbours.

The overriding message provided by the *De Excidio Britanniae* mirrors Patrick's complaints concerning his fellow countrymen, but Gildas goes far beyond anything which Patrick chose to offer, even at his most acerbic. He constructed an image of his own *cives* ('fellow citizens') as totally, and near-universally, steeped in sin, both in the present and throughout the bulk of their long history. His was (i,1,13) a 'mournful complaint' which 'deplored' 'the general loss of good' and 'the great black blot on *our* generation', which 'has heinous and appalling sins in common with all the wicked ones of the world' as well as 'inborn in it a load of ignorance and folly that cannot be erased or avoided' (i.e. original sin). He portrayed himself as presumptuous in thinking (i, 14) to 'stand up against the blows of so violent a torrent, against the rope of congenital sins that has been stretched far and wide for so many years together', even though his own small circle was presented – like Patrick's – as uniquely obedient to the Lord.

Gildas contextualized his contemporary polemic via a brief recapitulation of British history, in a format reflective of Stephen's speech before the high priest (Acts vii, 2–53; Gardner 1995). This portrayed the British past in terms of his interpretation of the unfolding relationship between the Britons and God over time. An unintentional consequence of this process was the presumption that contemporary visions of British ethnicity, as shared by Gildas and his audience, were equally valid in the late pre-Roman and Roman past. In practice, his position was highly retrospective, but that fact reinforces what can be extracted from his text concerning his own construction of British identity at the time of writing. Gildas's history was, of course, mythological in construction, relying as it did on the centrality of relations between man and God for a rationale. Such constructs are commonplace in post-colonial contexts (e.g. Hobsbawm and Ranger 1983 for post-colonial Africa) and occur widely across barbarian Europe. However, his conception of the origins of his own people offered no glorious pre-colonial golden age or prestigious ancestry, such as frequently develop within historical mythologies (see e.g. A. D. Smith 1999). Gildas stressed rather the negative at the opening of his work, particularly the evil of early British paganism, the traces of which he still recognized and abhorred (iv, 2, 3).

It was not, in origin, the island of Britain itself which was tainted by sin: rather that was portrayed, in a passage which owes something to Orosius (*Histories*, I, ii, 76–7; Higham 1991) as a highly desirable place, indeed as a promised land (iii, 3), 'like a chosen bride arrayed in a variety of jewellery' – for the British people as groom is the obvious inference. Unlike the Israelites in Israel, however, Gildas portrayed the Britons (symbolized by the island itself, but only once it was occupied: cf. 'Israel' for the Israelites in the Old Testament) as morally reprehensible from the beginning:

> Ever since it was first inhabited, Britain has been ungratefully rebelling, stiff-necked and haughty, now against God, now against its own countrymen, sometimes even against kings from abroad and their subjects. What daring of man can, now or in the future, be more foul and wicked than to deny fear to God, charity to good fellow-countrymen, honour to those placed in higher authority (for that is their due, provided, of course, that there is no harm to the faith).

Like Patrick's, Gildas's text privileges the élite, therefore, but his condemnation of his fellow Britons, here and in what follows, was mounted with overwhelming rhetorical power. It was pressed home by recourse to Holy Scripture in passage after passage, thus claiming for his strictures the highest possible moral authority recognized by this élite community. The theme was progressed through time, with the Britons (that is primarily the inhabitants of what had been the diocese but with some imprecision northwards) becoming ever more sinful than before. God, in consequence, was increasingly prone to cauterize their moral failings with 'plagues' of famine, of abundance, of rumours of barbarian attack, and the blindness which ultimately led them to inflict the Saxons on themselves. In the past, the weakness of the Britons had, on occasion, been treated with patience by the Lord, and even been mitigated by, for example (x, 1, 2), 'the brilliant lamps of holy martyrs', such as SS Alban, Aaron and Julius, through whom God had brought aid to His people. Such could be no longer the case in the present, with access to their shrines cut off by the Saxons 'because of the sins of the citizens' (x, 2), and 'people daily rush headlong to hell' (xxvi, 3) in an orgy of sin and self-destruction. Conforming and reputable Christians were acknowledged in the present, but in too few numbers to be seen by 'holy mother church', 'though they are the only true sons she has left'. Rather, 'all the controls of truth and justice have been shaken and overthrown, leaving no trace'. In contrast to the saints of Roman Britain, and the virtuous Ambrosius Aurelianus and his contemporaries, who fought the Saxons with some limited success, Britain's kings and other leaders in the present are wicked and oppressive tyrants steeped in blood (xxvi, xxvii) and her clergy are shameless and venal (lxvi). Her wider population consists of ignorant and anarchic fools in league with the devil.

Several themes run through this account, therefore, which have powerful meanings in the central Middle Ages in terms of Gildas's construction of the British people. One was a common and morally conceived history as a single people, which positioned the Britons *in toto* as the new Israelites, a people of the Lord, but one which had long been in a very weak position within divine providence. The diocesan population is thereby privileged over its parts. This people the Lord sought to chastise so as to return them to their proper obedience and status as the elect, sending a series of plagues (xx, 2–xxiii, 1) in the hope of repentence. Although God had then tested His people via their wars with the Saxons (xxvi, 1), and vouchsafed them several victories, alongside several defeats (xxvi, 1), Gildas certainly did not suggest that the protection of the Lord had been restored thereafter. Rather, He seems to have decided, in this construct, that they were undeserving of His aid against their enemies until they should reform themselves. Gildas's characterization of his countrymen in the present would certainly confirm that view, since they were explicitly portrayed as far worse in their behaviour than during the past time of God's testing. Their status as the elect was imperilled, but not yet lost (Garrison 2000: 157), and their history as told by Gildas led inexorably to this precise point.

Another fundamental theme which would later impact on the author of the *Historia Brittonum* was the vision of the Britons as an inherently unmartial race, which was incapable of successfully opposing external aggressors. This vision was introduced initially in the context of the Roman conquest of Britain, which was not contested by a people described (v, 2) as 'unwarlike and untrustworthy', and who were subdued not by force but by mere threats. When they then rebelled against Roman rule (this is apparently the Boudiccan rebellion) they failed to maintain their revolt when Roman armies arrived and (vi) 'the Britons offered their backs instead of shields to the pursuers, their necks to the sword. . . . Like women they stretched out their hands for the fetters. In fact it became a mocking proverb far and wide that the Britons are cowardly in war and faithless in peace'. Gildas renewed this refrain in the context of the ending of Roman Britain, which left the Britons (xiv) 'quite ignorant of the ways of war', whose efforts at military engineering were those of (xv, 3) 'a leaderless and irrational mob'. Once the Roman expeditionary forces had ended, he imagined that a British army (xix, 2): 'was stationed on the high towers [of Hadrian's Wall] to oppose them [the Picts and Scots], but it was too lazy to fight, and too unwieldy to flee; the men were foolish and frightened, and they sat about day and night, rotting away in their folly'.

In contrast, both the Romans and the several barbarian attackers were hardened and effective warriors. To illustrate Gildas's vision of the Romans as soldiers (xv, 2):

> A legion was soon despatched that had forgotten the troubles of the past. Soundly equipped, it crossed to our country by ship, came to grips with the dreadful enemy, laid low a great number of them, drove them all from the country, and freed from imminent slavery a people that had been subjected to such grievous mangling.

The Picts and Scots were horrible barbarians in Gildas's eyes (xix, 1), being 'readier to cover their villeinous faces with hair than their private parts . . . with clothes', but they too were capable and confident soldiers, who (xvi) 'broke through the frontiers, spreading destruction everywhere', and later (xix, 1) 'seized the whole extreme north of the island from its inhabitants'. So too were the Saxons effective and frightening warriors, being described as *ferocissimi* (xxiii, 1), wolves, lion cubs (xxiii, 3), dogs (xxiii, 4) and like the Assyrians, who featured repeatedly in the Old Testament as an empire-building people who utilized terror to sustain their tyranny.

When they gathered around virtuous leaders, such as Ambrosius Aurelianus, and placed themselves in God's hands, the Britons were thereafter granted some degree of success over the Saxons, but Gildas interpreted that contest not in terms of the martial qualities of the Britons but of God's trial of His people. Victory was in His gift, therefore, and earned not by the qualities of an effective warrior but by obediance to the Lord. The Britons' successes 'pretty well' ended in the year of the siege of *mons Badonicus*, in which Gildas himself seems to have been born (xxvi, 1). Since that time, war against the Saxons had ceased but civil wars had revived, and Gildas provided examples of such ungodly, internecine civil strife in his treatment of the kings of the day, in particular regarding the victories of Maglocunus against other (apparently) anonymous kings. The inference is that there was no hope for future victory against the barbarian Saxons through force of arms, but only through the grace of the Lord.

Gildas's text therefore denied the Britons any innate warlike qualities. His stance may have been owing to his own position within civil society. His text betrays a traditional, rhetorical education (Lapidge 1984), which would have fitted him for the thrust and parry of the court-room and local assembly, but not the battlefield, which had traditionally within provincial society been the responsibility of military professionals of low social standing – including barbarian recruits, of course – under professional officers. There can be little doubt that Gildas was a snob, but we should not underestimate the completeness of the separation of civil and military authorities in the late Roman Empire. It is important to recognize that the fifth-century lowland British élite would not have had any martial traditions of their own on which to fall back when the Roman army of Britain disappeared. Their historical mythology was Roman in origin, as were their central notions of the cultural and behavioural positioning appropriate to themselves. This helps to account for their employment of Saxon mercenaries, which has been widely acknowledged as modelled on recent and contemporary Roman practice in Gaul and elsewhere.

Gildas's position on warfare also derives from his very particular ideological stance. To acknowledge any martial qualities among his own people would be to reduce God's responsibility for whatever victories were achieved, so clouding the clarity of his conception of providential history and his agenda for his people for the future. Gildas seems to have been primarily an ideologue and not a man of action in the secular sphere. His text is a narrative about divine retribution for the failings of his people, which points the way towards redemption via the Lord (Trompf 2000). For Gildas, God's protection won by the moral reform of his people and led by its kings and clergy offered the only conceivable path forward.

Another theme was the illegitimacy of British civil authority in the present. Gildas was ambivalent towards the Romans in some respects, but he was prepared to acknowledge imperial authority, wielded by Roman *reges*, which he termed *imperium* on a world scale and *regnum* in a British context. Only imperial figures who set themselves against Christianity were *tyranni* (like Diocletian: ix, 1), and this underpins his vision of political legitimacy as derived ultimately from God alone. Gildas conceived the ending of Roman Britain (xii, xiii) in terms of the Britons lapsing into both moral and secular disobedience, hence the Arian heresy and the revolt of Magnus Maximus in tandem. Maximus was treated in this text as if British, in which Gildas was later widely followed by insular writers, and sent to Gaul by Britain (xiii, 1, 2):

> with a great retinue of hangers-on and even the imperial insignia, which he was never fit to bear: he had no legal claim to the title, but was raised to it like a tyrant by rebellious soldiery. Applying cunning rather than virtue, Maximus turned the neighbouring lands and provinces against Rome, and attached them to his kingdom of wickedness with the nets of his perjury and lying ... the throne of his wicked empire he placed at Trier, where he raged so madly against his masters that of the two legitimate emperors he drove one from Rome, the other from his life – which was a very holy one.

Britain's position under Roman protection therefore ended, for Gildas, in a great rebellion, led by a wicked tyrant, behaving in typically evil, British ways, against properly constituted and divinely ordained authority. It was this rebelliousness, combined rather uncomfortably with military incompetence, which had since left Britain defenceless against barbarian attacks. The two expeditions launched by the Romans in response to the British entreaties which he offered merely highlight these differences between

Roman legitimacy and military efficiency, on the one hand, and British immorality and incompetence, on the other. Thereafter, the only hope for British rulers, in Gildas's eyes, was for them to display the very highest moral standards, and so obtain the active protection of the Lord, but this was unacceptable to their people, leaving sub-Roman, British kingship with great problems regarding legitimacy (xxi, 4):

> Kings were anointed not in God's name, but as being crueller than the rest: before long, they would be killed, with no enquiry into the truth, by those who had anointed them, and others still crueller chosen to replace them. Any king who seemed gentler and rather more inclined to the truth was regarded as the downfall of Britain: everyone directed their hatred and their weapons at him, with no respect.

In the present, Gildas portrayed five contemporary rulers, each of whom was steeped in sins of various kinds (xxviii–xxxvi) throughout a section which he introduced by a highly ironic contents list, which set out to juxtapose their actual behaviours with that which he considered more appropriate to their station (xxvii): 'Britain has kings, but they are tyrants; she has judges, but they are wicked. They often plunder and terrorise – the innocent; they defend and protect – the guilty and thieving; they have many wives – whores and adulteresses' – and so on.

Contemporary British kings were portrayed by Gildas, therefore, as wicked men, bloody, brutal, ignorant, venal and dishonest, unworthy of respect or obedience, whose style of rule was contrary to God's plan for His people.

Not only did Gildas roundly abuse the British kings, but he also made use of a series of animal metaphors. This was in part to symbolize and further advertise their qualities, and it is noticeable both that Gildas used such imagery widely in his text and that later British writers followed suit (Edel 1984–5). However, these were also used in part to fix these kings and their activities within a schema of providential history derived from the Old Testament. His message seems to have been that the fate of the Britons could be expected to unravel under God's guiding hand in much the same way as had the lot of the Israelites following the fall of Jerusalem and their captivity among the Babylonians. So, for example, (xxviii, xxx) both Constantine and Aurelius Caninus were lion cubs (as were the Saxons, xxiii, 3), Vortepor a leopard (xxxi, 1), Cuneglasus a bear (xxxii) and Maglocunus a dragon (xxxiv, 4: but also incidentally a foal and a wolf at different points in his career). There is a reflection here of the four great beasts of Daniel's visions (*Daniel* vii, 1–8), with the first duplicated to provide a fifth to accord with Gildas's particular needs. This allusion establishes the point that Gildas believed British history had reached in the present, hence how it should be expected to unravel in the future. His historical sketch was founded on Jeremiah from chapter twenty-one onwards, and his framework makes grim reading. I addressed this issue in a paper published in Germany, from which I now quote in an attempt to lay out the schema itself:

> Like the Israelites, the British nation had fallen into a state of disobedience and moral depravity (*DEB* xxi); they had then ignored God's attempts to doctor them (xxii) but lapsed further into Godlessness, becoming collectively blind (xxiii) and employing Saxon mercenaries. Their revolt and the consequent destruction was 'just punishment for the crimes which had gone before' and directly likened to barbarian destruction wrought in the Old Testament on the Israelites (xxiv). Like Jerusalem, all the major towns were destroyed and their Christian communities killed. This Jeremiah look-alike disaster had then to be amended, to take account of a period of British resistance thereafter which finds no parallel in Jeremiah . . ., but Gildas reverted to his theme in chapter twenty six, with depopulated and ruined cities (cf. Jerusalem) but external peace (as during the Babylonian captivity). To continuing servitude of the British survivors he had already made reference (xxv) and this theme was repeated in twenty six: barring only a few righteous men (cf. Daniel), the Britons were now slaves of the belly and of the devil, and it is specifically this present state of affairs which Gildas laments, much as Jeremiah had done before him. It was at this point that Gildas turned to contemporary kings, characterising them by a variety of means including allegories drawn from the Book of Daniel, and it is these which illustrate Gildas's anticipation of divine deliverance of His people from their barbarian oppressors in the near future, provided only that they could be persuaded to return to Godliness.
>
> (Higham 1998: 141)

Although this interpretation has been contested, the vision of an author writing *against* Saxon occupation of Britain (Higham 1994) retains some merit. Although they appeared initially only north of the Thames (Figure 1), cemeteries reflective of an incoming Germanic culture were already widely established in two of the late Roman provinces (as far as they can be reconstructed) by the time Gildas was writing (Figures 2 and 3), and were then in the process of spilling over into the other two. If Gildas was, as has recently been argued (Higham 1994; K. R. Dark 1994), writing in the southern half of the western province of Britannia Prima, he had good reason to take notice. Given that his treatment of the Saxons in a past context was brutally condemnatory (xxiii–xxvi), he was clearly not impervious to their presence, and what that presence meant in the narrative terms which he had constructed. Indeed, his concerns regarding access to the shrines of the saints (x, 2) make it clear that he was highly conscious of one impact, at least, of the Saxon presence under current conditions, and these Saxons were obviously not

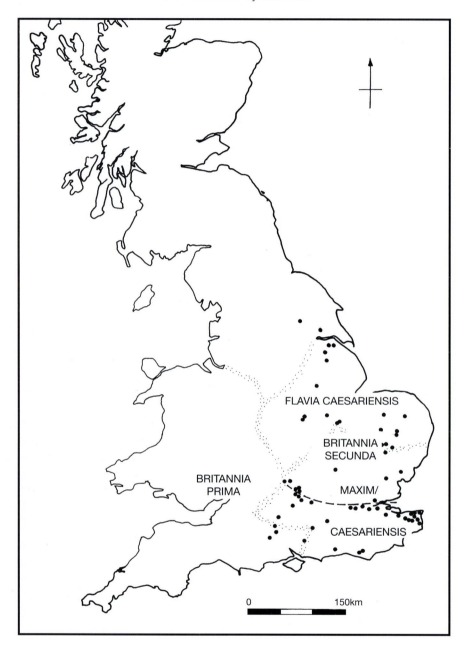

**Figure 1** Anglo-Saxon cemeteries in use by *c.* 475. The line along the Thames reflects the southern limit of known cemetery distribution by *c.* 450 (adapted from Hines 1990: 34)

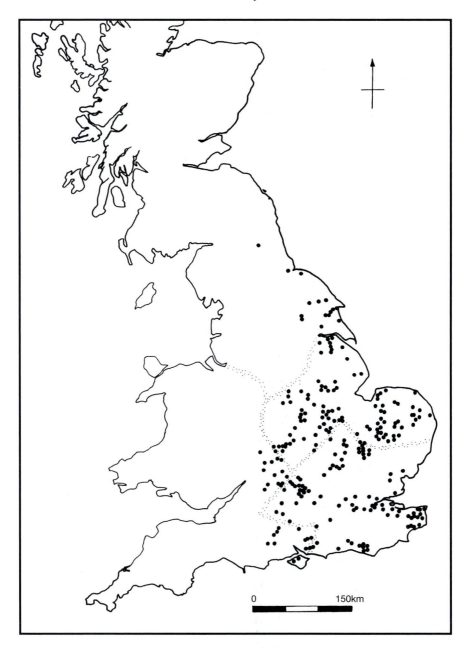

**Figure 2** Anglo-Saxon cemeteries in use by *c*. 520 (adapted from Hines 1990: 35)

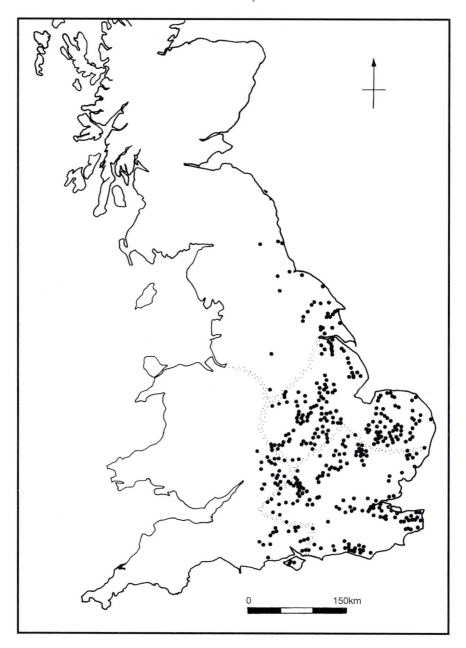

**Figure 3** Anglo-Saxon cemeteries in use by *c.* 560 (adapted from Hines 1990, p. 36)

considered just the placid farming immigrants or refugees so beloved of modern archaeologists, but an interventionist and feared presence from the perspective of the sub-Roman, Christian élite. Similar reactions were textualized in Lombardic Italy, where Paul the Deacon remarked:

> the churches were despoiled, the priests killed, the cities over-thrown, the people who had grown up like crops annihilated, and besides those regions which Alboin had taken, the greater part of Italy was seized and subjugated by the Langobards.
>
> (Peters 1974: ii, 23)

While such commentaries are clearly highly rhetorical, they do reflect the deep anxieties of provincial communities on the receiving end of barbarian colonization.

Here again, Gildas's testimony is inconsistent with attempts to rewrite the history of the British lowlands in the sixth century as a space still very largely characterized by British political authority (Morris 1973; Rutherford Davis 1982; K. R. Dark 1994, 2000). Parts of the indigenous political élite may well have survived even in eastern Britain well into the sixth century. There is very little evidence either way outside of the negative distribution of Anglo-Saxon cemeteries in areas such as Essex, and the scatter of Christian sites which seem to have survived through to the Christian era of Anglo-Saxon England. However, military power apparently lay from an early date with the incoming barbarians. This was being translated into power of other sorts, involving economic advantage, land-tenure and patronage, and a very different, 'Anglo-Saxon' society and culture was developing as a consequence, with its own historical mythology, of course, and its own identities.

Gildas's comments had a universality which defied any later attempt to localize them, despite efforts to argue for a specifically 'northern' text (Thompson 1979; Dumville 1984a), much as the Old Testament spoke of the Israelites in their totality when describing the destruction of Jerusalem. Rather, his message offered a morally constructed vision of British identity and national character as relevant in Gododdin (the Lothians) as it was among the Dumnonii (punned by Gildas as *Damnonii*, in Devon and Cornwall). For those who were familiar with his arguments, there was no escaping them on the grounds that they were applicable only to some other *Brittani* and an alternative section of the *cives* of *Britannia*. It is clear that medieval writers, from Bede onwards, read the text as applicable across the entire British people, so across all communities who acknowledged the idea of being British as relevant to themselves, or were adjudged such by others. Gildas was, in this respect, the last writer whose work survives who could conceptualize the entirety of the old diocese as 'British' in the present, and view the current Saxon presence as nothing more than a temporary, but terrible, punishment on God's people. Although he too looked forward to the expulsion of the

English, when the author of the *Historia Brittonum* referred to a 'British' Britain it was in the context of Gildas's wars between Britons and Saxons, which ended at Badon. Post-Arthur and in the present, the British lowlands were an English space. The later restriction of 'British' to non-'Anglo-Saxon' areas, even while retaining a title to the whole of *Britannia*, and the common division (as in the Welsh Triads – see Bromwich 1961) of the Britons into three (the old North, Wales and south-west) must be seen as post-Gildasian constructs, therefore. These ideas developed only as the Germanic colonial enterprise became established and began to be seen as permanent.

Although his words obviously had a contemporary context, Gildas's condemnations were not bounded in time, any more than they were in space. He argued his case across the story of the British past up to and including the present and, by implication at least, on into the future until such time as the Britons should return to their natural obedience to the Lord, as he urged. His was an intellectual and ideological package of historical causation which, within a particular Christian world-picture, was irresistible until such a time when God's protection of His people should be reinstated so totally that Gildas's moral crusade became irrelevant. One might add that Gildas does seem to have anticipated exactly this and cannot be held responsible for the uses to which his text was put in later centuries by scholars (such as Bede), who adopted positions regarding providential history, the identity of God's people and characterization of the 'Other' that he can reasonably have been expected to have opposed vehemently.

The cumulative impact on Gildas's audience was necessarily considerable, if we assume that they were susceptible to his vision and shared his assumptions. By placing the Britons, in their totality, as an elect which had been disobedient to God across many generations, so eventually falling outside divine protection, Gildas undermined 'Britishness' as a sustainable and valuable identity within the wider framework of a Christian world-order and ideology. By representing the Britons as an utterly unwarlike people, bent on civil conflict and incapable of defending themselves against other nations, he undermined and devalued any effort to mobilize against external enemies. By envisioning them as living under wicked tyrants, whose authority had no legitimacy and who were rebels against the Lord, he invalidated existing social and political structures. By representing the current clerisy as collectively unfit, venal and incompetent, he contested and undermined the other major facet of authority within contemporary society, that of the ecclesiastical establishment and its value system. By locking the Britons into a particularly disastrous episode in Old Testament history, the *De Excidio* mortgaged the future of the Britons as a people, since his reworking of biblical history would be fulfilled only with the total expulsion of the Saxons, and that could occur only – in this conception – following universal and full-scale moral reform. Gildas's ethnicity was arguably constructed in an Old Testament context and against the enemies of the 'New Israelites'. Until the Saxons had been swept away, therefore, no satisfactory case could be made for divine protection of the British people, since that was the principal demonstration of divine favour to which he looked. Gildas left the Britons, and particularly their leaders, still at the mercy of a vengeful Old Testament God. If that God had run out of patience with His people generations earlier, His perceptions of their morality and their obedience were the conditioning factors determining the major political issues of the day – hence the Saxon 'settlement' in Britain.

None of this would have been of particular importance had Gildas's text circulated only within his own lifetime or only among a small circle of like-minded literati. However, it escaped from that immediate readership, along with his reputation as a figure of authority in the insular Christian world, certainly within the sixth century. All this was to become the more significant as it was adopted after the seventh century as the defining narrative which characterized the Britons as a people, both among the British themselves and, far more dangerously, among the Anglo-Saxons. The *De Excidio* became, therefore, the founding text of British self-perception, and the narrative according to which the Britons were textualized historically by their neighbours. If Gildas's polemic undermined the providential status of the Britons, then that process in turn arguably encouraged the processes of accommodation which led to the formation of Anglo-Saxon society by devaluing existing insular concepts of group identity.

So Bede famously used Gildas's strictures (see Miller 1975a) to contest the status of the Britons as a chosen people in the present, even while silently omitting his characterization of the Saxons as merely a plague sent by God, and a rod by which He sought to correct His people. This adaptation enabled Bede to develop a new narrative of redemption, refocused on the English as God's chosen race and away from the Britons. Bede's enterprise was much facilitated by Gildas's development of his own narrative of retribution and had further consequences for the value placed on British culture in the eighth century (see Jenkins 1997 for the broader, theoretical context).

It is also important to recognize just how adaptable later writers would find Gildas's work. The lack of clear evidence of chronology, the absence of a date of composition and the poverty of place-names and personal names all leave Gildas's text very much hanging in space and time and open to a multiplicity of different interpretations. His ambiguity regarding the recent past likewise enabled others to use the text for purposes which could be totally at variance one with the other, as much in the Middle Ages as now. This ambiguity has been most marked in Gildas's comments regarding the so-called 'war of the Saxon federates' (*De Excidio* xxiii, 5–xxvi, 1: the term is Professor Thompson's), the outcome of which has generally been read as a great British victory – at the siege of Badon – which held back the Saxons for two generations (Frere 1967: 421, 427), but this is to over-interpret the text, perhaps in the light of the later accretion of commentaries and assumptions around it. For Gildas, the siege of *mons Badonicus* marked the year in which God's testing of His people ended, and it is not at all clear that He had judged them worthy to be granted total victory over the Saxons. Rather, Gildas's lamentations in the present suggest the very opposite (Higham 1994: 50–1). As I pointed out in that same volume (pp. 203–11), there is no sound basis in the *De Excidio* for reconstructing a period of British-dominated peace with the Saxons, i.e. an 'Age of Arthur' conditioned by British victory at Badon. If the foundations of British military revival cannot be identified safely therein, then they cannot be identified at all, barring dramatic new evidence. That said, the author of the *Historia Brittonum* certainly read Badon as an important victory, capable of being used to considerable rhetorical effect, even while acknowledging implicitly the subsequent victory of the Saxons as they poured in ever greater numbers into Britain in the sixth century. His account of the latter was arguably based on *Historia Ecclesiastica* i, 15, and he necessarily shared Bede's understanding of a 'primordialist' origin for the English nation, by immigration from Germany. Although their opinions have no authority regarding events in the fifth and sixth centuries, both these writers have had an enormous impact on the later perception of Gildas's text.

## Gildas and Arthur

Its very uniqueness as a named victory in the war against the Saxons encouraged Badon to be viewed as a critical British success around which patriotic comment naturally gathered. It has long been supposed that Gildas did not name the British leader, but Oliver Padel's re-examination of the Harleian text suggests that Ambrosius Aurelianus may have been intended (see the arguments offered by Padel 1994: 16, strongly supported by Wood 1999: 37). Reference to the victorious leader was almost obligatory if the victory were later to be exploited for ideological purposes. Arthur was certainly utilized to fill that space in the early ninth century, by which time the battle and Ambrosius already seem to have become detached – unless they were then deliberately parted. This latter seems the likeliest solution, since there was good reason for this to have occurred. The author of the *Historia Brittonum* was seeking to deploy Badon for nationalistic purposes, but had already constructed his vision of 'Britishness' very much in opposition to the Romans. Gildas's characterization of Ambrosius Aurelianus as pretty much the last Roman in Britain, whose parent had worn the purple (xxv, 3), arguably necessitated that a new and more quintessentially 'British' leader be credited. The weak linkage in the *De Excidio* between Ambrosius and Badon provided an opportunity for a later writer with his own, very different agenda to insert a new, and from his own perspective a more appropriate, leader of the Britons.

That Gildas neither named Arthur nor spoke kindly of the Britons over whom he putatively then reigned so gloriously, during the period of external peace in the present (when he wrote), is not an issue which is likely to go away. This problem has, however, been confronted repeatedly. For John Morris

(1973: 116): 'Gildas praises Arthur's government, but does not name him, for he names no one at all in the 80 years before his own day, save only Ambrosius; and his name is invoked in order to reproach his degenerate living descendants'. Gerald of Wales offered a more picturesque explanation, however, in the late twelfth century, which continues to resonate down the centuries (*Description of Wales* ii, 2):

> The Britons maintain that, when Gildas criticized his own people so bitterly, he wrote as he did because he was infuriated by the fact that King Arthur had killed his own brother, who was a Scottish chieftain. When he heard of his brother's death, or so the Britons say, he threw into the sea a number of outstanding books which he had written in their praise and about Arthur's achievements. As a result you will find no book which gives an authentic account of that great prince.
>
> (Thorpe 1978: 259)

This ingenious and imaginative solution to the problem reflects the common but entirely spurious belief in the central Middle Ages that Gildas was a scion of the royal house of Strathclyde, which still unfortunately has a habit of appearing in contemporary studies (e.g. R. White 1997: 3, 17). Caradoc of Llancarfan's *Life of Gildas*, written *c.* 1100, addresses the issue directly (v): 'Gildas, a most holy man, was a contemporary of Arthur, king of the whole of Great Britain' and represents him forgiving his slaying of his brother since 'he wished always to obey him'. However, Caradoc failed to explain the king's absence from the *De Excidio*.

The only incontrovertible facts are these: Gildas did not name Arthur; the victor of Badon was necessarily a much older contemporary of his own whose name he must have known (and Ambrosius remains a plausible candidate, as above); his choice of whom to name was his own, for his own reasons which can to an extent be explored (e.g. Higham 1994: 45), but the absence of Arthur from this text cannot be explained away or accommodated in any way which strengthens claims for his existence. Rather the opposite must be our position. Had Gildas named Arthur, then his historicity would be beyond reasonable doubt. His absence from our only near-contemporary text dealing with the putative 'Age of Arthur' permits any number of later appropriations of him, since silence fixes and disproves nothing.

## ALTERNATIVE IDEOLOGUES AND BRITISH AUTHORITY

Given that the construction of a specifically British identity had to be drastically reformed in the fifth century, outside of a Roman framework, Gildas's seminal and fundamentalist challenge to contemporary socio-political values, hence to their credibility, necessarily mattered. There were, however, considerable efforts to formulate a related but very much more valuable self-image and sense of group identity, which dovetails with several of Gildas's perceptions, contesting some even while still sustaining his view of the Britons as a chosen people.

Such developments one might expect to find among the courtiers and clergy gathered around contemporary kings, whose interests presumably included civil obedience and social cohesion under particular dynasts and their families. One can trace such forces at work within Gildas's own text. Gildas's kings, for example, were portrayed, however imperfectly, as judges, as employers of armed followers, as givers of alms, and as war-leaders, thus exercising patronage in various ways. More particularly, he recognized the presence of sycophantic courtiers around Maglocunus (xxxiv, 6):

> Your excited ears hear not the praises of God from the sweet voices of the tuneful recruits of Christ, not the melodious music of the church, but empty praises of yourself from the mouths of criminals who grate on the hearing like raving hucksters – mouths stuffed with lies and liable to bedew bystanders with their foaming phlegm.

The term which Winterbottom here translates as 'criminals' is *furcifer*, literally a 'gallows-bird'. Given that Gildas used the same word for the Picts and Scots (as an adjective, xix, 1) and the Saxons at Badon (xxvi, 1), it may be that he here had in mind the warriors of the royal *comitatus*, rather than rhetoricians or bards, but the matter must remain open (see Sims-Williams 1984). Whatever the precise implication, Gildas was here acknowledging the fact that at least one contemporary king had established a court which was vocally supportive of his activities and authority, so presumably providing ideological grounding for the regime. The author of the *Historia Brittonum* would later rekindle this process on behalf of the same court. Gildas's contempt for their input certainly suggests that, as one might expect, their views differed dramatically from his own, and that they were supportive of current kingly behaviours in ways which he considered unacceptable.

Gildas referred to contemporary British clergy who had gone overseas and across wide lands in search of ordination, ostensibly because they were deemed unfit by their peers within their own *parochia* (literally diocese: lxvii, 5). Given that he considered the seas surrounding Britain impassable except in the English Channel (iii, 1), this reads easiest as a reference to British clergy seeking ordination in Gaul. Likewise, the 'psalm-singing' Britons fleeing overseas from the Saxons a generation or two earlier should similarly be looked for in Gaul, where they presumably settled in Armorica (Brittany), rather than Ireland (as Thompson 1979: 222, in support of his vision of a 'north-western' Gildas). There is, therefore, in Gildas's own writing significant evidence for long-term and long-maintained contact with (most probably)

Gaul, and this is confirmed by visits to Britain by various late fourth- and early fifth-century Gaulish bishops (the latest known being Germanus in 429 and perhaps again *c.* 440). Christians passed also in the other direction in search of opportunity, with Pelagius leaving Britain for Rome in the very late fourth century and Faustus becoming successively abbot of Lérins (433) and bishop of Riez (452). In this respect, members of the British élite seem to have maintained close contact with Christians in a period which overlaps with the primary Saxon settlement (*c.* 425–50), and their separate identity as Britons was not seen as a bar to high office in Gaul.

Something close to 200 inscribed memorial stones are also extant in western Britain, which collectively betray connections with Gaul (Figure 4). The distribution of these is particularly interesting: only around a dozen survive in the north, most famously at Whithorn; there are about 150 in Wales; with the predominance very much in western Wales – and a further fifty or so are in Cornwall. Our understanding of these monuments rests heavily on the work of Victor Nash-Williams (1950), but has more recently been developed by Professor Charles Thomas (1991–2, 1994) and Jeremy Knight (1992, 1995, 1996, 1999). These inscribed stones are exceptionally difficult to date, but it is generally agreed that the sequence began around the mid-fifth century (but see now Handley 2001), when they were apparently a new departure and relatively unconnected with traditions of stone carving in later Roman Britain. The principal impetus seems to have come from mid- to late fifth-century Gaul, and more particularly from surviving areas of *Romanitas* there, particularly in the west. It arrived, and was successively reinforced, along the same channels of communication and contact which brought texts (including Jerome's new *Vulgate*) backwards and forwards. This was presumably part and parcel of the same contacts (particularly with Bordeaux) which brought quantities of continental pottery and other manufactures to western British sites, much of which came from the pottery amphorae containing the wine consumed in both court and church (Figure 5). Such merchants and their ships were mentioned by Adamnan (Anderson and Anderson 1961), referring, in the late seventh century, to the coast of Ireland in the second half of the sixth century.

In western Britain, the continental impetus seems to have been combined with another set of exemplars. Although few other types of Roman epigraphy were available as prototypes, milestones were still widely visible along the Roman roads by which most travellers still passed, and these often carried the names of the emperor as well as other information. Such markers may well have been attractive to tribal kings or chiefdoms with an interest in publicizing their own increasingly hereditary right to control space (Knight 1992: 50). While most surviving stones are memorial or grave markers, some, but relatively few, were set up at prominent locations away from cemeteries, perhaps with such advertising of heredity and power in mind. Also in western Britain, the Gaulish habit of Latin inscription met with a novel Irish form of

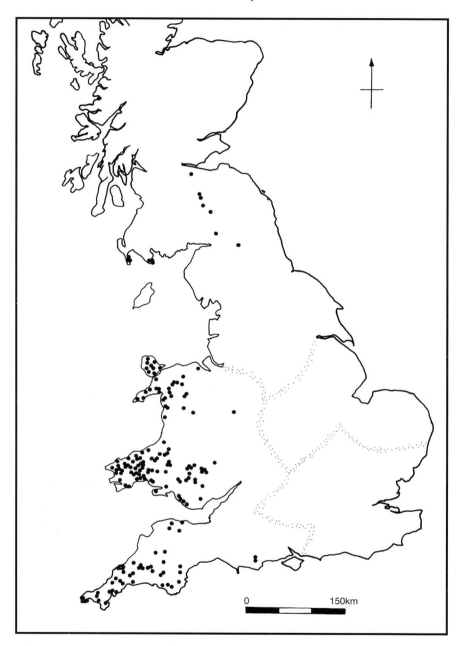

**Figure 4** The distribution of early medieval 'British' inscribed stones in Britain

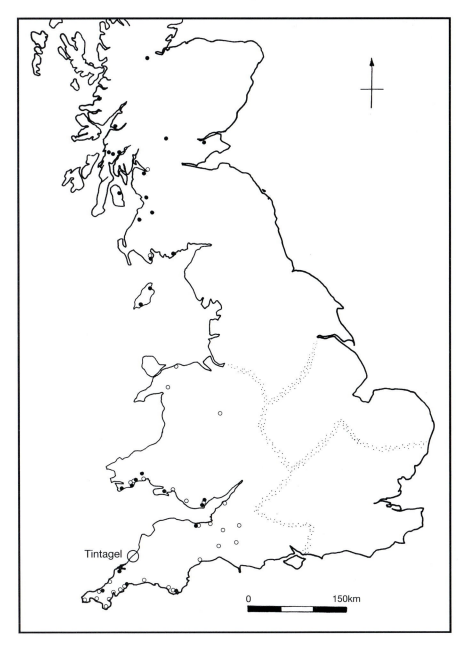

**Figure 5** Fifth- to sixth-century Gaulish and Mediterranean pottery imports to Britain in non-Anglo-Saxon contexts: solid circles represent Frankish 'E' Ware; open circles Mediterranean wares

lettering, known as ogam, which was also being developed for inscriptional purposes around the Irish Sea. The majority of these inscriptions are in Ireland (Macalister 1945), but a significant number of Latin-inscribed stones, particularly in Dyfed and Brycheiniog, also have shorter, ogam inscriptions along one edge. The inception of ogam may well have occurred during the later Roman period, or at least before the abandonment of such towns as Silchester, where an inscribed stone was found in the 1890s in a shallow well, filled up in the late fourth/early fifth century (Fulford, Handley and Clark 2000).

These western British inscriptions collectively provide important confirmation that Latin was a living language in the fifth and sixth centuries, and this in what had arguably been the least Romanized parts of Britain, where it seems unlikely that Latin had developed as a universal *lingua franca* before 400. They indicate in addition a high level of Latinity as a written language, at least among the élite – and perhaps particularly among the clergy – which also finds support in recent detailed analysis of literary style from fifth-century Britain (Howlett 1998). Latinity is evident not only in the phraseology but also in the names used, with a preponderance of Latin nomenclature in the putatively earlier examples, some of which also contain such words as *presbyter* (priest), *magister* (magistrate) and *protector*. The suggestion has also been floated recently that this highly developed Latinity blossomed into sophisticated structured writings which can still be seen on a minority of the inscriptions on stone in western Britain, which were arguably composed in a developed 'biblical style' and following identifiable, complex rules (Thomas 1998).

While these more advanced claims have still to be substantiated, they do at least conform to a broader picture of a well educated and well connected western British Christian élite in the later fifth to sixth centuries, who were very consciously seeking to occupy moral heights which were conceived in conventional Christian terms. They were developing a sophisticated and structured church with both monasteries and a diocesan structure. In the political context of the day Professor Thomas is arguably right to view this as a deliberate investment in Christian ideology, in response to the revival of paganism in the British lowlands under Germanic influence. Despite, or perhaps even in line with, Gildas's condemnations, therefore, the wider British élite community within, but barely beyond (excepting the north), those same five kingships which he castigated, can be seen to have been developing an intellectual counterblast, cast in providential terms, to the Germanization and paganization of lowland Britain and the construction of what was beginning to be 'England'.

Gaul – and ultimately Rome – were not the only areas with which this community in western Britain was developing contacts. Pope Celestine sent his own deacon to Ireland as a bishop in 431, and Leo the Great subsequently placed great store (in the years around 440) in the expansion of Christianity beyond the limits of the old Empire (Charles-Edwards 1993). Germanus may even have returned to Britain about that date, although the historicity and date of this second visit are contested. The effort to provide for Christians in Ireland necessarily depended on British support, and it is generally believed that the entire enterprise to spread the faith there fell into the hands of British priests within the first generation (Dumville 1993). Certainly, the British Patrick was later conceived as the key apostle in that arena, although he may well have been conflated with his Italian predecessor, Palladius. In the north, too, British clergy may have spread the gospel beyond Hadrian's Wall and even to the southern Picts (Thomas 1971). The story of St. Ninian (or Nynia) is very late and is adapted by Bede to his own agenda (*HE* iii, 4): his training was, therefore, at Rome, thus immunizing him, the patron saint and founding father of a current Northumbrian diocesan church, from the 'Otherness' and exclusion from the Christian fold which member-ship of the British race would otherwise imply within this text. If we assume that the underlying missionary narrative is realistic (as MacQueen 1990, but there must be some doubt of this), it provides evidence of a significant and sustained effort to Christianize parts of the British Isles which had lain outside the Roman Empire. That effort may well have been grounded in patterns of trans-frontier contact already developed during the Roman period (Whittaker 1994), but much of it belongs to the fifth century or marginally later.

Missionary activity proclaims, once again, a pro-active Christian leadership in western Britain, with the capacity both to identify the advantages of expanding the faith and to support the effort over a lengthy period, even in collaboration with the bishops of Rome. There is a significant difference between this outward-going British attitude to other insular peoples of long standing, which may well also be visible in the congruity of ogam and Latin inscriptions, and the absence of any known missionary effort towards the Germanic barbarians in lowland Britain. There is, of course, a caveat here, since both Professor Patrick Sims-Williams (1990) and Stephen Bassett (1992) have suggested that the Anglicization of western Mercia, where Anglo-Saxon cemeteries are notoriously scarce, was effected by incoming Germanic communities who accepted Christianity from the indigenous people but otherwise retained their own cultural practices (crucially language). This is, however, only one way to read the evidence, and others are on offer (e.g. Higham 1993b: 77ff. and now see Bassett 2000), which do not require that we dispute Bede's essential point (*HE* i, 22), that the Britons made no effort to convert the English. The reactions of western British clergy to contact with English priests *c.* 672, as reflected in Aldhelm's letter to Geraint (his *Epistolae* iv), confirms that the British side long contested the acceptability and orthodoxy of English Christianity.

We have, therefore, crucial evidence of a self-consciously Christian British élite across the two or three generations following the initial Saxon *adventus*, which was responding to this traumatic event and its consequences thereafter in intellectual and moral terms. It was seeking to reinforce its own membership of the family of Christian nations through an enhanced Latinity, the use of writing (Sims-Williams 1998), and the adoption of what were largely Gaulish cultural developments. These include memorial stones, the cult of saints, monasteries and a nascent parochial structure (Edwards and Lane 1992; Knight 1999). By so doing, the British intelligentsia was claiming the moral status of a people of the Lord and thereby seeking to redefine and defend its own sense of group identity and nationhood. At the same time it was exporting that same cultural package outwards to the Irish and perhaps elsewhere, in a deliberate effort to expand the community of the faith, to influence neighbouring communities, and so acquire power. Reasons for the first are obvious, and tie in with Gildas's strictures within the broader vision of providential history. The latter is, however, less clear-cut. The conversion of Ireland (on which attention has focused) has generally been considered out of sight of the Germanization of Britain (see, for example, Mytum 1992; Dumville 1993), if only because Patrick does not refer to such in either of his two surviving texts. That said, an accommodation with the Picts and Scots, both of whom had raided Britain in the past, may well have offered some advantages to a community in control of only the north and west of the old diocese. Missionary activity was certainly capable of interpretation within a framework of sacred text (as Patrick claimed), thus, by aligning the Britons with the apostles, adding value to British notions of their own group identity. Some practical outcomes might even be postulated, with 'Irish' dynasties established in both Dyfed and Brycheiniog, but the nature of Irish 'settlements' in Wales and elsewhere in Britain is still highly contested and the connection between British missionary activity and Irish 'colonization' barely explored. In practice, there is scant evidence for the movement of large groups of people from Ireland into Britain. However, whether or not the Britons anticipated military support from Ireland in the fifth century, they were certainly thinking in that vein in the tenth, when the author of *Armes Prydein* hoped for Irish warriors following the banner of *Dewy* (St David) against the English (see below, p. 193). British missionary activity should therefore be interpreted, *inter alia*, as an attempt to obtain power and influence via cultivation of particularly Cambro-Irish connections.

The narrow confines of this British Christian culture are revealed by the distribution of the inscriptions (Figure 4). It is very noticeable that it differs dramatically from evidence of late Romano-British Christianity (e.g. Mawer 1995; Figure 6). Assuming that the current state of knowledge is broadly reflective of the fifth/sixth-century distribution, then it does suggest that it was restricted almost exclusively to territory within 70 km of the Irish Sea. This is not, therefore, a phenomenon which can be evidenced widely across the old diocese, and it does seem to have been confined to areas at a distance from the Germanic-type cemeteries which were gradually becoming ever denser in distribution across the British lowlands during these same generations. Between the two, there lies a poorly understood but substantial

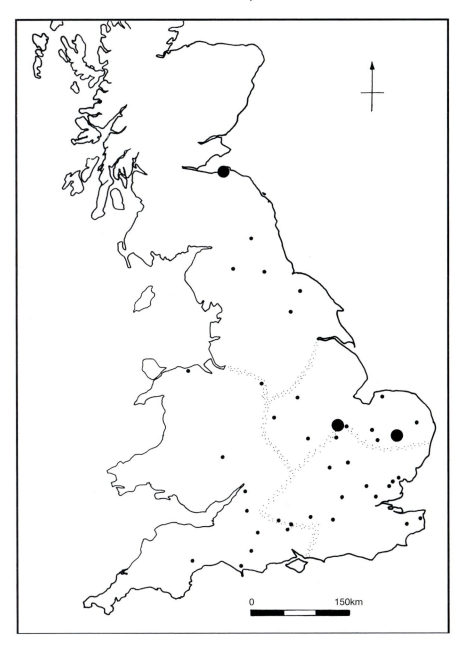

**Figure 6** The geography of Christianity in late Roman Britain as denoted by finds of accepted Christian significance: small circles represent 1–5 objects, large circles 6–14 (adapted from Mawer 1995: 144)

area in what is now largely the western Midlands and north-west of England. This central band of the old diocese displays little evidence of either memorial stones (excepting one example of a Latin inscription containing an Irish name at Wroxeter: Wright and Jackson 1968) or Germanic-type cemeteries throughout the fifth and sixth centuries.

In the eastern lowlands, by contrast, the Germanic archaeological evidence is impressive. A scatter of cemeteries came into use across central and eastern England by 450 and several more before *c.* 475 (Hines 1990), forming a triangular pattern – with gaping holes admittedly – stretching from Salisbury to Dover to York (Figure 1). During the next century, the density of this distribution increased dramatically (Figures 2 and 3), with hitherto apparently vacant regions increasingly colonized by Anglo-Saxon burial practices. However, although there was some expansion of the distribution into the north-east and the upper Thames valley, the general distribution changed little.

What this evidence means in political and cultural terms is far less clear, although many archaeologists, in particular, still focus heavily on the notion of a Germanic folk-movement as explanation (Hamerow 1994, 1997; Scull 1995; Chapman and Hamerow 1997), albeit the scale remains a matter of debate and many 'Anglo-Saxon' burials may in fact be of non-immigrant stock (e.g. Härke 1997, 1998). The frequent presence in 'Anglo-Saxon' burials of precious metals and fine metalwork (which are otherwise rarely noted at this date in Britain outside late Antique hoards) would certainly suggest that these cemeteries included a local or regional élite with impressive powers of wealth accumulation. These cemeteries do not generally occur in the vicinity of ancient mining. The acquisition of new supplies of silver to replace buried ornaments was necessarily, therefore, via trade, social exchange or tribute-taking (see the beginnings of a discussion of this issue in Wilson 1987).

That is not to suppose that this was a unified élite: in practice there were several different but interrelated Germanizing cultures in Britain, variously termed 'Saxon', 'Anglian' and 'Jutish' by Bede, for example (see the several, continental influences distinguished by Hines 1984; Hawkes 1989), which presumably reflect competing group identities. Within each and over time, visible symbols of identity were being utilized to express distinctiveness and independence from other Germanizing groups (as Suzuki 2000), but also from those Britons who had set their faces against cultural accommodation or had been excluded from this new social and cultural community. That said, the internal developments of regional group identity were always marginal in comparison with the chasm in terms of material culture and archaeological evidence between 'Anglo-Saxon' and non-Anglo-Saxon, 'British' communities. Bede's assumption that all the Germanic peoples in Britain could be deemed to be one for the purposes of providential history is certainly not entirely at odds with the archaeological record. It does, however, represent another and competing example of post-colonial historical mythology, this time based on a settlement myth allied to ideas about race derived from the Old Testament.

Two further phenomena need to be emphasized. The first is the extent to which Germanic material culture spread at a very early date across the heartland of the old diocese. This reflects the political geography of the Roman diocese, wherein civil power and wealth was clearly concentrated in the south and east. It is also, however, a phenomenon with an important cultural dimension. A computer-generated map based on the distribution of towns and villas in Roman Britain illustrates the point admirably (G. D. B. Jones and Mattingly 1990: 151, map 5.9; Figure 8). Comparison between Figures 7 and 8 demonstrate that Anglo-Saxon cemeteries were scattered across what had been the more Romanized half of the diocese, where towns and villas, so presumably the late Roman civil aristocracy, were primarily to be found. This was undoubtedly the zone with the richest agrarian economy and the most productive and numerous workforce. Whatever changes had occurred in these respects, there is little reason to suppose that the pattern of rural productivity across the old diocese was any different in comparative terms in AD 500, although the agrarian economy was clearly being reorganized into rather different modes of production outside a market economy. Germanic colonization had, therefore, from the beginning, taken root in the economic and demographic heartland of Britain, much as had Roman colonization when that first appeared four hundred years earlier.

These several distributions therefore seem to reflect a polarization of Britain *c.* 500 between an economically undeveloped and comparatively thinly populated, predominately Christian and 'British' west versus a comparatively well developed and well populated 'Germanic' and predominately heathen east. In between lies a broad middle band exhibiting neither memorial stones nor Germanic cemeteries, which had been comparatively poorly developed as an agrarian economy in all but its southern end (from Gloucestershire southwards) during the Roman period. It is important to note the extent to which self-publicizing Christianity had been silenced in the heartlands of the old civil diocese, which reflects, perhaps, an unwillingness on the part of surviving indigenous people there to value or advertise residual 'Britishness'. So, too, is there only a very little evidence of memorial stones in the broad middle band, which is now western England.

Yet scattered evidence does suggest some continuity of Christianity even within the lowlands into the sixth and even seventh centuries. British bishops in Wessex were mentioned by Bede in the context of the 660s (*HE* iii, 28) and he also noted a continuing cult at St Albans (*HE* i, 7, extending Gildas's comments with contemporary information). There were churches at Lincoln (M. J. Jones 1994) and Canterbury, various 'eccles' place-names (Cameron 1968; Gelling 1988: note particularly the example at Aylesford, Kent, where a late-Roman villa seems to have housed a Christian cult). There was also

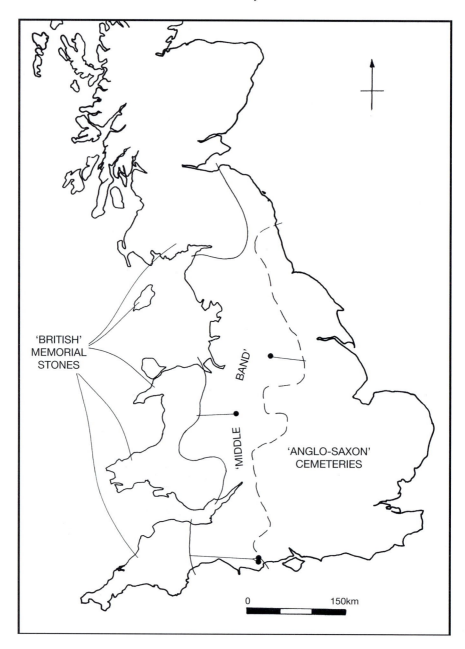

**Figure 7** The contrasting distributions of 'Anglo-Saxon' cemeteries and 'British' carved stones in the fifth and sixth centuries

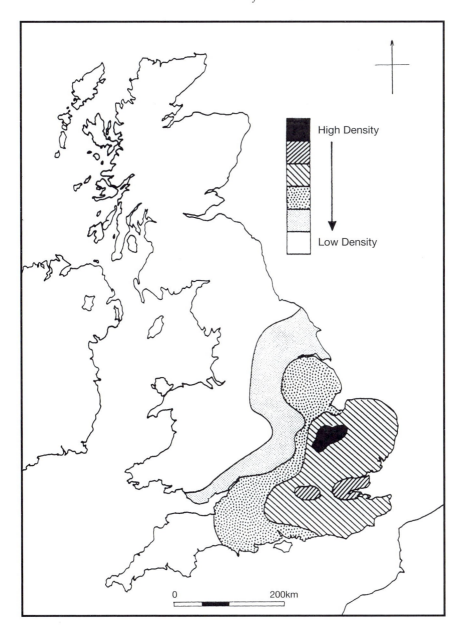

**Figure 8** Towns and villas in Roman Britain as indicators of the depth of Romanization: a computer-generated map (taken with permission from G. D. B. Jones and Mattingly 1990: 151)

a late sixth-century British cult of St Sixtus somewhere in the south-east (N. Brooks 1984: 20).

In what later became western England it is generally agreed that Christianity continued with fewer difficulties, perhaps based on a diocesan framework centred at such sites as Wall, Wroxeter and Gloucester (Bassett 2000). However, with the single exception of Wroxeter, no memorial stones survive and this seems to have been a markedly quiescent Christianity by comparison with neighbouring Wales.

Although the coherence and effectiveness of the British church inside Anglo-Saxon England is debatable (compare Higham 1997: 88 and Stancliffe 1999: 117–23), and probably variable from one region to another, there can be little doubt that some Christians were still *in situ* at the close of the sixth century. Overall, the early Christian archaeology of southern Britain may not have been as different from that on the continent as has long been imagined (e.g. M. J. Jones 2001). Its apparent invisibility may be, as much as anything, a matter of contemporary constraint for reasons of policy in Germanic-influenced areas, allied with impoverishment – supposing clerical lands to have been vulnerable to colonial acquisition. The division between a reticent and retiring Christianity in the lowlands and a strident, self-advertising cult in the far west and north had occurred already before the end of the fifth century and was to intensify thereafter.

## Summary

The ideological backdrop to the Arthur figure in Latin texts of the ninth and tenth centuries rests on the construction of a British identity, initially under the Roman Empire but then, more critically, in the generations after the end of Roman Britain. The evidence suggests that this 'Britishness' was developed by the insular élite for their own purposes in highly providential terms, so the Britons were defined by reference to their relationship with God. That in turn was seen as reflected in the experience of the indigenous community of the day, and it was their personal experiences, and perceptions coloured by those experiences, which led Patrick and Gildas to successively but independently textualize their own visions of what it meant to be British. The Germanic colonization of Britain particularly impacted on Gildas's vision of his people, the fatherland and contemporary rulers of the Britons. His 'lamentation' was constructed as a providential narrative of retribution expressed in Old Testament terms adapted to the whole British people of the old diocese. For Gildas, the Saxons marked not a new beginning for insular society but a terrible intermission in divine protection, and he wrote his 'lamentation' as a 'letter' rhetorically addressed to those in power in the hope that their renewal of the ancient allegiance to God, via a new morality, would bring a return of His protection.

Gildas wrote when (Anglo-)Saxon settlement had already begun the process of Germanic colonization in Britain, which was eventually to develop into Anglo-Saxon England. 'British' reactions – visible in terms of high levels of élite Latinity and well developed connections with Gaul – are evidenced only in the far west and north, i.e. the periphery of the old diocese, where Gildas too had focused his attention on contemporary kings. Although British Christianity, and communities still holding to a British national identity, probably survived rather better than we now appreciate in lowland Britain into the seventh century, their low profile contrasts dramatically with the more visible Christianity of (particularly) contemporary Wales. One must suspect that, elsewhere, Christian leaders adopted a very different, and less confrontational, approach to cultural expression. The lowlands were characterized not by militant Christianity but by accommodation and the adoption of an Anglicized identity. Anglo-Saxon England was arguably something which was constructed situationally, with important antecedents within indigenous society as well as Germany. However, the debt to the indigenous community could not be acknowledged by intellectuals on either side, whose understanding of ethnicity was necessarily derived from the construction of race in the Bible. There was, therefore, a natural tendency to maximize the scale of the divide, and construct a binary vision of history which polarized between Britons and Anglo-Saxons. When British writers in the central Middle Ages remarked on the fall of Britain to the Saxons there was no current 'Britishness' to be identified in the core of the lowlands. Rather, this identity was by now owned exclusively by the kingships, clergy and communities of the far west from Strathclyde in the north via Wales and Cornwall to Brittany in the south.

The several political issues which Gildas plotted through time, from the Roman conquest onwards, also led him to write up his own people as inherently un-warlike, cowardly and militarily incompetent, in terms which still resonated as late as the twelfth century, when William of Newburgh remarked (i, 2) that Gildas had declared the Britons 'neither brave in war nor trustworthy in peace'. Gildas interpreted the victories associated with Ambrosius in terms of divine testing of the Britons, rather than won by force of British arms, and additionally portrayed this, the only named leader of his countrymen, as 'Roman' rather than 'British'. With Ambrosius rendered ineligible, therefore, as an icon of 'Britishness', there seems to have been a dearth of legend centred on heroic Dark Age British leadership against the Anglo-Saxons capable of interpretation in a southern British context. When the author of the *Historia Brittonum* thought to address this issue and develop prototypes of British martial success in support of current political needs, there was very little on which he could draw from the long and barely recalled record of national disaster in the Dark Ages. It was this apparent lack of sub-Roman warriors with a reputation for victory over the Saxons which arguably precipitated Arthur's development, again for highly contemporary reasons.

# PROTOTYPE ARTHURS

The author of the *Historia Brittonum* was the earliest (at least, the earliest of whose works survive) to use the name 'Arthur' of a British warrior figure of the Dark Ages. Where did he derive the name, and what individuals can be identified with this name in the fifth or sixth centuries?

To take the earlier argument first, it has long been supposed that the name derives from the Latin *Artorius* (Bruce 1923; Malone 1925; Chadwick and Chadwick 1932), and has migrated from Latin to Old and Middle Welsh. This transition, it has been supposed, has been eased by virtue of the accident of its phonetic similarity to the Welsh word, *arth* ('bear'), but it represents the (admittedly rare) Roman cognomen, which was then adopted into Welsh.

The great strength of this position lies in the field of philological development. Given the known sound changes occurring over this period, the development of 'Arthur' from *Artorius* is 'phonologically perfect' (Professor Richard Coates, personal communication). The form 'Arthur' can alternatively be etymologized in Old Welsh as *arto-wiros*: 'bear-man', but problems with this origin develop in Middle Welsh, when the opportunity arises to distinguish between /u/ and /-u/. If the name were then considered to be a vernacular compound, the result should have been the name 'Arthwr', but in practice this never occurs. One must conclude, therefore, that the name was read and pronounced in Middle Welsh as 'Arthur' and not as 'Arthwr' because it was already an existing name which people knew how to pronounce (Professor Peter Schrijver, personal communication). This would seem to suggest that 'Arthur' was part of the naming stock of Britain from the Roman period onwards, and was fixed as a name whose pronunciation was taken as already established. This is easiest interpreted on the assumption that one or more historical Arthurs were remembered, so fixing the name for later generations.

It is, therefore, worth examining the early name evidence. While recognizing that the total database is small, Roman names are comparatively common in British writings in the fifth and sixth centuries. So Patrick, for example, and his father, both had Roman names. Thereafter, they were Celticized in the record and tend to fall out of use. That Brittonic names were already common among the British élite in the sub-Roman period is evidenced by Gildas, of whose five kings in the present, three have names constructed in the vernacular while two – Constantine, in Dumnonia, and Aurelius Caninus ('Aurelius the dog') – are Latin. These figures are far more likely to have been named in the fifth century than the sixth. The Latinity of many names on grave markers has already been remarked, with examples such as Bona ('Good'), the wife of Nobilis ('Excellent'), Paulinus, Latinus, Florentius, Salvianus and Caelextus occurring alongside both Brittonic and Irish names.

The Welsh genealogies were generally not recorded in surviving texts until very late – the Harleian genealogies representing the earliest substantial record from *c.* 1100, but arguably replicating a text of the mid-tenth century. The list for Dyfed, however, receives a degree of confirmation from an Irish text, the *Expulsion of the Deisi*, which survives in a twelfth-century manuscript. This MS confirms twelve generations down to the mid-eighth century, when it ends, so it is possible that both derive from a single mid- to late eighth century source (Miller 1977–8), which purports to stretch back to the foundation of the dynasty in the fifth century. Although this should obviously not be accepted verbatim as an historical record of the pedigree of a particular eighth-century dynast, such as Tewdwr or his nephew Maredudd (died 796), it may genuinely record an eighth-century tradition of family members with Roman names in earlier centuries. The whole opens with the earliest group in the Harleian MS providing a foundation legend, which includes Magnus Maximus, Constans and Constantine the Great, names which are arguably tenth-century additions (see pp. 213–14 for discussion and Figure 32), but there are several more localized and less outrageously implausible, putatively Roman-named ancestors, such as *Aircol* (Agricola) and *Petr* (Peter). These cluster around the Celtic name *Guortepir* (Vortepor), who may or may not be the historical figure addressed by Gildas or recalled on a memorial stone (Nash-Williams 1950, no. 138) found near Narberth but now in Carmarthen Museum, as VOTEPORIGIS PROTICTORIS, and in Ogham as VOTECORIGAS. It is quite possible, of course, that the inclusion of Vortepor in the genealogy owes something to one or both Gildas and the inscription (Maund 2000: 149, n. 33), and none of these sources are necessarily independent of the others. However, the name Arthur appears within this small group as an ancestor of the eighth-century kings of Dyfed.

These names may suggest that the Irish-connected, or Irish-originated, élite of the sub-Roman *Demetae* (in Dyfed) favoured Roman names (and titles) as well as both Irish and British ones – or at least that they were later presented as having done so. The first Harleian genealogy suggests that the early dynasty of Gwynedd similarly preferred a scatter of Latin names as the putative forebears of Cunedda, listing *Aetern* (*Aeternus*, meaning 'eternal' or 'immortal'), *Patern Pesrut* (*Paternus*) and *Tacit* (*Tacitus*; see, later, Figure 33).

The evidence is thin, of course, but it may imply that Latin names were far commoner among the secular élite in Britain before the second half of the sixth century. It has been suggested that if our Arthur warrior-figure derived from an actual *Artorius*, then he should have lived earlier than that. The Arthur of the second genealogy is represented as Vortepor's great-grandson, which would seem to place him rather late. The only candidate so far identified whose *floruit* is certainly early enough is one Lucius Artorius Castus, whose career was reconstructed by Malone (1925), in the second half of the second century. This Artorius led a military force as *dux* from Britain to suppress a local rebellion in Armorica, but is far better evidenced in his native Dalmatia (modern Croatia), where he later held high civil office. A tentative connection has been postulated between this Artorius and Sarmatian cavalry, who are evidenced at

Ribchester, in part in the hope that they might have been the prototype heavy cavalry of later medieval, Arthurian romance (Nickel 1975), but this is catching at metaphorical straws. Despite superficial similarities between the Arthurian cycle of the Middle Ages and the oral literature of the Steppes peoples (Littleton and Malcor 1994), there seems no real pre-Galfridian connection between these two Arthurs other than the coincidence of a shared name. Although there is no other reason to suppose that the career of this servant of the Roman Empire was particularly remembered in Britain, as was that of Magnus Maximus, for example, he does remain the sole candidate and it may be significant that the Arthur of the *Historia Brittonum* is described as both *miles* and *dux*, but never *rex*, and that might suggest a further connection. Without better information, however, the candidacy of Lucius Artorius Castus to be the 'historical' Arthur on whom the later figure was modelled (however distantly) must remain in the realm of speculation (Padel 1994), with its principal advantage being the lack of alternatives. The association should arguably be treated with considerable caution, therefore, and the real possibility remains that there were any number of historical Arthurs of relevance to this discussion and to the later use of the name, who are now entirely lost.

That said, the argument in favour of this Roman Arthur as the origin of the legends is infinitely stronger than that in favour of the British Riothamus, known to us *inter alia* from the letters of Sidonius Apollinaris (Loyon 1960–70: ii, 98). Unlike Artorius, Riothamus was both British and a figure of the sub-Roman period, but there his advantages cease. Riothamus led an army to Gaul in 468 as an ally of the Gallo-Roman field army and against the Franks and Visigoths, but was defeated by Euric in 469–70 and died soon after in the Morvan. The connection with Arthur (Ashe 1981, 1991, 1995, enthusiastically supported by Adams 1993) depends on two assumptions. First, to get around the problem that Riothamus was patently not called Arthur, his name must be construed as a title, which seems implausible (Padel 1995). Secondly, and equally fatally, this argument requires the acceptance as historical of constructions of the British hero as a war-leader on the continent, evidenced no earlier than *c.* 1100, to be found for example in the *Life of St Goeznovius*. Magnus Maximus arguably offers a far more accessible role model in a Welsh or Breton context, for a British army commander campaigning in Gaul than the relatively obscure Riothamus (Dumville 1977a: 181). The *Life* is far more likely to be adjusting a vision of the Arthur figure culled from the *Historia Brittonum* to accord with local Breton needs, than representing some oral tradition of an historical figure of the distant past.

Thereafter, there is a group of Arthur names within the secular élite in the late sixth century. A royal figure within Dyfed has already been mentioned (and will be again: p. 213). Secondly, Bishop Adamnan referred in the late seventh century to one *Arturius*, son of the Scottish (Dal Riatan) King Aedan, who was killed in battle before 597 (the traditional date of St Columba's death), but who had strong British family connections via his mother. Given that his father was reputedly of great age by this date, this Arthur could well have been born around the 560s–580s. Thirdly, Irish annals record the death of an Irish king in Kintyre at the hands of one Arthur in the mid-620s, and an Arthur also appears as the grandfather of one Feradach in a legal list of *c.* 697.

Several scholars have argued that this apparently sudden rash of Arthurs requires, or at least implies, that an Arthur figure of renown had recently caught the attention of these several families in western Britain. However, other names were also comparatively fashionable at various times, and across traditional ethnic boundaries (the English name Edwin, for example, occurs widely in late pre-Conquest Wales, without having been borne by a recent English king), so the case is weak, at best unproven. It is equally noticeable that great Welsh warlords, such as Cadwallon, failed to be reflected in royal naming over the next generation or so. This spate of Arthur-naming is therefore interesting but it certainly does not prove the existence of an historical figure of Arthur whose recent career was particularly well known in the mid- to late sixth century. This again might favour an earlier figure whose deeds were by this date legendary as the prototype.

The upsurge in Arthur-naming seems to be exclusive to Irish or Irish-connected families. This may simply reflect interaction of Irish in-comers with the name Arthur as a wonder-worker and folk-hero, upon arrival in Britain. Its adoption may, therefore, reflect a desire to capture whatever mythological kudos and religious potency already surrounded the name, with British/Welsh families avoiding its use primarily because of its newly acquired mythological connections (Padel 1994), which might have been considered un-Christian. Arthur remained in occasional use in Ireland thereafter, as, for example, in the *Annals of Ulster* 847, recording the death of one Artur son of Muiredach, king of western Life (Mac Airt and Mac Niocaill 1983), but barely exists among Welsh families until the later Middle Ages.

The name is not widespread elsewhere as far as the evidence allows us to judge. It is unknown in Anglo-Saxon England until an English *Artor Presbiter* occurs in Yorkshire in 1066, but this is not the Latin/British Arthur but an Anglo-Scandinavian name (Arnthorr is offered by Faull and Stinson 1986). The name is certainly not common in contemporary sources on the continent (Tatlock 1950: 218–26), so this is an improbable source – although it did occur in Brittany in the central Middle Ages, perhaps under the stimulus of the folk-Arthur. The two post-Conquest sub-tenants called *Artur* in Domesday Book (in Worcestershire and as a tenant of Eudo Dapifer) presumably derive from this source, but again there are few examples.

The alternative argument is that Arthur's name is unexceptional in an Old Welsh context, as the combination of *arto-* (Modern Welsh '*arth*', meaning a 'bear') and *wiros* (MW '*gwr*', meaning man/husband), as recently proposed by Thomas Green (1998). *Arth* is a comparatively common term in Old Welsh poetry, wherein it is used to describe and characterize warriors. In the *Gododdin*, for example, it occurs as an entirely conventional reference to a fierce animal in three places in the poem, as well as in the famous occurrence of the personal name. Nor is this unusual in the context of Welsh literature, since reference to powerful wild animals as symbols of, or metaphors for, boldness and ferocity was an integral feature of praise poetry (Edel 1984–5). The term is to be found twice in the *Armes Prydein* (e.g. line 170): 'two bears to whom daily fighting brings no shame', referring metaphorically but quite transparently to Cynan and Cadwaladr. In an early post-Roman context, examples are provided once more by Gildas (Jackson 1982). He included a convoluted reference to a bear in the opening of his condemnation of Cuneglasus (xxxii, 1):

> *Ut quid in nequitiae tuae volveris vetusta faece et tu ab adolescentiae annis, urse, multorum sessor aurigaque currus receptaculi ursi, dei contemptor sortisque eius depressor, Cuneglase, Romana lingua lanio fulve?*
>
> 'Why have you been rolling in the refuse of your old crimes even since the years of your youth, [you] bear, occupier of many and driver of the chariot of the bear's refuge, despiser of God and opponent of his will [literally 'depressor of his fate'], Cuneglasus, in Latin "tawny butcher"?'

Although Gildas's meaning remains somewhat obscure, the reference to a 'bear' here should be connected with the beasts of Daniel's dream, as a means of rhetorically fixing Cuneglasus in providential terms (as mentioned earlier). He was also arguably making ironical use of the practice of animal metaphor, by using the name of this dangerous animal in the context of a king as an insult, instead of the more normal praise (Jackson 1982). He was also perhaps punning bilingually on the name of a defended settlement, Dinarth, for which two candidates have been identified. The more plausible is Bryn Euryn near Llandrillo in the upper Dee valley (E. Davies 1929: 194–6; Edwards and Lane 1988: 27–9), the less likely is Hero Castle, also known as Dinarth, in Cardiganshire (Hogg and King 1963: 112). This was, therefore, an example of Gildas using an animal term in Latin for rhetorical purposes and it has nothing to do with the question of an historical Arthur figure, except as possible evidence that an *Arth-* place-name may have existed when he wrote, which might or might not derive from a personal name.

Animal names do, however, also occur from an early date in personal names. The earliest evidence goes back to the pre-Roman period, with leaders such as Cunobelinus. Similarly, the name Cuneglasus is based on the Old Welsh for hound (Modern Welsh, *ci*), and certainly does not translate into Latin as Gildas claimed (one must presume that this was intentional irony). Again, his audience was expected to appreciate his witty bilingual but pejorative remarks at this king's expense. Thereafter, note, for example, in the *Gododdin*, the personal name *Erthgi* ('Bear-hound': line 140, A14).

The most dramatic recent addition to the corpus of *Arth-* personal names is the stone drain cover discovered at Tintagel in 1998 in a fifth- or sixth-century context (Figure 9). This has part of a small, lightly inscribed (or cut/scratched) Latin inscription, reading: '*PATER / COLI AVI FICIT / ARTOGNOV / COL / FICIT*. Charles Thomas provided a translation to the national press (*Guardian*, 7 August 1998), which reads: 'ARTOGNOU, FATHER OF A DESCENDANT OF COLL, HAS HAD [THIS] MADE [OR BUILT]'. This, however, ignores the beginnings of repetition, evidenced in the last two words which are not translated (*COL* – the name, and *FICIT* – made). There is also a small cross, above *pater*, which is stylistically similar to the main inscription. The whole looks like a broken practice piece, which is important as evidence of literacy at this high status site, but final assessment must await detailed reporting by Professor Chris Morris and his expert advisers.

There are, of course, real difficulties in equating this *Artognou* with 'Arthur', since it represents a completely different British name, *Arthnou*. This is just one of numerous vernacular names which contain the element *arth-*. The Llandaff Charters refer in passing to individuals called *Arthan, Arthbleid, Arthcumanu, Arthfael, Arthmail* and *Arthuo*, as well as *Arthur* (W. Davies 1979). *Arthrwys* likewise occurs in the *Gododdin*. While Arthur is not well evidenced in early Wales outside of Irish-connected families, names containing the element *arth* are comparatively common. There is, therefore, some space

**Figure 9** The 'Arthognou' inscription found at Tintagel (photographed by Paul Johnson, copyright University of Glasgow: courtesy of Chris Morris and Coleen Batey)

for the possibility of a folk connection between the name Arthur and the Welsh *arth*. However, the Middle Welsh forms must weigh against a vernacular origin for the name itself as 'bear-man', since that would give Arthwir, which in normalized Old Welsh spelling would appear as Artguir, later Arthguir, and modern Arthwyr (Professor Richard Coates, personal communication). Rather, the name retained a form in the Middle Ages which implies a derivation from the Latin *Artorius*.

## BEARS AND GODS

There is some doubt at present regarding the survival of the European brown bear in Britain at this date. Martial (died *c.* 102) remarked on Caledonian bears shipped for combat in the Coliseum, and Welsh hunting laws of the latter part of the central Middle Ages refer to bears, which suggests that they were then still encountered in the far west. However, the claims made for the occurrence of 'bear' as a place-name element in England are weak, and most are probably explicable as personal names (as Barham in Kent). Derek Yalden argues (1999: 112) against the conventional wisdom that brown bears died out in Britain in the tenth century, since archaeological evidence of their survival past the Roman occupation is minimal. Later evidence is typically highly portable (as the claws found at York, Coppergate) or comes from tame creatures (as found at both Colchester and Carlisle in post-Conquest contexts).

If the brown bear was already declining early in the first millennium AD, then the dual pressures of increasing land clearance for farming and capture for sport during the Roman period can only have speeded that process, pushing breeding populations in lowland Britain towards extinction. An isolated find from Binchester (County Durham) in the fourth century may confirm what we might in any case suspect from the better-known history of the wolf, that the population will have survived longer in the hill country of the north and Wales, and longest of all in Scotland. In that case, the bear may well have been characteristic only of those parts of Britain beyond the apparent reach of Anglo-Saxon colonization by the middle centuries of the first millennium. It may, therefore, have been a particularly apt point of reference for stories constructed in the vernacular and localized in those parts of the north and west where Old Welsh was widely spoken.

The bear is an animal renowned for its great strength, its preference for remote places, its skill in hunting and living off the wild, the fluidity of its stature, and its solitary nature. These are many of the characteristics displayed by the folk-hero Arthur. Given that the greatest hero-figure of surviving Old English literature seems also to be named for the bear (*Beowulf* = 'Bee-wolf' which is generally read as a metaphor for 'bear'), the naming of characters with superhuman strength after the strongest natural predator perhaps had a compelling logic in story-telling circles. One might suppose that the decline of the bear population towards extinction led to a process of substitution within stories which had previously featured wild animals or animal deities. Thence an 'Arthur' developing from *Artorius* and perhaps originally recalling the Roman soldier of that name was available to be conflated into a British folk-hero and then historicized into a quintessentially British warrior type who was to become renowned as a symbol of British resistance to Germanic invasion and conquest, as that story was eventually developed in the hill country of what had been the diocese of Roman Britain.

The history of the brown bear in Britain may, therefore, have some connection with the emergence of Arthur from what one might assume to have been a number of other possible candidates, as a quintessentially British warrior figure. His name may simply have carried a richer and more appropriate panoply of meanings than any putative rivals', as being particular to the political and cultural geography of western or northern Britain from the sub-Roman period onwards.

In this context, we need to return to the issue of the mythological Arthur, the Arthur of local wonder-tales, whose primacy over the historical Arthur has been championed most recently in a stimulating article by Oliver Padel (1994). Examples of these local legends first emerge into history at the same date as the warrior-figure of Arthur, in the *mirabilia* attached to the *Historia Brittonum*. If the story of Arthur's visit to the 'Otherworld' in *Preiddiau Annwn*, or the various stories summarized in *Pa gur yw y porthaur?* predate the *Historia*, then the Arthur of heroic mythology is evidenced even earlier, but these works are impossible to date with any degree of certainty.

There is an important question here, which is not definitively answerable, as to which came first, Arthur in wonder-stories or Arthur the valiant, the epitome of British martial virtues? The likeliest solution would seem to be that the author of the *Historia* did not himself construct his local stories about Arthur but merely textualized them within his own terms of reference, having come across them earlier in life. In contrast, he had far greater responsibility for the warrior Arthur. To that extent, the likelihood is that the folk-Arthur precedes, and was the immediate blueprint for, the Arthur *miles* who famously led the Britons to repeated victories in the *Historia*'s chapter 56. That said, the folk-Arthur seems in turn to depend on the Roman personal name, which had been adopted into local wonder stories from the name stock of the Empire. Just as the great outlaw figure of medieval England bore a Norman French name – Robin (albeit 'Hood' derives from Old English) – so too does the great hero-figure of the British wilderness carry an élite name, descended from Latin.

These stories about Arthur were woven into the topographical and antiquarian perceptions of the Brittonic world in a remarkably consistent fashion across both time and space (Padel 1994). Early medieval communities were comparatively adept at identifying external agencies in the landscape (although they did on occasion make mistakes). They could often, therefore, distinguish the unnatural shape of a burial mound, for example, from the natural contours of a small hill, but were less successful in establishing those responsible or the likely date of construction. In the Anglo-Saxon world, some massive earthworks were associated with human figures – both famous (as Offa) and obscure (such as Wat) – who were believed responsible for their construction (Edwinslow, for example, where the burial mound proved to be much earlier than the famous king). Others were linked to superhuman agencies such as pagan gods (Woden is the commonest). There was, of course, some exchange across the grey area separating these two categories.

A very similar naming process occurred in the Brittonic world and association with Arthur was a common mechanism for explaining unnatural landscape features. This seems to have occurred over a very long period, and was still taking place within the past few centuries, making the early stages in the process difficult to distinguish and to interpret. For example, the smaller of the two henge monuments at Eamont Bridge near Penrith in Cumbria (Figure 10) is late Neolithic or early Bronze Age, but it is unlikely to have been termed 'the Round Table' (Leland 1535x1543, ix, 7, fo. 62: ed. Smith 1964: v, p. 48), now rationalized to 'King Arthur's Round Table', before the insular development of that table in the period 1150–1300, and it may well have been conferred far later. That said, Leland's alternative name, 'Arture's Castel' might be earlier, comparable as it is with the 'palace of the warrior Arthur' (*palatium ... Artuir militis*), identified as 'Arthur's oven' near Stirling (destroyed in the eighteenth century), described by Lambert of St Omer in 1120 (Dumville 1974–6: 107). Similarly, the 'King Arthur's Chair' or 'Bed' located in the centre of a fortified Iron Age enclosure at Warbstow, Cornwall, looks suspiciously like a medieval rabbit warren and is apparently a comparatively late addition to the archaeology of the site (Figures 11 and 12). There is, therefore, a long history of Arthurian folklore and local naming, active even in areas where a Brittonic language was no longer spoken in the later Middle Ages, but where a 'Celtic' identity survived or might to advantage be recovered.

That said, there is a particular pattern to many of these Arthurian place-names. Take, for example, 'King Arthur's Bed', which is nothing more than a man-shaped hollow in a natural Tor on North-hill on the edge of Bodmin (Figure 13), surrounded by stones with the appearance of troughs, in which he was reputed to feed his dogs, the earliest record of which is Dr William Borlase's account in 1754 (Padel 1994: 29). Or consider 'King Arthur's Hall', also on Bodmin (between St Breward and Garrow Tor: Figure 14), which is an orthostatic structure of considerable size and antiquity, but first noted only in the sixteenth century. We have references to neither at a particularly early date, but both reflect the common occurrence of such stories attached to the type of wild moorland locations which are appropriate to the haunts of bears, and thence to the mythical wild hunt. Parallels with the development of the Irish Finn or Fionn have been suggested for a very long time (e.g. Chambers 1927; Van Hamel 1934; Murphy 1953) but have recently been reinforced (Ó hÓgáin 1988; Padel 1994) and are convincing. Like Arthur, Fionn too was

**Figure 10** King Arthur's Round Table, a late neolithic henge monument near Penrith, Cumbria.

**Figure 11** 'King Arthur's Chair' or 'Bed', Warbstow, Cornwall

**Figure 12** The fortifications of the Iron Age enclosure at Warbstow, Cornwall

**Figure 13** 'King Arthur's Bed', Bodmin, Cornwall

**Figure 14** 'King Arthur's Hall', Bodmin, Cornwall

historicized as the martial defender of his people (against the Vikings) but originated as a mythical hero-huntsman within the world of magic and religion. His earliest historicization seems to have been in the context of efforts by Leinstermen to regain the Boyne Valley in the fifth and sixth centuries (Ó hÓgáin 1999), and in his use retrospectively by missionaries keen to have him prophesy the coming of Christianity.

It is crucial to stress that some localized stories were certainly already in existence by the early ninth century, since the *mirabilia* listed in the *Historia Brittonum* refer (in chapter 73) to two such instances, one in Builth and the other in modern-day Herefordshire. In both cases what were probably ancient (Bronze Age or Neolithic) burial mounds were explained by reference to Arthurian stories, incorporating various folklore motifs. It is worth quoting this chapter of the *Historia* in full:

> *Est aliud mirabile in regione quae dicitur Buelt. Est ibi cumulus lapidum et unus lapis superpositus super congestum cum vestigio canis in eo. Quando venatus est porcum Troynt, impressit Cabal, qui erat canis Arthuri militis, vestigium in lapide, et Arthur postea congregavit congestum lapidum sub lapide, in quo erat vestigium canis sui, et vocatur Carn Cabal. Et veniunt homines, et tollunt lapidem in manibus suis per spatium diei et noctis, et in crastino die invenitur super congestum suum.*

> (Faral 1929: 61)

> There is another wonder in the region which is called Builth. There is a pile of stones there and one stone positioned on top of the heap has the footprint of a dog on it. When he hunted the boar *Troynt*, *Cabal*, who was the hound of Arthur the warrior, made an imprint on the stone, and Arthur afterwards collected up the heap of stones under the stone in which was the footprint, and it is called *Carn Cabal*. And men come and they carry the stone in their hands for the space of a day and a night, and on the next day it has returned to the top of the pile.

This site is well established, being Carn Gafallt, a hill 466m high above the Caban-coch Reservoir, near Rhayader in the upper valley of the Wye (Figure 15). On its southern edge are several burial cairns (at SN 943644, above Talwrn), one of which may perhaps be the *carn* to which this author refers (although *carn* is ambiguous, meaning both 'hoof' and 'cairn'). Alternatively, the name may even then have defined not the individual cairn but the entire hill, which would connect with the vision of Arthur as a giant-figure. The notch which particularly characterizes the skyline of the hill, which gives it something of the appearance of a saddle, may imply that the connection with 'horse' (Modern Welsh *ceffyl*) was primary in the formation of the name, and the Arthurian connection secondary.

**Figure 15** Carn Gafallt, in the upper valley of the Wye

This story is, of course, the earliest evidence available for the currency of the tale of the hunting of the great boar Twrch Trwyth, which plays a major role in the central medieval Welsh story *Culhwch and Olwen*, which has been claimed as the earliest vernacular Arthurian text (Bromwich and Simon Evans 1992). The great hunt motif, however, at this date may have been free-standing, since it is far from being a necessary part of the winning of Olwen in marriage, which is the dominant narrative in the story as textualized.

The presence of a (magical) stone bearing a mark reminiscent of a hound's print (a fossil seems the likeliest genesis of the story), has therefore been explained by reference to this mythical hunt. Just how magical this tale was becomes clearer when we recognize that this is an enterprise led by an Arthur-figure whose name may have recalled the vernacular 'bear', with his hound called 'horse', attempting to slay the 'essential boar' (*Twrch* is pig/boar, *Trwyth/Troynt* meaning 'decoction'). *Twrch Trwyth* has been convincingly argued to have been mythological in origin (Bromwich and Simon Evans 1992: lxix). This was arguably a local etymological story, therefore, derived from a wider tale of Arthur the huntsman and already known in a local context to the author, who is generally acknowledged to have had a particular interest in this region of Wales (at least since Lloyd 1911: I, p. 223; Lot 1934: 111), and included these wonder-tales appended to his Gwynedd-centric *Historia*. It might conceivably have been the accident of Arthur's dog and the hill itself bearing the same name which led to the etymology becoming established.

In this context, it is only the *miles* which qualifies Arthur which betrays the author's concern to tell this story in a manner which clearly makes the connection with the historicized figure of chapter 56.

The second example runs as follows:

> *Est aliud miraculum in regione quae vocatur Ercing. Habetur ibi*
> *sepulcrum juxta fontem, qui cognominatur Licat Anir [or Amr], et viri*
> *nomen: qui sepultus est in tumulo, sic vocabatur Anir; filius Arthuri*
> *militis erat, et ipse occidit eum ibidem et sepelivit. Et veniunt homines*
> *ad mensurandum tumulum in longitudine aliquando sex pedes,*
> *aliquando novem, aliquando duodecim, aliquando quindecim. In qua*
> *mensura metieris eum in ista vice, iterum non invenies eum in una*
> *mensura, et ego solus probavi.*

> There is another miracle in the region which is called Ergyng [Archenfield]. There is there a grave next to a spring, which is called *Llygad Amr*, and the name of the man who is buried in the tumulus, is called *Amr*; he was a son of the warrior Arthur, and he himself killed him in that very place and buried him. And men come to measure the grave, which is sometimes six feet long, sometimes nine, sometimes twelve, sometimes fifteen. Whatever length you measure on one occasion, you do not repeat that measure, and I have tried myself.

Here is another local wonder-story, which seeks to associate a burial mound with the historicized Arthur, and it is unlikely to be accidental that these two stories are grouped together. Again, the epithet *miles* reflects the author's concern to make clear the connection between this Arthur and the champion of his chapter 56. However, the story itself is older than this text, even if its particular phrasing is probably the author's own, if only because he explicitly avers that he himself had previously demonstrated its veracity in person. Again the story is etymological in inspiration: *Llygad* is 'an eye' (Modern Welsh), and is apparently used here as a metaphor for the spring (as the source of tears/water). *Amr*, however, is a term with a closely related meaning: Modern and Old Welsh *amrant* translates as 'eyelid' (as in the *Gododdin*), and Modern Welsh *amrantiad* as 'wink'. The spring was, therefore called 'Eye Eye', so metaphorically 'Fountain Spring'. It should arguably be seen as the source of the River Gamber, in which case the etymology was eventually lost as that became anglicized. Only once *Amr* had acquired a meaning as a personal name, the addition of *Llygad* became necessary, and the Arthurian narrative presumably developed thereafter as explanation. *Amr* seems an improbable personal name. The transition arguably occurred owing to the superficial similarity between *Amr* and *Arthur* (cf. Brutus, Britto and *Britannia*), i.e. only when Arthurian stories were developing in the region. That this had apparently already occurred by the early ninth century again demonstrates the vigour of Arthurian folk stories at an early date, and the capacity of such tales to capture new sites and develop new variants of the common stock of tales.

Such was similarly the case in Cornwall and Devon by the early twelfth century, when the canons of Laon, 'twenty years or so before Geoffrey of Monmouth wrote his *Historia*, . . . found Cornish men holding their country to be Arthur's, pointing to his chair and oven, and heartily believing him still alive' (Tatlock 1933: 465). This 'oven' can arguably be identified with the remains of what was probably a smelting furnace on the eastern edges of Dartmoor (SX674812) but the 'chair' or 'seat' has not been identified, unless this be at Warbstow. In this region, therefore, Arthur would seem to be a secular, saviour figure or folk-hero outside of time, so undead, invoked by a local community which had long held to a cultural and political identity which was in origin British, even while open to Anglo-Saxon cultural colonialism from Wessex. The *Anglo-Saxon Chronicle* records a West Saxon vision of the gradual contraction of this British enclave. It was colonized, without much success, by the English diocesan system and Exeter was effectively established as an Anglo-Saxon town under Æthelstan, but all without much apparent effort to win the hearts and minds of the inhabitants. Local resistance to papal authority was a feature of the early tenth century (Rumble 2001: 239), and Arthurian folklore should be read similarly as a stock of local tales retained to sustain local identity and contest unsympathetic, external authorities, from which the local community felt to an extent culturally estranged. In this context, there is some overlap between the idea of Arthur as culture-hero of significance to the self-definition of a community whose statehood had been lost, and the adoption of a patron saint as reinforcement of state formation (think of SS Patrick, Oswald, Cuthbert, Edmund and Edward the Martyr: Thacker 2000). It is very noticeable that eleventh- and twelfth-century Welsh literature (from *Culhwch and Olwen* to Caradoc of Llancarfan's *Life of Gildas*), was increasingly inclined to position Arthur in Devon and Cornwall with his court at Kelliwic ('Grove-settlement', which, as Padel noted, again associates Arthur with the wilderness).

This Arthurian element in the landscape had the added advantage of both human characterization, in the sense of the role of a pseudo-historical figure in the stories, but at the same time superhuman attributes. The grave of *Amr* reflects a magical fluidity in stature. Arthur – like a bear – was considered capable, for example, of moving the massive stones which commonly formed parts of Neolithic and Bronze Age burial and ritual monuments throughout the region, such as Arthur's Stone, Cefn-y-Bryn, on the Gower, which is reckoned to weigh some twenty-five tons (Figure 16). In the folk explanation recurs the theme of a pebble in Arthur's shoe, which annoyed him so much on his way to fight at Camlann that he shook it out on the Welsh mainland to fly off seven miles onto the Gower. Latterly, the stone was reputedly used in folk rituals by girls from Swansea who brought food offerings and sought to

**Figure 16** Arthur's Stone, Cefn-y-Bryn, on the Gower

test the fidelity of their sweethearts under a full moon (Bord and Bord 1976). Another, very similar monument is Arthur's Stone, near Dorstone in the Golden Valley (Herefordshire), in ninth-century Archenfield. Again, the name is attached to a massive capstone, this time covering part of a chambered Neolithic long cairn (Figure 17). Arthur emerges, therefore, as both a giant and of superhuman strength, used to explain the otherwise inexplicable in the landscape.

Whether this Arthur – the superhuman demi-god or force of nature – or the historicized Arthur of pseudo-history came first is an issue which has repeatedly been raised (at least since Rhŷs 1891) and on which there are diverse opinions. To separate the historical figure from the elemental may, however, be to impose modern standards of historicity on a past which did not distinguish in that sense between one set of stories and another. Clearly, it is admissible to recognize the interlocking nature of their histories and to expect constant interchange between so-called 'historical' works in Latin and vernacular folk tales. The Arthur of wonder-stories is, of course, an Arthur which had become established within the vernacular. Bears are creatures of great strength and seldom seen, living generally far from mankind in the woods and hills. It is precisely these sorts of locations, on the Welsh and Cornish hills and scattered thinly across southern Scotland, that many of these legends are located (Figures 18 and 19). The cultural province of the landscape-Arthur is markedly similar to that of early British Christianity, to the extent to which

**Figure 17** Arthur's Stone, Dorstone, Herefordshire

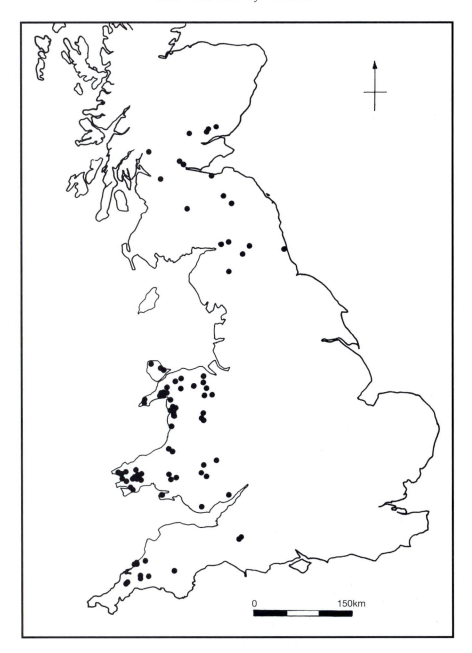

**Figure 18** The distribution of Arthur-names in the British countryside (based with permission on an indicative list compiled by Elizabeth Johnson)

**Figure 19** Craig Arthur, Eglwyseg Mountain, near Llangollen

that is depicted by the memorial stones (Figure 4, earlier).

Arthur therefore seems to have originated as the Roman name *Artorius* but then was developed orally as an agent of legendary power and thus a focus of story-telling among the Britons of the early to central Middle Ages, particularly connected with the wilderness and high, exposed places. Some connection with a bear-god seems possible, such as have been identified in other Celtic regions (MacCullough 1911; Ross 1967), but the evidence is poor. The only convincing cult site in Europe is that at Berne in the Roman period, although one at Drôme is possible, and stone figures of bears at Limoges, and Armagh (in a post-Roman context), may have religious meaning. In Britain, a bear-cult of *Matunus* has been postulated at Risingham in the north and the horned god, *Cernunnos* appears flanked by a bear and another poorly defined animal figure at Meigle in Perthshire (again in a post-Roman context). Such has led Ross to suggest that (p. 349) 'although fragmentary, this evidence [of a bear cult] is impressive, and it is obvious that in later times the divine qualities envisaged as being possessed by the bear would become transferred to find expression as heroic epithets in a heroic milieu'. There is, however, a distinct circularity to this argument, which would be untenable in a Romano-British context without assumptions drawn from later, medieval evidence. If the folkloric Arthur of the ninth century had significant associations with a bear-god cult popular in Roman Britain, then that fact remains to be established and the cult seems overly coy about declaring itself.

## CONCLUSION

This discussion has predictably been inconclusive in regard to establishing the origins of the historicized Arthur of the ninth and tenth centuries. It has, however, begun to explore the context in which the legendary persona originated and then developed. That context was first and foremost ideological. The insular élite was attempting to develop its own identity in the sub-Roman period as a people within providential history, i.e. as a people of the Lord, as is reflected in the writings of Patrick and Gildas, and in inscriptions on stone. This was made the more necessary in consequence of Germanic colonization of the more Romanized parts of the old diocese from the second quarter of the fifth century onwards. British identity then had to be repositioned to confront English group membership. The defining factors in the sixth century were arguably language, religion and an independent historical mythology – with all that these entailed in terms of self-image. Thereafter, as the religious divide broke down, élite groups keen to confront the Anglicizing colonial process sought to reinforce their historical mythology by providing heroic icons supportive of both virtuous leadership and a military reputation, in contra-diction to Gildas's polemic, the spate of Saxon victories and the fact that English control by the eighth century extended across the greater, and wealthier, part of the island. The Arthur of early British Latin literature was developed for that purpose. The name arguably derived from the stock of Roman names, i.e. from an original figure whose name (like that of Ambrosius) was Roman. No such figure seems entirely satisfactory, but the history of Lucius Artorius Castus would at least conform with the non-royal but military figure which we encounter in chapter 56 of the *Historia Brittonum*. Arthur's appearance in the *mirabilia* of that same work strongly suggests that this legendary figure had been taken up thereafter into a vernacular story cycle and perhaps even conflated or in some sense connected with the Welsh *arth*. That conclusion would also seem implicit in his role as a quintessentially British hero-figure – as opposed to a Roman one – in chapter 56 of the same text, wherein he appears among a succession of British secular leaders (Vortigern, Vortimer, Emrys = Ambrosius, Maelgwn, Urien, etc.). Arthur derived, therefore, in all probability, from the folkloric re-imagining of a legendary figure of Romano-British history whose name was remembered but was attached to a hero and wonder-working figure during the sub-Roman period. The capture of the old heartlands of Roman Britain by Germanic warriors arguably refocused 'Britishness' in the far west, where evidence of Romano-British religion is weakest, and it seems just possible, but far from proven, that an indigenous bear-cult might have influenced the folklore.

Arthur's advantage over rival figures for prominence in memory and legend may have lain in the depth of his cultural integration and the scarcity of pan-British candidates. If the Britons had virtually no pre-Roman history of their own, as both Gildas and the *Historia Brittonum* would seem to imply, and no imperial family to boast of during the Roman period, then a general leading troops from Britain to quell revolt on the continent might have become 'owned' within the diocese as a quintessentially 'British' hero-figure. Arthur's advantage may have lain to an extent in the accident of his name's connection with the brown bear, hence his cultural adaptability or duality, bridging the Roman *Artorius* and the British *arth*. The latter was a well used name element in early Wales, and the gradual extinction of the bear itself, allied to its reputation for strength and fortitude probably encouraged the development of a humanized hero-figure surrounded by wonder-tales attached to wild places. Whatever the precise relationship, these clearly developed before our earliest surviving manifestation of the historical legend.

Latin names seem to be characteristically early in the sub-Roman period, and the small clutch of Arthur names conferred on the children of the secular élite in the second half of the sixth century should be considered Latin rather than vernacular. However, these names may already reflect an Arthur of widespread but localized stories of magical type, the hero of which was a mythical huntsman figure. In other words, the origins of the name in Roman Britain may already have been forgotten. The passage of the hero-figure from mythical huntsman to humanized warrior and protector of his people is eased both by comparison with the Irish Fionn, given that the early names were carried by Irishmen, and by the general assumption that early military leaders were both great huntsmen and leaders of men. So too was the wilderness considered the appropriate place for man to connect with God (e.g. *DEB* xxv, 1–2). Even the historicized Arthur of the *Historia* was in many respects supra-human, particularly regarding the 960 opponents whom he supposedly slew at Badon, and this too points back to the wonder-figure of superhuman strength as the prototype.

The most plausible conclusion is, therefore, that the historicized Arthur of the central Middle Ages had his roots in a Roman *Artorius* who had been taken up and developed within British folk stories already widespread by the beginning of the ninth century. Thence he was adopted into overtly political, 'historical' texts in order to provide a prototype of the successful British warrior, which was an image necessary to sustain current political agendas. There is good reason to look for the historicization of Arthur in the context of British Christian ideology developed to contest the vision of an unmartial and cowardly race as imagined by Gildas and taken up by Bede. The historicized, warrior Arthur was, therefore, created to sustain the vision of a martial people of the Lord, gathered around unconquerable champions of superhuman strength, whose steadfastness in resisting the heathen barbarians who had taken over the diocesan heartlands would eventually be rewarded with victory by God (see Chapter III). The likeliest origin was a military leader of repute in Roman Britain who had become legendary and who later evolved into a 'pan-Brittonic . . . folkloric hero, a peerless warrior of giant-like stature who leads a band of superhuman heroes that roam the wild places of the landscape' (Green 1998: 9).

The folk-tales continued, of course, and William of Malmesbury noted their popularity even while attempting to establish the figure of history which he had found in the *Historia* (Mynors, Thomson and Winterbottom 1998: i, 8.2, p. 27):

> This Arthur is the hero of many wild tales among the Britons even in our own day, but assuredly deserves to be the subject of reliable history rather than of false and dreaming fable; for he was long the mainstay of his falling country, rousing to battle the broken spirit of his countrymen, and at length at the siege of Mount Badon, relying on the image of our Lord's Mother which he had fastened upon his arms, he attacked nine hundred of the enemy single-handed, and routed them with incredible slaughter.

So began the vision of two Arthurs, the figure of fable and the figure of sub-Roman history, but the latter was arguably based on nothing more substantial than the Arthurian material in the *Historia Brittonum*, to which we must now turn our attention.

# CHAPTER III

# CONTESTED HISTORIES
## Anglo-Saxons and Britons c. 730–830

— ·◆· —

> Then in those days Arthur fought with the kings of the Britons
> against them [the Saxons], but he himself was the *dux bellorum*.
> (*Historia Brittonum* 56)

The *Historia Brittonum* was written in Wales *c.* 829–30. It will be argued in
this chapter that it was conceived as a highly political text, and very much in
the context of Anglo-British relations. Our understanding of it must begin
with an appreciation of the political and ideological situation over the previous
century or so, that is with the immediately antecedent experiences of his own
generation and the two previous, which will have significantly influenced the
stance adopted by its author. The work of Gildas, which the author both used
and sought to rebut in important respects, has already been considered in the
previous chapter. This chapter will, therefore, begin with Bede's *Historia
Ecclesiastica*, which the author likewise both used and contested, and move
then to a brief résumé of political relations between Mercia and its neighbours,
particularly the Welsh kingships, before examining in more detail the *Historia
Brittonum* itself.

## BEDE AND THE BRITONS

The English conversion to Christianity irrevocably changed the ideological
landscape of Britain and the conflicting positioning of British and Anglo-
Saxon élites. Looking back on the seventh century from the next, Bede
developed a vision of providential history which was in open competition with
that of earlier British thinkers, as exemplified by Gildas. To add insult to
injury, he took the British writer's story line about divine retribution and the
path towards redemption for his own people, but then massaged it into a
providential history for the *Angles seu Saxones* which entirely undermined
and ultimately denied the moral and ideological positioning of the Britons.
So the 'Angles or Saxons' – Gildas's abominable gallows-birds – were
repositioned as the people of the Lord within Britain, in post-Roman history

and in the present (see the very different perceptions of Hanning 1966; Goffart 1988, 1990; Higham 1995; Houwen and MacDonald 1996; for parallels for his general reconfiguring of the past, see Hen and Innes 2000). It is from Bede's work onwards that the historian can sense the presence of a common 'English' identity, expressed primarily through claims to a common descent and origins mythology, common language and a literary tradition (Foot 1996). One could even argue that Bede invented the English nation, and that he did this quite consciously in contradiction to earlier perceptions of the Britons.

During and then beyond Bede's adult lifetime, a series of newly Christian English kings in Mercia developed what can best be described as a proto-state, based in part on their patronage of the Church. This drew into a new and increasingly unified Mercia the bulk of what had been a predominantly 'British' West Midlands, at least as regards élite culture, lying between the eastern zone of pre-Conversion English cemeteries and the kingships of Wales beyond. Hitherto, this central belt of southern Britain had to some extent shielded the more self-consciously 'British' west from Anglo-Saxon colonialism and the pressures of Anglicization. From the late seventh century onwards that was no longer the case and Wales was increasingly vulnerable to cultural as well as both military and political colonization. It is not just an Anglo-centric perspective to point to the power of Anglo-Saxon culture and identity to expand at the expense of 'Britishness' and other Celtic identities. The principal pressure post-700 came from Mercia, as regards all of the politics, culture and economics of the Welsh kingdoms.

Bede's vision of the historical development of Britain dominates the ideological landscape, although other Germanic writers clearly shared his vision of the Britons as a people fallen from grace, to be compared with the fallen angels who had become devils (as Felix's *Vita Guthlaci* 34: Colgrave 1956). Bede completed his great historical composition in 731, having written his own *gens* into biblical and providential history as a people of the Lord at the expense of their neighbours and rivals. It is clear from the very beginning of the work that it was written from a very specific ethnic and dynastic position, but the extent to which it was written against others has not perhaps been sufficiently recognized. The dedication, for example, was to the Northumbrian king of the day, the embattled Ceolwulf, and Bede seems to have paid particular attention to his political sensibilities in several areas of the work (Kirby 1979–80). The sources to which he admitted were exclusively English and 'Roman', omitting reference to either Britons or Mercians (although his assistant, Nothelm, became archbishop in 735 under Mercian patronage so may have been a Mercian himself), suggesting that the partiality of his approach to the past was quite intentional. It was also, perhaps, not entirely honest, for he certainly drew on British sources and traditions, even excepting Gildas, whose work he did acknowledge, and seems to have obtained information direct from churchmen with a knowledge of the British north, at least (Kirby 1966).

In preparation for his great narrative, Bede first (*HE* i, 1) constructed Britain as an idyllic setting suitable as a promised land for God's people and he implied that only with the arrival of the English language (hence the Anglo-Saxon settlement) was the providential enterprise for Britain as a whole. He then offered a potted history of Roman Britain. This allowed the Britons a martial reputation in the distant past (so fighting off Julius Caesar: *HE* i, 2) and an early and honorific status as a people of the Lord (*HE* i, 4): 'the Britons preserved the faith which they had received, inviolate and entire, in peace and quiet, until the time of the Emperor Diocletian'. That positioning was then reinforced, since (*HE* i, 6) 'even Britain attained the great glory of bearing faithful witness to God', with extended treatment of St Alban, based on a version of the *Passio Albani* but with reference to Gildas (*DEB* x–xi), and mention of the latter's Aaron and Julius. Bede was content, therefore, to develop an uncontroversial starting point for his narrative of retribution, with the Britons fully within the fold of salvation history.

The first hint that the status of the Britons was under threat comes in the late Roman period with the Arian heresy, which established (*HE* i, 8) 'the way for every foul heresy from across the Ocean to pour into an island which always delights in hearing something new and holds firmly to no sure belief'. Bede was here using Gildas (*DEB* xii, 3) but by paraphrasing Acts xvii, 21 he was casting the Britons in the role of the unbelieving Athenians. Pelagius – who was absent from Gildas – was then introduced as a British arch-heretic, characterizing Britain as a source, as well as recipient, of heresy.

Bede continued with his Gildas-derived story, to tell of the wickedness of Magnus Maximus and the unmartial state of the Britons, who were twice rescued from the attacks of the barbarians by Roman expeditions but ultimately abandoned to be massacred, since they were incapable of defending themselves (*HE* i, 12). This martial decadence was paralleled by new moral failings. A great famine (to be viewed in biblical terms as divine punishment) was followed (after Gildas) by plenty, the vice of luxury and a host of crimes, which were then punished by (divine) retribution via the invitation to the Saxons (*HE* i, 14): 'As events plainly showed, this was ordained by the will of God, so that evil might fall upon the miscreants.'

By this point, therefore, the Britons were being positioned by Bede, very largely via development of the material offered him by Gildas, as an unmartial race whose position within divine providence had been placed in jeopardy by their own moral shortcomings (see Higham 1995 for a fuller exposition). By contrast, the 'Angles or Saxons' were developed as a courageous people with a prestigious history characterized (like the Israelites) by migration and legitimized by virtue of the divine ancestry of their leaders (*HE* i, 15), in line with the Woden-descent still acknowledged as a necessary element of royal authority in eighth-century Anglian genealogies. With the collapse of Roman protection, it was the English who now took over that role, and this is the first of a series of mechanisms by which Bede was to develop a congruence between the roles and moral positioning of the Roman Empire, in the past, and the Anglo-Saxons, in the present, in Britain. In his description of the Saxon revolt, Bede massaged the moral of Gildas's story, stressing the role of the Saxons as divine agents, and the judgement of God upon the Britons, and reversing Gildas's portrayal of the Saxons as 'Other' – devils, wolves, Assyrians, gallows-birds, an abomination, and so on. In Bede's narrative, the Anglo-Saxon settlement was entirely in accord with God's long-term plans, as opposed to Gildas's vision of the Saxons as just one more scourge sent as a corrective by the Lord to bring his British Israel back to obedience.

Thereafter, Bede departed from Gildas to introduce material from the *Life of St. Germanus*, using that to emphasize the dependence of the heresy-prone Britons on overseas clerics capable, for example, of winning 'a victory by faith and not by might' over the Saxons. Germanus, as a representative of Catholic Europe, was countering that most British of heresies, Pelagianism, and had putatively to visit Britain twice to this effect. The heretical nature of the Britons was thereby confirmed within this text, and Germanus's activities provide a valuable precursor to Augustine's efforts to establish his Roman authority over the Britons.

Bede then reverted to Gildas's narrative, with an account of the further moral decline of the Britons (based on *De Excidio* xxvi, 3). From this retrograde people, Bede distinguished his own *gens*, who were still unbaptised but foreknown by God (*HE* i, 22), for 'He had appointed much worthier heralds of the truth to bring this people to the faith'.

For Bede, the Britons had reached their lowest ebb in providential terms by about 600. It was at this point that Bede introduced Augustine, the Roman apostle of his own English people, so further reinforcing the Roman/Anglo-Saxon moral axis on which his vision of history depends. Bede quoted from Pope Gregory's correspondence to the effect that he had granted to Augustine authority over all the bishops of Britain (*HE* i, 27, 29) – which necessarily included the British bishops. The refusal of the British clergy *en masse* to acknowledge Augustine's authority and accept the practices of the Catholic church at Augustine's Oak (*HE* ii, 2) could then be interpreted by Bede as the final, damning act of disobedience of the Britons towards God's representatives on earth, hence to God Himself.

Having, therefore, plotted the decline of the Britons from a position of ancient excellence under Roman rule, Bede constructed their denial of Augustine as the ultimate evidence of their fall from grace. This freed him to depict the Britons from then up to the present time – hence throughout the English Christian era to date – as so disobedient to God as to have fallen outside His protection. Consequently, there was no legitimate ideological bar to the continuing processes of Anglo-Saxon conquest and colonialism inside Britain – in contrast to Bede's apparent disquiet at the Northumbrian invasion of Christian Ireland *c.* 684 (*HE* iv, 26). Nor was there any bar to English supremacy in a quasi-Roman guise, hence the establishment of successive *imperii* by successful English (particularly Northumbrian) kings over English and British kingdoms alike. Bede somewhat ungraciously recognized the current supremacy of Æthelbald of Mercia over the south (as a *subiecta* as opposed to an *imperium*), and this too is very likely to have included British subjects. In the present (*HE* v, 23), 'the Britons oppose the English through their inbred hatred, and the whole state of the catholic Church by their incorrect Easter and their evil customs, yet being opposed by the power of God and man [i.e. Englishman] alike, they cannot obtain what they want in either respect'. British leaders who had, in the past, sought to overthrow English supremacy could legitimately be construed as evil figures and heretics outside of the Christian fold and without proper authority, and Bede's Cadwallon is a victim of this rhetorical positioning (*HE* iii, 1).

Bede had, therefore, disposed of the Britons as a people of the Lord in the present, positioning them instead much as the Jews were seen throughout Christendom as a once elect people who had fallen from grace by their own ill deeds (O'Reilly 1995: xxxv). As a replacement, he had stamped on the ideological landscape a powerful vision of the English as a chosen race. This vision clearly still had a utility for the Northumbrians at this date. There should be little doubt that many inhabitants of northern England and southern Scotland still thought of themselves as Britons, or were considered as such by others – particularly if their English was poor (Faull 1977; Higham 2001a for references). In the current context, however, it had an even greater utility further south, where Mercia had absorbed considerable British populations and also still had an eye to further expansion towards significant pools of at least semi-independent British kingdoms in Wales (Bassett 2000). Mercian cultural and political colonialism can only have been aided by Bede's construction of a pan-English ideology supportive of ethnic supremacy within a Christian framework, albeit his Northumbrian-centric vision strongly implies that support for Mercian colonialism was never his purpose.

## WELSH–MERCIAN INTERACTIONS

During the eighth century, the more easterly Welsh kingdoms had a long and much contested frontier with English Mercia, while the 'southern Welsh' of Cornwall interacted primarily with Wessex. During most of the century, Mercia was ruled by just two, long-lived kings, Æthelbald (716–57) and Offa (757–96: see e.g. Scharer 1982: 159–278). By insular standards, the increasingly well organized and integrated kingship of Mercia was assuming the status of an insular, conglomerate 'super state', the principal power in England below the Humber, to be compared with the (admittedly much greater) Carolingian kingdom of Pepin and Charlemagne, across the Channel. Indeed, King Offa's receipt of correspondence from Charlemagne (Whitelock 1955, no. 197) represents him as an equal, albeit at the same time referring to

English exiles whom Charlemagne was protecting from Offa's wrath. Alcuin, the Northumbrian cleric in Charlemagne's service, addressed Offa as 'the glory of Britain, the trumpet of proclamation, the sword against foes, the shield against enemies' (Whitelock 1955: no. 195).

Taking advantage of the power vacuum created by the death of Wihtred of Kent and the departure overseas of the powerful Ine of Wessex, Æthelbald had by 731 established himself as the dominant king of southern Britain, as Bede asserts. A charter granting land at Ismere, Worcestershire, in 736, famously terms him 'king not only of the Mercians but also of the provinces which are called by the general name "South English".' In the witness list, he appears as 'king of Britain' (Whitelock 1955: no. 67). Æthelbald took direct control at different times of London (from Wessex, Kent and the East Saxons) and Somerset (from Wessex), and seems to have dominated the Southumbrian church, with a reforming agenda, through the appointment to the primacy of Cuthbert, erstwhile bishop of Hereford (Wormald 1982; Kirby 1991; Keynes 1990, 1995; Hill and Worthington forthcoming).

The power of this Mercian ruler had dangerous implications for even those of his neighbours not included in the 'South English'. The brief annalistic continuation of Bede's *Historia* (Plummer 1896: 363), written in Northumbria, referred under the year 740 to Æthelbald's ravaging of part of Northumbria '*per impiam fraudem*', while the Northumbrian army was engaged against the Picts. A second entry in this same text for 750 records the 'rebellion' of the West Saxon king against Æthelbald and *Oengusum*. This latter was Oengus I (729–61), the powerful Pictish king who had dominated the north since the 730s, when he extended his authority over Dalriada, but his power was slipping in 750, when the Strathclyde Britons defeated and killed his brother, Talorgen. It is telling that the same annal noted that Eadberht of Northumbria extended his *regnum* in this same year. This coupling of the powerful Mercian and Pictish kings may imply some sort of understanding between them, to share *imperium* respectively over the south and north of Britain (Charles-Edwards 1991: 25). The same annalist, in noting Oengus's death, remarked that 'from the beginning right to the end he had ruled his kingdom as a tyrannical hangman with cruel crimes', which does suggest that he was remembered in Northumbria with particular venom. If this reconstruction is apt, the Welsh had good reason to look to Northumbria, as well as to the Strathclyde Britons and Scots, as potential allies in their own conflicts with the Mercians.

A Mercian king capable of raiding Northumbria was clearly a danger to Wales. Bede was keen to stress that the Northumbrian 'overkings' of the seventh century had exercised hegemony over British kings as well as English. There is every likelihood that the Mercians likewise expected to dominate the far west, where the active co-operation with the Welsh on terms of comparative equality, which characterized the early years of Penda's reign, seems to have ended. There is fragmentary evidence of English attacks in this period. The *Anglo-Saxon Chronicle* is extremely sketchy concerning Mercian activity prior to Egberht's reign but it does refer to Mercian and West Saxon action against the Britons in 743 and West Saxon again in 753. This was arguably against the Cornish, but a charter of King Ithel in the Llandaff collection (W. Davies 1979: no. 192), supposing it to be genuine, does refer to the return of eleven churches around Hereford to the Welsh bishop around the mid-century, following a period of Saxon devastation in the region. Although the implication of Felix's *Life of Guthlac* is of Welsh attacks on Mercia (admittedly at a slightly earlier date), the little evidence available seems to suggest that the Mercians were more normally the aggressors.

Under Offa, this appearance of a powerful Mercia interfering in its neighbours' affairs comes more clearly into focus. Looking back on the period with ninth-century hindsight, Asser ('Life of Alfred' 14) termed him 'a vigorous king, who terrified all the neighbouring kings and provinces around him'. Although there were periods of successful opposition (as in Kent), Offa effectively, and on occasion brutally, made himself the direct arbiter of political affairs throughout East Anglia and the south-east and established control of a number of well endowed minsters, reinforced by new papal privileges, as a means of consolidating his control (Keynes 1990, 1995). So, too, did Offa's Mercia invest in historical mythology, developing the legend of royal descent from the continental Anglian kings of yore as a political myth capable of reinforcing his dynastic position. King Æthelræd of Northumbria became his son-in-law in 792, which implies that he was accepting subordinate status at this date. Furthermore, one explanation for the collapse of the Northumbrian silver *sceatta* coinage in the 790s must be the possibility that either Æthelræd or his rival and eventual successor Eardwulf had had to pay tribute to Offa. Whatever the cause, the available bullion did apparently drop below the levels needed to sustain the currency (for general discussion see Metcalf 1987; for the particular argument, Higham 1993a: 149, 167).

There are several references to war between the Mercians under Offa and the Welsh (e.g. W. Davies 1990; Hill 2000). The *Annales Cambriae* notes the battle of Hereford in 760 and the devastation of south-western Wales by Offa in 778. Thereafter, an English raid in the summer of 784 refers merely to 'the Britons', which may imply widespread damage to more than one kingdom. A late manuscript of the *Annales* refers to the devastation of Rheinwg by Offa in 796, which might refer either to Dyfed or part of Brycheiniog, and a battle occurred at Rhuddlan on the Clwyd in 797, which suggests Welsh counter-attacking against the English tenure of the coastal plain in eastern Powys once both Offa and his son were dead. As W. Davies has remarked (1990: 67–9), the evidence collectively appears to refer to English attacks on the Welsh kingdoms, rather than the reverse, which certainly implies secure Mercian control of western Cheshire, the north-east Welsh coastline, the upper Severn valley and other points of departure. All in all, there seems sufficient evidence to suggest that Offa thought of Wales, rather than his northern neighbour, as the appropriate theatre for military activity outside southern England. Its very foreignness may well have encouraged him to treat it as a fit place to plunder and blood his thegns.

Anglo-Saxon aggression towards the west, centred in the eighth century, coincided with a decline in overseas contacts between the Irish Sea coastlands and the continent. One feature of the British west during the sixth and seventh centuries had been fortified political centres of high status at which access to exotic goods was concentrated and whence distribution occurred: Tintagel is only the best evidenced of these (Nowakowski and Thomas 1990; Morris and Harry 1997; Figure 20). These developed as centres of craft specialization and manufacture, with concentrations of precious metals within the archaeological record. The level of overseas trade is much disputed, and there is a case for arguing it to have been comparatively small in scale (Bowman 1996; Wooding 1996). However, even small-scale exchange of exotic goods had some potential to sustain social hierarchies. One recent discussion has proposed that the ingredients existed here for the development of a full-scale market economy in the later sixth and seventh centuries (Campbell 1996). That this did not occur has been explained in terms of poor quality land, the scale of population, social attitudes to capital accumulation and problems of a location peripheral to European seaways. Another factor might be Anglo-Saxon tribute-taking and raiding deep into British territory, which drew off a significant proportion of the surplus, disrupted production and reduced the availability of precious metals below levels capable, for example, of minting a coinage. Offa's own high-quality coinage, by contrast, clearly implies access to considerable quantities of silver, which probably derive from a combination of mining (in Somerset, for example), the re-minting of foreign issues (primarily at London) and tribute.

There are two further pieces of evidence of which we need to take account. One is the great earthwork, long-known as Offa's Dyke, which was built by the Mercians against Powys, and runs for some 103km from Rushock Hill on the north side of the Herefordshire Plain to Llanfynydd near Mold (Fox 1955; Noble 1983). Recent research led by David Hill (1985, 2000) from the University of Manchester has done much to bring this massive undertaking into focus, particularly its actual extent and probable purpose (Figures 21 and 22). However, we still rely on the testimony of Asser around a century after the event for Offa's responsibility (Stevenson 1904; Keynes and Lapidge 1983), and there is a difficulty with his assertion that it stretched 'from sea to sea', which now seems unjustified by the archaeological record. It may be that Asser's phrase is little more than a figure of speech, derived from his knowledge of the *Historia Brittonum*, which offers *a mari usque ad mare per latitudinem Brittanniae* ('from sea to sea across the width of Britain') in the context of the Roman Wall (*HB* 23), and *paene a mari usque ad mare* ('almost from sea to sea') to describe the English conquests in Britain (*HB* 42). Both arguably in turn derive from Gildas's comment on the great Saxon raid, *de*

**Figure 20** Tintagel's natural harbour and the lower terraces

**Figure 21** Offa's Dyke: an aerial view of the earthworks on Llanfair Hill, Llanfair Waterdine, between Knighton and Newcastle (courtesy of Clwyd–Powys Archaeological Trust)

**Figure 22** Offa's Dyke: from Carreg-y-big looking northwards towards Orseddwen, near Oswestry (courtesy of Margaret Worthington)

*mari usque ad mare* (*DEB* xxiv, 1): Gildas was, himself, a frequent (and confusing) user of *paene*. It was certainly Asser's vision which is enshrined in the much later Welsh text, the *Brenhinedd Y Saesson* (*Kings of the Saxons*: T. Jones 1971), which included notice of the dyke's construction inserted between entries for the years 783 and 795. Apparently so as to explain Offa's decision, the author of this text reversed the pattern that he had received from existing annals, making the southern Welsh somewhat improbably attack and ravage Mercia in 777 and 783. The earlier text must clearly be preferred and this explanation be dismissed as a late rationalization from a south-west Welsh viewpoint developed so as to explain construction.

Whatever else Offa's Dyke signified, two things can be said about it. One is that it represented a massive statement about the power and authority of the king who commissioned it, which necessarily dwarfed those of his western neighbours (Figure 23). Secondly, it belongs in the context of a contested frontier and, however temporary its meaning, the Dyke represents a Mercian contrived, military boundary, constructed to exercise control. That boundary is inclusive of numerous lands which had traditionally been part of Powys, throughout its length, as Gerald of Wales was later, in part, to affirm.

In parallel with the Dyke must be considered the Pillar of Eliseg (or Elise). This well known monument stands in Valle Crucis, near Llangollen, and lent its name to both the vale and the nearby medieval abbey. It was thrown down

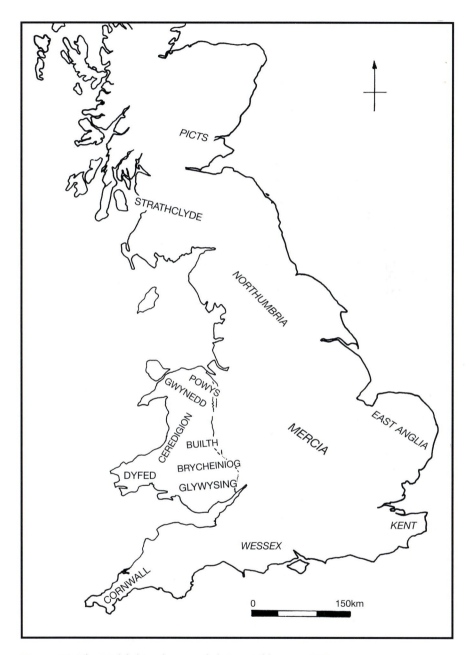

**Figure 23** The Welsh kingdoms and their neighbours *c.* 800

in the Civil War and was in pieces when the inscription, which is now largely weathered away (Figures 24 and 25), was recorded by Edward Lhwyd in 1696. Lhwyd's reading (Nash-Williams 1950: 123, no. 182) is given below (pp. 166–7), but it is important to note at this point that it bears witness to a successful war prosecuted by Eliseg, great-grandfather of the king *Concenn* who erected it in the ninth century (following Howlett 1998: 29): 'who united the inheritance of Powys from the hand of Catem through his own forces from the power of the English both with his own sword and with fire'.

*Concenn* – otherwise Cyngen – ruled Powys from 808 until he departed for Rome, where he died in 854/5. Working back across the generations, Eliseg's activities seem to belong to the mid-eighth century, thus perhaps the very early years of Offa's reign (Macalister 1928: 304; Nash-Williams 1950: 124). The claim that Eliseg was successful in war suggests that this was a period during which some land which had been lost previously to the Mercians was regained for Powys. The siting of the pillar seems to indicate that this included Valle Crucis itself, behind which lies the Clwyd valley and Rhuddlan. It may be that some other of the areas characterized by English place-names, which lie west of the dykes (Gelling 1992: 106–11), might also be indicated. However, neither the Dyke nor the Pillar of Eliseg seem to have marked a frontier for very long, even supposing the latter ever had. It may be better not to think in terms of fixed boundaries or other clear demarcation between Welsh and English kingship during most of this period, with all the of territory, tribute, renders and loyalties deeply contested in a wide band along the March and far into Wales.

There are some indications that Welsh élites may have had other concerns, related to processes of acculturation in western and northern England. In 600, the Welsh language was arguably commonly spoken across the bulk of the north, and at least as far east from Wales as the southern Pennines. Similarly, British clergy were the dominant religious agency throughout at least Herefordshire, Shropshire, parts of Staffordshire and Cheshire (see generally, Sims-Williams 1990; Bassett 1992, 2000; Gelling 1992; Higham 1993b), as well as northern England, and there may well have remained at least pockets of British speakers deep inside Anglo-Saxon England (in Derbyshire, for example, and in Wessex, where Ine's law code *c.* 700 recognized Britons among the 'gentry' classes). During the later seventh and the eighth centuries, these conditions gradually ceased to apply. The north was consolidated under Anglian control to become an increasingly 'English' culture province. Penda and his sons seem to have taken more direct control of the border shires (Lloyd 1911: 194–5; Brooks 1989). The Welsh language seems to have died out in most areas which were to become English by about 800 and the Mercian diocese of Lichfield was established in the north-west Midlands, either replacing or refocusing British priests who may still have been based at existing church sites, such as Wall. English bishoprics were founded also for the Hwicce and the *Magonsæte* in the West Midlands. Alongside these, royal monasteries

**Figure 24** The Pillar of Eliseg in the landscape

**Figure 25** The Pillar of Eliseg: detail of the inscription (courtesy of Derek Seddon)

(as at Wenlock: Thacker 1985) arguably diverted religious patronage away from older British foundations, like the famous British monastery at Bangor-on-Dee, to themselves (Higham 2001b). Some British religious centres were refounded, enriched and Anglicized, and St Albans must be the primary example of this in eighth-century Mercia, but most were probably impoverished and struggled to survive in the new cultural milieu.

This hundred-and-fifty-year period witnessed, therefore, the contraction of British culture and the loss of a large part of the community which might have thought of itself as British. That cultural and social identity was transformed into forms of provincial 'Englishness' in areas where English ecclesiastical and political hierarchies had achieved dominance. This does not seem to have involved massed expulsions of the local population and large-scale immigration, although some surviving members of the British élite may well have departed. Rather, this was a process which has been described rather helpfully by the term 'ethnocide' (Megaw and Megaw 1997: 117): 'a process by which Others are forced "to transform themselves to the point of total identification, if possible, with the model proposed to or imposed on them".' In this case, the term 'forced' may be an overstatement. Group identity is highly variable in detail but its maintenance requires commitment. That in turn depends upon circumstances in which membership is valued and delivers tangible benefits (e.g. Hargie, Saunders and Dickinson 1994). Given the little we can surmise about western and northern England during this period, it seems unlikely that continuing British identity had many attractions for the local population. Its position *vis-à-vis* providential history was undermined by recent events and 'Britishness' was increasingly a bar to social and legal status and hence access to power and patronage.

This is not to suggest that notions of a pan-British national identity were well established around 800 in Wales. Paradoxically, it was arguably better developed among English writers, who ignored local identities in favour of a single vision of British identity, with all that that carried in terms of rejection by God. Although it is clear that the texts to be discussed below have embedded in them the idea of a pan-British ethnicity and national history, there was very little expression of this in the political sphere. Kingship was local and territorial and political consciousness was necessarily small in scale. The basic pattern of Welsh kingship was already established when Gildas wrote, with authority invested in specific dynasties. The vision offered by his work of some sort of hierarchy of kingship, focused on Maglocunus (W. Davies 1982: 104; Higham 1992b), does not seem to have become entrenched, although the notion of primacy was on occasion resurrected in Gwynedd and noticed elsewhere – as in the *Annals of Ulster* 815 (816). While there had been some reduction in the actual number of territorial kingships by the eighth century, particularly in the south-east where kingdoms were particularly fragmented, there had been little real consolidation. Although there is some evidence of royal officials of a generic type, there was little apparatus or administrative machinery capable of enabling kings to rule large territories or groups from a distance (W. Davies 1982, 1990). Nor is there any good reason to consider that political agglomeration was either inevitable or even desirable in the context of the early or central Middle Ages. Succession was frequently contested, given that candidates for the kingship could emerge from a comparatively broad royal community, which included, in the male line, the sons, brothers, cousins, grandsons and great-nephews of previous kings, plus a tighter group of maternal kin. Where more than one dynasty had in the past provided kings, not all the candidates need have been related, and this has a particular relevance for Gwynedd, where several figures apparently from outside the dominant dynasty on occasion seized power (in general, see Beverley Smith 1986). As with any part of Britain at this period, it is as important to consider the individual goals of kings as the broader objectives which may be identified across a dynasty (for a slightly later context, see Maund 1998). As the remains of Offa's Dyke imply, therefore, Mercia's relations were not generally with the Welsh *in toto*, but with particular rulers within specific territories, whose policies might well vary both from one territory to another and from one dynastic king to his successor.

That said, there was at least a residual sense of common culture, as expressed both through the vernacular language, a distinctive Christian tradition of learning and authority, and a common historical perspective, and this reflected a 'British' group identity in the eighth century which could be compared with, for example, Bede's contemporary vision of 'Englishness' (Wormald 1978, 1995). The way in which early poems and their cast-lists of long-dead characters, some of which originated in northern Britain, were taken up, re-energized and to an extent reformulated within local court cultures in Wales during this period provides one entrée to this construct. Sections of the Welsh élite valued, and retained for centuries, the idea of a British nation which had formerly occupied and controlled the entirety of the old Roman diocese and beyond, roughly as far as the Antonine Wall. The leaders of this nation could be construed as having fought heroically against Anglo-Saxon colonialism during the sixth century. This vision retained considerable potency within political literature, for fairly obvious contemporary purposes. The Cambro-Latin tradition of learning provided another marker of identity. The nine Latin prayers of Welsh origin, for example, which found their way into a Mercian manuscript of *c.* 650–750, demonstrated a wide knowledge of the Bible and an ability to use biblical context as a means of enriching and deepening the meaning of borrowed words (Howlett 1992). The same style is evidenced in the *Historia Brittonum* (as discussed later) and other Cambro-Latin texts (Howlett 1998).

Another possible insight is offered by the *Annales Cambriae*, which notes, under the year 768, that 'Easter is changed among the Britons', giving responsibility for this fact to Elfoddw, later noted as 'archbishop' of Bangor when he died in 809. The entry is generally assumed to be reasonably accurate and it is important to note that it was almost certainly written in distant

Pembrokeshire, far from Elfoddw's primary sphere of influence. If, as it implies, the adoption of the Roman dating of Easter was synchronous throughout Wales, this at least suggests a successful co-ordination by the several regional leaders of British Christianity, across numerous kingdoms, of a decision to which all had adhered. To all intents and purposes, this was a national policy, which may imply a sense of nation and a common religious identity expressed via synods and a fairly comprehensive system of communication. The *Historia Brittonum* refers retrospectively to 'a *magna synodus* of the clergy and laity meeting together in one council' in a fifth-century context, but the idea presumably had some contemporary meaning – it certainly was not a contemporary or accurate account of a fifth-century event! Similarly, the meeting of British churchmen which reputedly took place at Chester around 600 need not have been as exceptional an event as the thinness of our information might otherwise suggest, and I have suggested elsewhere (Higham 1993b) that that meeting may have been sited to bring together clergy from the 'British' West with others of the same tradition from deep inside Anglo-Saxon dominated England.

Why the Welsh should have decided to adopt Roman and English mechanisms for determining Easter is unclear, and there seems no good reason to limit ourselves to Lloyd's view (1911: 203) that they had collectively persuaded themselves that they were 'by a meaningless conservatism, cutting themselves off from the religious life of Christendom'. Certainly, greater contact with English religious communities resulted, as Asser's career and the flow of manuscripts separately indicate. However, the Welsh had a long history of direct contact with Frankia, and had long been connected with Ireland, and could obtain a wider literature from these sources even before the mid- to late eighth century.

Given this context, the abandonment of long-established and entrenched opposition to English religious practices and authority may have had a political context. We can only speculate, but Mercian pressure may well have helped to place conformity on the agenda and been relevant to the outcome. Offa had established himself in west Kent *c.* 764 and presided in person over the appointment of Archbishop Jænberht (765–92) at a church council held at his own court. Within a few years he had taken control of east Kent as well. Relations between the Mercian king and the archbishop seem to have remained co-operative for some years, despite Jænberht's close family connections with the local Kentish élite and its royal family, which ultimately seems to have destroyed their working relationship (Brooks 1984: 114–17). Delivering Welsh conformity on the question of Easter just might have been a strategy employed by Offa to encourage the acquiescence of the archbishop in his own assumption of royal prerogatives in east Kent. We cannot know, but the timing and the structure of power make this sort of scenario seem plausible, and any archbishop at Canterbury would wish to be the first to resolve the controversy between Augustine and the Britons, as famously recorded by Bede. If he was involved, then it suggests that Offa was treating Wales as an appendage of his own kingship, to be managed in various respects as best suited his own political needs. Whether or not this is correct, Offa's control of Kent was increasingly contested in the 770s and he responded by having Lichfield raised to archiepiscopal status in 787. This elevation was retained only until the death of its first incumbent in 803, but the presence of a new Mercian archbishop in the West Midlands may also have had implications for its Welsh neighbours.

Offa was, as he intended, succeeded by his son and anointed heir, Ecgfrith, but he died in the December of the same year as his father (796), leaving a distant relative, Coenwulf (796–821), to seize the kingdom (see Walker 2000 for a useful discussion of the dynastic politics). Coenwulf similarly imposed himself on Kent and East Anglia, but found his kingdom under attack from Northumbria in 801. However, he seems to have been generally successful in first restoring and then maintaining Mercia's dominant position. If anything, Coenwulf was even more aggressive than his predecessors towards the Welsh. He is likely to have been responsible for the cryptic comment in the *Annales Cambriae* for 798 that Caradog king of Gwynedd was 'killed by the Saxons'. The term used, *jugulatur*, implies assassination or execution rather than death in battle. This impression is confirmed by the entries in a late manuscript for 816 and 818, which suggest Mercian forces in Snowdonia, Rhufoniog and Dyfed, while the Harleian text for 822 reads: 'The fortress of Degannwy is destroyed by the Saxons and they took the kingdom of Powys into their own control'. Coenwulf himself died at Basingwerk, and this fact is likely to be connected with his ambitions in Wales, where it seems that he was attempting permanent land seizures, and perhaps even total conquest.

The traditional assumption that these attacks effectively mark the beginning of the end for Powys as a Welsh kingdom may be too extreme, given that King Cyngen died in Rome some thirty years later (Sims-Williams 1994), and was probably active as king to the 850s. However, it does seem that Coenwulf had taken Offa's policies towards the Welsh a stage further and was interfering in Gwynedd in the far west, as well as taking booty and establishing a degree of control over the northern territory of Powys.

Coenwulf may have been encouraged in his aggressive stance by renewed conflict in Gwynedd, and his intervention may link back to the fact that Caradog had died at English hands. Two members of the dynasty disputed the succession between 813 and 816. Cynan Dindaethwy was a son of Rhodri, who had died in 754 as 'King of the Britons' (according to the *Annales* which was, of course, written for his descendant Owain). Hywel is either considered his brother or Caradog's son, in which case he was a distant cousin. Cynan was driven out in 814 but returned, only to be expelled once more in 816 and die in the same year. His death was deemed significant enough to receive mention in the *Annals of Ulster* (Mac Airt and Mac Niocaill 1983), wherein he was described somewhat grandiosely as *rex Brittonum*, but he was the last

Welsh king to be named in this text until Rhodri Mawr's victory over the Vikings in 856. Hywel then went on to rule his troubled kingdom until 825, when he too died, so it was he who had to confront full-scale Mercian intervention west of the Conway.

### Summary

What we might usefully term the long eighth century – from the conversion of the Mercians under Wulfhere to the 820s – was, therefore, a period which saw the English élite arguing their case to be the chosen people domiciled within the old British diocese, hence as natural and legitimate heirs to the imperial Romans as rulers of Britain. A necessary part of this repositioning was the denial of the Britons of any status within salvation history as a people of the Lord in the present – that is since the initial English conversion by Roman missionaries. This ideological assault was combined with political and military pressure, which, while by no means consistent or continuous, rarely let up for long. Ideological and political processes were generally mutually supportive, as Bede was aware: his historical *magnum opus* massively privileges 'English' as opposed to 'British' history. Patronage and power within southern Britain were largely in English hands and probably expected so to remain.

In this context, both British group identity and British political and ecclesiastical authority were in retreat across Britain. The earlier 'middle band' of western England (Figure 7, earlier), which had been characterized by neither British memorial inscriptions nor Anglo-Saxon cemeteries, was taken ever more firmly under English control during this period, and was in large part cut off from Wales within a new frontier dyke system. At the same time new raids, booty-taking and active conquests were periodically directed at the British kingdoms of the far west, whose long-term survival was arguably placed in considerable doubt.

## RECLAIMING THE PAST: WRITING BRITISH HISTORY IN THE EARLY NINTH CENTURY

It was this *saeculum horribile* which contextualized a major British response to Bede and the ideological substrate of English colonialism. Only one piece of 'historical' writing survives from the ninth century which was composed in northern Wales, beside which we can place a single extended inscription on stone, written between 808 and 854, and almost certainly after 821 (Macalister 1935; but Howlett 1998: 31, suggests 810–30). These two very different works offer us our first opportunity to consider how spokesmen of the Welsh élite interacted with the past in this era of Anglo-Saxon expansion, and the uses to which they thought to put it within their own world. A re-examination of this material, and an exploration of its authors' several objectives, provides us with the necessary opportunity to reassess the role of Arthur within the *Historia Brittonum*, which is the text in which it is now generally believed that he first appears as an 'historical' figure.

## The Immediate Context

Coenwulf's death in 821 was significant enough around the shores of the Irish Sea to receive mention in Irish Annals. However, his aggression towards Wales was initially continued by his brother and successor, Ceolwulf I (821–3), and it was only his 'deprivation' of the kingdom that brought Mercian pressure on the Welsh to a sudden halt. Although it may initially have seemed, on recent past experience, only a matter of time before a new king would establish himself and renew westwards expansion, Hywel's death (825) actually coincided with an extended crisis within Mercia. Ceolwulf clearly lost his throne in the context of factional conflict and his successor, Beornwulf (823–5), likewise failed to sustain his rule. A charter pertaining to land in Sussex dated 825, and drawn up following the council of the English church at *Clofesho* in October 824, remarked on the multitude of disputes which had erupted within the English political élite (Sawyer 1968: no. 1435), and several other land books reflect the reacquisition of lost lands by clerics, particularly in the south-east, where the intervention of Mercian kings had been particularly resented. These movements reflect an active contest for power within Mercia, which impacted widely on all its neighbours. Beornwulf's efforts to reimpose his authority by force proved disastrous: Egberht of Wessex defeated him in Wiltshire at *Ellendun*, deep in West Saxon territory, leading the local élites of the south-east to seek the protection of the West Saxon king. Egberht was thereby propelled into the role of overlord south of the Thames. Beornwulf then attempted to reassert himself by invading East Anglia but met his death there in battle. It was not until Wiglaf seized power in Mercia in 827 that a longer-lived regime became established, and this had necessarily to work out a new and very different relationship with its neighbours.

Whether or not the result of *Ellendun* and Beornwulf's subsequent death influenced the attempt is unclear, but Merfyn Frych's seizure of power in Gwynedd *c.* 825 was arguably made a great deal simpler by the collapse of Mercia's capacity to intervene. Additionally, the ideological positioning of his reign was necessarily affected by this sudden spate of crises, the meaning of which was presumably a matter of considerable discussion in Wales in the 820s. At its simplest, Mercia's collapse into dynastic crisis created space for a new nationalist rhetoric in Gwynedd.

Merfyn's origins have often been sought in Powys, but this connection is largely dependent on the view that the *Llywarch Hen* poetry was in some way connected with his patronage. In practice, that assumption is now looking increasingly fragile, and the alternative suggestion has been proffered that this body of literature may belong to eighth- or ninth-century Brycheiniog rather than Powys (Sims-Williams 1994). Merfyn's other known connection is with the Isle of Man, and this seems by far the stronger. His challenge for the kingship of Gwynedd was, therefore, that of an outsider, at the head of a sea-borne force coming from the north. He was, however, either the maternal grandson, or son-in-law of that King Cynan who had died in 816, and this presumably provided a degree of legitimacy and support within Anglesey. David Kirby has suggested (1976) that his success reflected a shortage of appropriate candidates from within the established royal dynasties inside Gwynedd, due to successive exclusions and recent deaths. That said, however strongly he and his heirs insisted that they belonged to the first dynasty of Gwynedd, Merfyn was then and subsequently seen as the founder of a new dynasty. He was, therefore, something of an external candidate for the kingship of Gwynedd, whose legitimacy was less than secure by reference to his royal descent.

The hold on power of the new ruler of Gwynedd was probably, therefore, particularly fallible in the few years following his coup in 825, and especially vulnerable to pressure from England. It was his good fortune that such did not recur in the next few years, providing his factional leadership with the necessary time and space to secure the kingship and place it beyond the reach of potential rivals. In 829 Egberht of Wessex established himself as king in Mercia and as overlord of Northumbria, and the prospect loomed of a single successful warrior king in control of all southern Britain, and dominant even over Northumbria. However, Wiglaf recovered Mercia within a year. Even so, King Egberht putatively led an army into Wales in 830 and 'reduced them all to humble submission to himself' (*Anglo-Saxon Chronicle*: Whitelock 1955: 186). Submission to this powerful but non-Mercian warlord, however temporary, was perhaps of some value to Merfyn, who is most unlikely to have felt as seriously threatened by Wessex as his predecessors had been by the Mercians. By submission, he acquired widespread recognition and a degree of protection, but only the accident of an *ad hoc* balance of power between Egberht and Wiglaf stood between Wales and further English aggression, until, that is, Viking raids began to capture the attention of English kings from 835 onwards.

In practice, Merfyn proved particularly successful, dying still in control of Gwynedd in 844 and passing on his kingship to his more famous son, Rhodri Mawr, with only a single, recorded outbreak of violence which might (but need not) point to dynastic opposition. It is, however, important to emphasize the fact that Merfyn's success was far from predictable in the late-820s. Rather, his position is likely to have been quite precarious. Given its author's use of Merfyn's fourth regnal year (probably 829–30, although the author offers 831) in his computation of the recent past (*HB* 4), it is clearly within this short period at the beginning of his reign that we can place authorship of the *Historia Brittonum* (Dumville 1972–4a).

# THE *HISTORIA BRITTONUM*: AUTHORSHIP AND PURPOSE

Although several editions exist, the popularity of the *Historia Brittonum* in the Middle Ages, and its susceptibility to textual development and emendation, have made it a difficult text to establish effectively. Pending all David Dumville's long-promised editions of the several recensions (1985–), the editions of Joseph Stevenson in 1838 and, more particularly, Edmond Faral (1929) are to be preferred as representing the earliest surviving manuscript, being the BM Harley MS 3859 of *c.* 1100 in an Anglo-Norman hand. This was arguably itself a copy of a text, now lost, written at St David's about 950x975. Several separate works – the *Historia* (including the lists of *civitates* and *mirabilia*), the *Annales* and the British genealogies – were copied into a single manuscript (Dumville 1977–8). Material from later recensions has been incorporated in the edition of Mommsen (1891–8) and these have also been introduced, along with some minor errors of typology, into Morris's text (1980), although they are distinguishable therein with some difficulty.

This problem of a highly complex textual history has been the source of numerous difficulties of interpretation, not least of which are issues of authorship and historical reliability. All those who have accepted the late attribution to 'Nennius' (more properly *Ninnius*: see most recently P. J. C. Field 1996), have also accepted the preface which is found only in the handful of texts derived from the Corpus Christi College, Cambridge, MS. 139, written in 1164 (Dumville 1972–4b). Both attribution and preface are, perforce, absent from all other, and earlier manuscripts, and this must weigh against their claim as part of the original text of *c.* 829–30, as has been recognized for at least three quarters of a century (Chadwick and Chadwick 1932: 153). That said, David Howlett (1998: 103) has latterly offered a rather different defence of the originality of this preface, suggesting that it was composed in the same Cambro-Latin style as the main ninth-century text, which might imply that it was not so far distant from the original as Dumville had supposed. This preface, which is published in detail but without translation by Dumville (1975–6), famously claims, *inter alia*, that:

> [I] have heaped up everything that I have found, as much from the annals of the Romans as from the chronicles of the holy fathers (that is, of Jerome, Eusebius, Isidore [and] Prosper), and from the annals of the Scots [Irish] and Saxons [English], and what many learned men and scribes have tried to write down from the traditions of our ancient [? times]. For what reason I am unaware, whether because of very frequent plagues or disasters of warfare, they have left it rather intractable.

This notion of a 'heaping up' has encouraged many historians in the twentieth century to imagine that this text therefore contains within it comparatively unaltered and much earlier source materials (the classic statement is that of Myres in Collingwood and Myres 1936: 329–30, but see also Hanning 1966: 91). It is David Dumville's great achievement that he has demonstrated the weakness of this approach, and begun the process of redefining the style of this work as a 'synchronizing history' of a type common in Ireland at this date (Dumville 1986). This may be too narrow a label, however, and Thomas Charles-Edwards proposed (1991) that we should also think of this as a 'synchronistic history', which exhibits characteristics of both *historia gentis* (the history of a people) and *historia ecclesiastica* (Christian history). Latterly, the *Historia* has been reviewed once more and interpreted as a full, national pseudo-history (Coe and Young 1995), albeit with considerable debts to a wider Cambro-Irish intellectual community (Dumville 1994). It has additionally been heralded as a particularly fine example of the sophisticated 'biblical style' of Welsh Latin text (Howlett 1998: 74–83), within which the authenticity of specific sections as original to the text – including those on Patrick and Arthur – can be demonstrated stylistically.

What became clearer during the course of the 1990s was the extent to which we should see this as an authored text, and not just a collection of pre-existing source materials lumped crudely together by a poorly qualified copyist and editor. That said, it may not be entirely helpful to see its purpose in terms merely of 'sermonizing' in the modern sense of the word (Green 1998), even though the author himself used the term *sermo* to characterize it (*HB* 55) and probably intended that it be read out loud to an audience.

The text goes far beyond this. Although it is not clear from internal evidence what title, if any, the author intended his work should bear, we should be in no doubt that it was written as a history, within the context in which that term was understood at the time. Certainly it has a moral purpose, motivation, causation and consequence. Furthermore it has a nationalist or ethnic context, so can be viewed as an example of a common type of medieval writing, the national history or history of a race, within the broadest possible meaning of 'history' or 'metahistory', as that is now conceived (White 1973, 1978). It is a history of one community within Britain which is constructed in part at least against other communities (R. R. Davies 1994). More particularly, it offers a unique but complex, political and ideological position of immediate relevance to the court of King Merfyn, and in that respect it must be viewed as a text written for pressing and current, political purposes. Like the works of Gildas and Bede, this is a providential work, which focuses on the relationship between God and His people as modelled on the Testaments. It is therefore a story about both retribution and redemption, and one which seeks to place the Britons, as a people, in the present, the past and the future, in an honourable and valued position within the history of salvation. As such, this is a complex foundation myth which has been developed by a member of the local élite, primarily for consumption within that local leadership but also, to a lesser extent, by some at least of their competitors.

The actual name of the author is of relatively little significance. We know of a clerical author named *Ninnius* in the early ninth century and he may have been the author of this work, but our information about him is so slight that there is little difference between an ascription to this named author and the far safer assumption which is followed here: the work is presently best considered anonymous.

The *Historia* has traditionally been used by scholars for a variety of purposes, chief among which has been as a source of information to be mined for facts about the fifth and sixth centuries, and particularly Arthur's role therein (see recently Bachrach 1991; Charles-Edwards 1991; for a more cavalier approach see e.g. Castleden 2000). However, many of the source materials used seem only to date to the late eighth or early ninth centuries, i.e. to the generation of its author or perhaps of his parents (Dumville 1986). Take, for example, the list of *civitates* (*HB* 66), which it is usually assumed was original to the *Historia* and written by the same author, although it follows the *Annales* and genealogies in the Harleian text. While the total of 28 towns presumably derives from Gildas (*DEB* iii, 2), the actual sites chosen are clearly not consistent with a date much earlier than 800, even if some of the unidentified names have not been made up by the author (a possibility mooted by Jackson 1938). Most obviously, the English genealogical material incorporated in chapters 57 to 61 includes Offa's son Ecgfrith, so is unlikely to predate his consecration in 787 and may indeed belong to the sole year in which he actually reigned (796). This English-derived material was therefore not quite up-to-date when incorporated in the *Historia c.* 829–30, but it was only one generation adrift. It is highly retrospective regarding its earlier figures and cannot be relied upon without independent verification as evidence for a much earlier epoch, despite the reservations argued by Charles-Edwards (1991).

We should focus, therefore, on what this work can tell us about the thought-world of its author and his political and ideological objectives in writing it (Hanning 1966; Dumville 1986, 1994). It was, after all, as far as we know, the first work of its kind to be written by a British scholar since Gildas's historical introduction to his polemical attack on the rulers and clerical élite of his own day, the *De Excidio Britanniae*, in the late fifth or early to mid-sixth century. It is only in this context that we can begin to understand his references to Arthur and the other putative figures of history alongside whom he makes a brief appearance.

To recapitulate to this point, therefore, the *Historia Brittonum* is a history which offers a vision across time from a particular British or Welsh perspective, and which has obvious (and less obvious) debts regarding its specifics to a variety of other sources. It is, however, not a simple amalgam of other existing pieces. It is a highly original piece of writing. Indeed, it must be stressed that its originality has to date generally been underestimated. Like much other early to central medieval history, it is important to realize that this is an ideological and rhetorical tract, which has been written both for, and against, particular ideas and specific groups.

At a detailed level, this is a work which has been written very much with Merfyn and his patronage in mind, and to a significant extent against other rulers, both within Wales and without. There is sufficient internal evidence for us to be confident that it was written in an area under Merfyn's control and quite possibly at his court, for the king himself. That is the 'social logic of the text' (Spiegel 1997). It is in that context a work of dynastic propaganda, the function of which was to validate and sustain Merfyn's kingship. This does not mean that it was necessarily written by a north Welshman: Asser's *vita* of Alfred, for example, provides a significant parallel, where an outsider under royal patronage and protection was the author of a highly supportive, personal history. In fact, the few internal clues available suggest that the author had a particular knowledge of, and interest in, the central or southern marches, and he even reveals to us that he has been, in the past, in Gwent (*HB* 72) and the upper valley of the Wye (*HB* 73). His knowledge of all of Old Welsh, Latin, Old English and perhaps some Old Irish (Dumville 1986, although there may be some doubt of his competence in Old Welsh as a written language: Coates and Breeze 2000: 37) points to a multi-cultural background which was unlikely to fit particularly well with what little we know of Gwynedd. Rather, such suggests the more cosmopolitan interface between southern Wales and England, perhaps in a Welsh monastery or minster-type community in an area of Irish influence such as Builth or Brycheiniog, or Gwent to the south. Although his Latin is in some respects rather limited, it is competent and flows effectively: he was apparently a learned man by the standards of the day. David Howlett's investigations (1998) suggest that he was conversant with scholarly styles of Latin composition in Wales at that date, and incorporated these successfully in his own text. He seems also to have ingested current ideas about Old Testament comparisons for local events and individuals, which were, by the 790s, beginning to circulate via works composed in Carolingian France (Garrison 2000). This suggests that the author was close to the forefront of continental scholarship at this date, with access to several recent Carolingian texts. He was perhaps attracted to Gwynedd by a patron who was in need of the diversity of his intellectual skills and talents, in much the same way that Alcuin left York for Charlemagne's court a generation earlier, and Asser departed St David's two generations later to join Alfred's circle. These parallels would suggest a figure whose learning was well known even outside his own immediate environment. Once in Gwynedd, however, the author seems to have been keen to present himself as more *Guenedotian* than the *Guenedotians* (the people of Gwynedd), and there should be little doubt that his text was written expressly for Merfyn and his circle. Again, the parallel with Asser writing under Alfred's patronage is a pressing one.

In its broadest interpretation, however, this work is more than a mirror of Merfyn's specific and immediate needs, since it repositions the Britons within providential history in ways which appear to have been novel. This was still apparently undertaken in Merfyn's political interest, since there are hints that the king was being positioned as the leader of the whole 'British' people, or that the history of the 'British' people was being refocused onto his political position in the present. However, it does place this vision on a wider canvas, as a general *apologia* which seeks to legitimize the Britons (particularly in this context the Welsh) as a people of the Lord, fully established within the history of salvation. In particular, it seeks to contradict Gildas's vision of an unmartial British race steeped in sin, even while respecting the *De Excidio* as a framework document for chronological and ethnological purposes. Likewise, it contests Gildas's particular positioning of the Britons within an Old Testament context and offers an alternative, and far more favourable, Bible-inspired interpretation of the aftermath of the *adventus Saxonum*. It is, therefore, a work about identity, which offers an insight into the 'subjective ethnic consciousness of an individual or a group of people' (Pohl 1998: 21), in this case the author and his immediate and intended audience at Merfyn's court. It offers unique insights, therefore, into visions of group identity among the rulers of Gwynedd in the 820s, and the efforts being made to redeploy 'the Britons' as a term owned and used by a particular political élite.

The *Historia Brittonum* was also written to counter the use to which English authors had put Gildas's work. In this respect, the *Historia* sets out to contest the past with Bede as much as Gildas, both of whose historical works the author clearly knew well (Dumville 1994). To this purpose, it privileges a particular vision of British national identity across time, pulling together the past, the present and the future – via prophesy – into a single, linear and progressive narrative. That narrative consistently demands that the British be valued over and above other insular *gentes*, as a people of the Lord.

Precisely how we evaluate the author's intentions depends to an extent on how different sections of his text are perceived. So, for example, the comparatively benign approach to certain seventh-century English kings and saints has encouraged some recent commentators to imagine the author to favour some sort of accommodation with the English now that they were accepted as fellow-Christians (Charles-Edwards 1991), or even be looking towards peaceful coexistence with them in ways which might be considered 'anglophilic' (Dumville 1994: 413–14). This is, however, to privilege some passages over others, since his acerbic comments on the Anglo-Saxons are easily as numerous as these more accommodating phrases. In practice, the author's vision of history was biblical and he should be seen first and foremost as interested in the positioning of his own people in salvation history. Where it was necessary that that be done at the expense of the English, then that was what he offered. Furthermore, there is a great deal of damaging comment on the English implicit in his text, and little which is complimentary, to support the directly hostile remarks that he does include. So, too, does he destroy the reputation of Vortigern, the British king held responsible for the *adventus*

*Saxonum* and for making dynastic alliance with its leaders, in so doing invalidating any political initiative in the present to reach accommodation with the English. There may be some prevarication, therefore, but we should be in no doubt that the Saxons of the distant past, and the Mercians of recent history, were viewed by this author through hostile eyes, and the expulsion of the English was a core part of his agenda.

## BRITONS, TROJANS AND ROMANS

Following an unusually full list of contents, his schema of chronology (*HB* 1–6) and an in-part Gildas-derived, geographical introduction (*HB* 7–9), the author fixed the Britons (*HB* 10) within legendary Roman, thus Trojan, history, connecting Virgil's Aeneas with an eponymous grandson, Britto, after whom *Britannia* could then be construed as having been named (although Brutus was treated as an eponym in chapter 7). The Britons were thereby immersed in the classical story told by Virgil of the Trojans even before Rome was founded (as noted as long ago as Duchesne 1894: see Carley 1994 for Irish parallels), so claiming a lineage equal, or even superior, in antiquity, hence status, to the Romans. The Fall of Troy was an appropriate analogy to the loss of Britain from a British but not an Anglo-Saxon perspective, which had considerable capacity to add value to Britons in the present. Besides this claim, English connections with Rome – dating from the very late sixth century and made a central plank of English history by Bede – seem hopelessly jejune.

This vision was then synchronized with Old Testament chronology, to make Britto a contemporary of Eli the High Priest. By this means the Britons were placed within providential history and their presence in Britain asserted at a far earlier point than any other insular *gens*. The Britons were represented as coming to Britain in the third age of the world, the Picts 'at least 800 years' later, the Irish in the fourth age and the Saxons a mere 429 years ago (*HB* 12–16: for a critical appraisal of the more recent dating mechanisms, see Dumville 1972–4a).

The author had a second origins story (*HB* 17), which derived ultimately from a table of nations, apparently from a fairly recent source (Goffart 1983), despite his reference here to 'old books of our elders'. This bracketed the Albans and Britons with the Franks and the Latins as descendants of Hessitio, the son of Alanus, son of Japheth, son of Noah, and traced their descent from Adam and 'the Living God'. Their putative kinship with the Franks and particularly the Romans conferred military and moral stature and this descent likewise makes a powerful claim for inclusion as a chosen people of the Lord.

The opportunity was taken among these origin stories to make claims concerning the legendary Cunedda's expulsions of the Irish 'from all the British regions' (*HB* 14). Cunedda would later (*HB* 62) be reintroduced as the gloriously martial ancestor of Maelgwn (Maglocunus), king of Gwynedd, whose fame derives primarily from Gildas (*DEB* xxxiii–xxxvi). This is by far the earliest literary evidence for Cunedda. Although his sons have attracted numerous concerns, his historicity was long accepted almost without question by modern scholars (e.g. Kirby 1976). However, although the case for his historical reality has since been resurrected (Gruffydd 1989–90), its frailty was exposed by Dumville (1977a), and Cunedda can be viewed more safely as a retrospective construct than a proven figure of the sub-Roman period.

In this context, Cunedda's functions in the *Historia* are twofold, and neither need be historical. The first centres on the construction and unity of Gwynedd, his eight sons (and on occasion one grandson) acting as eponyms for the various districts of which the eighth-century kingdom had been formed. He is a founder figure, therefore, of political value to the rulers of Gwynedd, much as Brutus and Britto were conceived as founders of the British people within this text. The foundation legend found expression both as a narrative and also genealogically, and helped to validate the expansion across the mainland of a dynasty whose earliest authority was probably confined to part only of Anglesey (e.g. White 1978). Gildas had vilified Maglocunus at the climax of his polemic against the morality of contemporary British kings, although he does seem to have recognized, however grudgingly, the exceptional power of this ruler. He termed Maglocunus 'the dragon of the island' and 'higher than almost all the generals of Britain', who had 'driven out many of the aforesaid tyrants from both ruling and even living' (*DEB* xxxiii, 1ff.). Although *insula* elsewhere in this work normally refers to Britain, in this instance it could mean Anglesey (it is generally so treated), so Maelgwn was perhaps in the process of establishing his dynasty on the mainland. The explicit connection made between Cunedda and Maelgwn in the *Historia Brittonum* reflects the cultivation of legends relating to both as potent political icons drawn from Gwynedd's construction in the past, useful in the present at Merfyn's court to consolidate his power across the whole kingdom. Our author necessarily shed Gildas's hostility and represented Gwynedd's most famous king Maelgwyn (*HB* 62) in a carefully sanitized form as *Mailcunus magnus rex apud Brittones . . . in regione Guenedotae* ('the great Maelgwn king among the Britons . . . in the region of Gwynedd').

Secondly, the two references to Cunedda in this work were arguably in large part intended to invoke existing political legend to support Merfyn's external candidacy. Cunedda supposedly founded the first dynasty of Gwynedd from *Manau Guotodin* in a blaze of martial valour, acting as the saviour not just of Gwynedd but of 'all the *regiones* of Britain'. The story probably lost nothing from the implicit connection with heroic poetry concerning Gododdin, which was presumably circulating and being progressively readapted in early ninth-century North Wales. Merfyn's recent campaign for the succession, launched also from the north but from that other 'Man' in the Irish Sea, could only benefit by being connected with, thus validated by, this legendary expeller of foreigners (the Irish) and protector of the British race. This suggests that

Merfyn, in turn, was positioning himself as a leader capable of facing up, on a national level, to the danger from external, 'foreign' aggression, albeit now English and from the east.

The author normally used the term *Eubonia* for the Isle of Man, but made the necessary connection to bear this interpretation in his geographical preface (*HB* 8), '*Eubonia, id est Manau*', the latter being the vernacular term, *Manaw* (cf. Old Irish *Manu*). The heroic origin story was therefore supportive of Merfyn's authority and prowess and connected the very recent past – in which the Britons of Wales were under pressure from English armies and Mercian colonialism – with a past already appropriated by heroic legends focused on Gwynedd. Cunedda's legendary exploits against external powers in the distant past were intended, therefore, to inspire and be emulated in the present, even if the scale of his putative successes might seem beyond the scope of current leaders (cf. Patterson 1987: 158ff.), implying as it does the aim of expulsion of the Anglo-Saxons from Britain.

This was not the sole means taken to develop the military reputation of the Britons, *contra* Gildas. The author had greater difficulties when he grappled with that issue in the context of Roman and later conquests, but he did what he could. Extenuating circumstances were invoked to excuse the former and its totality disguised. Not only were the Romans depicted as the rulers of the whole world (as Gildas, *DEB* v, 1), but the sub-Roman history of the Britons, as constructed by Gildas, was redeployed ingeniously but entirely spuriously to the Conquest period: the Britons were represented, therefore, as unused to weapons already in the time of Julius Caesar, and suffering from the combined attacks of Picts and Scots (*HB* 15). Furthermore, the Britons successfully repulsed Julius Caesar's initial attacks (*HB* 19), under the improbable leadership of one Dolabella (apparently lifted from the description of the wars following Caesar's death in Orosius's *Histories*), only succumbing, after three great battles, to the overwhelming forces with which he later returned (*HB* 20). The numbers – three years, 300 ships, three battles – reflect both sacral history and Welsh vernacular narrative style. This was a careful depiction of the story available to the author in existing histories, the rhetorical trick being to minimize damage to the reputation of the Britons, who, in difficult circumstances, had fought hard, well and in apparent unison. The unmartial vision of the Britons as offered by Gildas was replaced by one which was far more complimentary to the Britons at war against the odds with powerful and better-equipped external aggressors.

Thereafter there is an annotated catalogue of emperors and their dealings with Britain, which in part reflects the available information but in part the impression which the author intended to give. His selection and portrayal of particular incidents or careers was designed to enhance the standing of the British people and its rulers in various ways. He declared, for example, that the payment of taxes to Rome ceased in the time of Claudius, instead thereafter being paid to 'British emperors' (*Britannici imperatores*). Their putative authority implies equality for the Britons with the Romans as an imperial nation. This construct necessarily contests Bede's acquisition of *imperium* in a post-Roman, British context on behalf of a series of early English kings (as *HE*, ii, 5), with authority over the Britons as well as the Anglo-Saxons.

Bede had derived a story from the non-contemporary *Liber Pontificalis* (arguably misinterpreting the places and persons) that a British King Lucius had sought and gained baptism from Pope Eleutherius (*Chronica Maiora* 4131; *HE* i, 4). The author of the *Historia Brittonum* developed his own variant of this tale (*HB* 22) to include the rulers of the entire British people, so claiming that the British élite had accepted Christianity from the aptly named pope '*Eucharistus*' even before the Roman emperors, and hence long before the English. This established an exceptionally early genesis of the Britons as a people of the Lord and an early connection with the papacy, which was an issue to which the author would return. Once again, the primacy of the Britons as a people at the heart of salvation history was crucial to the writer's message.

The obligatory reference to the building of the Roman walls follows (*HB* 23). Then Carausius – whose poor reputation carried dangers for British reputations – was portrayed as a Roman tyrant, seizing authority with the support of Roman armies over the British kings. Constantine II, on the other hand, son of the first Christian emperor, was stated (*HB* 25) to have died in Britain and his lettered tombstone claimed as still to be seen outside *Caer Segeint*. There follows a brief wonder-story, which contrasts with Gildas's reference to Roman extraction of precious metals from Britain (*DEB* vii), that he had sowed three seeds, of gold, silver and bronze on the pavements of the city, that no man should ever live there in poverty. This very particular attention to *Seguntium* (Caernarfon), fixed by reference to an apparently current landscape feature, effectively lays claim to the highly prestigious, even venerable, Christian emperor. Constantine II was, therefore, being interpreted as a figure with particular connections with Gwynedd (cf. the second Harleian genealogy, which claimed him for Dyfed), to the obvious benefit of Merfyn's court, in complete disregard of the fact that he died in civil war, in 340, in the Alps. This treatment of an existing monument within the historical narrative of the *Historia* compares with the *mirabilia* which he attached to it, and goes some way to confirming that both were by the same hand. It should be stressed, however, that no Roman period inscriptions currently surviving in Wales name Constantine (Collingwood and Wright 1995). Nor do any sub-Roman, British memorial stones, such as might have been confused by this author with the fourth-century context, although one found at Penmachno does recall a figure named Carausius (Nash-Williams 1950: 92, no. 101).

The author offered several versions of the story of Magnus Maximus (herein Maximianus) and the ending of Roman Britain, which drew on Gildas and other sources. The hallmarks of his stories are, first, the departure of Britain's soldiery to ultimate resettlement in Armorica. It is this emigration of warriors which then contextualized Britain's occupation by external peoples and 'the citizens" expulsion, contrary to Gildas's vision of divine punishment of the Britons as habitual sinners. Secondly the martial prowess of the British soldiers is repeatedly emphasized: they are depicted as killing Gratian and overthrowing Roman rule (*HB* 27–8) and 'the Romans did not dare to come to Britain to rule anymore, for the Britons had killed their generals'. This achievement was restated in triplicate at the beginning of chapter 30, where the author reverted to a Gildas-derived vision of appeals to Rome against the Picts and Scots, but he added his own, presumably contemporary gloss on the Roman expedition, which – like recent English raids one may presume – 'returned in great triumph, having despoiled Britain of gold and silver with bronze and all precious raiment and honey'. Roman intervention was not perceived herein, therefore, as an unmitigated benefit – reflecting more Gildas's jaundiced remark on the coining of the island's precious metals early in the Roman occupation (*DEB* vii). The ending of Roman Britain is told as a story developed to sustain the notion of the British as a martial race still in obedience to God, *contra* Gildas and Bede, even while conforming to the received events provided by the former. It also carries warnings directed at British (i.e. Welsh) rulers in the present who might seek the assistance of external (i.e. English) armies.

## VORTIGERN AND THE *ADVENTUS SAXONUM*

There follows a long and complex treatment of the arrival and establishment of the Saxons during the reign of Vortigern (herein *Guorthigirn*), within which several source stories are rather crudely interleaved to make up a group of passages which provide the central focus to the entire work. The major pair of narratives derive respectively from a Welsh *vita* of St Garman/St Germanus and an account of Vortigern's dealings with Hengist, the two being interwoven to emphasize that they are being combined by the author into a single story to both describe and explain the first crucial phase of the loss of Britain. The interleaving both establishes their (putative) contemporaneity and stresses the common factors in each, which centre on Vortigern's political and moral failings, in contrast to the high moral status and valour of the Britons as a race. The centrality of Vortigern to all these stories is difficult to over-emphasize. Indeed, the author takes care to stress his universal responsibility by reference to the tight dating of his *imperium* in Britain, when he welcomed the Saxons into Britain, in his culminating chapter of the historical narrative (*HB* 66).

Germanus's life has been used in three passages (*HB* 32–5, 39, 47), although there is one further reference to St Germanus, which tidies him away by recording his return *ad patriam suam* (by which the author, following Bede, apparently meant Gaul), once Vortigern was dead (*HB* 50). These passages not only occur three times but make widespread internal use of sacred number – particularly three, multiples thereof, and forty. These are used to bind in the value system implicit within the text by reference, for example, to the trinity and the deeds and lives of Moses and Christ. To give just one example (*HB* 47), Germanus stood upon a rock for forty days and nights addressing Vortigern: comparison with St Luke iv, 1 clearly establishes Germanus as a Christ-figure and Vortigern as Satan, while Moses similarly led the Israelites through the desert for forty years and himself spent forty days and nights on a mountain top, speaking with the Lord, while his people plotted to construct idols (*Exodus* xxxi, xxxii). The author's intention was seemingly to construct the Britons within the ideological context of the Israelites, and so to invest them with particular meanings within sacred history.

The first section provides a Germanus-centric story of a dynastic revolution in Powys, by which the saint disposed of the wicked king Benli and substituted Catell (or Cadell). This story suggests a Powys-originating text, since it assimilates a local saint, Garman or Harman (as Llanarmon-yn-Ial, near Ruthin, and several other cult-sites further south), with the more famous bishop of Auxerre. The latter's late fifth-century life refers to two visits to Britain to combat heresy, the first of which we can date by reference to the *Chronicle* of Prosper of Aquitaine to 429 (see discussion in Thompson 1984). Germanus emerges in the pages of Bede's *Historia Ecclesiastica* (i, 17–21) as a force for Roman and divine guidance among the heresy-prone, fifth-century Britons. Contact between this region of Gaul and Wales in the late fifth and sixth centuries is well evidenced (Knight 1995, 1996), so his appearance in this hagiographical context could be independent of Bede. However, the author of the *Historia* certainly knew the *Historia Ecclesiastica* and regularly contested Bede's construction of the Britons as a race, and this may well have influenced his treatment of St Germanus herein, whose role as an orthodox Christian leader is being commandeered for the Welsh interest.

There are hints too of vernacular texts. The scene in which Germanus discoursed with King Benli's gate keeper is highly reminiscent of the early but incomplete Arthurian poem *Pa gur yw y porthaur?* (*Black Book of Carmarthen*, xxxi), which was also apparently used by the author of *Culhwch and Olwen, c.* 1100 (Bromwich and Simon Evans 1992; Padel 2000). It is quite possible that this passage was at least influenced by some such work, if not this one.

St Germanus's authority has here been appropriated to Powys in particular and the Britons in general. He emerges as a miracle-worker, feeding his followers by miraculous means (as Moses, then Christ), predicting dire future events (as Moses) and adding his authority to the royal candidacy of a ruling dynasty. This version is, however, a story told from neighbouring Gwynedd, which is using local claims for Germanus's authority to represent divine intervention but at the same time to undermine the authority of the ruling dynasty of Powys in the present via a particular portrayal of it in the past. The *liber* (book) which the author stated that he had used is not likely to be a text of any antiquity, and composition during the reign of Catell of Powys (d. 808) certainly seems possible (Dumville 1986), given that the focus of the first element in this story is Germanus's responsibility for the foundation of Catell's dynasty by his earlier namesake. It may be that our author found the basis for his material in a saint's *vita*, since the claim that royal authority was owed ultimately to the intervention of a saint is a classic topos of the genre.

Benli was disposed of by divine retribution, the first of two kings of Powys who would suffer this fate in this text. His name was perhaps connected with the hillfort name Foel Fenlli (Dumville 1986), which is also near Ruthin, which may imply a comparatively localized legend as source. Germanus then baptised Catell, his sons and the whole *regio* (he probably means the entire population of Powys), raised him to the kingship and made him the founder of the current dynasty. The author made subtle use of this story to undermine the status of the king of Powys in the present. By implication, he invited his audience to contrast two dynastic foundation tales – his version of Powys's and that of Gwynedd's, to which he has already referred in passing and which we must assume was well known to his immediate audience. Catell's nine sons set up a comparison between Gwynedd's heroic founder, Cunedda, and Catell, represented herein devoid of military prowess and pre-existing status. Instead he is a lowly servant or slave (*servus*) of the wicked Benli, 'a beggar lifted up from the dunghill' who had given the saint shelter. The name means 'chattel' or 'cattle', so is of low status, particularly when compared with Cunedda, which is one of the numerous 'hound' names favoured by British leaders. This version of his dynasty's foundation is unlikely to have found favour with Cyngen of Powys in the present, suggesting that we have here a reflection of contemporary controversy and competition (Dumville 1994: 411): a significant contrast exists between this vision of Powys's dynastic history and that recorded on the orders of this same Cyngen, probably at a date between 821 and 854, on the Pillar of Eliseg. It is at least worth considering in passing whether or not the latter commission may reflect reaction at the court of Powys to 'publication' of the *Historia c.* 829–30, or vice versa.

The second passage which is based on this putative *vita* (*HB* 39) juxtaposes the saintly Germanus and the sinful Vortigern, within the context of a great synod of the entire clergy and laity of Britain. The British are associated with the sanctity of Germanus, and their reputation as a people of the Lord protected accordingly – in contradiction to Bede's perception as much as Gildas's acerbic remarks (e.g. on the council members, *DEB* xxiii, 2). Vortigern, alone, is herein depicted as accursed and condemned, and his flight from the synod quarantines him and so avoids contamination of the status of his people. The author thereby reasserted the providential positioning of the Britons in general, scapegoating Vortigern as uniquely and solely responsible for the loss of Britain. The blatant, illicit and incestuous act of which he was found guilty by Germanus and the whole council of the Britons left him exposed to punishment by God, and the Saxon arrival could be interpreted in that context as divine punishment of the ruler, without danger to the moral status of the British community once he be removed. It is an important point to bear in mind that Vortigern was associated by contemporaries in both kingdoms with Powys, not Gwynedd, so this text undermines the dynasty of Powys in the present. Incest fits well with the numerous accusations of unlawful intercourse levelled at contemporary kings by Gildas, and the inspiration may have derived from this source, if any such was needed.

This story is continued in chapter 47, with the saintly Germanus vainly seeking the bigamous and incestuous Vortigern's repentance and following him to Dyfed, where he befell a fate very similar to that of king Benli, destroyed in his fortress by heavenly fire. Dyfed and its rulers were thereby tainted by his ending, which seems heavily influenced by the Old Testament stories of Sodom and Gomorrah. The author had also come across – or himself developed – other stories of Vortigern's ending, all of which are uncomplimentary in the extreme and which presumably circulated freely in the court of Gwynedd. These he added in the next chapter, taking every opportunity to denigrate the reputation of this putative precursor of the neighbouring dynasty (cf. Geary 1994), who was also identified herein as the same man who had let in the Saxons:

> he was hated for his crime by all men of his race, the powerful and the weak, unfree and free, monks and laity, the weak and the strong, he fled from place to place until at last his heart broke and he died, without honour. Others say that the earth opened and swallowed him up . . .

The second major strand in this textual pastiche was the story of Vortigern and Hengist. This is the central crux of the *Historia*, since it is the arrival of the Saxons at this date which led inexorably to the English domination of Britain in the present, which the author was seeking to explain as well as oppose. Here he made every effort to dilute the ideological force of the disaster which the *adventus Saxonum* was considered to be from a British perspective. Apart from a small passage based on Bede, this story has been interpreted as anonymous but English or, even more specifically, Kentish in origin (Morris 1980; Dumville 1986; Charles-Edwards 1991), but the rhetorical force of the story is clearly the author's own and he seems to have used Gildas and Bede more extensively within it than has hitherto been recognized. A Germanic source is suggested in part due to the recurrence of the motif of the Saxons' treacherous use of knives (*sahs*), against the Thuringian nobility in Widukind's tenth-century history. This connects with a popular mechanism by which to explain the etymology of 'Saxons' by reference to their *saxas* (Waitz and Kehr 1904: vi, vii, fn.1). It is not particularly surprising if this uncomplimentary etymology was circulating in Wales in the early ninth century. It could obviously be contrasted with advantage to the Trojan-derived origin story and process of naming which the author was claiming for his own people. The central idea of a murderous banquet was, however, already a well used motif in European literature, dating back to Herodotus and forward to Harald Hardrada (Yorke 1993: 46). Elements of this story may well have derived ultimately from England, but it is here incorporated into a larger narrative of the *adventus*, which is told from a rhetorical stance which is the author's own.

His sources were, therefore, several. The banquet motif may have been English in origin, and the Kentish genealogy certainly was (from his collection of eighth-century Anglian genealogies). However, the author had apparently reformulated his sources in obedience to his own rhetorical needs (most obviously in his treatment of Vortimer: *HB* 43–4), and we should see these passages as authored rather than copied or even edited.

This material again occurs in three passages (*HB* 31, to which a chronological computation has been added, presumably by the author; 36–8; 43–6). Following Gildas (or Bede, whose version of Gildas apparently named Vortigern: Jackson 1982), the *Historia* (*HB* 31) places responsibility for the presence of the Saxons in Britain squarely and exclusively at Vortigern's door. Instead of the Jeremiad constructed by Gildas, however, whose *tyrannus superbus* and council were afflicted with a corrective blindness by the God of the Israelites, the author offered his own package of motives: Vortigern feared the Picts and Scots (after Gildas), a Roman invasion, or Ambrosius – the other figure arguably of this generation to whom Gildas had made reference, on whose work these comments were ultimately based. Vortigern is developed through this text as a political figure making his own decisions, albeit one who is both politically inept and morally bankrupt. He was, however, given total, personal responsibility for what occurred. The author consciously distances himself here and elsewhere from the vision of a sinful *gens*, which Gildas constructs, but the rationalization which he offers is only that, and is too often accepted as an authoritative statement of Vortigern's 'real' priorities. Necessarily, the writer recognized in the present that the Lord has not yet provided the necessary help to rid Britain of the Saxon incomers (*HB* 27). However, by making Vortigern's actions intelligible in a political context, responsibility for them rests exclusively at his door and the *Historia* is rid of that vision of a God of retribution, perpetually prescribing unpleasant medicines for the Britons until they should repent, which was one of Gildas's more damning messages.

In passing, the author also took the opportunity to undermine the value attached to English claims of descent, hence their place in providential history, and this should be contrasted with the origin stories of the Britons, their early presence in providential history and their claimed descent from the 'Living God' in chapter 17. He offered a genealogy of Hengist and Horsa (cf. Bede, *HE* i, 15), which is the first section of a Kentish royal genealogy to which he again referred in chapter 58. Bede's source constructed a line of descent from Hengist back to Woden, but this had been taken further back by the later Anglian source which our author used, via four further Germanic names to *Geta*, the reputed son of God. To this the author added: 'this is not the very God of Gods, amen, God of armies, but one of their idols, which they worshipped'. Such comments undermine any attempt to view this author as an Anglophile, and underline his determination to distinguish the Britons as a people of the Lord from neighbours tainted by non-Christian practices in the post-Roman period.

There follows a version of the Saxon rebellion which has departed a long way from the terse comments of Gildas, on which it was ultimately based (albeit in part via Bede) – compare, for example, *DEB* xxiii with the paraphrase offered by *HB* 36. This version develops, contextualizes and humanizes Gildas's story, adding in places and characters as necessary. So Gildas's 'east side of the island' becomes Thanet, probably under Bede's influence (*HE* i, 25), and it is worth noting that St Augustine cannot come out of the implicit connection with Hengist entirely untarnished. The author appears to offer a vernacular version of the name (*Ruoihin*), but this has recently been interpreted as a misreading of Old Welsh *rwych* ('gift'), attaching to Thanet in an existing Welsh text (Coates and Breeze 2000: 32–8). This presumably refers to the same general story of Vortigern's land-grant as is offered herein, which derives ultimately from Gildas so may have had any number of iterations in British circles. Even so, this passage of the *Historia Brittonum* was no simple translation of an existing passage in Old Welsh, since other phrases betray debts to surviving Latin works (see below, p. 148). The author also added an interpreter named *Cheritic* (Ceredig). The name is British but famously occurs in the West Saxon royal genealogy, although that may not have been accessible in Gwynedd at this date. More significantly, it also occurs in Bede's *Historia* (iv, 23: *Cerdice*), wherein it is one of a tiny number of British personal names offered, and that occurrence may have been the catalyst for its adoption here. Although the problem of communication between Vortigern and Hengist will have been an obvious difficulty from the perspective of Merfyn's court, this can only be viewed as imaginative reconstruction by an author who has clearly improved on received stories about the past.

The resulting narrative has far more meaning in a ninth-century context than Gildas's, and that presumably drove its development. It has a powerful message. It was exclusively Vortigern, not the Britons, who was *iners* – 'ignorant' or 'idle' – hence prey to Hengist's wiles, and it was Vortigern, alone, who became drunk and besotted with Hengist's daughter. Vortigern was no Adam, but he was tempted by this Saxon Eve in a clever reformulation of the fall of man in Genesis, with Hengist cast as the serpent. 'Satan', therefore, 'entered into Vortigern's heart'. The consequence was Vortigern's treacherous stupidity in giving away Kent to the Saxons (over the head of the innocent, local British king, *Guoyrancgon*), the admission of more Saxons and his adoption of Hengist as his principal adviser.

Hengist supposedly then brought over his son and nephew, Octha and Ebissa, who were, much to the puzzlement of Northumbria's historians today, established on the borders of the Picts. Cavalier references to first the Scots and then the Picts, both of whom appear together in Gildas, suggest a story which has been developed far from its origins. The inclusion of a Saxon attack on the Orkneys – which were often seen as a touchstone of conquest in Britain following the (garbled) accounts of the Claudian invasion in Orosius, Jerome and Bede – confirms this impression. Bede had similarly used the 'Mevanian Islands' of Man and Anglesey to emphasize his claim for the universality of Edwin's *imperium*, aware perhaps of the prominence of off-shore islands in stories about the Roman conquest. This may also have influenced our author, who had earlier made much the same point about the kingship of Britain (*HB* 8).

Welsh texts, such as the Triads, frequently distinguish three zones in Britain: British Wales and the west, the north, and the south, and there is good reason to suppose that this author thought in a similar way. He therefore seems to have taken this opportunity to establish a synchronous Saxon occupation in both the north and south, so enabling him to place initial responsibility for the *adventus* in its totality – i.e. the loss of both – squarely on Vortigern's shoulders. This strategy obviated the need to allocate further blame among the Britons at a later stage, which would have had serious implications for his providential stance. His Saxon settlement in the north has often been treated as potentially historical, but is better viewed as a construct of the author.

This narrative resumes in chapter 43, with an upbeat tale of British victories against the Saxons under the command of Vortimer (*Guorthemir*), Vortigern's son, which is most unlikely to derive from an English source. The opportunity for this story lies in the generalities offered by Gildas (*DEB* xxvi, 1), and the author took every advantage of the scope offered by his vagueness, but once again the story is developed far from the original, with characters and battles named, and sacral numbering. Its rhetorical purpose is arguably to ameliorate the depressing and morally damaging story of the loss of Britain, seizing the opportunity offered by Gildas's allusion to unnamed victories. The author thereby claims a martial reputation for the Britons, if Vortigern be excluded, and represents the Saxons as un-warlike, not just routed but fleeing from Britain, 'clambering aboard their keels like women'. So the *Historia* contested Gildas's vision of the military ineptitude of the Britons with some subtlety, reusing for the Saxons the term *muliebriter*, which the earlier writer had used for the Britons in the context of the Roman conquest. This message had obvious utility in the 920s, when English attacks on Wales had suddenly ceased, and its ideological message is clear. There is no reason to imagine that any features added by the *Historia* to Gildas's minimal outline of the 'war of the Saxon federates' are historical, and many reasons to suppose that they are not. Nor should we imagine the author to have felt respect for Hengist (Dumville 1994), who is depicted as scheming and conniving, without any answer to the Britons' cold steel, once they were led effectively.

Although Vortimer later appears in Welsh genealogies (e.g. Bartrum 1983: no. 13), his inclusion seems a consequence of rationalization and he is not credited with descendants. His historicity is necessarily fragile in the extreme. There is much to be said for the view that he is an imagined figure constructed by this author for his own purposes. If so, he was developed both as a moral antithesis to his wicked, Saxophile father, and as a secular type for St Germanus (e.g. Brodeur 1939), developed so as to be capable of defending the martial reputation of his people. This author was particularly prone to conceptualizing the past in terms of doublets, or paired characters, as occur widely in vernacular Welsh literature (e.g. Bromwich and Simon Evans 1992), and Vortimer has considerable value in that context.

While this putative expulsion of the Saxons did much to reclaim British history and invest it with ideological value, it could not – given the current realities – be maintained in a text written when the Anglo-Saxons had taken over most of what was perceived as once 'British' Britain. The tragedy therefore resumes: Vortimer is represented as dying at the height of his success and the Britons failed to bury him on the coast, as he had instructed, so as to defend their possession. Analogy here would seem to be with boundary burial, which was practised by the Irish and Welsh and the early English (Charles-Edwards 1976; Higham 1992a). This ritual may have been used in Wales at this date against the English, given the inhumation that was reportedly discovered beneath the Pillar of Eliseg (as discussed later). The author necessarily recognized that the Saxons returned and conquered, as was the will of God, but he minimized the ideological damage caused, representing them as cunning and duplicitous, rather than brave. There followed, therefore, the treacherous slaughter motif, noted earlier, in which 300 unarmed British *seniores* were killed at dinner (note the sacral and poetic numbering once more), and the capture of Vortigern led to his ransoming himself by ceding more territories. On this reconstruction, the (temporary) loss of Britain was part of God's plan, which could not be contested by mere mortals, but it was nothing for which the Britons should, as a people, retrospectively blame themselves or feel embarrassed by, since they had throughout been both virtuous and brave (Vortigern excepted). Nor was it something from which the Anglo-Saxons in the present should gain moral status, since they had achieved power only by dishonest means.

The author added to these two basic narratives two further bodies of material. One (*HB* 48, 49) was genealogical, serving to connect Vortigern with the ruling families of ninth-century Builth and Gwerthrynion, represented by Ffernmail and his father Teudubir, and connecting them via Vortigern to Gloiu, an eponym for *Caer Gloiu*, Gloucester. Given the damnable memory of Vortigern already fostered herein, this was clearly not intended to rebound to their credit, and this is arguably another example of the *Historia* serving the interests of Merfyn and Gwynedd by undermining the ideological and dynastic positions of contemporary British kings elsewhere in Wales. Additionally, this genealogy disputed claims being made in Powys and elsewhere for connections between Vortigern and Magnus Maximus, whose authority as a founding figure was widely favoured by the Welsh dynasties (discussed later).

The remaining material (*HB* 40–2) is based on a Gwynedd-centric story, which was probably in origin a foundation story for the hill-fort of Dinas Emrys, which has very properly been termed a folk-tale (Dumville 1986). It certainly contains a number of folk-tale motifs. The fatherless boy who is to be sacrificed may be one such but it also represents Ambrosius as a Christ- or Moses-figure, and has obvious Christian resonance, particularly bearing comparison with the contest of Moses and Aaron with the magicians of Pharaoh (Exodus vii, 8–13).

The story is managed for rhetorical purposes and was probably very largely, in this guise at least, the work of the author of the *Historia* himself. He was perhaps working up the kernel of an existing folk-tale to suit his own purposes (*contra* Dumville 1994: 414, who assumes that the author merely 'recognized' an existing prophesy in his work). It provided a further opportunity to castigate Vortigern, who is represented herein as pagan (Charles-Edwards 1991: 19–20, but the treatment is not consistent), as well as to associate Gwynedd with the magical Emrys, who reveals himself as the virtuous Ambrosius of Gildas's account, and whom the author developed thereafter as 'king among all the kings of the British nation'. The very land of Snowdonia is represented as being proof against Vortigern's wickedness, to the considerable benefit of its rulers, and the prophesy of final British triumph being made manifest in Gwynedd lends its authority in turn to the locality and its ruler. The mantle of British leadership is, therefore, being placed once again on Merfyn's shoulders. That the worms contested three times suggests a Triadic construction as well as sacral numbering, but the message is apparently contemporary (see later, pp. 159–60 for fuller discussion).

## ST PATRICK AND ARTHUR

Following this long and highly rhetorical (nineteen chapters) treatment of Vortigern and the settlement of the Saxons, the author moved on to two new characters, St Patrick and Arthur. As became apparent in the last section, his historical method depended to a large extent on the development of characters set, for rhetorical purposes, in doublets or contrasting pairs. This duality was primarily morally constructed, but he also used racial identity and lay versus clerical roles to set up the necessary tensions. We have, therefore, the saintly bishop Germanus, constructed against the accursed king Vortigern, the brave and warlike Vortimer leading British forces versus the devious and cowardly Hengist, whose Saxon soldiers fled like women, Vortimer again as the courageous and virtuous son of an immoral and craven father, the virtuous and wise prophetic child and future king, Ambrosius, set against the poorly advised, bigamous, pagan and satanic Vortigern, and so on. All of these figures are constructed as contemporaries, albeit of different ages, within the overall context of Vortigern's reign. It is his rule which opens this section of the text (*HB* 31), and it is his death which brings it to an end.

To this point, and including the seven chapters (50–6) which focus on Patrick and Arthur, the post-Roman passages of this work are structured ultimately, if at times extremely distantly, around the sequence of events as laid out (albeit with exceptional imprecision) in Gildas's *De Excidio Britanniae*. Gildas referred (*DEB* xxiii) to the invitation to the Saxons from the 'proud tyrant', their arrival, reinforcement, treaty arrangements and settlement in the east of Britain. In the following chapters, he described their revolt and war between Saxons and Britons, which ended in the year of the siege of Mount Badon (*DEB* xxvi, 1).

We come now, however, to the last section in the *Historia* which has these characteristics, and this section does to an extent offer a linking mechanism or 'bridge' constructed to connect Vortigern's reign with later, English-derived history (Charles-Edwards 1991: 21; Dumville 1994: 429). This is not, however, its sole or even its primary function. Patrick and Arthur are another morally constructed pair of (putative) contemporaries, somewhat on the lines of Germanus and Vortimer. Like them, both are virtuous, but one is clerical and one martial. Unlike them, both are Britons. They were transported into this chronological framework by the author of the *Historia Brittonum* even despite Gildas's failure to mention either, and their contextualization and historicization within this Gildas-derived framework has no validity whatsoever. It was clearly the author's decision to do this, perhaps inspired by connections in his Irish sources between Patrick and Germanus, and by his decision to associate Arthur with Gildas's Mount Badon – assuming that that was not received wisdom already at this date. It must be said, in that context, that this is plainly the earliest text surviving to make this connection and it does seem to have been this author who first attempted it. Hereafter, the Gildas-centric structure of the *Historia* had to be abandoned, since Gildas's own 'historical' narrative gave out at this point, some forty-four years before his date of writing. The author's treatment of St Patrick and Arthur therefore represents his final portrayal of a 'British Britain', before his enforced acknowledgement of Anglo-Saxon domination, characterized in this text by Anglo-Saxon source materials adopted as a framework.

For rhetorical purposes, it seems to have been felt important for the moral legitimacy of the Britons, as developed in this work, to be reinforced at this point. Vortigern's wickedness and the successes of the hated Saxons had been balanced within the previous section by a series of virtuous British and Christian exemplars, but it was Vortigern's reign which structured events and his actions which led to disaster. It was not enough, therefore, simply to single out Vortigern and to build connections between him and neighbouring dynasties whom Gwynedd opposed. For all his hard work at shoring up the status of the British people to this point, the author seems to have been concerned that the result was at best a moral ambivalence characterized by divine punishment. With the disastrous reign of Vortigern brought to a conclusion in a mêlée of variant horrible ends (*HB* 47, 48), the author sought to people the subsequent historical space with British figures whose reputations could sustain his key message – that the Britons had long been, and were still, both a Christian people, doing God's will and beloved by God, and a martial race, capable of preserving themselves against external attack and taking advantage of divine aid when it appeared. This whole section seems therefore to have been developed to act as a counterweight to the morally deficient reign of Vortigern, and so provide a vision of unsullied British achievement post-Vortigern, to be proclaimed triumphantly prior to the subsequent acknowledgement of Saxon supremacy in the present and recent past. It serves to insulate the present from Vortigern's moral bankruptcy, which might otherwise be thought to condition all later history. By so doing, the author was laying claim for his people to an heroic, Christian history, post-Vortigern, and the central role in providential and salvation history as that pertained to Britain.

This contrast had, of course, a powerful message to his own contemporaries, regarding the connections between Christian behaviour, divine providence and success in war. From a Welsh perspective, his message was a hopeful one, offering ideal exemplars for his people and its leaders. As behoved a priest writing for a king, he began by offering St Patrick as his model of the impeccably virtuous British cleric, beloved of God, but he had other frameworks in mind as well, as will become apparent.

What follows is a carefully reworked précis of stories focusing on St Patrick. The source material was written in Ireland, in connection with the claims to primacy of the monastery of Armagh. The principal texts used were Muirchu's *Life* (Hood 1978), written within the period 661–700, and Tirechan's *Memorandum*, which arguably dates to the same general period (Bieler with Kelly 1979), but there are additional comments which are not known in Irish sources until rather later (Dumville 1986: 13). None of this material has any historicity regarding Patrick's career, and there is no evidence that our author had access to Patrick's own writings, other than via secondary texts. Although Patrick was an historical figure, therefore, the author's approach is historicizing, written on the basis of texts which are primarily hagiographical in tone and far from 'realistic'.

The author's treatment of this Irish material is highly selective and designed to further his own rhetorical purposes. So, for example, he neglects the numerous stories of Patrick's miracles and church foundations in Ireland, and concentrates instead on specific features of his ministry, in particular the divine inspiration and Roman authority which originally dispatched him, and parallels between his career and biblical exemplars.

This Patrician material is contextualized chronologically within the broader narrative by the introductory comment, at the very start of chapter 50, that

St Germanus returned home after Vortigern's death. Patrick's story starts, therefore, as Vortigern dies, as a captive in Ireland, and it has arguably been placed at this point within his chronology by the author for rhetorical purposes. Patrick's captivity is, therefore, symbolic of the captivity of his British countrymen under the diabolical Vortigern, and his escape equates with theirs from Satan once he was dead – again, contrast Gildas (*DEB* xxvi, 3), whom he is seeking to 'correct'. We are expected to position his putative continental education, in which St Germanus was supposedly involved, and the inception of his career as a missionary, after Vortigern's death, thus establishing the next time frame within this episodic narrative.

What follows is a value-laden and highly rhetorical account of Patrick's career, designed to establish his exceptional place in providential history. So it was by God's will that he was educated, and he was long at Rome. Following God's unwillingness to allow Palladius the honour of converting the Irish, Patrick the Briton was sent (*HB* 51) by the extraordinary combination of 'Celestine the Roman Pope and Victor the angel of God, moved and persuaded by the bishop St Germanus'. Both Celestine's and Victor's participation derives from Tirechan (*Memorandum* 56, but see Patrick's *Confessio* 23, for *Victoricus*, from which the latter derived).

As the apostle of the Irish at the behest of Rome, Patrick's career could be represented as quintessentially orthodox – note the way in which his activities were blessed by the continental clerical establishment and begun in the name of the Holy Trinity (*HB* 52). This emphasis was presumably designed to contest English perceptions of Welsh Christianity in the past as flawed and even heretical (as Bede's repeated assertions on the subject, as well as Gildas's on the subject of Arianism).

This account reaches its rhetorical climax in chapters 54 and 55. The first of these establishes, in detail, the case for Patrick to be numbered among the miracle-working apostles of the New Testament and develops him as a wonder-working Christ-figure. This comprises lists of his achievements, both as to miracles performed and also as a bishop, with fabulous totals of alphabet-tables written, churches established, bishops consecrated, priests ordained and laity baptised. The whole is sprinkled liberally with sacral numbers – 3,000 priests ordained, 12,000 baptised, seven kings, three petitions, etc., all of which were designed to sustain the rhetorical positioning of Patrick as a British apostle operative at the close of Gildas's time-frame within the spiritual framework of the New Testament. This material is based on Tirechan, particularly chapter 6, but the numbers have been changed, in part to accord with the vision of totality which the author seems to have felt was reflected in the number 365, which occurs three times.

There are additionally resonances of the Old Testament Moses in chapter 54: he fasted for 40 days and nights and petitioned the Lord on Eile hill, for example. These connections are made explicit in the following chapter by four direct comparisons, which are taken verbatim from Tirechan (*Memorandum*

53, 54). The first, for example, was concerning conversations with an angel in the burning bush (Exodus iii, 1–15, but see also Mark xii, 26; Luke xx, 37; Acts vii, 30–4), which was widely perceived as a revelation of God vouchsafed only to the elect. This extended comparison with Moses is a powerful tool, since he was the single most important character of the Old Testament, and the archetypal figure of prophet, priest, lawgiver, judge and shepherd, and this would seem to be why the author quoted this material in full. The fourth, which may even have been adopted at a later date into the Arthurian tradition (as *The Stanzas of the Graves*), is the obscurity of his tomb, for 'he was buried in secret, no-one knowing [where]', which derives via Tirechan from Deuteronomy (xxxiv, 6).

Patrick was, therefore, offered as an exemplar of British Christianity, to bear comparison with Christ and the apostles. Part of his value to this text is as a Christian saint of the front rank who was recognized internationally at this date and whose authority could stand comparison with English candidates for sanctity. His career provided an opportunity to refute many English claims, including those of Bede and others concerning the positioning of the Britons outside divine providence and about the exclusive relationship, via Augustine, between Roman orthodoxy and the English. At the same time, the author was contesting via this exemplar Gildas's vision of a sinful clerisy in the present, at the time of writing. So, too, did the British Patrick famously convert a barbarian race, centuries before the English missionaries of the eighth century got to work in northern Germany. This is the first of two passages which challenges the moral implications of Bede's claim (*HE* i, 22) that it was a great crime against God that the Britons never preached the word to the English. Likewise, the scale of his achievement, as expressed via the numbers of his miracles and converts, and so on, was intended to outshine that of any comparable figure.

More importantly, Patrick's likeness to Moses was heavily emphasized. The author was clearly attracted by Moses, having already made implicit reference to his deeds in his portrayal of Germanus. Patrick's positioning was on a completely different level, however, and was entirely explicit. Moses refounded the Old Testament Israelites as a people of the Lord following their exile under pagan rule in Egypt, leading them to the Promised Land and providing them with the ten commandments. Gildas (*DEB* xxiii, 2) had portrayed his *tyrannus superbus* – hence Vortigern in this text – as a Pharaoh-figure, and again made use of Pharaoh's army lured to its ruin in the Red Sea (*DEB* xxxvii, 2) in the context of the five British kings of the present. That the *Historia* here positions Patrick immediately after Vortigern as a Moses-figure cannot be accidental. Explicit comparison herein suggests that the author was seeking to develop Patrick as a figure representative of the renewal of the British as a people of the Lord, entering the Promised Land of Canaan following a period of spiritual exile (in a plague-ridden Egypt) conditioned by Vortigern's iniquity and the *adventus Saxonum*. But the biblical Moses was also the central figure of the Covenant, and a prophet through whom God has given dire warnings to his people about the future (Deuteronomy xxxii, 19–23), which had obvious parallels for the Britons in the present.

It is possible that the author was also making connections between St Patrick and the present court of Gwynedd. Patrick's putative original name, prior to his assumption of *Patricius* when consecrated bishop, is given as '*Mann*' (Faral 1929: 36, but Morris 1980: 75 offers the reading '*Maun*'). Patrick was, therefore, perhaps being constructed symbolically as a second figure of renewal of the British people, following the martial achievements of Cunedda from *Manau Gododdin*, who expelled the Irish from western Britain. He takes his place as the British apostle of the Irish and a Moses-figure for his own British *gens*. Merfyn's origins in the Isle of *Manau* then imply that he could be construed in the present as the third such figure of renewal, within the context of a work of particular relevance to the court of Gwynedd at this date. As elsewhere, the author's treatment seems full of wit and subtlety.

## ARTHUR AND THE OLD TESTAMENT

From Patrick, the author passed to Arthur, whom he developed in a single, extended chapter (*HB* 56) as an archetype of the triumphant, British war leader and Christian warrior, thus as the secular counterpart to the sanctified Patrick. Like the latter, Arthur was also being constructed in an Old Testament context. Patrick was quite explicitly compared with both New and Old Testament figures, but his development as a type of Moses is the dominant influence on this text. Although the author's immediate source was Irish hagiography, the biblical quotations used derive ultimately from Deuteronomy (xxxiv, 6, 7), and our author certainly had a good enough working knowledge of the Bible to be aware of that fact. The book ends with the death of Moses and the succession of his military lieutenant and *minister*, Joshua son of Nun, to his role as leader of the Israelites. Joshua is depicted throughout as a war leader rather than a prophet, who was triumphant over his people's enemies with God's aid. He was never a king but he conquered many kings. Arthur's position in this text as the great warrior – but not a king – whose narrative follows that of Patrick reflects an awareness on the part of the author of this sequence in the Old Testament. He was making a conscious effort, through Arthur, to further develop a new providential position for the Britons as the new Israelites overcoming their enemies and occupying the Promised Land.

Joshua was contextualized as a younger contemporary of Moses by the words: *Et factum est ut post mortem Mosi servi Domini* ('And it happened that after the death of God's servant, Moses . . .': Joshua i, 1). Similarly, Arthur and his English enemies were situated chronologically by the phrase *In illo tempore* ('At that time'), looking back to the ending of Patrick's ministry, his great age at death and his unlocated tomb, both of which he putatively shared with Moses. As Joshua's story follows that of Moses, so Arthur's follows that of Patrick, again implying a sequence modelled on Joshua.

Arthur's 'historical' role was constructed by reference to Hengist's death and his son, Octha's, putative reappearance from the north to take up the leadership of the Saxons in Kent, hence against the Saxons. In this sense, his role developed that of the earlier Vortimer and took up where the latter's had ceased. Since the author was developing the south-east-centric vision of the Anglo-Saxon settlement which he had already established in Vortigern's reign, Arthur is necessarily placed rhetorically as both a doublet with Patrick and as the antithesis of the pagan Octha.

Arthur was introduced as follows: 'Then in those days Arthur fought with the kings of the Britons against them [the Saxons of the kingdom of Kent], but he himself was the *dux bellorum*'. The phrase *dux bellorum* has attracted considerable attention throughout the last century, and efforts have been made by historians to read into it all sorts of meanings. It simply translates, however, as 'leader in battles', or 'war-leader', and no expansion of this into a title or military command is warranted by the text. However, it is crucial that we recognize that it has a biblical derivation, which has not previously been acknowledged. An electronic search of the Vulgate produces only one instance in which *dux* and *bellum* occur together, which occurs in the opening lines of the Book of Judges, which follows the Book of Joshua (my emphasis):

*Post mortem Iosue consuluerunt filii Israhel Dominum dicentes quis ascendet ante nos contra Chaneum et erit* dux belli?

After the death of Joshua the children of Israel consulted the Lord saying who shall go up before us against the Canaanites and be *the leader in battle*?

Our author has adapted the generic term *bellum* slightly to the plural, presumably in deference to his listing of twelve battles immediately thereafter. This is not the only occurrence of the phrase in early Christian works: Sulpicius Severus used *dux bellum* twice of the war-leader of the Judaeans in his *Chronicorum libri* (written 403/4), having almost certainly derived it from this same reference in Judges. There is no particular reason to think this text was accessible in ninth-century Wales. The same phrase was used by Bede in his 'lesser chronicle', which he incorporated into his *De Temporum Ratione* ('On Time'), completed in 703 (line 1637), then reused in his 'Greater Chronicle', written in 725 (see the year 4410). In both instances, Bede used *dux belli* of St Germanus in his capacity as commander of the Britons in the 'Allelujah Victory' over the Saxons and Picts. His source for this event was Constantius's *Vita Germani* ('Life of St Germanus'), which he summarized. Constantius has (xvii, 15, on p. 264) *Germanus ducem se proelii profitetur* ('Germanus offered himself as commander for battle'), and Bede seems to have paraphrased this as *Germanus ipse dux belli factus* ('Germanus himself was made leader of the battle'). This may, therefore, have been constructed without reference to Joshua. When he came to write the *Historia Ecclesiastica*, some years later, Bede seems to have returned to Constantius's text, for he now followed his wording precisely (*HE* i, 20). Either or both of Bede's chronicles *could* have been read by the author of the *Historia Brittonum*, who certainly had a considerable interest in time and dating, but I am unaware of any particularly good reasons to suppose that they were. Whether or not he did, his reading of the work of Tirechan signposted the end of the Book of Deuteronomy so obviously that this author's development of his Patrician material via Arthur is most likely to derive directly from his engagement with the Book of Joshua and the opening of Judges, where, alone, Joshua's role was spelled out in a single phrase. This recurrence of what is an unusual and somewhat tautological phrase therefore strongly implies that the author of the *Historia* was constructing Arthur as a British type of Joshua on the strength primarily of his own reading of Deuteronomy, Joshua and Judges.

There is some additional circumstantial evidence which confirms that he was interested in this section of the Bible: repeated use of the number 12 early in the book of Joshua (iii, 12; iv, 2, 3, 4, 8, 20), particularly regarding the twelve stones from the river of Jordan and the twelve tribes of Israel, and the fact that Joshua's battles occur exclusively in the first twelve chapters, seems to have encouraged the numbering of Arthur's battles as twelve. This use of apostolic number also positions him as a Christ-figure, albeit a type of warrior-Christ.

To summarize to this point, Moses had been partnered by, and then succeeded by, his younger aide, Joshua son of Nun, who won a succession of glorious and God-given victories as leader of the Israelites against the Canaanites. So was Patrick, who was explicitly depicted as the British Moses, represented as having been partnered, and succeeded as the central figure in this part of the narrative, by the vigorous young warrior, Arthur. Like Joshua, Arthur was similarly constructed as universally victorious with God's aid over the pagan occupiers of the Promised Land (but in his case this Promised Land was Britain, a connection made earlier by Gildas). Although it remained implicit, this metaphorical meaning would presumably have been recognized by those of his audience with a sound working knowledge of the Bible, particularly given the degree to which it was signposted in chapter 55. It is difficult to overemphasize the centrality of this biblical allegory to the text and its importance for us in attempting to understand this, the earliest Latin 'Arthurian' passage, since it impacts emphatically on both the presentation and characterization of Arthur, in detail and overall.

It is, therefore, only with the biblical context fully appreciated that the author's purpose and use of language can be approached. Arthur was included as the British Joshua, the *dux bell(or)um* of the latter-day Israelites, to reposition the Britons post-Vortigern in salvation history and to contest the unflattering constructions of the Britons as a people by both Gildas and Bede. Gildas had already invoked Pharaoh and the plagues of Egypt to contextualize the Britons under Vortigern. Here, the author was extending this reference to Exodus and developing both a Moses and a Joshua figure as leaders of the New Israelites (the Britons), and so avoiding Gildas's recourse to Jeremiah's 'Lamentation' and the symbolism of the fall of Jerusalem and sack of the Temple. His characterization and the language of discourse is therefore biblical in key respects, particularly as to Arthur's role as *dux* rather than *rex* and his position *vis-à-vis* the British kings of the day. Comparison of this author's language with, for example, Gildas's use of *dux* for Maglocunus and Bede's for such English figures as Penda, and such issues as the relationship between this *dux bellorum* and the *imperium*-wielding kings of the seventh century therefore cease to be of any real significance.

## ARTHUR'S BATTLES

There follows arguably the most contested passage in the *Historia*, which is of such importance to our exploration of Arthur in this text that I quote it in full (after Faral 1929: 38–9), with a translation:

> *Primum bellum fuit in ostium fluminis quod dicitur Glein. Secundum, et tertium, et quartum, et quintum super aliud flumen, quod dicitur Dubglas, et est in regione Linnuis. Sextum bellum super flumen quod vocatur Bassas. Septimum fuit bellum in silva Celidonis, id est Cat Coit Celidon. Octavum fuit bellum in castello Guinnion, in quo Arthur portavit imaginem sanctae Mariae perpetuae virginis super humeros suos, et pagani versi sunt in fugam in illo die, et caedes magna fuit super illos per virtutem Domini nostri Jesu Christi et per virtutem sanctae Mariae virginis genitricis ejus. Nonum bellum gestum est in urbe Legionis. Decimum gessit bellum in litore fluminis quod vocatur Tribruit. Undecimum factum est bellum in monte qui dicitur Agned. Duodecimum fuit bellum in monte Badonis, in quo corruerunt in uno die nongenti sexaginta viri de uno impetu Arthur; et nemo prostravit eos nisi ipse solus, et in omnibus bellis victor existit.*

The first battle was in the mouth of the river which is called *Glein*. The second, and third, and fourth, and fifth [were] on another river, which is called *Dubglas*, and it is in the region of *Linnuis*. The sixth battle [was] on a river which is called *Bassas*. The seventh battle was in the wood of Caledonia, that is *Cat Coit Celidon*. The eighth battle [was] in the castle of *Guinnion*, in which Arthur carried the image of saint Mary the perpetual virgin on his shoulders, and on that day the pagans were put to flight, and a great slaughter was upon them through the power of our Lord Jesus Christ and the power of Saint Mary his holy virgin mother. The ninth battle was fought in the city of the Legions. The tenth battle was waged on the bank of the river called *Tribruit*. The eleventh battle occurred on the mountain which is called *Agned*. The twelfth battle was on the mountain of Badon, in which there fell in one day nine hundred and sixty men from one charge [of] Arthur; and no-one slew them except he alone, and in all battles he was the victor.

It has been suggested repeatedly that the author had some sort of written source, which has been postulated as a battle-catalogue poem in the vernacular (initially by Chadwick and Chadwick 1932: 154–5), of a type known otherwise commemorating the martial achievements of kings such as Cadwallon, Cynan Garwyn and Urien. Such a source has some limited potential to confer historicity on the battles themselves in this context, hence on Arthur himself. However, for several reasons, this argument now seems far less powerful than hitherto, although this section may well have been written with an awareness that such poems were in circulation. Supposing the author to have been writing in Gwynedd, Cadwallon perhaps provides the most appropriate analogy. *Moliant Cadwallon* is one of two surviving undated poems which focus on this famous king of Gwynedd. Several recent commentators have argued that they may post-date the king's death by many generations, but a contemporary provenance is strongly defended in some quarters (as Williams 1935; Breeze 2001, who offers a translation of the second example, the *Canu Cadwallon ap Cadfan*). The *Moliant* is printed twice in the *Bulletin of the Board for Celtic Studies* (Williams 1935; G. C. G. Thomas 1968–70) and translations are provided by Skene (1868: I, 433ff.), Rowland (1990: 495–6) and Breeze. I quote just two verses from Rowland's translation to provide a flavour of the text:

> The encampment of fameworthy Cadwallon
> on the summit of Digoll Mountain
> seven months with seven battles daily.

> The encampment of Cadwallon by the Severn
> and from the opposite side to Dygen,
> Freiddin the burning of Meigen.

The Arthurian battle-list places one battle at a river mouth, six beside rivers, one in a wood, one in a fort, one in a city and two on hills or mountains. The places of combat are generally compatible with those reflected in this and other battle-catalogue poems, in which rivers, mountains, élite residences, regions, fords, woods and wells all occur. Jackson thought that it might be possible to detect in the Latin text some resonance of Old Welsh poetic structure, which would tend to support the general assumption of a vernacular source. Additionally, the ingenious theory was proposed that Old Welsh *iscuit* ('shield') has been replaced by *iscuid* ('shoulder') by scribal error in a written, vernacular text prior to translation into Latin (Bromwich 1975–6).

Even if we were to allow this hypothesis, and imagine that some such now lost text underlies Arthur's list of battles, to further suppose that it should be read as conveying historically accurate information capable of reconstructing a 'real' career has considerable dangers. In the case of Cadwallon, we have other material which enables us to contextualize and to a very limited extent reconstruct his life. Without similar material, Arthur's battle-list is impenetrable and cannot be treated as historical in any modern sense of the word. That said, it has exercised a fascination for historians over centuries, with attempts made to locate these various conflicts in each and every part of Britain (contrast, for example, Skene 1868: 50, with Collingwood 1929; Crawford 1935; and Morris 1973). As Jackson remarked as long ago as 1959, 'a great deal of nonsense has been written in the attempt to identify them', and events subsequently have only borne this out further. He argued (in 1945) that only two names were established with any real certainty: *urbs Legionis* was arguably in this context Chester (although Caerleon remains a possibility) and 'the wood of Caledonia' lies in Scotland, perhaps in Strathclyde. To these might be added Lindsey for *Linnuis* and *Bremenium* (High Rochester in Northumberland) for *Breguoin*, which was substituted in a later recension of the *Historia* for the otherwise unknown *Agned* (Jackson 1949). Otherwise, the battles of this list are unlocated and, at present, unlocatable.

The discussion has, however, to this point, privileged the most 'historical' scenario. That there ever was a pre-existing list is no more than a hypothesis (as pointed out by Green 1998). Hints of vernacular poetry may be illusory or have other causes. Nor is there any particular reason to think that the image of Mary would have been considered any more appropriate to a shield cover than a surcoat or tunic of some sort in Wales in the ninth century (Padel 2000: 11). The whole argument is upheld more by length of service and the authority of its several proponents than the quality of the case propounded. That the entire chapter was written in 'biblical style' (Howlett 1998: 69ff.) suggests that this text was authored in Latin and was not translated literally into Latin from the vernacular. Provided this judgement is upheld, the only safe conclusion is that this battle-list was the author's own work.

As already noted (above), the numbering of the battles is transparently biblical. It is, of course, the apostolic number, but it is probably more relevant to this text that the first twelve chapters of the Book of Joshua detail the victories of the Israelites under God's guiding hand. The biblical treatment of Joshua's wars is far more extensive, of course, than that offered by the *Historia Brittonum* of Arthur's, but its author had only just remarked, in the context of St Patrick, his need to abbreviate his narrative. His intention was apparently, therefore, to convey his messages within as brief an account as was practical, and that arguably determined the form which he adopted, which can best be described as an annotated list. Assuming that similar lists were a well known and valued method of praising Welsh leaders of the more recent past, this will have been seen as entirely appropriate to the circumstances.

How did the author construct this list, given that the general framework and end-point were already established by virtue of his biblical exemplars? If the notion of a pre-existing battle-list be set aside as at best unproven, at worst implausible, we are free to return to the text and explore other possibilities. It was recognized as long ago as the 1930s (Crawford 1935) that Arthur's battle-names need not actually signify historical battles, let alone a string of victories which were all broadly contemporary and achieved by one man. Indeed, many may not represent conflicts of any sort, for the list seems to have been made up from very disparate sources, if sources at all. The battle of Chester is by far the best known of those listed, if this is the correct identification, but it occurred in the early seventh century and was a Northumbrian slaughter of Powysian warriors and, famously, clergy (Bede, *HE* ii, 2). We cannot be certain that another earlier battle had not taken place there or thereabouts, which was a British victory. However, the case seems far-fetched. The inclusion here of *urbs Legionis* is as likely as not to derive either from the historical battle or the synod of that name, which was later entered under the year 601 into the *Annales Cambriae*. If it was the disastrous battle which was being recalled, its inclusion here might just, of course, be mischievous, given that it was a famous defeat for Powys and the Cadelling dynasty. Alternatively, this might have been read in the early ninth century as an effective rebuttal of Bede's rhetorical treatment of the battle, which he used as crucial evidence for the developing 'Otherness' of the Britons in providential terms and their vulnerability to divine vengeance or punishment following the Augustine's Oak contretemps.

Reference in battle-catalogue poems to woods as the locations of battles is commonplace, but the choice herein of the Caledonian example may reflect the author's desire to represent his hero as triumphant even on the very edges of the old Roman diocese at its furthest extent. Alternatively, it has recently been suggested (Green 1998) that this battle owes debts to the magical enlistment of the trees, ranked by species, which is a feature of the early vernacular poem *Kat Godeu* (*Book of Taliesin* viii). That poem or its underlying stories could have been accessible to the author. In that case this battle derives from mythology. This context was again used for Merlin in the central Middle Ages (Jarman 1960, 1978). The poem *Pa gur yw y porthaur* similarly features an Arthurian battle of *Trywruid* which may have been the source of this author's *bellum in litore fluminis quod vocatur Tribruit* (Green 1998). However, the borrowing could equally have occurred in the opposite direction, since current opinion dates the poem later than the *Historia* (Padel 2000: 15). The replacement of *Agned* by *Breguoin* in some late recensions arguably derives from a 'battle of the cells of *Brewyn*' to be found in the poetry of Taliesin, who attributed this victory to Urien of Rheged (Skene 1868: 350; Jackson 1949). Additionally, Padel (1994; and see Wood 1999: 38) has argued persuasively that Badon itself was detached from Ambrosius Aurelianus by the author of the *Historia* to be given to Arthur.

It seems, therefore, that the battles of various heroes of the past, both historical and mythological, have been swept up into this list. This may help explain the apparently wide spatial distribution which the names seem to suggest. Even Crawford's very sensible suggestion (in 1935), that the list originated as a general list of events, now seems unnecessary, however, since there is no reason to imagine this sweeping up to have been done by anyone other than the author of the *Historia*. This writer had after all already demonstrated a powerful tendency to construct lists, including an earlier battle-list for Vortimer (*HB* 44) which was patently synthetic. The inclusion of English place-names, reference to the *Lapis tituli*, which is arguably a reference to Bede's notice of a 'monument bearing Horsa's name' in Kent (*HE* i, 15), and his concluding sentence, which borrows both *ciulas* ('keels') and *muliebriter* from Gildas, all lead towards this conclusion. There is additionally a list of *civitates* (*HB* 66\*), which owes little more than its total to Gildas (and Orosius), but which is in detail a broadly contemporary text (Jackson 1938). This battle-list is, therefore, one which our author arguably compiled himself, deriving his inspiration from multiple sources but helped out by his own knowledge and imagination. There seems little prospect that the Arthurian section of the *Historia Brittonum* is based on a pre-existing battle-list in the vernacular, let alone one of any antiquity and authority.

By this reading, Arthur's battles could include locations or happenings of all sorts, battles which had otherwise been recorded anonymously or been assigned to someone else, legendary or mythological places or made-up stories. We should assume that the list is highly rhetorical and was intended to convey a particular message, rather than detail historical events. The vision of Arthur as a pan-British war-leader, a veritable *dux bellorum*, which is offered by the author, is certainly complemented by the list. It seems to have been constructed with that purpose in mind, representing him as triumphing in a wide variety of contexts, both historical and legendary, known and unknown, across all Britain. Given that the dominant imperative seems to have been to achieve twelve victories, the author constructed a remarkably improbable scenario, with his second, third, fourth and fifth battles all being fought on the River *Dubglas, in regione Linnuis*. The driving force was arguably, therefore, his construction of a British type of Joshua, to accord with his repositioning of the Britons as the New Israelites and Britain as the Land of Canaan, with powerful messages in the present regarding divine protection of his people and their role within God's plans for their island home.

That is not to say that this list is without value to our exploration of the positioning of Arthur in this text. Indeed, it offers us a great deal. First, and most obviously, is its role in sustaining the vision of an exemplary British warrior and war-leader, who is the necessary counterpart to the saintly bishop, Patrick. It is a fundamental of the text that Arthur, like Joshua, be constructed as both victorious with God's aid and victorious over the enemies of God's people. Like Joshua, Arthur was a leader of the whole people, not part of it battling with other parts. The apparently wide distribution of his victories implies that the author was keen to portray all the English as his enemies. There must be no recurrence of Gildas's lamented civil wars among the Britons (*DEB* xxvi, 2), or his peace between Britons and English (which is one possible interpretation of *DEB* x, 2), in this reformulation of a heroic, British past, post-Vortigern.

Second is the rhetorical development of the relationship between Arthur, representing the Britons in arms, and the Christian God. This development is both extraordinarily transparent and of considerable interest, yet it has passed largely without discussion by modern historians, owing to their concern to recover a 'real' Arthur for the history of the fifth or sixth centuries. It is this aspect of the list which is likely to have offered the author's contemporaries the clearest messages. By representing this *dux bellorum* as victorious in twelve battles, the author was representing him as a Joshua figure. Joshua and Christ were generally seen as in key respects synonymous in the early Middle Ages (in Hebrew, the name Joshua = Jesus), so Arthur (like Patrick) was also conceived as a Christ-figure, but in this case as a secular and martial type of Christ. Such symbolism was already pervading notions of kingship by this date, particularly in Carolingian circles, so these connections may well have been thought of particular value to Merfyn. The author may well also have intended that his audience should contrast his Arthur with the descent from a pagan god which he had already attributed (*HB* 31) to Hengist (whom he had already identified with Satan) and so his son Octha, against whom Arthur is represented as fighting. Octha and the Saxons were the Canaanites in this construct, hence quintessentially 'Other', and the Christian God and His people were ranked against them under Arthur's leadership.

This image of the Christ-warrior is reinforced within the list on two occasions. The first is the extended description of the battle *in Castello Guinnion*, where victory over the *pagani* was attributed quite explicitly to the potency of both Christ and Mary. This is a construction of British victory over the Saxons under Arthur's leadership and under the active protection of Christ and his virgin mother. This passage may owe something to Bede's portrayal of St Oswald's victory over Cadwallon (*HE* iii, 2), and may have been intended to contest the moral values explicit therein. Oswald, too, was connected with Joshua by a Celtic writer, in this case Bishop Adamnan (Anderson and Anderson 1961: 198–201). However, the Britons did not use the English strategy of representing their warriors posthumously as saints, necessitating a rather different construction of divine assistance to Arthur. We have here, therefore, a powerful claim for both Christ and Mary weighing in on the side of the Britons in war against the (Anglo-)Saxons – of obvious relevance in the present, when Mercian kings had suddenly begun to appear fallible in battle and English power seemed to be crumbling. Just as the Old Testament God had repeatedly delivered his enemies into the hands of Joshua, therefore, so now were Christ and his mother represented as delivering the Saxons into Arthur's power.

The second occasion is rather more subtle, coming in the concluding remark: 'and in all battles he was the victor'. This does, of course, reflect Joshua's career, but the choice of *victor* herein recalls the reference (*HB* 51) to 'an angel of God named *Victor*' in the context of Patrick's despatch to the Irish from Rome, and again, Magnus Maximus's son (*HB* 29), who was reputed killed by the Germanic Count Arbogast. Repetition of the term may not be accidental, and its general purpose was perhaps to construct links between these several passages concerning exemplary British figures of the past, both pre- and post-Vortigern, and between both Patrick and Arthur and divine agency. There are connections here also with Gildas, who termed Badon the *postrema victoria* ('final/last victory': *DEB* ii) and used *victores* (but of the Saxons), *vinco* and *victoria* in his treatment of 'the war of the Saxon federates' (*DEB* xxv, 3).

A third emphasis is on Arthur's personal prowess. The twelfth of his battles was accounted *mons Badonicus*. This was the only battle which the author recovered from Gildas, and it is the only one which is certainly historical in an early sub-Roman context, even given that it is improbably attributed to Arthur. It was this, the last and the most nearly historical, in this context, to which the author attached his claims for Arthur as the great supra-human warrior-hero. His Arthur had slain 960 in a single charge, 'and no-one slew them except he alone'. This is, therefore, the point at which the author emphasized his claim for the legendary valour and martial skills of his hero-figure. It is tempting to postulate that this claim reflects the author's source for his Arthur figure in localized wonder-tales, as a superhuman figure of folklore and wider stories of the mythological Arthur (Padel 1994). That said, this too has a biblical connection, for: 'On that day the Lord magnified Joshua in the sight of all Israel, and they feared him, as they feared Moses, all the days of his life' (Joshua iv, 14). Supposing the author to have been aware of this passage, he may well have wished to 'magnify' similarly his British type of Joshua. It is difficult to imagine a more effective demonstration of such 'magnification' of a warrior than to exaggerate out of all proportion the number of the enemy laid low by his charge. The total may derive from sacral numbering ($3 \times 3 \times 100 + 3 \times 2 \times 10$).

## THE IMAGE OF ARTHUR

We have, therefore, a complex vision offered us, as an audience, in this text. On one level, the Arthur of the *Historia Brittonum* is an exemplary British warrior of the past, who was ferocious in battle, the bane of his enemies and invariably successful. The scale of the claims regarding his prowess suggest connections with superhuman wonder-working Arthur-figures in the landscape and mythology, albeit the name itself probably derives from the name-stock of the Roman Empire, presumably via legendization of some such figure as the second-century Roman officer already discussed (p. 76). The author also mobilizes Christian motifs in order to establish that he was the beloved of the Lord, leading the Britons/Israelites in wars fought against the pagan 'Other' – the Saxons/Canaanites. He is the twin construct or doublet of the exemplary Patrick, the legendary bishop, the Moses-figure and New Testament apostle. Joshua followed Moses in the Old Testament narrative and successfully undertook the conquest and settlement of the Promised Land (Joshua xi, 15), as the leader of his people in war against the unbelieving peoples of Canaan. His death sparked a discussion with the Lord as to who should be the next *dux belli* ('leader in battle') of the Israelites. Similarly, Arthur as *dux bellorum* ('leader in battles') is depicted as having waged successful warfare against the pagan Saxons. Following the portrayal of Patrick as a Moses-figure, Arthur completes his labours and refounds the Britons as a martial people of the Lord within the Promised Land of Britain – which is an idea to be found in both Gildas and Bede. Arthur's prowess is demonstrated by the numbers of the enemy he has slain, and in this respect, as in others, he is akin to Joshua, whom the Lord 'magnified'. Both Patrick and Arthur are positioned here and developed, therefore, in highly rhetorical ways.

The author's objective overall would seem to be to counter the damaging impact on British perceptions of their own history which was necessarily exerted by Gildas's vision of British moral bankruptcy and cowardice. There followed Bede's more recent and even more damning positioning of the Britons as having passed outside providential history. Gildas had developed the downfall of his people via a series of plagues such as befell Egypt (Exodus vii), then correlated the *adventus Saxonum* with the Old Testament fall of Jerusalem to the Babylonians and Chaldeans (Jeremiah), turning implicitly to Daniel's dreams in the present. The author of the *Historia* repositioned it to his own rhetorical advantage. Like Gildas his starting point was the captivity in Egypt (Vortigern), but he then depicted Patrick and Arthur bringing their people back in triumph to the Promised Land as the new Israel. The *adventus Saxonum* obviously could not be omitted from a ninth-century *Historia*, since otherwise Anglo-Saxon England, hence the loss of Britain, had no rationale. By focusing that story exclusively on Vortigern, however, the author minimized its potential damage. With the Pharaoh-figure of Vortigern dead – perhaps even swallowed up by the earth, much as the Old Testament Pharaoh had been swallowed by the Red Sea – the portrayal of Patrick and Arthur reflects the author's concern to recover the status of the Britons, develop virtuous exemplars and confirm their centrality to providential history. The Moses–Patrick, Joshua–Arthur analogies were fundamental here, since Moses is the Old Testament figure to whom 'the Lord used to speak face to face, as a man speaks to his friend' (Exodus xxxiii, 11), and through whom God provided the commandments. He was, however, also the figure through whom God informed his people that he would punish them in the future for their inconstancy, albeit they would still be the elect. That message was fundamental to the construction of an ideological defence of the British as a people, in the circumstances of Anglo-Saxon occupation of the bulk of southern Britain, and attacks and attempts at further conquest early in the ninth century, since it assured the author's audience that even these recent difficulties could still be interpreted as the temporary punishment of His people by God.

Was there any historical reality behind this portrayal of Arthur in the *Historia Brittonum*? In defence of Arthur's historicity it has to be recognized that historical figures were sometimes used as the bases for the author's characterizations. Vortigern, for example, is based upon Gildas's *tyrannus superbus*, as named by Bede, even though there are few points of comparison between these two constructs. Others are similarly fictionalized, historical figures, including SS Germanus and Patrick. That said, Horsa, Hengist and Octha are probably best viewed as legendary, albeit figures who had already been historicized by earlier writers. We certainly cannot be sure that even Vortimer was actually invented by the author, although that seems very probable. From his perspective, the English figures were historical, in as much as they derived from existing texts. However, the author's rhetorical needs must be considered the decisive feature of his vision of Arthur, as of other figures of the past. His Arthur need have carried over little beyond the name and the general notion of a great warrior from whatever model the author had available, and that model is likely to have been mythological rather than historical by this date, as the story of Arthur's prowess at Badon implies. The option of a wonder-working Arthur-figure was clearly available to the author since he incorporated him into his text (*HB* 73), while there is no hint that an 'historical model' was accessible, and many signs that it was not. Had the story of some such figure of Roman Britain as Lucius Artorius Castus retained any sense of chronological or historical reality, then the construction of Arthur in the *Historia* would have had difficulty gaining acceptance within the audience for which it was intended. A by-this-point legendary figure embraced by folklore offered no such difficulties and was far more adaptable to the author's needs.

Overall, the biblical model provided his framework and his central characterization, and this requires that we acknowledge that the historicity of this Arthurian construct was of no particular relevance to the purposes for which this figure was developed. Whether or not this story bore *any* relationship with reality is unknowable, and to a large degree irrelevant to our reading of the text. What is clear is that the author was engaged in the construction of a past full of achievements and capable of providing a sustaining self-image for a political community in the present (cf. McKitterick 1997), and that was the central meaning of the 'Arthurian' passage.

It is the *mirabilia* which the author appended that confirm the availability of the folklore Arthur to this author. It has recently been suggested that the *mirabilia* were included so as to point to the 'eternal qualities of the wonder of God's dispensation in the natural world' (Dumville 1994: 431–2), but their distribution and treatment suggest a more politicized set of motives. The lack of such manifestations of God's power in central Mercia or Wessex, for example, arguably reflects the author's view that those were Godless spaces. It has already been suggested that the author probably came from the southern or south-central Marches of Wales and this list strongly implies a personal knowledge of the local topography and folklore of that region, from the pre-1974 counties of Herefordshire and Radnorshire southwards to Glamorganshire (Figure 26). The major part of this list (*HB* 68–74), to which the fullest stories are attached, was arguably therefore, the author's own, apparently concocted from existing personal knowledge or oral testimony. This view is sustained particularly by his personal affidavits concerning two instances in Gwent and Builth (*HB* 72, 73), which demonstrate his personal responsibility for parts at least of this text.

To this core have been added several further examples. The first entry relates to Loch Leven, which has no obvious connection with the remainder. Warm springs and salt springs both occur in Bede's idealized description of Britain (*HE* i, 1), which may account for the references to the 'hot lake in the *regio* of the Hwicce' (Bath) and the unnamed salt springs in the same *regio* (*HB* 68: presumably Droitwich). Both occur in English-controlled areas in the early ninth century, but ones not far distant from Welsh territory and only lost to British kingships in the seventh century. They are, therefore, here being reclaimed for 'British' Britain. Within Wales, Builth and Brycheiniog, Gower, Gwent and Ceredigion are all represented in the main grouping. To this list has then been added four miracles in Gwynedd (*HB* 75), told with minimal detail and with only one extended to recall a legendary event, which may well have been added rather hastily to the author's own existing area of knowledge to avoid causing offence among Gwynedd's ruling élite, which was, of course, his primary audience. Almost as an afterthought, two Irish examples are tacked on at the end, without even the terminology which distinguishes the remainder (particularly use of the terms *miraculum* or *mirabilia*), and without even notice of their being Irish.

The geography of the *mirabilia* was, therefore, apparently intended to reflect the locality of God's people within the British Isles, from southern Pictland through Wales and what was traditionally thought of as Welsh territory in western England, over to Ireland.

Disregarding Arthur's putative son, Amr (see p. 89), which may derive in any case from the river name Gamber, only two figures of antiquity are named in the *mirabilia*. The first is St Illtud, whom tradition associates with sites from Breconshire to Gower but most particularly with Llantwit Major (Henken 1987), and it may even be that the author had some particular past connection with this cult. The second is Arthur himself (in detail, see pp. 87–90). Again, we have here a doublet of British hero figures, one of whom is clerical and the other martial. One of the key mechanisms of the author's story-telling in the main part of his text is recoverable also, therefore, in the *mirabilia*.

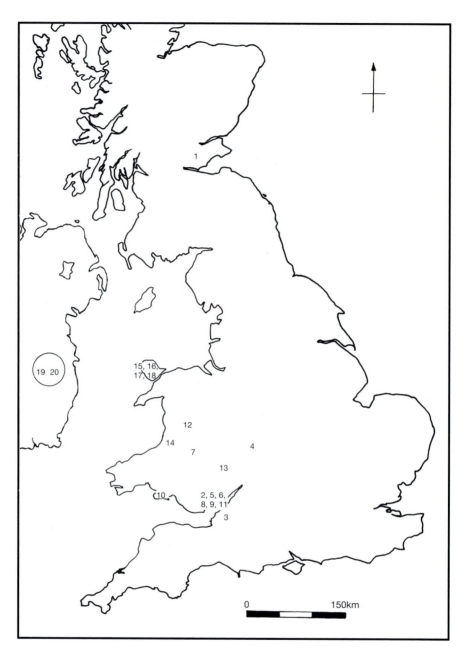

**Figure 26** *The mirabilia* of the *Historia Brittonum*: 1 Loch Leven, 2 The Severn Bore, 3 Bath, 4 Droitwich, 5 The Severn Bore, 6 Llyn Lliwan, 7 Spring of *Gwrhelic*, 8 Ash-tree beside the Wye, 9 A cave in Gwent called *Vith Guint*, 10 The altar at Llywynarth, 11 Spring in Gwent at *putei Mouric*, 12 Carn Cafel, 13 Tomb of *Amr*, 14 Tomb on *Cruc Maur*, 15 Raised beach, 16 A moving hill, 17 A marvellous ford, 18 Stone in *vallem Citheinn*, 19 Loch Lein, 20 Loch Echach

Where Arthur appears in these stories, it is worth noting that in both instances Arthur is given the epithet *miles* ('warrior'). One is set in Builth and the other in Ergyng (Archenfield), so these are tales concerning, and perhaps derived from, the upper Wye valley. What is significant in considering this Arthur is the fact that, in all these highly rhetorical contexts, the hero-figure is developed primarily as a warrior, stories around whom make him exceptional. In no instance is there a case for arguing Arthur as a king, and this was certainly not the vision which the author of the *Historia Brittonum* had in mind. We can be reasonably certain that all three passages in which Arthur appears were original to the author. Therefore, repetition in each instance of the term *miles* was presumably the author's, reflecting an apparent desire to connect the Arthur of chapter 56 with the *mirabilia* of chapter 73 (see p. 89). In that case the image of a Joshua figure and soldier of the Lord leading God's people in battle in a particular historical context was being integrated with existing local etymological legends, from which the author arguably derived the name. The basic idea of a superhuman and martial figure of folklore connects easily with the biblical image of the 'magnified' Joshua. The author's portrayal of Arthur at Badon can, therefore, be construed both as a reflection of the folkloric Arthur of local mythology and as the biblical Joshua, *minister* and martial factotum of Moses. These two concepts have been brought together in this text rather wittily by a well read and well travelled Welsh scholar to provide a metaphor in the past for his patron in the present.

Why Arthur, and not some other hero-figure from the British past? This is a much harder question to approach and we must recognize that most such alternative figures have been lost to us, although indigenous hunter-gods of the Roman period such as Mabon/Mapon (Ralegh Radford 1952–3) offer other alternatives which do occur in medieval Welsh poetry. Like Arthur, Mabon was used as an explanation of landscape features (hence *locus maponi* in the Ravenna Cosmography, and the place-names Lochmaben and Lochmabenstane). Mabon was, however, a specifically north-western deity, with a cult centred (at least in the Roman period) in the far north and north-west of the old diocese, in modern Dumfriesshire.

It is important to bear in mind that Gildas offered a single exemplar of virtuous leadership in the aftermath of the *adventus Saxonum* in the person of Ambrosius Aurelianus. This 'Divine' Aurelianus does seem to have been historical, in as much as Gildas referred to his grandchildren as being active in the present, although his name just might have been in part the butt of Gildas's wit. However, his very Romanity, as developed by Gildas (*DEB* xxv, 3), may well have disbarred this figure in the eyes of the author of the *Historia*, since his need was for a quintessentially British hero-figure. Since 'Britishness' had been constructed against Romanity in the early passages of this work, this was a serious obstacle. Additionally, the use to which he put Gildas's chronological framework required that the latter's brief reference to war between the Britons and the Saxons (*DEB* xxv, 3; xxvi, 1) be stretched to encompass the exploits of both Vortimer and Arthur. Ambrosius Aurelianus occurs at the very start of this period, as leader in the first battle. The author of the *Historia* accepted him, therefore, as a contemporary of both Vortigern and Vortimer, occurring as the child Emrys, a son of a Roman consul, and referred to him (*HB* 48) as 'king among all the kings of the British nation', with authority over (*HB* 42) 'all the kingdoms of the western part of Britain'. Like Arthur, this Emrys has parallels with the Irish Fionn, who also occurred as a child-figure and seer capable of foretelling good in the future (Ó hÓgáin 1999), but his positioning within this text was necessarily contrary to development as the peon of martial qualities which the author required. With Ambrosius Aurelianus disqualified, therefore, as too Roman, some other, quintessentially British, warrior figure was necessitated by the rhetorical needs of the writer, and this figure could not be derived from Gildas, since he named no other. Whether or not there was much choice is unclear, but Arthur's reputation was developed by the author to fulfil a very particular role, the framework of which was biblical. A mystical and magical hero-figure clearly gave maximum opportunity for this Arthur to be historicized in the image of Joshua, the 'magnified' leader of the Israelites in war. It was arguably reasoning of this sort that led the author to substitute Arthur for the overly 'Roman' Ambrosius as the victor of Badon and to initiate and then develop his role within the text.

The notion of Arthur's historicization has been developed against the twentieth-century assumption of his historicity (see discussion in Green 1998), but it must be recognized that these are fundamentally modern distinctions. The *Historia* was written within an intellectual milieu dominated by wonder-stories in the Bible and saints' lives, as well as secular and mythological vernacular narratives. Its author used a large cast of characters drawn from a wide spectrum of current story-telling, without distinguishing legendary figures from historical: to him Hengist, Joshua, Moses, Brutus, Britto, Lucius and Cunedda, for example, were all as authentically historical as Maelgwn, Cadwallon, Patrick and Germanus. Arthur was merely one more such figure, whom he developed and contextualized, like the others, as he saw fit within his own purposes. The author of the *Historia* had his own agenda, which he pursued to some success, but the historicization of Arthur would not have featured among his objectives. Rather, his Arthur served those objectives, and was neither more nor less 'historical' in his portrayal than any of the other figures whom he took from legendary sources and developed along the way. The 'historical' Arthur is a modern obsession which is thankfully absent from the early ninth century, when a far less rigorous vision of the boundaries of history was dominant.

Taking, for a moment, an exclusive view of the evidence, the Arthur of the *Historia Brittonum* may have derived from very small beginnings. Although Arthur was developed as an icon for the entire British nation throughout history as an invariably successful and Christ-beloved warrior, this development was only demonstrably based on two occurrences of the name in etymological stories located in and around the upper Wye valley. It is possible, but not necessarily probable, that this locale does represent the origins of Arthur as folk-hero, and that it was the *Historia* which bridged two contexts, one highly localized and based on folklore, and one historicized and conceived on a national stage. Such a transferral of an idea from the local to the national arena in order to fix national identity in putatively immutable and ancient forms has significant parallels elsewhere in both place and time. To offer a single example, in post-unification Germany (from 1871), the 'Heimat idea' was transformed from local origins to represent a (supposedly) timeless German nation, visible down the ages. The concept was adopted because of its rhetorical value to those seeking to construct German nationalism (Confino 1997). Similarly, Arthur's particular utility lay in the re-envisioning of a muscular and God-protected 'Britishness' in an early ninth-century context, in the particular environment of Merfyn's court. Arthur was similarly developed, therefore, as an aspect of nationalist rhetoric, and previous manifestations could conceivably have been very localized, given that no further evidence of his location in the countryside is available for over a century.

## THE ENGLISH HISTORICAL FRAMEWORK

The author's depiction of Arthur leaves him universally victorious but he still needed to manage the transition to the Anglo-Saxon domination of his own day. He began this process within chapter 56, with a brief reference to the Saxons' response to defeat. This was to bring in from Germany vastly inflated numbers of their own people and their kings. The English obtain no moral advantage from this process, but it did usefully explain English success and introduce the framework of English genealogies and regnal lists (Dumville 1986), which were used to provide a structure for the remainder of the 'historical' narrative. Bede's *Historia* clearly underlies much of the material which has been added into this structure, but the author also had northern British sources. Whether or not it is realistic to argue for a set of north-British annals (Hughes 1973; Dumville 1976–7) must remain a moot point (Charles-Edwards 1991), but the author certainly incorporates material from contemporary, Welsh perceptions of the heroic age in the 'Old North'.

This material serves important functions in this text. First, by quoting English royal genealogies from the very end of the eighth century, it constructs connections with the lifetime of the author and his audience, who could be expected to recall such names as Offa and Ecgfrith. The Anglian originals would equally have begun each genealogy with the name Woden, but this descent from a pagan god arguably had a particular, and uncomplimentary, meaning within this text.

Second, it frames this interlude of English domination in suitably English terms. We are not entitled to assume that the author was without an alternative source of British king-lists and genealogies – rather such must surely have been available for Gwynedd at least and he quotes the recent descent of the royal house of Builth (*HB* 49). This was, therefore, a conscious decision. The emphasis on Northumbrian kings implies that the author was conscious of Bede's focus on the royal houses of Bernicia and Deira, and his construction of their centrality to seventh-century Britain.

Third, the author focused attention on specific events which were capable of sustaining his rhetorical purposes. In particular, he was keen to undermine the current perception of English domination as irresistible, and likewise Anglo-Saxon claims (as Bede) to be the principal people of the Lord within Britain. His method was to direct attention towards instances of English military failure, particularly against Celtic opponents, so portraying the Anglo-Saxon conquests as fragile and capable of being reversed. This was in line with the prophesy, which he had constructed (or at least included, in *HB* 42), connected with the young Ambrosius Aurelianus and revealed to Vortigern, that looked towards the eventual expulsion of the English from Britain.

He therefore developed his primary genealogical source material for the Bernician royal family to include comment on two details. One was the ultimately Bede-derived reference to Ecgfrith's death in battle with the Picts, after which the Northumbrian expansion was halted and efforts to levy tribute on their northern neighbours abandoned (*HE* iv, 26). This was clearly included to mark the failure of Anglian imperialism in the north and the humbling of both king and army in the act of invading a Celtic neighbour. It should be remembered that this was presented by Bede as a lamentable moment in the history of his own people, when (quoting Virgil) 'the hope and strength of the *regnum* of the English began "to ebb and fall away"'. Our author seized upon Bede's unusual admission of weakness to his own advantage. Its relevance to recent English invasions of North Wales is obvious.

The second expansion was his reference to Oswiu's putative marriage with the British Riemmelth, from an unknown source if source there was, included perhaps so as to claim the presence of British blood within even a leading English royal family and construct bridges between the Britons and Northumbria. Given the recent discomfiture of both as neighbours of Mercia, such connections had some political merit in the present and began the process of distinguishing between one English kingdom and another, to which he later returned.

In chapter 61, the author developed the Deiran genealogy so as to provide an extended, rather repetitive but triumphal story of the victory of a hero of Gwynedd, Cadwallon, whose memory Bede had, of course (*HE* iii, 1; Higham 1995: 133–5), sought to damn:

> Osfrith and Eadfrith were the two sons of Edwin, and with him they fell in the battle of *Meicen* [Bede's Hatfield], and the kingship was never revived from that stem, because not one of that family

survived that battle, but they were all killed with him by the army of Cadwallon, king of the country of Gwynedd.

Again, this was the glorification of a Celtic triumph over the English, and this time it was one which could be simplified to rhetorical advantage (for one of Edwin's sons did supposedly survive, only to be killed later by Penda) and claimed for Gwynedd. The detail is not entirely consistent with Bede's story (*HE* ii, 20), but the changes enhance Cadwallon's role and omit all reference to Penda's part. In other brief references (*HB* 62), the author remarked on the bravery with which the otherwise unknown *Dutigirn* fought against the English, and the achievements of five British poets, of whom only two are otherwise putatively known to us by their work. Maglocunus and Cunedda are reintroduced at this point, in reference to the greatness of the former and the successful slaughter and expulsion by the latter of that other incoming group, the Irish. Their presence again highlights the martial pretensions of the court of Gwynedd and the author's positioning of his patron as the champion of the Britons against their enemies in the present.

The regnal years of Ida's successors were then used (*HB* 63) to frame the Augustinian mission (which occurs too early in this context) and the exploits of Urien and other British leaders in the north. However, it would be a mistake to imagine that the author lifted these direct from a reliable, northern British, historical text. Rather, he turned to Gildas for appropriate phrasing. He adapted the latter's '*Ex eo tempore nunc cives, nunc hostes, vincebant*' ('From that time now the citizens, now the enemy, were victorious': *DEB* xxvi, 1) as '*In illo autem tempore aliquando hostes, nunc cives vincebantur*' ('During that time, however, sometimes the enemy, sometimes the citizens were overcome'). He then used sacral number to define Urien's siege of *Metcaud* (Lindisfarne), as lasting three days and three nights (paralleling Christ's entombment before the resurrection: see p. 207), which harks back to Vortimer's three putative sieges of Thanet (*HB* 43). Urien was then murdered by Morcant from jealousy, 'because in him [Urien] before all the kings there was greater valour as the renewer of battle'. This last phrase is suggestive of a poetic idiom, but the author's purpose was arguably to draw attention to another occasion when the English had been driven off the British mainland by British forces acting in unison, this time spearheaded by the famous but legendary Urien. The island of Lindisfarne is here a northern parallel for Hengist's island of Thanet, where Vortimer had once before (*HB* 43) putatively cooped up the English and expelled them overseas. Urien is being presented as another example of the successful, British warrior 'type', therefore, alongside Cunedda, Vortimer and Arthur. Lindisfarne's famous role as the seat of an Irish monastery and bishopric may also have empowered this story and made the scene particularly poignant.

The red and white worms of prophecy (*HB* 42) had striven together three times. Vortimer's victories can be imagined as reflective of the first and

Arthur's the second. Urien's siege of Lindisfarne presumably represents the third occasion, with the English poised on the very edge of Britain. Following an ensuing period when the red worm would be seen to be much weaker (which aptly describes the later seventh and eighth centuries), it would then become stronger and drive the white out of Britain altogether. The key messages would seem to be in the present to beware British disunity and civil conflict, since that had in the past undermined success against the Saxons, and to work towards the final victory which had been prophesied. From the perspective of the court of Gwynedd, both Vortigern's family and the 'Old North' were suitable theatres in which to explore the issue of disunity, and to point up the terrible consequences of internecine strife and the crime of regicide. This is, therefore, a passage which supports a vision of Merfyn Frych – whose origins were northern – as the deliverer of his people from the Saxons in the present, at the head of a united nation and with the full compliance of his fellow kings. Not only were Cunedda, Vortimer, Arthur and Urien couched as metaphors for Merfyn himself, but so too was the red worm or dragon of prophesy, supposing that is that Merfyn's famous freckles (from which derive his by-name 'Frych') indicate that he had red hair. What this passage does not offer is a reliable basis for the reconstruction of an historical Urien Rheged (Sims-Williams 1996).

The outcome of Urien's death was the disastrous reign of Æthelfrith, whose great achievements against the Britons and the Scots were acclaimed by Bede (*HE* i, 34), but were not, for obvious reasons, highlighted in this text, which passes rapidly on to Edwin and his role as the first Christian king of the Northumbrians. At this point, the author included notice of Edwin's occupation of Elmet, in West Yorkshire, and expulsion of *Certic* (Ceredig), its king, which must be presumed to have derived in part from Bede (*HE* iv, 23), in part from a northern British source, which may well have been poetic. Thereafter, the story is based in large part on Bede (*HE* ii, 9, 14), with somewhat garbled references, for example, to the baptism of Eanflæd, Edwin and his people. He departed abruptly from Bede's account of Edwin's baptism, however, with the challenging remark:

> If anyone should wish to know who baptised them, *Rum map Urbgen* [Rhun son of Urien] baptised them, and for forty days he did not cease to baptise the whole race of *ambrones* and through his preaching many believed in Christ.

Urien's attempted eviction of the English may have failed, therefore, but the author is insistent, even against the testimony of Bede (which he clearly knew), that Urien's son had baptised the Northumbrians. By making this claim, the *Historia* challenges Bede's damning accusation that the Britons had never preached to the Saxons. This putative missionary work develops Patrick's mission to the Irish into a general theory of British missionary achievement and their claim to take their place alongside the apostles (Charles-Edwards 1991: 28). Rhun in his turn is developed as a Moses or Christ-figure by the claim of forty days spent baptising, which may perhaps have been intended to trump Bede's claim that Paulinus spent thirty-six days ($12 \times 3$) at Yeavering in the same activity (for the sacral numbering see Hopper 1939). The warrior Urien, in this case, gives way to his clerical counterpart and son, the two characters once again being constructed as a contrasted doublet of virtuous British figures, the one martial and the other clerical. Although it is customary to accept Urien as an historical figure – he is after all a significant figure in poetry attributed to Taliesin – Rhun's historicity as a missionary must be considered fragile in the extreme (Higham 2001a: 17–19).

The author was clearly striving for the moral high ground for his people, and this is emphasized by the terminology he used. *Ambrones* is a rare term which derives from a Gaulish tribe in antiquity, but the author of the *Historia Brittonum* probably took it from Gildas, who used it (*DEB* xvi) as an adjective to define 'wolves' when using that as a metaphor for the Pictish and Scottish raiders besetting the Britons. Winterbottom (1978: 21) translates it as 'greedy', but this loses something of the sense of menace, which might be better conveyed by 'ravenous'. In this text it was used of the Saxons, so the ungrammatical *Saxones ambronum* of chapter 57 as well as the above, and carries a highly derogatory meaning. The further the author could distance the English from the status of a people of the Lord, and portray them as a barbarian race outside divine providence, the more laudable Rhun's efforts to Christianize them, and the higher the moral status of the British people as an apostolic race. There is additionally a sense here, as in Oswiu's British marriage, of connection between Britons and Northumbrians, both of whom had suffered from Mercian power in recent years, and this foreshadows the last passages of the text. This is, therefore, a rhetorical construct with powerful messages for the Britons of Wales in the early ninth century, and these messages were arguably central to the author's development of his text. The historicity of a Bishop Rhun son of Urien, with a ministry among the northern Angles (as, *inter alia*, Phythian-Adams 1996), was irrelevant to his agenda.

There follows a final pair of narrative chapters (*HB* 64, 65), structured around what is essentially a king-list for Northumbria, but with additional information. The author's attempts at synchronization seem less than successful (Dumville 1986), with, for example, Cadwaladr's death inserted into Oswiu's reign, apparently on the assumption that his death from the plague should be placed in the great plague years of the 660s, as recorded by Bede. The *Annales Cambriae* placed his death in 682 (p. 210), although that need be little more accurate. The central, and novel, feature of these final, historical passages is the author's unprecedented portrayal of British disasters. This is a clear reversal of his policy hitherto and is the more interesting for that. We have, therefore, the destruction of Cadwallon, *regem Guenedotae regionis*, 'with a great slaughter of his army', by Oswald. This accords considerable kudos to the royal saint of Northumbria, so may perhaps have been intended to once again make connections with the current Northumbrian court of the long-lived King Eanred (*c.* 811–40). There follows the death of Cadwaladr, putatively in Oswiu's reign, and the deaths of the British kings with Penda at *campo Gai*. From the perspective of Gwynedd, this last is mitigated by King Cadafael's escape the night before, so is damaging only to the other dynasties and kingdoms represented in this campaign.

Much seems to hang on the construction of the last figure discussed, at the end of chapter 65. This was Penda of the Mercians (d. 655), whose appearance here breaks the chronological sequence which had to this point structured the text, being interpolated after Ecgfrith's death in 685. Earlier references to the Mercian king make it quite clear that the author knew his floruit, even though he credited the king with a mere ten regnal years and so set considerable problems for scholars seeking to construct the history of Mercia in the early seventh century (e.g. Brooks 1989). His portrayal at this point was, therefore, both intentional and purposeful, for closing his historical narrative with Penda arguably offered considerable advantages to the author. He highlighted Bede's several references to his killing of Christian kings, claiming that he achieved this *per dolum* ('through guile', which harks back to his vision of Hengist), and naming both Anna of the East Angles and Oswald of the Northumbrians, whom he here termed *sanctus*. More particularly, he highlighted Penda's famed paganism:

> *ipse victor fuit per diabolicam artem. Non erat baptizatus et nunquam Deo credidit.*

> he was himself the victor through devilish art. He was not baptised and never believed in God.

The audience of the *Historia* was left, therefore, with a damning image of the only Mercian king to be discussed in any detail in this work, the brother of Eobba and son of Pybba. His reputation was developed and exploited so as to undermine the authority of the Mercian dynasty *in toto*, as provided by the author in chapter 60 down to Offa's son Ecgfrith, which was derived in all its branches from Pybba via his various sons. The author was, therefore, closing his historical narrative with a portrayal of the Mercians as represented by the iconic pagan, Penda, so as enemies of God and of all Christians, their kings ensnared by the devil himself. His repetition of *victor* at this point may serve to remind his audience of the opposition between his victorious Christian exemplars, the angel Victor and the Britons Patrick and Arthur, and the equally victorious but pagan and barbarian, hence damned, Penda, using devilish arts and guile, who represents a latter-day Hengist-figure at the head of the Mercians.

Returning to the prophecy of chapter 42, following three great efforts to expel the Saxons by British leaders (Vortimer, Arthur and Urien), a period of

British weakness was destined to follow. During this phase the English 'have seized many peoples and countries in Britain', reaching *paene a mari usque ad mare* ('almost from sea to sea'). The phrase is derived, out of context, from Gildas's great Saxon raid *de mari usque ad mare* (*DEB* xxiv, 1: our author used it again in *HB* 23), but it does well describe the situation under the great Mercian kings of the eighth and early ninth centuries, when English armies were raiding deep into Gwynedd itself. The strength of the great, Mercian white worm was not, however, God-given, but derived from Satan, which crucially left intact British claims to be a people of the Lord in the present.

It was also apparent to the court of Gwynedd in the present that Mercian *imperium* was unwelcome to other peoples within England, who might be considered potential allies to Gwynedd in the 820s. Wessex is passed over in silence, perhaps because of Egberht's pretensions to himself become the ruler of Mercia as much as on account of his current claims to overlordship in Wales. There is, as suggested earlier, some evidence of hostilities between Northumbria and Mercia within the author's probable lifetime. This perhaps contextualizes his several attempts to make connections with Northumbrian figures and even recognize them as fellow Christians: hence his claims for their primary baptism by the Britons; the Irish-converted Oswald's military prowess and sanctity; Oswiu's British marriage and destruction of the diabolical Penda; and Cuthbert's holiness. The East Anglian victory over Beornwulf of Mercia in 825, in which he died, may similarly have suggested that King Anna, who was well known at this date as the father of a troop of saintly daughters and patron of the Irish St Fursa, as well as a royal saint in his own right, might to advantage be featured in this text as a victim of the Mercians. The text does, therefore, make some effort to differentiate the Mercians from other English peoples, apparently for contemporary political purposes. In this respect, it is far more subtle in its approach to contemporary ethnicity than Bede's *Historia Ecclesiastica*, which notoriously treats all Britons as one people within a providential context.

The historical narrative of the *Historia* ends with a final *computus* (66), which places the key events to have affected Britain in a universal chronological context:

> Vortigern, however, held empire in Britain from the consulships of Theodosius and Valentinian [425], and in his fourth regnal year the Saxons came to Britain, in the consulship of Felix and Taurus [428], in the 400th year from the incarnation of our Lord Jesus Christ. From the year when the Saxons came to Britain and Vortigern received them even to [the consulships of] Decius and Valerian are 69 years.

At this point of closure, the author emphasized the centrality of the arrival of the Saxons and Vortigern's personal responsibility therefore within his construct of British history. By making this occur in Vortigern's fourth regnal year, he made one further implicit connection with the present, which would seem to have been Merfyn's fourth regnal year. Furthermore, he suggested that the Saxons had, to date, resided in Britain for 400 years, having arrived in the 400th year from the incarnation (arguably a mistake for 'the passion'). Such calculations certainly suggest that he had in mind prophecies concerning the duration of their stay, comparable to the example referred to by Gildas (*DEB* xxiii, 3), which alluded to 300 years, and the view that the time for their expulsion was at hand. Merfyn was presumably the figure to achieve this end.

## CONCLUSIONS

The *Historia Brittonum* was written within a political context which was conditioned by recent Mercian attempts at conquest in Wales. Its overriding purpose was to construct a salvation history for the Britons in both moral and political terms, capable of underpinning the contemporary positioning of King Merfyn's court. It was written against the Mercians, and in support of the continuing existence of a separate British people on whom God would confer ultimate victory. To this end, the British were construed as a people of the Lord, with a series of virtuous exemplars, both clerical and martial, developed in support of the moral positioning and valorous nature of their race, against blueprints derived from the Bible and elsewhere. In important respects, this message was constructed against the received wisdom derived from Gildas's earlier work. This was a text written to establish and reinforce a new group identity, therefore, with Merfyn at the head of a united people and positioned as a potential, national messiah within a tradition which stretched back to Cunedda, Vortimer, Arthur and Urien. In pursuit of this objective, the author adopted a variety of rhetorical strategies (see Smith 1999: 57ff.), including claims of genealogical descent for the Britons from heroic or divine ancestors, as well as cultural and ideological descent within the Roman and Romano-Judaic traditions. By so doing, he sought to define the 'British people', both within and without Wales, as a single filiation of interrelated kin groups, whose shared past featured a collectively owned golden age of heroic achievements capable of repetition, under appropriate leadership, in the present and near future.

At the same time, the Anglo-Saxons in the distant past were portrayed as a people without moral status, thus reinforcing Gildas's vision of them: they were outside of the Christian community and descended from pagan gods; they lacked courage and fortitude, and their successes were explicable by reference to their guile and Vortigern's wickedness, as much as God's over-arching design. By this portrayal, the author was seeking to reverse the ideological stance adopted by Bede, who constructed the English as a courageous people in the eye of the Lord, even when still pagan, and the Britons as 'detested by God and man alike'. That ideology had sustained the expansion of Anglo-Saxon

England at the expense of its British neighbours during the eighth century. Now, in the ninth, the author of the *Historia Brittonum* proposed a very different scenario, a very different position for both *gentes* within providential history and a very different outcome as to control of Britain. In the recent past, however, his strictures were reserved primarily for the Mercian dynasty, to which end Penda was particularly singled out as satanic. There is a real effort in the latter part of the text particularly to construct bridges between the Britons and the Northumbrians, and to recognize too the legitimacy of East Anglian Christianity, which arguably reflect recent conflicts between both these peoples and Mercia. Indeed, the death of Beornwulf of Mercia in 825 at the hands of the East Angles was arguably critical to the positioning of the *Historia* in 829–30.

The author was also making specific claims on behalf of the court of Merfyn of Gwynedd *vis-à-vis* his rivals. He took several opportunities to bolster the military reputation of this specific people and its past rulers and to claim for them a position of leadership among the Britons. He deliberately devalued the moral authority of neighbouring kingships, with a particular emphasis on the powerful and well established kingship of Powys, which we can therefore assume was considered the main external competitor to Merfyn among the northern Welsh. Hywel, his predecessor and dynastic opponent, had been connected with Rhos, while Merfyn represented the branch of the royal family more closely associated with Anglesey. Derogatory remarks concerning Powys therefore had a context both in terms of competition between Merfyn and Cyngen and between the two rival branches of the dynasty which had earlier contested power in Gwynedd. Merfyn's putative marriage into the dynasty of Powys (to Nest, sister of King Cyngen) makes little impact on the rhetoric of this text, although it does reveal a pragmatic attitude among the dynasts themselves, despite the rhetoric of their supporters.

This was, therefore, a history written in pursuit of present, political and ideological concerns. The extent to which such purposes dominate the text becomes clear on close examination, passage by passage. This fact is nowhere more evident than in the single, extended passage dealing with Arthur and it must be stressed that this narrative provides no insights capable of reconstructing a 'real' contribution to early British history. This author's Arthur was first and foremost a biblical construct, developed as a British Joshua and coupled with Patrick as a type of Moses, as a means of envisaging a British golden age post-Vortigern, under God's guiding hand. His status and the terms used in his definition were conditioned by that purpose and his battle-list was highly contrived, arguably by the author himself, from various sources, none of which were demonstrably early or authoritative. The idea for the name almost certainly came from the folkloric and legendary figure already known to the author before he began this composition, probably before he removed to the court of Merfyn Frych, which he had experienced directly in the Upper Wye Valley.

To pursue the issue of contested histories, however, we need to turn, if only briefly, to the only other British text which certainly derives from this generation, that inscribed on the Pillar of Eliseg.

## THE PILLAR OF ELISEG

As already noted, the Pillar of Eliseg is a round shaft which has given its name to Valle Crucis, in which it is erected, near Llangollen (Figures 24, 25). It now stands at about 2.12m, following its resurrection in 1779, but was arguably some 3.66m prior to its being thrown down and broken as a deliberate act of iconoclasm in the seventeenth century (Macalister 1935). The inscription was recorded by Edward Lhwyd in a letter to the Rev. Dr Mill, principal of Edmund Hall, Oxford, written on 14 September 1696, following observation of the monument while still in pieces. This reading has since been generally confirmed by Macalister (1922), so far as is possible given that the last sixteen lines are now missing, and is that printed by Nash-Williams (1938, 1950: 123). The text is translated as follows (based on Howlett 1998: 29–30):

> † Concenn son of Cattell, Cattell
> son of Brohcmail, Brohcmail son
> of Eliseg, Eliseg son of Guoillauc
> † Concenn therefore great-grandson of Eliseg
> built this stone for his own great-grandfather Eliseg
> † It is Eliseg who annexed the inheritance of Powys . . .
> from the hand of Catem through his own forces
> from the power of the English
> both with his sword and by fire
> † Whosoever shall read this hand-inscribed text
> let him give a blessing on the soul of Eliseg
> † It is Concenn who attached 1100 yokes [of land] with his own hand
> which to his own kingdom of Powys formerly belonged
> and in his presence . . . mountain
> the monarchy . . . greatest of Britain
> Concenn, Pascent, Maun Annan
>
> . . .
>
> † Britu, moreover, [was] the son of Guorthigirn
> whom Germanus blessed
> and whom Severa bore to him, the daughter of King Maximus,
> who slew the king of the Romans.
> † Conmarch painted this writing
> at the command of his King Concenn
> † The blessing of the Lord [be] upon Concenn
> and his own in his whole family

and upon all the land of Powys
until the Day of Judgement. Amen.

Even recognizing the problems of decipherment, which are ultimately insoluble, this inscription provides us with another and very different vision of the past, from the perspective of Powys as opposed to Gwynedd. Gwynedd's ultimate victory in the dynastic competition between these two gave its court the greater opportunity to reconfigure the history of the Britons according to its own agenda and in its own image. However, that does not mean that it was either any more accurate or meaningful in the early ninth century.

What the Pillar of Eliseg offers, therefore, is an opportunity to contrast passages in the *Historia Brittonum* with a near-contemporary statement of the history of the ruling dynasty of Powys. Cyngen (*Concenn*) had set down his own genealogical descent from Eliseg, and paid tribute to his great-grandfather's martial achievements against the English. He then seems to have set out his own claim for similar achievements (but the text is partly illegible). These passages offer an image of periodically effective military leadership within Powys over the previous fifty to eighty years, and up to the present, which is to be credited to the royal dynasty. This picture is very different to that found in the *Historia Brittonum*, wherein the recent record of the dynasty is damned by omission.

More particularly, Vortigern is treated with great honour in this text, as a figure of extraordinary repute to whom the current generation look back with proper reverence. The contrast is so extreme as to imply that some causal connection between this exceptionally lengthy inscription and the *Historia* seems very possible. Here, Vortigern was the founder of the dynasty and married to Severa, the daughter of the great Magnus Maximus, to whom most Welsh dynasties later looked for authority as both the last Roman emperor and, paradoxically, the putatively British figure who finally expelled the Romans from Britain: see for example, the Harleian genealogy of Dyfed's kings, in which *Maxim Guletic* appears twenty-three generations above the mid- to late tenth-century Owain map Elen. Instead of his having a son fathered incestuously on his own daughter, as *per* the *Historia*, herein Vortigern's prestigious marriage produced Britu. We can either equate this figure with Britto in the *Historia Brittonum*, and thus read him as an eponym for the Britons, or with Faustus, given the Germanus connection in both texts (as suggested by Howlett 1998: 32). Whichever, Britu's parentage combines the authority of the great warrior-emperor Magnus Maximus and the British 'emperor' Vortigern, without any hint of incest or other moral irregularity. These were, therefore, being constructed as the fathers of a Powys-centric British nation. If the name Maun was intended to represent the young Patrick, his moral authority was also being arrogated by the dynasty to itself.

This is a powerful series of claims, which combine to demand for Powys and Cyngen's own dynasty a central role in the genesis of the post-Roman,

British race. At the same time it contests the version of history to be found in the *Historia Brittonum*, honouring the figure of Vortigern and according him a special and prestigious place in the history of Powys and of Britain. Just as the *Historia* was designed to sustain and glorify the king of Gwynedd in the present, so too was this much shorter but more dramatic text intended to glorify king Cyngen, by reference to his ancestors and their achievements as well as his own.

There is a case for supposing that the cross with this inscription was originally erected over the tomb of Eliseg himself. Resurrection of the stone in 1779 was accompanied by some exploration of the mound on which it had stood, and a near contemporary account exists (Nash-Williams 1938). A slab-constructed and covered grave was excavated, beneath a layer of large pebble-stones, within which lay the disarticulated bones of what seems to have been a single male burial. The surviving description asserts that: 'there was a large piece of silver coin found in the coffin, which was kept; but that the skull was gilded to preserve it, and was then deposited with its kindred bones'. The coin, even more than the pebbles, imply a post-Roman rather than a prehistoric burial.

That Mercian pressure over recent decades had been the principal feature of Welsh political life in the 820s has already been suggested. The Pillar of Eliseg provides further evidence not just of Welsh contention of territory (see earlier, p. 108) but more particularly the desire to proclaim particular Welsh claims and the authority on which those claims were based. This inscription is, therefore, an ideological statement by a king of Powys. He sought to advertise his own achievements and contextualize them by reference to those of his ancestors, and his authority alongside theirs, in defence of his own position as king in this vulnerable, marcher kingship, where Mercian attacks had arguably been most common and heaviest. It is also a statement about the relative authority of Cyngen's own forebears, the founding fathers of his dynasty, and the status of that dynasty within the context of political and dynastic rivalry with Merfyn of Powys.

It is clear from the accounts in both the *Historia Brittonum* and the Pillar of Eliseg that Vortigern was, in the early ninth century, believed in both Gwynedd and Powys to have had a founding role in the dynasty of Powys. From that point, the very different current needs of the two authors and their respective audiences required very different treatment. The one damns him as the accursed ruler with sole responsibility for the *adventus Saxonum*, the other honours him as a great figure capable of lending status and authority to his putative descendants in the present. That these accounts are both driven, and dominated, by the current agendas of their authors, and more particularly their patrons, underlines the unreliability of either and both as windows on the career of a 'real', historical Vortigern. Their truths are ninth-century truths, therefore, which are potentially lies when transposed to the fifth or sixth centuries.

The Arthur of the *Historia Brittonum* is a casualty of this same comparison, since he is a figure who was developed from sources of negligible 'historical' value, for reasons of politics and ideology which are all too apparent. It is dangerous to view the *Historia Brittonum* as history at all, if that term is understood today as an attempt to record past events. This text simply does not lend itself to interrogation for this purpose. Neither the *Historia* nor the Pillar of Eliseg has anything to tell us about the sub-Roman period. However, both offer crucial insights into the political and ideological positioning of the northern Welsh élites in the early decades of the ninth century, and how they thought to utilize the past in pursuit of power for particular groups in the present.

# CHAPTER IV

# TEXT IN CONTEXT

## The *Annales Cambriae c.* 954

———— •◆• ————

> The battle of Badon, in which Arthur carried the cross of our Lord
> Jesus Christ for three days and three nights on his shoulders and the
> Britons were the victors.
>
> 

*Annales Cambriae*, year 72 [AD 516]

The *Annales Cambriae* is the second, Latin text written in Wales to refer to
Arthur, around a century and a quarter after the *Historia* had been written.
Our understanding of its authorship, and of how Arthur and other figures
were constructed within it, necessarily begins with an exploration of the
politics, the ideological environment and the cultural world in which it was
written and to which its author reacted. There were many differences between
the world of the *Annales* and that in which the *Historia* had been conceived:
for example, the *Annales* were written in the middle of the Viking Age, in the
context of a newly unified Anglo-Saxon England, and in Dyfed as opposed to
Gwynedd. All these factors and more had important implications, indirectly
at least, for the author's agenda in the later text, hence on the way that Arthur
would be portrayed. A second feature of the period is the increasing quantity
of vernacular literature which has survived, when compared with earlier
centuries, which purportedly reflects the world in which it was written. This
chapter will begin, therefore, with an overview of political developments in
Wales and England and move towards a more detailed examination of the
*Annales* via an exploration of other literature of relevance to our discussion
of the development of Arthur.

It will also be argued that the author of the *Annales* was very conscious of
the *Historia Brittonum*, which emerges as an influential text during the
following century, even despite the changing political agenda. Its author
was the spokesperson of a political community in North Wales which was
concerned more than anything else to reinforce the credibility of the jejune
second dynasty of Gwynedd. On recent experience, the foremost threat in
829–30 was the prospect of renewed Mercian expansion, and it was that threat,
therefore, which his work particularly contested. In practice, the collapse of
Mercian hegemony and the increasing intervention of Viking forces in insular

affairs from the mid-830s onwards rendered the threat of Mercian conquests in Wales less than for a century previously. However, the danger of English intervention remained significant, outside particular periods when the Vikings or internal discord absorbed the energies of its rulers. The *Historia* retained, therefore, its relevance as a national, providential history for the Britons, written against the English. It served to raise awareness of 'Britishness' and to claim a special place within the history of salvation for the Britons as a people. It sought too to add value to group membership, and to lay a claim on the future, by offering a collective past and the prospect of survival and even ultimate victory *vis-à-vis* the English in Britain. It also retained its message within a Welsh context, as an advertisement for the superior legitimacy and authority of the dynasty of Gwynedd. Its very authorship suggests a degree of political sophistication at the court of Merfyn Frych, capable of engaging with the writing of history as an instrument of power. There is little to suggest that anything directly comparable was occurring elsewhere in Wales or England at that date, although Wessex obviously caught up under Alfred, two generations later.

The *Historia* certainly survived and eventually proved popular. There is all too little evidence as to how quickly or widely it was disseminated before the eleventh century, but it does seem to have been read in southern Welsh monasteries within about half a century of its composition. It could be argued that the expansion of the dynasty of Gwynedd across large parts of Wales was legitimized and aided by the messages offered by the *Historia*, in which case that, in turn, perhaps led to its wider circulation.

## ENGLAND, WALES AND THE VIKINGS

Although the earliest known Scandinavian raids on southern Britain were in the 790s, it was only during the 830s that these began to impact to a large extent on the Anglo-Saxon kingdoms. Thereafter, Viking armies increasingly absorbed the energies of the English and, from the 860s to the 890s, even the survival of Anglo-Saxon kingship was in question. Their intervention created new opportunities for British élites, who were on occasion now freer than hitherto to pursue their own agendas. They might seek to join with the Vikings to attack and even destroy the English enemy, they might join with the Christian English against the heathen, or they might do neither and pursue very different agendas of their own outside the over-arching political and racial rhetoric of the day.

In practice, it is clear that the British were divided as to how to react, as one might expect from the diversity of competing kingships and their local histories. On the whole, kings, leading families and religious communities pursued their own immediate political interests, seeking support from, and alliance with both Vikings and Anglo-Saxons as appropriate. However, few

Welsh kingships during this period successfully rid themselves of the influence of one or other of the Vikings or the English for long, and the ninth and tenth centuries can perhaps, in this context, be summarized as a struggle between Vikings and Anglo-Saxons for supremacy among the Britons (W. Davies 1990).

Both the West Saxons and Mercians sought to retain political influence in Wales and prevent the Welsh allying with the Vikings. Egberht's son, Æthelwulf, joined with Burgred of Mercia in 853 to constrain the Welsh to acknowledge Mercian superiority by force of arms. The details are unclear but an invasion is indicated by Asser's passing reference to devastation. Burgred was forced out of England by the Vikings in 874, and this presumably gave the Welsh greater political freedom, since Danish armies in England rarely seem to have attacked their territories (the campaign of 894 being the exception). However, they were increasingly the object of damaging raids by Viking fleets operating principally from Dublin around the Irish Sea coasts, from the 850s onwards. Asser claimed (Stevenson 1904; trans. by Keynes and Lapidge 1983, chap. 54) that a Scandinavian fleet which attacked Devon in 878 had overwintered in Dyfed, 'slaughtering many of the Christians there', and this was just one of many occasions during the ninth and tenth centuries when St David's was attacked. The western promontaries and coasts of Wales were highly vunerable to sea-borne attacks and seem to have suffered considerable damage, particularly over the mid-ninth and later tenth centuries (W. Davies 1982, 1990). The rate of activity is to an extent reflected in the common occurrence of Viking place-names along the coasts of Wales (W. Davies 1982: 118).

The principal political process within Wales which impacted directly on authorship of the *Annales* was the aggressive acquisitiveness of Merfyn's son Rhodri, often termed 'Mawr' – 'the Great' (844–77), and his immediate descendants. Rhodri had presumably been named after his maternal ancestor in the eighth century, as part of Merfyn's efforts to establish his family as legitimate kings in the dominant line. His reign and that of his son Anarawd were particularly successful, with the acquisition of both Ceredigion (in 872) and Powys (perhaps by the late 850s, certainly by the 880s: Figure 27). Rhodri's grandson Hywel Dda ('the Good') obtained Dyfed, apparently by exploiting a strategic marriage, in 904, and eventually (942–50) secured control of Gwynedd and Powys as well. It may be that the *Historia's* devaluation of the legitimacy of rival dynasties privileged the expansionism and the self-confidence of Merfyn's successors, some of whom came closer than any earlier king known to history to a unitary kingship of the Welsh. This rapid expansion of the dynasty was accompanied by new military achievements: Rhodri defeated the Danes under Gorm in 856, although he was temporarily driven out in 877 and was, according to the *Annales Cambriae*, killed by 'the Saxons' (presumably Ceolwulf II of the Mercians (874–9)), but was 'avenged by God' via his sons at the Battle of Conwy in 880. Both he and his sons attacked the southern Welsh kingdoms repeatedly and Anarawd allied himself

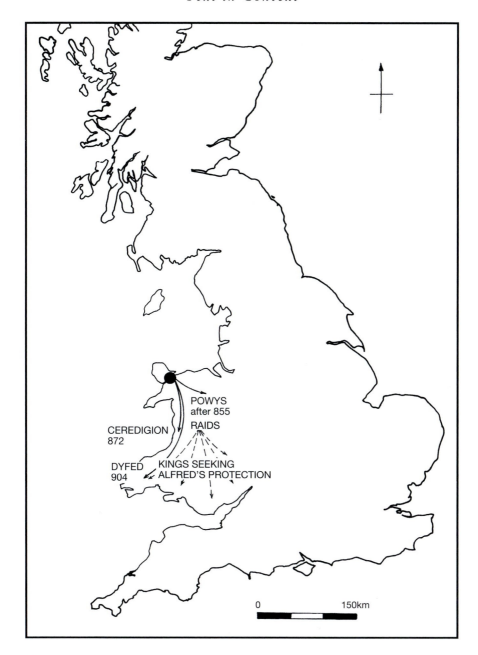

**Figure 27** The expansion of the second dynasty of Gwynedd

with the Danish kingdom of York at some point between 878 and *c.* 885, against Alfred's son-in-law Æthelræd of Mercia. Gwynedd's kings had become a more significant force within insular politics than at any point since the heady days of Cadwallon in the 630s and could, with justification, pose as national leaders of the British people, even despite widespread opposition.

Mercian attempts to maintain influence in eastern and northern Wales were certainly on occasion a real threat. Rhodri's death, along with his son, at the hands of the English has already been noted and Ealdorman Æthelræd certainly sought to exercise hegemony over the central and northern Welsh in the late ninth century. War as far west as the Conwy suggests that Powys was open to English armies at this date, and English influence seems to have spread widely. A fragment of a ninth-century cylindrical cross shaft at Llanrhaeadr-ym-Mochnant (near Oswestry) is of Mercian type, as is the Pillar of Eliseg, of course (earlier, Figures 24 and 25). In the same church, a slab cross bears the incomplete legend † COCOM/FILIU/EDELSTAN-. Readings are contested but it arguably translates as 'The cross of Gwgan son of Æthelstan' (Ralegh Radford and Hemp 1957). The latter is clearly the OE personal name, which was presumably borne in this instance by a member of the local aristocracy in the tenth or eleventh centuries, and other English names (particularly Edwin) were also adopted by Welsh families. There is similarly an Anglo-Scandinavian style, extended wheel-head cross (known as the *Maen Achwyfan*) at Whitford, near Holywell (Figure 28), and another at Penmon, Anglesey. All these instances imply English or Anglo-Scandinavian cultural penetration during the Viking Age, which reflects the growing integration of Wales with the rest of southern Britain.

Æthelræd's widow, the Lady Æthelflæd, built several *burhs* in the West Midlands. In 916 she 'sent an army into Wales and destroyed *Brecenanmere* [arguably the crannog on Llan-gors Lake in Brycheiniog], and captured the king's wife and 33 other people', apparently in retribution for the killing of the otherwise unknown Abbot Egberht a few days earlier (Figure 29). While the Mercian threat of total conquest had receded, therefore, military intervention and efforts to enforce political hegemony continued. Æthelflæd died as superior ruler of northern and central Wales, so may well have been in receipt of tribute as well as military support and a degree of deference from its kings.

## HEROIC POETRY

In this context, it is important to note that several Welsh courts were arguably patronizing heroic saga poetry in the vernacular, at around this date. The chronology of the earliest poetry is contested but the genre had already begun to be recognized in Gaul by the sixth century (Moisl 1980–2). However, there are grave difficulties of dating poems prior to about the ninth century. The

**Figure 28** The Anglo-Scandinavian style cross at Whitford, near Holywell (courtesy of Clwyd–Powys Archaeological Trust)

**Figure 29** The crannog on Llan-gors Lake in Brycheiniog (courtesy of Clwyd–Powys Archaeological Trust)

problem is compounded by the lateness of most surviving manuscripts. That said, it is generally supposed that the 'poems of Llywarch the Old' (*canu Llywarch Hen*) cycle date from approximately this period. Llywarch Hen was a figure of the northern British heroic age, alongside such characters as Urien of Rheged. Urien occurs in poetry putatively composed by Taliesin, in the *Historia Brittonum* and in tenth-century genealogies, and is therefore normally presumed to have been historical. Llywarch is less securely so and was by this date a figure of legend. It has been suggested that he was created

176

under the patronage of the second dynasty of Gwynedd as a legitimizing ancestor figure (Ford 1970), since he is positioned herein on the borders of Wales, urging on his sons to their deaths against the English. However, that view has received little support to date (Rowland 1990: 8).

If the Llywarch Hen cycle should not be associated with the second dynasty of Gwynedd and their acquisition of Powys in the tenth century, it may be that composition was connected with the court of Brycheiniog around AD 900 (as proposed by Sims-Williams 1993), which was experiencing pressure from two sides, from both Gwynedd and Mercia (as above). This vernacular literary tradition constructed myths of cultural and ideological affiliation by allusion to, and lamentation concerning, the heroic spirit which animated ancestral communities in a past golden age (A. D. Smith 1999: 57ff.). Such had powerful, validating messages in the present, and would have been particularly appropriate at a court keen to underline its own British identity *vis-à-vis* Mercian Angles but at the same time to resist the claims of Merfyn's son or grandsons and their aggressive stance towards England. If the latter were believed to be descended from Llywarch, then his depiction as 'aged, pathetic, impotent and possibly a parricide' (N. J. A. Williams 1978: 264) has obvious propaganda value in the struggle to remain independent of Gwynedd, but this vision depends on somewhat questionable links being credible at this date. The tradition was certainly synthetic and Williams suggested that it was for a time as inclined as the Finn Cycle in Ireland to absorb otherwise independent stories, individuals or incidents.

Rowland (1990: 75–6) has suggested that one of the two groups of poems about Urien may be earlier than the *canu Llywarch*, and the interest in, and characterization of, Urien evident in the *Historia Brittonum* would support the idea of a degree of contemporaneity with the composition of that work. Again, the dating is to an extent speculative, and there are voices still favouring a sixth-century date (Breeze 1997a). However, Rowland suggested that the *Pen Urien* cycle in virtually its surviving form might belong in the late eighth to mid-ninth centuries. These poems would certainly appeal to an audience keen to construct national heroes against the English, with sentiments such as (Rowland 1990: 477–8): 'He [Urien] made of the Bernicians after battle a burden of biers', and, after his death, 'The chief support of Britain has been carried off'. The use of northern heroes within texts constructed in Wales had considerable potential to develop a pan-British, and far more inclusive, vision of 'Britishness' than a literature contained entirely within the Welsh peninsula, and this may well have encouraged the practice. These were nationalistic writings, therefore, of value to particular élites at the time of composition.

Another group of poems often thought to belong to the ninth century features the figure of Cynddylan and his family, who are associated with a series of places in Shropshire, such as the river Tern, Baschurch, the two Ercalls and the Wrekin (*Dinlle Ureconn*: Figure 30). This is the *canu Heledd* ('Song of Heledd') Cycle. The date of composition is again unknown, with opinion

**Figure 30** The Wrekin (*Dinlle Ureconn*) behind Roman Wroxeter: the Brittonic name occurs in poetry associated with Cynddylan and also in the regional people name *Wr(e)ocensæte*

varying from as late as around 1100 (Dumville 1977d) back to the ninth century (Williams 1932; Breeze 1997a) and variously the late ninth or early tenth century, or the mid- to late ninth century (Rowland 1990). The idea behind this group may have come from the *Marwnad Cynddylan* ('Elegy of Cynddylan'), which Rowland has suggested may be a near-contemporary elegy composed shortly after Cynddylan's putative date of death in the mid-seventh century. Such is the hunger for historical source materials for this region at this date that, even with the problems recognized, this poetry is frequently discussed as if relevant to the reconstruction of history in this region in the first half of the seventh century (Kirby 1977; W. Davies 1982: 99–102; Gelling 1992: 72–4; Bassett 2000). However, even the *Marwnad Cynddylan*, which is dated early on linguistic grounds, contains detail which might imply a rather later date of composition, at least in the form which survives. Reference, therefore, to an archbishop suggests familiarity with Lichfield as an archdiocese post-787 and the slaughter of 'book-clutching monks' may owe more to Bede's description, in 731, of the Battle of Chester than some otherwise unknown massacre at Wall or Lichfield. Even in other respects, the testimony of this poetry conflicts with other sources (e.g. Williams 1932), which implies that it does not offer a reliable version of early seventh-century events in this area. Rather, the author seems to have had little knowledge of the period (Rowland 1990), beyond a level of awareness of, for example, Penda and the battle of *Cogwy* present in the *Historia Brittonum* (*HB* 65). While some of the place-names used are probably authentically Welsh, others are English. Overall, it is safer to suppose that this was a landscape with which the poet was familiar *c.* 900, looking back on the disasters which befell the Welsh at Offa's hands, which has been used as a backdrop for action inserted for rhetorical reasons into the heroic past.

This poetry should be disallowed, therefore, as a source for the seventh century. Far more valuable is the insight to northern Welsh political thinking at the time of composition, even if that cannot be defined as rigorously as we might wish. In this context, eulogy in the vernacular of heroic British leaders in parts of Shropshire lost to Mercian arms in the seventh century should arguably be viewed in the context of the contest between Gwynedd and Mercia in the present for control of Powys and the north-west Midlands. In other words, the underlying message of these well crafted poems is a claim to current English territory on behalf of Merfyn's descendants.

By writing an heroic British history into a part of the 'middle band' of Britain (see Figure 7 earlier), these poems reclaim it for the British past, thus potentially for a British future. The same process can be seen elsewhere in other poorly dated Welsh literature, with reference to places such as Gloucester and Glastonbury (particularly in the Triads: Bromwich 1961) as ancient British centres. Again, therefore, the principal theme of this literary output should be interpreted in a much later context than its putative subject, which was merely a convenient vehicle for current issues and a type of title deed.

It is worth noting that none of these three groups of poems certainly refer to Arthur, although there is some doubt whether or not the *canu Heledd* contains a single Arthurian reference (Rowland 1990: 186, note 4, decides against). This is arguably no accident, given that it ties in with the comparative scarcity of Arthurian references in early Welsh poetry more generally (Sims-Williams 1991). No 'Arthurian' saga poems *certainly* predate Geoffrey of Monmouth's *Historia* (1130s), although that does not automatically mean that none existed, nor that all were derivative of his construct of Arthur (Jackson 1959b). They are, however, even then somewhat scarce, occurring principally in the Black Book of Carmarthen (mid-thirteenth century) and the *Book of Taliesin* (early fourteenth century) but absent from other early collections. As Sims-Williams remarks, this scarcity within early horizons does suggest that Arthur had not attained, in the Welsh verse of the central Middle Ages, the dominant position he was later to achieve. His absence should not, therefore, surprise us in this intellectual climate. Arthurian poems which might be this early are very different in type, belonging to the world of magic and mythology. A typical example generally dated around 900 is *Preiddiau Annwn* ('The Spoils of the Otherworld'), in which Arthur carried off a great cauldron from the 'Otherworld' in his ship *Prydwen*. The story resurfaces in *Culhwch and Olwen, c.* 1100, with the 'Otherworld' now metamorphosed into Ireland.

The one historicized Arthur-figure that was certainly already accessible before 900 was the Joshua/Christ type of warrior offered as a national hero in the *Historia Brittonum*. If the central, anti-English, nationalist agenda had been hijacked via this work by the second dynasty of Gwynedd, then this Arthur may well have seemed inappropriate for inclusion in these cycles: the Llywarch Hen poems arguably belong in a context resistant towards Gwynedd – so also to its new political icons; if Urien was being developed independently as a national hero of the Old North in Wales in the late eighth to early ninth centuries, it was perhaps necessary that he be free-standing and not overshadowed by the Arthurian construct within the *Historia*, within which he had in any case an honourable position as a British hero of value equal to Vortimer and Arthur; the *canu Heledd* cycle was located on the English borders, where it might have been politically dangerous to establish a heroic cult of Arthur capable of being captured in the interests of Powysian separatism, if such was then still a potential political force. Such hypotheses are incapable of real testing, of course, but they do serve to remind us that Arthur was by no means the automatic British hero figure in any historicized context at this date. Rather, he remained, throughout the later ninth and early tenth century, a very particular construct, arguably borrowed from folkloric sources, within a Gwynedd-centric and biblically framed Latin text, where he appeared for typological purposes.

## *Y GODODDIN*

An example of poetry which does make reference to Arthur is the collection of elegiac stanzas known today as *Y Gododdin* ('The Gododdin'). This survives in two versions, which were themselves composed at different dates, both written in a single Welsh vernacular manuscript of the second half of the thirteenth century, known as the *Book of Aneirin*. To be precise, only the first version (A) is explicitly connected with the title, since the second has been appended to it by a second hand. The two texts are significantly different and not just variants one on the other, despite considerable common material which most scholars have assumed points back to a single original (Hehir 1988). The text has been published (Williams 1938) and translated (Jackson 1969; Jarman 1988: it is Jackson's numbering of verses which is used here, but Jarman's line numbers, so as to facilitate reference to either edition), and ingenious attempts made to reconstruct an 'original' text (Koch 1997; but see Isaac 1999).

There remains a real possibility of initial composition of *Y Gododdin* in the mid- to late sixth or seventh centuries (Cessford 1997, opts for 550–640; Breeze 1997a: 13–20 provides an elegant case for the sixth or seventh centuries; Dumville 1988 suggests a date for the central events, but not composition, *c.* 540). However, it is hazardous to assume that any single passage or phrase can definitely be dated so early. The depth and complexity of the textual history likely to underlie particularly the 'A' text, which seems to derive from the later source of the two, is the key factor in this caution. Even the 'B' text, which is traditionally thought to derive from a ninth-century source, was probably copied from a text no earlier than the tenth century (Dumville 1977d; Isaac 1999), although a tentative case has been made for a common tradition for the two versions in the seventh century in the north, following which divergence might have occurred due to the separation of the textual traditions between northern Britain and Wales (Charles-Edwards 1978, but see the critical review in Dumville 1988). *Y Gododdin* likewise reflects a variety of interactions with other literature at various stages in its development. The *Moliant Cadwallon*, for example, alludes to 'the destruction (or grief) of Catraeth, great and famous' (Jarman 1988), which suggests that the subject of *Y Gododdin* was known to the author of that work at some unknown date in or after the early seventh century (Rowland suggests the tenth century). It was certainly known in southern Powys by the late twelfth century (Williams 1972a) but that does not take us far back beyond the date of composition of the extant copies. It is quite possible that the 'original' was composed in the British North but then went through any number of reformulations during later centuries.

The *Gododdin* cannot, therefore, be treated at face value as an historical source for a particular military campaign launched against *Catraeth* (which may or may not represent modern Catterick) from Edinburgh (Jackson 1969). It can, however, be explored as a repository of British ideology in the early to central Middle Ages, capable of delivering valuable meaning to a variety of different audiences, a flexible vehicle, as well, which has been adjusted repeatedly to the needs of this task.

Both texts are collections of eulogistic elegies, mourning dead heroes but celebrating their achievements, in terms which have been described as 'intricate, witty, skilful and exciting' (Hehir 1988: 79). The heroes are Britons, representative of several localities, although most are attributed to Gododdin in the Lothians. Collectively they were styled *Brython*, in opposition to an enemy variously termed *Deifr* or *Dewr* (Deira or Deirans), *Brynaich* (Bernicia, but only in text A) or collectively *Lloegrwys* or *Saeson* (Angles or Saxons). Although *lloegr* can mean any neighbouring people (Cessford 1997), the 'Englishness' of the historical Deirans and their kings was so well established in Wales in the central Middle Ages that we can probably assume that this enemy was then at least assumed to be English. The heroes of the poems were, therefore, positioned or perhaps later repositioned within a very specific ethnicity which was constructed in large part in opposition to 'Englishness' from a viewpoint which lay inside the 'British' north in the heroic age.

Many of the heroes were distinguished by high birth and lineage, and claims concerning their lordliness and nobility, which contrast with the 'mongrel' characterization of the enemy (as B19), who were anonymous and generally denied any respect or status in this regard. Away from the battle-field, the emphasis is on aristocratic courtliness, meekness and gentleness, and shyness in front of women, although there is also frequent reference to the champion's portion and boasts at the feast, which then had to be fulfilled.

Above all else, the two most important qualities, which are both emphasized and praised, are martial prowess and loyalty to the leader and patron. This emerges in various forms, but bravery in battle, reliability as a comrade, effective use of weapons, the number of the enemy lain low, earning one's mead, constancy and stubbornness in the face of attack and fierceness are all held up as exemplary qualities. Many warriors are praised metaphorically, by reference to the attributes of the boar, the serpent, the wolf, the lion and the bull, and the currency of this language is sustained by the several personal names which derive from fierce animals, such as the 'bear-hound', *Erthgi*, in A14.

In general, therefore, this material defines and advertises the value-system of an aristocratic audience, their code of honour and their concern to achieve fame and avoid public shame (Jackson 1969). The poem praises the *comitatus* of Mynyddog, Lord of Edinburgh and ruler of Gododdin, both individually and collectively, as willing to die rather than fall short of the promises made to their lord during the year's feasting which he had provided. The presumption of martial honour and military prowess relate to a group of warriors who are drawn from several regional communities, so can be viewed as in a sense representative of the British people as a whole in war against the English.

This emphasis on valour and the honour of the warrior, which is frequently repeated, contests Gildas's vision of an un-warlike and dishonoured people whose cowardice was proverbial. It has much in common with the efforts of the author of the *Historia Brittonum* to construct a martial and heroic past for the Britons. Such would have had a particular relevance to the second dynasty of Gwynedd, who were attempting to establish themselves as lords of men in new areas and attract loyal service from men whose ancestral kin had hitherto looked to other patrons.

It is in the context of the qualities to be praised in a warrior that the name Arthur appears in the *Gododdin*. This occurs in verse B38, which is verse 102 of Jarman's edition (pp. 64–5: his translation follows):

> He charged before three hundred of the finest,
>   He cut down both centre and wing,
> He excelled in the forefront of the noblest host,
> He gave gifts of horses from the herd in winter.
> He fed black ravens on the rampart of a fortress
>   Though he was no Arthur.
> Among the powerful ones in battle,
> In the front rank, Gwawrddur was a palisade.

Jackson's translation differs quite significantly (1969: 112), but not as regards the phrase in which the name 'Arthur' appears.

It is unsustainable to insist on an early date for this reference to Arthur. As Jarman noted (1989–90), the stanza contains some Old Welsh orthographic features alongside a number of later or medieval features, so there is no clear message as to its date of composition. Since the verse does not appear in the 'A' text, it is impossible to tell whether or not it was present in any versions of the collection which predate the separation into the two which survive, but there seems a probability that it did not. However, the phrase is almost identical to that in the elegy to Urfai, two verses earlier, whose advice was heeded 'though his father was no prince' (compare the *Cyn ni bai ef Arthur* of line 972, with *cyn ni bai gwledig* in line 951). This correspondence might encourage some confidence that this is not a very late and isolated interpolation, but present in, say, the ninth or tenth century. Jarman listed this line among possible interpolations in the introduction to his edition (p. lxiv), but that is on the assumption that we have an essentially single-date, early text which has later been altered in various ways. The textual history may well be far more complex than that would imply, with composition effectively occurring over a long period, and Jarman later proposed (1989–90) that it would be hazardous to argue that this line is earlier than around 1100.

The hero of this verse is Gwawrddur, who also occurs in combination with Arthur in poem xxv in the *Book of Taliesin*, but this connection need not be independent of *Y Gododdin*, and is not particularly early (Jackson 1959b). Gwawrddur is being praised primarily in the context of his martial valour in open battle (lines 967–9), and secondarily as a generous gift-giver in a more peaceful context, back home (line 970). There then comes brief mention of Arthur, as the paragon without compare in regard to the slaughter of innumerable warriors in a siege situation. The author then reverts to his earlier vision of open battle, with Gwawrddur depicted as a bulwark of the army in the vanguard.

While the notion of providing food for carrion birds is commonplace, the image of a siege or attack on a fortified site is a rarity in *Y Gododdin*. *Caer* occurs only five times (with a sixth in the related *Gorchan* of *Tudfwlch*), twice as a metaphor for a hero who is staunch in battle and once of Eidyn (Edinburgh). The other instances are that connected with Arthur and one very vague reference in line 456.

It may well, therefore, have been reference to the slaughtering of foes in the context of a siege, which brought Arthur as an exemplar to the author's mind at this point. While we can only hypothesize, the likeliest explanation is that the author knew the *Historia Brittonum*'s chapter (*HB* 56) dealing with Arthur, and could anticipate that his audience knew it as well, since it is here that the allusion would seem to take us. The relevant reference is to Badon Hill where Arthur putatively slew 960 men in one day in a single charge. Gildas famously termed the conflict at Badon an *obsessio* ('a siege': *DEB* xxvi, 1), thus providing the necessary connection between siege warfare and Arthur's reputation. Badon was termed a '*bellum in monte Badonis*' by the author of the *Historia*, and it is reasonable to suppose that this was still understood as a siege. The author was apparently offering a witty aside here, therefore: Gwawrddur was a good man to have beside you on the ramparts but, of course, his achievements would not stand comparison with the sort of numbers of enemies slain postulated of Arthur at Badon in the *Historia*.

Arthur was not the only figure used in the *Gododdin* as an exemplar. The principal such hero is Cynon, who was named as one of three leaders of the host in A18 but who was acclaimed as the pre-eminent warrior in several passages (e.g. lines 210, 383, 390–401, 638). Cynon was, therefore, apparently internal to the matter under discussion, and not, like Arthur, imported from outside the story. There remains the possibility, however, that this figure may have been conflated with the Cynan called upon in the *Armes Prydein* to lead the southern British against the English (Williams (ed.) 1972b: 44–6), who was probably the legendary founder of Brittany, Cynan Meiriadoc. The name appears repeatedly in various dynasties in ninth-century Wales, and it was via Cynan ap Rhodri's daughter, Esyllt, that the second dynasty of Gwynedd claimed descent from the first dynasty (Faral 1929: 50). Promotion of the martial reputation of a Cynan/Cynon in the context of *Y Gododdin* would certainly do the Gwynedd dynasty no harm in the ninth and tenth centuries. Other names famed in Gwynedd's history also occur in *Y Gododdin* or the satellite works which came to be associated with it. A significant example is Cadfan in one such satellite, the *Gorchan Cynfelyn* (Jarman 1988: 74–5) in the line *Wyr Cadfan colofn graid* ('The grandson of Cadfan, pillar of battle'), which arguably alludes rather wittily to the well known inscribed memorial stone erected by King Cadwaladr to his grandfather Cadfan at Llangadwaladr (Nash-Williams 1950: 57). The names Caradog (killed by the English in 798) and Gwriad (Merfyn's father) likewise occur.

There is also the obscure figure of Elffin, who was used as a paragon in the context of combat in the verse celebrating Eithinyn (A38), but who does not otherwise occur in *Y Gododdin* and so may have been external to the warrior group featured in the text. The name recurs in a poem of around 900 called *Dwy Blaid* as a younger contemporary of Urien, in the *Annales Cambriae* (722) and in the fifth Harleian genealogy, in the context of a king of Strathclyde whose floruit is likely to have been in the late seventh century, who was clearly 'known' in some sense in Wales in the second half of the tenth century. In the cases of both Elffin and Arthur, the poet offers virtually nothing beyond the name, but seems to have expected his audience to recognize his meaning for themselves.

Can we identify this Arthur? If this allusion post-dates the *Historia Brittonum*, as seems very likely on the basis of current scholarly opinion, then the search need not continue. Arthur's exploits therein at Mount Badon are entirely appropriate as a source and this must be by far the likeliest explanation. Only if we could be reasonably sure that this reference predates the *Historia* and belongs to the north, need the search be widened. Then the simple answer must be 'no', but there are at least options appropriate to this context. It is possible that a pre-*Historia* poet could have had in mind one of the two northern Arthur figures who did lead armies around 600 (see pp. 76–7), either one of whom *may* have established a particular reputation as a warrior of unusual ferocity. Neither is, however, particularly strong a candidate. Both were arguably Irish, which would seem to rule them out in this context, and in any case we have no independent evidence such as the *Historia* provides that such a reputation actually existed in either case. It is at least as likely, if that is the appropriate context, that the reference is entirely misunderstood and is to some other Arthur of legend or some other now-lost folkloric past at the time of writing.

In summary, therefore, the *Gododdin* was probably circulating, and was arguably being reformulated to some extent, in the ninth/tenth or eleventh centuries. The central messages concerning faithful service and courage in battle have a wide relevance to a martial community but the likeliest context would seem to be within the general framework of the rise to power of the second dynasty of Gwynedd, which, like the legendary Mynyddog of *Y Goddodin*, needed to emphasize the relationship between generous lordship and faithful warriors from numerous British peoples. If the reference to Arthur derives from the *Historia Brittonum*, as seems most likely, then that connection is perhaps strengthened marginally, given its authorship under Merfyn's patronage. In that case, *Y Gododdin* provides no independent evidence capable of supporting claims for Arthur's historicity (as argued, for example, by T. Jones 1964: 12–13), since the *Historia* had already effectively historicized Arthur for its readership. Even if there was no such connection, the allusion must be to a current understanding of Arthur at the time of composition, and, as Padel (1994, 2000) has pointed out, Arthur appears in this text only to not actually appear. With this in mind, Jones's view that reference to Arthur in *Y Gododdin* substantiates the historicity of the Arthur of the *Historia* necessarily falls, but a witty reference to the *Historia* is by far the simplest and safest solution to the conundrum.

# ASSER

Given that the *Annales* was almost certainly written at St David's, the writings of the most famous son of that monastery two generations earlier provide us with a degree of access to the thought-world and political arena in which its anonymous author grew up. This was a world in which political pressures were tending to bring southern Wales into closer contact with Wessex than hitherto, and to construct significant personal relationships between key players on both sides of the Cambro-English divide which were very different from contemporary relations between Gwynedd and England, but it was not without tensions.

Aggression from both Gwynedd and Mercia (and arguably the Vikings as well) in the late ninth century led the southern Welsh kings to turn for protection to King Alfred. Asser, writing in 893 but looking back to the time when he was first summoned by Alfred (*c.* 885), wrote:

> At that time, and for a considerable time before then, all the districts of right-hand [southern] Wales belonged to King Alfred, and still do. That is to say, Hyfaidd, with all the inhabitants of the kingdom of Dyfed, driven by the might of the [?]six sons of Rhodri, had submitted himself to King Alfred's royal overlordship. Likewise Hywel ap Rhys (king of Glywysing) and Brochfael and Ffyrnfael (sons of Meurig and kings of Gwent), driven by the might and tyrannical behaviour of Ealdorman Æthelræd and the Mercians, petitioned King Alfred of their own accord, in order to obtain lordship and protection from him in the face of their enemies. Similarly, Elise ap Tewdwr, king of Brycheiniog, being driven by the might of the sons of Rhodri, sought of his own accord the lordship of King Alfred. And Anarawd ap Rhodri, together with his brothers, . . . came to him in person; when he had been received with honour by the king and accepted as a son in confirmation at the hand of a bishop, and showered with extravagant gifts, he subjected himself with all his people to King Alfred's lordship on the same condition as Æthelræd and the Mercians.
>
> (Keynes and Lapidge 1983: chap. 80)

St David's, too – according to Asser – anticipated considerable benefits from Alfred's patronage of their favourite son, and a degree of protection even from their own local king.

Anarawd had been in alliance with the Danish leadership at York, but that seems to have left him exposed to English pressure, leading him to submit to Alfred. His treatment is directly compared by Asser with Ealdorman Æthelræd's (Alfred's son-in-law), but looks rather more like that afforded the Danish Guthrum of East Anglia, Alfred's godson and earlier rival for power in the south. His political status was presumably in some senses comparable to the kings of York. Gwynedd's kings were, therefore, significant players in the complex insular politics of the late ninth and early tenth centuries. They were feared by other Welsh kingdoms and dynasties, who resisted their claims to be the natural leaders of the Britons against the ancient racial enemy. Rather, aggression from Gwynedd forced other Welsh dynasties to develop closer ties with Wessex. Alfred presumably preferred a divided Wales to the prospect of a hostile block of Welsh territory, which the outright success of Gwynedd's leaders might have brought about. To accommodate the political needs of the southern dynasties, he posed as protector of Christianity within Britain overall, and patron of monasteries among the Britons as well as the Anglo-Saxons. Alfred may even have sought to accommodate Cornish ethnic sensibilities when he gave significant local estates (including Exeter) to Asser, his Welsh secretary, confidant and eventual bishop.

Alfred's ultimate accommodation of Gwynedd, however, rendered his protection far less meaningful in southern Wales, and the region's kings had good reason to be disenchanted with Alfred's leadership in the late 880s. Given the frequency with which Asser offered Welsh translations of English place-names throughout the text, it has been argued that his eulogistic *Life of Alfred* was aimed at a British audience (most recently, Keynes and Lapidge 1983: 41–2, 56). In that case, the *vita* might have been undertaken by Alfred's Welsh associate to recover lost ground in southern Wales. There certainly are signs that Alfred and his immediate advisers sought a pan-Christian alliance within southern Britain, accommodating Britons and Danes, as well as West Saxons and Mercians, under his overall leadership. However, there are alternative visions of Asser's motivation, and the *Life* may equally well have been written for the king himself, his court and his heirs (J. Campbell 1986; Scharer 1996), without a specifically Welsh readership in mind. In this context, Asser's translation of place-names into Welsh need be no more than the affectation of an author keen to demonstrate his own trilingualism on behalf of a patron whom he could confidently assume valued scholarship highly.

Asser was a learned member of the St David's community, whose access to, and knowledge of, (primarily) religious literature was obviously extensive, and whose work was in large part a pastiche of quotations from other works (Scharer 1996). Not surprisingly, there are some indications within his text of the same intellectual background as is identifiable in the *Historia Brittonum*, with which he seems to have been familiar (as argued by Howlett 1998). So, far example, he offered (*Vita* 1) something of an apology for Anglo-Saxon pagan worship in antiquity, such as had provided an opportunity for invective on the same subject in the *Historia* (*HB* 31). Asser extended the identical genealogy back into safe, Christian territory, to Adam. His use of *muliebriter* of the Vikings (*Vita* 18) picks up rather too neatly to be coincidental in its use for Hengist's Saxons in the *Historia*. So too do we find a special interest in connections with Rome, and acceptance of the providential position of the English as a race, both of which foreshadow the vision enshrined in the *Annales Cambriae*, which arguably used a St David's chronicle already in existence when Asser was there.

In many respects, Asser's perceptions were compatible with those of the later work and contrary to the nationalistic agenda of the *Guenedotian Historia*. Like the *Annales*, he was very matter-of-fact about English attacks on the Welsh. He was, however, neither prepared to follow Gildas in denigrating his own people as cowardly, nor Bede in imagining them outside providential history. On the other hand he did not follow the *Historia*

*Brittonum* in claiming for them a particularly impressive martial reputation. Asser's ideological neutrality was not shared by the 'official' vision of English/West Saxon history emanating from Alfred's court. This was embodied in the vernacular chronicle, completed in or by 892, which Asser of course used extensively. This version of the past developed Bede's vision of the Britons as a despised race abandoned by God, to include successive English victories over a cowardly enemy, even though the Old English Bede then entering circulation toned down his hostility to the Britons considerably (Tristram 1999). So, for example, a series of essentially fictitious events were developed for the fifth and sixth centuries, which include the following examples:

> 457: In this year Hengest and his son Æsc fought against the Britons in the place which is called *Creacanford* and killed 4,000 men; and the Britons then deserted Kent and fled with great fear to London.
>
> 473: In this year Hengest and Æsc fought against the Britons and captured countless spoils and the Britons fled from the English as from fire.
>
> 552: In this year Cynric fought against the Britons in the place which is called Salisbury [Old Sarum], and put the Britons to flight.
>
> (Whitelock 1955: 154–6)

These and similar entries may well have seemed necessary to develop the martial self-belief required by the English to resist Viking armies in the present. However, such disregard for British sensibilities can have done little for Anglo-Welsh relations at a time when Alfred's natural allies in southern Wales were already disenchanted with his wider policies. Efforts made in nearer contemporary Chronicle entries to present the Vikings as ravagers of Celtic lands as well as English arguably did too little to appease Welsh sentiment, supposing that the Chronicle's message in some sense reached Wales.

## THE *ARMES PRYDEIN*

In 919, King Edward asserted his direct kingship in Mercia. From that point onwards, the pretext of protection by a West Saxon king from Mercian aggression dissolved and the Welsh kings became little more than satellites of an increasingly powerful and united kingdom of the Anglo-Saxons, which had less need than hitherto to consider their interests or sensibilities. The extent of their absorption into the greater polity is highlighted in the reign of Æthelstan. His early charters include as witnesses Hywel Dda of Dyfed, Idwal of the expanded Gwynedd, Gwriad (possibly of Gwent) and Morgan of Glywysing, alongside several of their kin and the kings of the Strathclyde Britons and the Scots. All were, on occasion at least, in attendance on the English king and at his court. Hywel's name continues to appear well into the 940s and recognition of some sort of primacy in Wales is at least hinted at in his prominent positioning in these witness lists, even on occasion before the English æthelings, which suggests a degree of political sensitivity in England towards Wales, but there were dangers in this increasingly unequal set of relationships that the Welsh kings might be reduced to the status of ealdormen or royal officials. On the admittedly much later authority of William of Malmesbury (Mynors *et al.* 1998: ii, 134, 5–7), Æthelstan reduced the northern Welsh to dependency at Hereford, placed a heavy tribute on them and dictated a new boundary on the Wye. Thereafter, he evicted the Cornish from Exeter, which he refortified, and established the Tamar as their boundary. This was a significant departure from the more diplomatic approach of his grandfather towards the Britons, which reflected his much reduced dependence on their co-operation and heightened ability to coerce.

Æthelstan's dealings with the western Britons fall into the much bigger picture of his attempt to establish himself as the dominant political force in Britain via the seizure of York (927), and campaigns in Scotland (934), in which his Welsh clients participated. His ambitions were contested, however, and brought into being an alliance of the Irish Sea Norse, the Scots and Strathclyde, which he defeated spectacularly at *Brunanburh* in 937.

The obvious omission from this alliance was the Welsh, given the comparatively harsh treatment they had received at his hands. If William of Malmesbury's notice of an annual tribute should be taken literally, it must have been a heavy addition to local obligations, amounting to 'twenty pounds of gold and three hundred pounds of silver, and . . . 25,000 oxen, besides as many as he might wish of hounds . . . and birds of prey'.

Although the earliest text is in the early fourteenth-century *Book of Taliesin*, the prophetic vernacular poem *Armes Prydein* ('The Prophesy of Britain') is generally agreed to have been written in this early to mid-tenth-century context: Sir Ifor Williams (1972b) argued strongly for the date range 927–37, or 'about 930', although a date between 934 and 937 might be more appropriate, since that was necessarily the period during which the north-western powers were establishing common ground for the campaign of 937. Alternatively, it might date to the very early 940s (as now argued by Breeze 1997: 5) when Idwal of Gwynedd rose against English hegemony in alliance with the Norse.

This poem is the first surviving example of a well known genre of medieval Welsh prophetic poems. These typically react to present tribulations – in this instance both English taxation (line 21) and 'Germanic' ('Other') tenure of 'British' ('our') lands – by recalling past heroes and glories while at the same time looking forward to complete success in the immediate future.

This is not, however, an isolated text in intellectual and political terms. That the author could allude to stories about the Saxons as exiles, Hengist and Horsa, their acquisition of power by treachery and their early connection with Thanet all suggest that he was familiar with the *Historia Brittonum* (see *HB*

31, 36, 43: hence their portrayal, for example, as 'churls [who] now wear a crown after the secret slaughter', 'the scavengers of Thanet' and 'the scavengers of Vortigern'). St Garmon also recurs (lines 145–6), alongside reference to 404 years of English occupation, which suggests some familiarity with the *Historia*'s closing *computus* (*HB* 66), albeit that was now adapted to new purposes. In important respects this is a recapitulation, albeit in a different, vernacular idiom, of important themes embedded in the earlier Latin text. The poem similarly offers a redemptive narrative developed within the context of providential history which is enshrined in the past but connected via prophesy with the politics of the present and future. These themes are, however, reshaped to accord with the rather different political realities of the early tenth century: the new English kingship was of such stature that an alliance between the Welsh, the Irish, Cornwall, Brittany, Strathclyde, the Scots and Dublin was seen as a necessary prerequisite of victory. The greater breadth of geographical and political horizons, as compared with the *Historia*, was arguably in part due to the experience of Welsh leaders meeting a wide spectrum of western European political leaders at Æthelstan's court or in his armies. In part, it reflects the wide connections of Dyfed and its links with Clonmacnoise in Ireland (Grabowski and Dumville 1984: 225–6) and the southern British lands. There is certainly a far greater sense of an Atlantic-edge family of peoples in this text than the earlier *Historia*, which had a comparatively insular perspective on recent political events.

That said, Æthelstan's political connections there and current Viking operations necessarily rendered the expectation of aid from Brittany far-fetched. Similarly, the prospect of Irish intervention is difficult to take seriously. Such aspects sustain the suspicion that this work verged on political naivety. This piece, far more than the *Historia*, might merit the term 'sermon'.

The hoped-for outcome was framed in conventional British terms and it is symptomatic of the author's vision that it is difficult to see what the other parties were supposed to gain from it. This close focus on the Britons, combined with the vernacular idiom, suggests that this work was written for a comparatively local audience (lines 125–6 of Rachel Bromwich's translation):

> The Cymry will prevail through battle
> well-equipped, unanimous, one in word and faith.

The prospective victory was represented as so complete that tenure of the southern British lands would be recovered by the Britons, from Manau (Gododdin) to Britanny and from Dyfed to Thanet, for (line 134): 'how much of the country do they [the Saxons] hold by right?' 'None' is, of course, the implied response and the illegitimacy of their tenure is a recurring theme herein, as it was in the *Historia*. Indeed, once again the terms used relate back to the *Historia*, and this new work looks forward implicitly to the imminent fulfilment of the prophesy of the boy Emrys to Vortigern (*HB* 42).

Topographical detail in the text suggests that the author was localized in southern Wales: St David is the principal saint, who was expected to lead the Irish into battle (lines 129–30); his miracles have been overturned by the Saxon (line 140), and he will lead all the combatants to war (line 196). Dyfed, Caerwent and the Wye all seem very familiar and it is specifically southern taxes which are to be contested (line 78), collected by officials based at Cirencester. Williams plausibly suggested a monastic writer from the south acting as spokesperson for his own vision of Welsh 'nationalist' opinion, perhaps even from St David's itself, alternatively from a satellite community.

Such a viewpoint was necessarily opposed to contemporary royal policy in Dyfed, but the poem was presumably composed for the court in an effort to effect change in the nationalist cause. Hywel Dda was a descendant of the bellicose Rhodri Mawr but one who had long pursued a policy of compliance towards King Æthelstan and the English. Hywel had particular reasons for restraint as the founder of a new kingship comprising Ceredigion and Dyfed, via marriage to the niece of Rhodri ap Hyfaidd, the last king of the native line of Dyfed, who was beheaded in Powys arguably by order of Hywel's father Cadell, *c.* 905. He was, therefore, still probably attempting to secure and reinforce his local power base and saw unequal alliance with the English court as an appropriate mechanism by which to further that ambition. It would be wrong to suppose him an anglophile, but Hywel was apparently a realist who sought to work with the English court to build up his own position in Wales to the point where he might become a veritable 'King of the Britons' – a position which he all but achieved after 942 (Kirby 1976–7).

The *Armes Prydein* was appealing first and foremost for a united British response, as a people of the elect under the guidance of God, the Trinity and the 'Son of Mary' (recall the *Historia*'s reference to Mary in an Arthurian context). To fulfil the prophecy concerning the expulsion of the Saxons, which was embedded in the *Historia*, they would fight under leadership of impeccable legitimacy and martial prowess (e.g. lines 12–14):

> The Britons will rise again when they prevail
> for long was prophesied the time when they will come,
> as rulers whose possession is by [the right of] descent.

'They' in this context are two famous leaders of the distant past, Cadwaladr of seventh-century Gwynedd and the more problematic Cynan, who has generally been interpreted as Cynan Meiriadoc, the associate of Magnus Maximus and legendary founder of Brittany (Williams 1972b: 46; Bromwich 1961: 316–18), but whose name offers connections with *Y Gododdin* and other more recent Welsh hero-figures as well. The author's choice of two figures implies recognition of some division of opinion within Wales, north versus south, perhaps between the different descendants of Merfyn as much as their opponents. His British unity is constructed on a certain duality, therefore, with paired exemplars used in much the same way as occurred in the *Historia Brittonum*. These two figures appear repeatedly as deliverers of their people in other early prophetic verse, but it is unclear whether their popularity in this role merely reflects the usage of the *Armes Prydein* or was already established at the time of writing.

This highly politicized and nationalistic text makes no direct reference to an Arthur figure. Admittedly, as already noted, Cadwaladr and Cynan are referred to as 'two bears to whom daily fighting brings no shame' in line 170, and the term occurs also in line 113, but these puns are easiest interpreted as examples of animal metaphor such as are typical of early Welsh poetry. Compare, for example, the *Book of Taliesin*, poem 53, wherein bears, lions and dragons all occur in a poem focusing once more on Cadwaladr. There is nothing here to suggest that a pun on the name 'Arthur' was intended, although that cannot be entirely ruled out. Once again, therefore, a British vernacular text full of political meaning was being written in Wales within about a century of the *Historia* with little or no reference to the Arthur-figure featured therein. This instance is more remarkable than either of those discussed above, for not only did the author apparently have knowledge of the earlier Latin text but it also purported, like the *Historia*, to be a national rally to arms. The Arthur-figure of the *Historia* was certainly constructed within a providential context as a national hero and might have recommended himself for use in this work.

We can probably assume, therefore, that the author of the *Armes Prydein* knew of Arthur at least as presented in chapter 56 of the *Historia*, so the decision to omit him from this work was arguably his own. It may be that, even while using it, this southern Welsh author was keen to distance himself from certain aspects of this Gwynedd-centric text. Perhaps to make use of Arthur might have been construed as dynastic propaganda, particularly if the *Historia* broke new ground in constructing Arthur in this guise. It is noticeable that the author departs from the story-line of the *Historia* in various ways, not least by repeated reference (lines 27, 137) to the damnable Vortigern as 'Gwrtheyrn Gwynedd'. Williams explained this connection, which is unique in Welsh literature, by reference to a local story of his death in Caernarvonshire, where a tumulus *Bedd Gwrtheyrn* at Nant Gwrtheyrn reputedly covered a stone coffin. However, this supposes both that this southern Welsh author was aware of this obscure and localized, northern topographical etymology and that he deemed it sufficiently compelling to put aside the strong messages enshrined in the *Historia* connecting Vortigern with other parts of Wales. Such a solution is unlikely, though not impossible. Here again, therefore, it seems probable that the author has consciously deviated from the Gwynedd-centric version of British history which he knew from the *Historia* for his own political and ideological purposes. This may, therefore, carry a hint of continuing tensions between the southern Welsh and their bellicose neighbours in Gwynedd.

In the last resort, it seems likely that Arthur was not considered best suited to the particular needs of this work, which also makes little use of most of the other morally constructed figures of Vortigern's reign. Vortigern himself appears, as do Hengist and Germanus/Garmon, but in different guises and for different purposes. Vortimer is omitted and neither Patrick nor Arthur occur. If there is a single figure in this text who occupies the rhetorical space shared in the *Historia* by Patrick and Arthur, it is undoubtedly St David, who is depicted both as a saint and as the symbol, banner and even leader of the British (and Irish) in arms. He is introduced prior to either Cadwaladr (first appearance line 81) or Cynan (line 89), in line 51, in close association with God. Thereafter, the two kings are little more than heroic and victorious captains of men under his patronage and general overview. It is with the image of the British people granted insular supremacy by the Creator God at the instance of their national saint, and with David actually at their head, that the poem concludes (lines 192–9). This is a thoroughly south-western Welsh – and clerical – vision of the ideological landscape, which has displaced much of the characterization and rhetoric offered by the Gwynedd-centric *Historia Brittonum*, and from this perspective Arthur's absence should occasion little surprise.

## THE *ANNALES CAMBRIAE*

Despite such nationalist protests as the *Armes Prydein* represents, Wales seems to have been comparatively closely supervised by English kings up until *c.* 950, with the co-operation of local rulers who were generally disinclined to chance the wrath of their powerful neighbours. At Æthelstan's death (939), the north and the northern Mercian Danelaw revolted and were joined by Idwal of Gwynedd, but both Mercia and north Wales were crushed in 942 and the Viking Kingdom of York in 944. Instead of rising in arms with him, Hywel Dda took advantage of Idwal's failure and secured Gwynedd and Powys, presumably with English acquiescence at the very least, and he ruled them thereafter without any obvious sign of tension with England until his death in 950.

King Edmund's murder in 946 brought Eadred to the throne, who completed the subjugation of the north. Hywel on occasion attended his court (see, for example, Eadred's grant of land to Wulfric in 946: Whitelock 1955: 552), but his health was apparently poor and he seems to have been incapacitated during his final years, leaving the running of the regime very largely to his clerical lieutenants. Eadred's death, in 955, opened a series of succession crises, and of immature candidates for kingship, which left the English establishment ill-equipped to impose itself on Wales. The names of Welsh kings cease to occur on witness lists of English charters during the reign of Eadwig (955–9), and it seems unlikely that their attendance at the English court was thereafter anything like as commonplace as it had become during the previous generation. There were exceptions, of course, particularly in Edgar's famous passage up the Dee rowed largely by his Welsh clients (in 973). Thereafter, however, Wales is not mentioned in the *Anglo-Saxon Chronicle* for seventy years, until the rise to power of Gruffudd ap Llywelyn. Instead, the several texts are full of notices of Viking activity. This does not mean that all interchange ceased, but it does suggest that it had a lower priority than hitherto inside England. Thereafter, for two or three generations, Welsh kings were arguably freer than earlier in the tenth century of English interference. They were not, however, free of Viking raids, which were considerable in the later part of the century.

It is during this cusp period, when close English supervision of Wales was just starting to slacken, that the *Annales Cambriae* seems to have been written in the form which survives, although, of course, some changes may have been made in the course of the initial copying. This is a chronicle which was copied into the same British Museum Harley MS 3859 as the *Historia Brittonum c.* 1100 in an Anglo-Norman hand. A reliable edition is that of Faral (1929: 44–50) and there is a text and translation, with additional, marked material from later texts (for which see Dumville 1977–8) in the Phillimore series (Morris 1980). The last entry records the death of Rhodri ap Hywel in 954 (sometimes corrected to 953), and the text was structured only so as to encompass a paschal cycle of 532 years plus one, from *c.* 444 to 977 (again on occasion slightly amended). This interest in the paschal cycle was probably commonplace in Welsh monastic circles at this date, and is replicated in the *Historia Brittonum* (*HB* 16). It was almost certainly written, therefore, in the reign of Owain (d. 988), Rhodri's brother and successor, with whom the first two genealogies which follow in the same Harleian collection begin (Faral 1929: 50–7).

It seems very likely that the chronicle can be dated more precisely than this. There is no reference to the death of Owain's brother Edwin, who seems to have died a year or so after Rhodri. Nor are there any further events in Owain's reign, such as King Eadred's death in November 955, which seems a critical omission given the inclusion of King Edmund's *obit*. These omissions suggest a date for the *Annales* virtually contemporary with its last entry, so in or about 954–5 (as also suggested by Grabowski and Dumville 1984: 224, 226). The Harleian collection of genealogies is almost certainly contemporary, and seems to have been undergoing emendation at this date for reasons which connect with the political thinking behind the *Annales*.

The *Annales* has a particularly important role in our understanding of the pre-Galfridian Arthur for several reasons. It is by far the earliest attempt to provide an absolute date for Badon and is the earliest reference also to Arthur's death at Camlann. These specific entries, or various amended versions thereof, have formed the basis of the vast majority of twentieth-century attempts to locate King Arthur in time, in and around the early sixth century, on the assumption that one at least of them derived from a contemporary or near contemporary source and could be relied upon.

This is, therefore, a text which is often accorded a high level of historical authority. It has, for example, been judged a 'sober historical document using good sources, not an annalized fiction' (Jackson 1959a: 4), and the Camlann entry 'looks like a plain statement, free from legend' (Ashe 1991). Ashe went further thereafter in this passage in his arguments in favour of an historical Arthur:

> since (so far as is known) everyone named in the dozens of non-Arthurian entries did exist, there is a presumption that a real Arthur underlies these questionable phrases. Some of the entries are misdated or influenced by legend, but they never mention definitively fictitious persons.
>
> (Ashe 1991: 8–9)

One might, of course, contest specific instances, but the general truth of this argument is acceptable, even if its presumptions are not, since from this author's perspective Arthur had already been historicized by his presence in earlier text.

Additionally, the *Annales* has generally been credited with a degree of independence from the *Historia Brittonum* in regard to its Arthurian material, so has been read as capable of confirming his historicity. This is a complex area since there are both obvious similarities but also as obvious differences in the 'factual' material offered by the two texts, which has led to varying opinions on this important issue. So, for example, it has been postulated that these two authors perhaps used an existing but now lost 'Northern History' or 'Northern Chronicle' but in different ways, or used similar but not identical sources (Jackson 1953, 1959a; T. Jones 1964; Charles-Edwards 1991). This is obviously an area which will repay detailed examination.

### Structure and Framework

The underlying structure of this chronicle was established by Kathleen Hughes (1973), who divided the text into three sections: early material which was based on an Irish original (now lost), which had in turn been structured around Isidore's chronicle (up to 613); early seventh- to late eighth-century material which derived in part from northern British sources, which had themselves been structured around northern English material; and a set of annals written and kept at St David's, apparently from the mid-790s onwards, to include the latest entries. The *Annales* is, therefore, a text constructed in Dyfed, or what should by this date perhaps be termed Deheubarth, in a major monastic and diocesan centre and under the patronage of a branch of the second dynasty of Gwynedd, on the basis of the interpretation of literary and oral materials available there in the mid-tenth century. Above the level of the individual entry, however, it is not merely a straight copy of any one of these sources, but a composition in its own right.

The Harleian text is set out on a palimpsest in columns several to a page, each year opening *an'*, with every tenth year (although the numbering is not entirely consistent) numbered, the starting point being about the year 444. Some argue for slightly different starting points (Alcock 1971: 39, 49, opted for 447; Grabowski and Dumville 1984 prefer 445), but the conventional start date is retained here for the sake of consistency with published editions (Faral 1929: 44). So, for example, 514 is *an'.lxx* (year 70) and 524 is *an'.lxxx* (year 80). The whole of the surviving work was written as one continuous text, rather than the framework being set out initially and then filled in with entries where appropriate, but this need not have been true of the tenth-century text of which it is a copy.

Most years throughout have no entry, but there are significant differences in the density of material across the three periods. The last section is certainly the least problematic and most historical in its content, as well as being the best represented with sixty-nine entries over a period of 158 years. In several sections, as 807–17, it is a near complete sequence of annual entries, albeit the individual entries are mostly brief, the exception being 814 which is extended but is then followed by a blank year. This may suggest that the original entry ran across into the space allocated to the following year. This close sequence focuses almost exclusively on Gwynedd, and it may be that some sort of account of the immediate background of Merfyn's succession travelled south with his descendant, Hywel Dda, or his supporters, when (or soon after) he took over Dyfed in 904.

The general approach of our author is reasonably clear, with references to the deaths of kings and bishops in Wales (particularly Gwynedd and Dyfed), intra-Welsh warfare, attacks on Wales by the English and the Vikings and a few key happenings in other areas. Several Irish entries suggests that the author had access still at this date to the Irish chronicle on which the earliest section was based, at least up to the late ninth century (Grabowski and Dumville 1984: 213). The main focus rests, however, on the community of St David's and the current dynasty of Deheubarth. This material is reasonably authoritative, although it is obviously partial and has resulted from a complex process of decision-making, which has determined both what should be included or excluded and how inclusions should be worded. In this sense, the author's work should be read as a text of considerable power which has privileged particular visions of the past while obfuscating or ignoring others.

A very different picture emerges from the central section, which has only forty-five entries spread across 182 years, and nowhere more than three annual entries in consecutive years. The material can be subdivided into two unequal parts, the earlier being dominated by a string of events many of which ultimately derive from Bede's *Historia* and its late eighth-century continuation (Plummer 1896: I, 361–3). This has come, in part at least, via one or more texts which have a northern bias but from a 'British' perspective, with additional 'British' material, so was probably compiled in the 'British' north. Strathclyde is the obvious option given the degree of interest in its kings in the eighth century. Entries include, therefore, such events as the battle of Chester (613), the death of Ceredic (616: arguably of Elmet, of whom mention occurs in *HB* 63), Edwin's reign (617, 630) and baptism (626), Cadwallon's death (631), Oswald's death (644), right through to Bede's death in 735, and those of Oengus (736) and Talorgen (750) of the Picts, the latter 'killed by the Britons', the death of Beli son of Elffin (722), of Strathcyde, and those of his son *Teudubr* (750) and grandson *Dunnagual* (760), all of whom occur in the fifth Harleian genealogy. Parts at least of this would seem, therefore, to be based on a northern British text written in the second half of the eighth century but heavily dependent on Northumbrian sources for anything before *c.* 700. The *Historia Brittonum* arguably provided a second route by which material originally textualized by Bede reached this author.

A small number of Welsh figures and events have been inserted into this framework, but these are a minority (from 613 to 735 only seven entries are certainly Welsh) and there is a noticeable absence of clerical figures, which contrasts with the later section and suggests that little of St David's's own history for this period was available to the author. After 750, there is a greater emphasis on Welsh affairs, with notice of Rhodri's death in 754 and references to several Mercian events with a relevance to Wales, including attacks launched against Dyfed and other areas from Mercia, which continue on into the early ninth century. These were presumably added from living memory as much as anything else, hence from oral sources available in the late eighth century, when a chronicle began to be kept at St David's. An interest which extends back into the seventh century is the Easter controversy, with a reference implicitly to the Synod of Whitby in 665 [664] which presumably derives ultimately from Bede but was perhaps incorporated here to contextualize the northern Welsh adoption of Roman computation in 768.

As Hughes argued (1973), therefore, this does look like a chronicle which incorporates an earlier annalistic text begun at St David's in the late eighth century, in part at least because of a new interest in the Easter controversy. However, there is no reason to think that the present form predates the mid-tenth century, when this much shorter text was combined with new sources to construct a half millennium-long chronicle. Its author used an Irish chronicle of early tenth-century date, various written, largely northern sources and other locally available material to reconstruct the past into a chronicle framework (Dumville 1977–8). The poverty of early Welsh entries in a work of which the contemporary focus lay in Wales does imply that there was little available to the author capable of being developed into annals for the period before *c.* 750. This may, of course, reflect damage done by the Vikings to local libraries in recent years, particularly given that the author noted the burning of Mynyw (the bishopric of St David's) in 810, which may well have destroyed much of the community's stock of texts. There were several further instances of damage done to the site during the Viking Age which had the potential to seriously limit the materials available to a mid-tenth-century author.

Reference to Rhun's putative baptism of Edwin does, however, suggest that the author was familiar with the *Historia Brittonum*, which should not surprise us if that had already been consulted in the same vicinity by the author of *Armes Prydein*. The appearance of both texts in a single early manuscript likewise suggests that they came together comparatively early. There is certainly a considerable overlap between the coverage offered particularly of the seventh century by the two texts, and this impression of familiarity will be reinforced as we consider the sources for the earliest part of the text.

### The earliest section of the Annales

The mid-tenth-century author had the greatest difficulty in attempting to compose material capable of entry into the earliest section of his chronicle, since he seems to have had no British material available in a chronologically organized format. His Irish chronicle was a now-lost text of the Clonmacnoise-group which had been written recently – arguably in the first half of the same century (Dumville 1984b: 53; Grabowski and Dumville1984). This is apparent both from comparison with later, surviving Irish annals and from a survey of the material included. So St Brigid (454, 521), St Patrick (457), Bishop Benignus (468), Bishop Ebur (501), St Columba (521, 562, 595), Gildas (570), Brendan of Birr (574) and Constantine (589) all derive from the Irish text, although not necessarily at the same dates or in the same order. Even so, the first century of the *Annales Cambriae* is particularly sparse. From 444 to 612 there are only twenty-three entries, including only ten in the first century. There are only seven 'British' entries *in toto* (if we exclude the death of Gildas which derives from the Irish source), which have been included up to AD 600, as follows (Faral 1929: 45):

[516]: *Bellum Badonis, in quo Arthur portavit crucem Domini nostri Jhesu Christi tribus diebus et tribus noctibus in humeros suos et Brittones victores fuerunt.*

[537]: *Gueith Camlann, in qua Arthur et Medraut corruerunt, et mortalitas in Brittania et in Hibernia fuit.*

[547]: *Mortalitas magna, in qua pausat Mailcum, rex Genedotae.*

[573]: *Bellum Armterid.*

[580]: *Guurci et Peretur moritur.*

[584]: *Bellum contra Euboniam et dispositio Danielis Bancorum.*

[595]: *Dunaut rex moritur.*

('[516]: The battle of Badon, in which Arthur carried the cross of our Lord Jesus Christ for three days and three nights on his shoulders and the Britons were the victors.

[537]: The *gweith* [battle of] Camlann, in which Arthur and Medraut fell, and there was a mortality [i.e. plague] in Britain and in Ireland.
[547]: The great mortality [i.e. plague] in which died Maelgwyn, king of Gwynedd.
[573]: The battle of Armterid.
[580]: Gwrgi and Peredur died.
[584]: Battle against the Isle of Man and burial of Daniel of the Bangors.
[595]: King Dunawd died.')

These entries divide around 570, after which, excluding only the death of Daniel (the reference to the Isle of Man in this year derives from the Irish chronicle), all the material arguably belongs to northern Britain: Armterid is often equated with Arthuret (Cumbria), and Gwrgi and Peredur, and Dunawd, occur as descendants of *Coyl Hen* ('Old King Cole') in the Harleian genealogies xii and xi respectively. It has been suggested (Miller 1975b, 1975c) that these entries offer an historical watershed for the northern Britons, therefore providing the earliest entries in some sort of northern British chronicle or historical narrative, as suggested earlier from the second half of the eighth century. It may, however, be overly optimistic to argue for anything more substantive than a late eighth-century cleric at or around Glasgow attempting to fit various undated genealogies and some vernacular poetry into his own chronicle framework, which was then used in combination with material from the *Historia Brittonum* and a new generation of poetry by a mid-tenth-century cleric at St David's. The poem *Dwy Blaid* (perhaps written within fifty years of 900), for example, refers to enmity between Dunawd and Owain (Urien's son), Gwallawg and Elffin, and Morgant (Urien's putative murderer) and the poet, of whom Gwallawg and Morgant are both associated in the *Historia* with Urien. These entries may have been constructed synthetically, therefore, from a range of interrelated and non-contemporary materials, so must be considered less than historical. Both the dates and the events are therefore unreliable.

Daniel is the only clear, 'Welsh' addition to these northern entries. Given that he was the putative founder of the principal cult sites of both Gwynedd and Powys, reference to his death was perhaps obligatory when writing for a king who derived his paternal descent from Rhodri Mawr and whose father had recently ruled over these territories. This entry is not, however, necessarily accurate either in regard to his date of death or the inclusion of both Bangors (Higham 2001b). Without further evidence, it is hazardous to assume that it derives from anything more authoritative than cult-centred stories circulating, or written down, at Bangor on Menai, which are likely to have been as devoid of chronological parameters as most other saintly *vitae*. These may well have been extended to take in Bangor-is-y-coed during the later ninth century as part of efforts to legitimize the dynastic seizure of power in north-east Wales, with which Owain's immediate ancestors were, of course, involved. The term here used (*dispositio*) focuses attention not on the saint's death or burial, as is more normal in this text, but on the disposal of his property, hence his monasteries and lands. Their descent was of interest to his successors, and thus likely to have featured in a *vita*. The term recurs in this text only in the entry for 606. Daniel's entry could, therefore, have been inserted by the tenth-century author on the basis of either current oral testimony derived from Bangor, or a now-lost *vita*, comparable perhaps to that of St Garman to which reference was made in the *Historia*, virtually wherever he chose in the early part of his text.

The risk of a comparatively cavalier positioning of Daniel has an obvious relevance to our discussion of the dating of the Arthurian entries in the *Annales*, but we should first consider the earlier group of three non-Irish entries as a whole. There are apparent links between them which imply that they were inserted with a common purpose: Arthur occurs in two, in one of which he is depicted as the victor of Badon; the fame of both Badon and Maelgwn Gwynedd derive ultimately from Gildas, whose death follows as the (Irish-derived) entry for 570. In a sense, a knowledge of Gildas's *De Excidio* would seem to be the key to the author's perception of events, with dates of death for all three figures then developed to accord with the content of the Irish Chronicle. That said, the detailed chronology this author adopted causes difficulties when set against the specifics within Gildas's text. His battle of Badon (516) occurs only thirty-one years before Maelgwyn's death in 547. Gildas, on the other hand, seems to remark that he was born in the year of Mount Badon (*DEB* xxvi, 1), in the forty-fourth year before the date of composition, when Maelgwn was very much alive (*DEB* xxxiii–xxxvi, as interpreted by Winterbottom 1978; Sims-Williams 1983; Dumville 1984a; Higham 1994). These two constructs are clearly incompatible (as noted *inter alia* by T. Jones 1964: 5), but it may be that current editions of the *De Excidio Britanniae* are corrupt and the forty-four years relate to some other passage of time. It was not read in this way by Bede (*HE* i, 16), whose text of the *De Excidio* was far earlier than the earliest extant (and see Brodeur 1939: 246–7; O'Sullivan 1978: 156). It is quite possible, therefore, that the author of the *Annales* would have read Gildas's chronology much as did Bede (Wiseman 2000), in which case Badon should have occurred around forty-four years *after* some other event, as opposed to *before* the present (i.e. the date of Gildas's composition). That said, the author does not oblige us by constructing some significant event some forty-four years either earlier or later than 516.

This view has another weakness, in that it assumes that the author of the Annales had access to Gildas's text and had studied it closely, which is far from demonstrable from internal evidence. The achievements of Ambrosius Aurelianus are noticeably absent from the text, which seems strange unless the author believed them to predate 444. Consider, additionally, the name forms used. There is little overlap but that which does occur fails to develop any connection. For example, Gildas's *insularis draco ... Maglocunus* is replaced by the form *Mailcum, rex Genedotae*, which arguably paraphrases the *Mailcunus magnus rex apud Brittones . . . in regione Guenedotae* of the *Historia Brittonum* (*HB* 62). It seems unsafe, therefore, to assume that the tenth-century annalist was personally familiar with the *De Excidio*. The St David's copy may have been a victim of the high rate of destruction of texts which seems to have occurred on site.

It has long been recognized (e.g. T. Jones 1964: 21) that the first Arthurian entry, concerning Badon, is unusually long by comparison with other entries in this text (and particularly the first section thereof). This has led to the suggestion that all but the briefest notice of the battle might be a later interpolation, that brief notice therefore having a greater probability of historicity than the whole. However, the author does use extended entries where he considered them appropriate (as e.g. for 722, 814) and there is no additional reason to consider this entry other than as written *c.* 954. The case has already been postulated for the author's familiarity with other Welsh 'historical' material in general, and the *Historia Brittonum* in particular, and a comparison of the Arthurian chapter in the *Historia* (*HB* 56) and the two Arthurian entries in the *Annales* (entries for 516, 537) brings this relationship into focus. Koch (1996, accepted by T. Green 1998) has already made a case for the author having used the *Historia* as a basis for the Badon entry, on the strength of repetition of the putative mistake in copying implicit in his reference to *humeros suos* ('his arms' see pp. 144–5). It was argued in the previous chapter that this view is a hollow one, which might risk us losing Koch's contention regarding the present issue, but in practice this can be defended on much better grounds. Detailed examination of the Arthurian entries exposes the recurrence of particular words as being so frequent that there seems little doubt that the author of the *Annales Cambriae* wrote both entries with the *Historia Brittonum* open before him. These entries are quoted once more but with the material in common with *HB* 56 in roman (see p. 144 for text of *HB* 56 for comparison):

> [516]: Bellum Badonis, in quo Arthur portavit *crucem Domini nostri* Jhesu Christi *tribus diebus et tribus noctibus* in humeros suos et Brittones victor*es* fu*erunt*.
>     [537]: *Gueith Camlann*, in qu*a* Arthur et *Medraut* corruerunt

That is not the end of probable borrowings, since the *Historia* also uses the term *Gueith* in the very next chapter (*HB* 57: *Gueith Lin Garan*), and the phrase *tribus diebus et tribus noctibus* soon thereafter (*HB* 63, dealing with the siege of Lindisfarne) in sections which the author of the *Annales* had apparently read. With these latter borrowings also in roman, the text reads as follows:

> [516]: Bellum Badonis, in quo Arthur portavit *crucem Domini nostri* Jhesu Christi tribus diebus et tribus noctibus in humeros suos et Brittones victor*es* fu*erunt*.
>     [537]: Gueith *Camlann*, in qu*a* Arthur et *Medraut* corruerunt

This would leave only five words, out of thirty-one, as original, of which one is a personal name and another generally interpreted as a place-name.

The author was not copying directly, therefore, but he was plagiarizing heavily and he clearly found the language of the received text within the *Historia Brittonum* well suited to his purposes. Those purposes too were also heavily dependent in this area on the same text. He had presumably read therein of the period following Vortigern's death, which was characterized by biblical typology as an insular golden age. The central mechanism relied upon elevation of the reputation of Patrick as a type of Moses, and construction of Arthur as a type of Joshua, the latter leading the Britons to victory as a people of the Lord fighting under divine protection. It is not surprising that the author of the *Annales* should wish to incorporate this golden age early in the paschal cycle which framed his own chronicle.

While the *Historia* focuses explicitly and exclusively on Patrick and Arthur in its efforts to re-establish the Britons as the latter-day Israelites post-Vortigern, this period in the *Annales* encompasses a group of six entries, which collectively establish the age of the saints in western Britain and Ireland, via the births of SS Bridget and Columba and the deaths of SS Patrick and Bridget, Bishops Benignus and Ebur, and Arthur and Medraut.

This difference reflects to an extent, of course, the tenth-century author's dependence on an Irish chronicle as his framework document, but he was still making choices. Several of these entries, not just the notice of Badon, are framed in exceptional terms. Consider, for example, the language of death used in this chronicle: the normal term used of kings, be they British or English (excluding violent deaths), and some clergy, is *moritur* (or a variant thereon). *Obiit* is used almost exclusively of figures whose Christianity the author wished particularly to emphasize, plus some great foreign patrons of the church: thus (St) Gildas, (St) Kentigirn, the Welsh hero-figure Cadwaladr (Owain's paternal ancestor), the Irish-educated and putatively saintly King Aldfrith of Northumbria, Oengus and Kenneth of the Picts and Cyngen of Powys (who died at Rome), while Pope Gregory and Pepin of Frankia exceptionally *obiit in Christo*. Only two figures 'departed to the Lord' (*ad Dominum migratur*), St Patrick and Bishop Elfoddw, the 'archbishop' of Gwynedd who was lauded in this text for bringing the Welsh into conformity with the Roman Easter in 768.

Bishop Ebur, who *pausat in Christo anno CCCL aetatis suae* ('rests in Christ, 350 years his lifetime'), was similarly exceptional. Ebur is a Cambro-Latin rendering of the Irish Íbar (the bishop of Beggary Island), and the entry has apparently been taken from the precursor of the Clonmacnoise-group of texts (Grabowski and Dumville 1984: 220–1). However, the early Latin Irish chronicles which survive have *quies* rather than *pausat*, as Brigid in this text. *Pausat* is used only in the entries for 501 and 547. The selection for inclusion in the *Annales* of this entry was perhaps to take advantage of the extended life-span, which has some potential to connect this epoch in Cambro-Irish history with the Old Testament listing of Adam's descendants in Genesis v.

This group of entries seems, therefore, to develop the interpretation of the Britons as a people of the Book, a chosen people of God enjoying a golden age of heroic Christianity, at the outset of the text. The idea perhaps came from the *Historia*, which initially tied the Britons into Old Testament history (*HB* 11), then used Patrick and Arthur to represent British types of Moses and Joshua (*HB* 50–6). However, it also reflects the author's own familiarity with the Bible and Dyfed-centric Cambro-Irish connections in the present, and his vision of a shared past. It has an important role to play in a text which sought to provide a summary of the history of the British Isles from a south-western British perspective, since it focuses on the claims of the Britons and Irish collectively to be the chosen people within Britain. It constructs for them, therefore, a shared position in this early period within God's designs. Again, this would seem to reflect particularly close links between St David's and Clonmacnoise during the author's own lifetime, but it may also reflect something of the connections between St David and Ireland envisioned in the *Armes Prydein*, which had been written comparatively recently in this same region.

The primary people of the Lord in this text was, therefore, a joint Cambro-Irish construct well suited to long-running visions of history in the south-west of Wales, which are well illustrated in the *Life of St. David* written by Rhigyfarch of Llanbadarn *c.* 1100 (Wade-Evans 1944: 150–70). Rhigyfarch claims Patrick for Dyfed, and portrays him as only with difficulty dissuaded from establishing himself at St David's (chap. 3). His mission was, therefore, in some senses owned at St David's in the central Middle Ages. This construct was, at the same time, competing with Gwynedd-centric visions of a militant British nation of the past under the leadership of Cunedda, founder of the first dynasty of Gwynedd, which had gloriously expelled Irish incomers as unwelcome interlopers, as celebrated in the *Historia* (*HB* 14, 62). This was, therefore, a contested vision of history, which had meaning primarily at the time of composition in the mid-tenth century.

Interest in the papal alteration of the dating of Easter also reflects an awareness of this issue on the part of the tenth-century author. Connections between the papacy and the British nation were renewed latterly, via the good offices of Elfoddw, and (as already noted) the author's approval of Elfoddw, 'the man of God', was reflected in the choice of language already used of Patrick to record his death. Elfoddw had, of course, been active under the patronage of Owain's ancestors, since his genealogy was traced back in the male line to the first dynasty of Gwynedd, and he might be construed as a second Patrick as the 'renewer' of his people within providential history. The author was also careful to include other connections between Wales and Rome, such as Welsh kings making pilgrimage, as in 854, 885 and, more particularly, the case of Owain's own father, Hywel, in 928. He was, therefore, seeking to project an image of the Britons as a people of the Lord in conformity with, and connected to, Rome and the wider Christian world, under the leadership of Owain's branch of the second dynasty of Gwynedd, which had a particular claim on the Roman connection in the recent past.

To return to the fifth-century entries, it must be significant that there is no reference to such notorious figures as Vortigern, who might otherwise have disturbed the representation of this glorious past, nor of the (Anglo-)Saxons, who are very noticeably absent until their conversion (herein in 595). Vortigern's absence might be explained by reference to his dating in the *Historia* (*HB* 66) to the late 420s, i.e. prior to the beginning of the *Annales*. However, the author's disinclination to refer to the English in derogatory terms, for example as pagans or as usurpers who had stolen Britain, is a fundamental difference between the *Historia* and the *Annales*. The approach of the latter is to treat English Christians (such as Bede, Aldfrith, Osred) very much in the same way as Britons, although there are signs of stress when dealing with Offa's death: he did not just die but died *morte*, much to the relief, one suspects, of contemporaries in Dyfed. Such vehemence is not difficult to excuse on the part of a contemporary Welsh cleric, regarding a king whose depredations on Wales exceeded those of all other Christian kings. Offa apart, however, there is no sense of racial antagonism nor a nationalistic claim to the whole island of Britain herein, as is explicit in the *Historia* and the *Armes Prydein*. There is no use of pejorative language (e.g. *ambrones*), such as characterizes the *Historia*. Equally, there is no rancour towards English kings in the present: the latest mentioned is Edmund, whose murder the author noted accurately and without prejudice (the term used is *jugulatus est*, which is identical to his wording of the death of a Welsh figure in 951). The *Annales* were written, therefore, by an author who accepted, or was at least prepared to accommodate, the current political dominance and religious positioning of the English, very much in line with the policies attributed above to Hywel Dda.

There is a current political agenda herein. This comes over strongly in the last few entries. In 943 [942] Idwal of Gwynedd and one of his sons had been killed by the English, and his grandson Cyngen was poisoned in 946. The Saxons laid waste Strathclyde in the same year and murdered a certain Cadwgan son of Owain (of Morgannwg?) in 951. Hywel Dda's dynasty in south-west Wales, by contrast, was unaffected by recent conflict with the English. Rather, Hywel was still at least an occasional visitor to the English court in 946 (Birch 1887: no. 815), where he seems to have been treated with honour. However, following his death in 950 as *rex Brittonum* (Figure 31), his sons became locked in a mortal struggle with Idwal's sons for control of all western Wales. As already mentioned, Hywel Dda had latterly ruled in Gwynedd/Powys as well as Dyfed and Ceredigion, but his sons rapidly lost control of the former and were hard pressed by their cousins even in their core

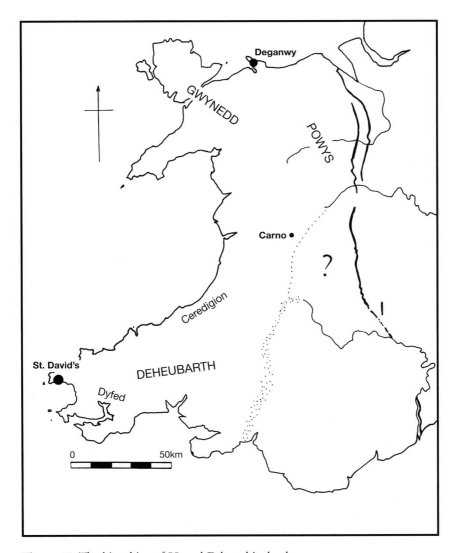

**Figure 31** The kingships of Hywel Dda at his death

territory. The battle of Carno, in 951, was later interpreted as between Hywel's and Idwal's sons, who gained access to the Upper Severn Valley by this victory. The latter were later credited with having ravaged Dyfed twice in 952 and Ceredigion in 954 (T. Jones 1952: 7). The death of Hywel's son, Rhodri, in 954, only four years after his father and at a time when this war was going badly, presumably deepened the crisis, bringing Owain to the throne of Deheubarth in the middle of a dynastic emergency. The *Annales* was written, therefore, under the patronage of a new and highly insecure king whose position was under threat not from the English but from his own cousins in northern and central Wales, who had had the upper hand in recent warfare.

Idwal's side of the family had a recent history of defiance towards the English and naturally adopted a nationalist, British agenda. Owain also laid claim to the leadership of the British nation *in toto* – at least that is surely the message coming out of the Harleian collection of British genealogies – but he was struggling to compete with his cousins in the mid-950s. The *Annales* reflects, therefore, his political agenda at that date and his need to distinguish his own position from that of the current leadership of Gwynedd. The care with which the *Annales* avoided reference to the Saxons as pagans and interlopers reflects Owain's need to accommodate the English leadership in the present and seek protection against aggression from Gwynedd, a stance which was by this date traditional in southern Wales. He was pursuing a strategy of accommodation towards the English kingdom, therefore, in pursuit of his own dynastic and political agenda, very much as his father had done before him, and the local dynasty even earlier, back at least to the previous century.

This political stance may have secured Owain's survival. In 955, three Welsh kings witnessed King Eadred's grant of Alwalton to Ælfsige Hunlafing (A. J. Robertson 1939: no. 30), which was one of the ailing king's last known acts, if indeed he actually attended to this matter in person. The three kings were Iago the son of Idwal of Gwynedd and Powys, Morgan the son of Owain of Morgannwg and Owain of Deheubarth. Their attendance on the English king implies that he was seeking to impose a general peace on the warring princes of Wales only months before he died. The charter stresses the universality and high stature of Eadred's rule in Britain, titling him 'King of the Anglo-Saxons and *casere* [emperor] of all Britain, *Deo gratias*'. The Welsh leaders were presumably expected to sign up to this vision and acknowledge their own dependence as part and parcel of their role as witnesses. However, Eadred's death (in November), then the struggle for power between his nephews Eadwig and Edgar, which led to a division of the kingdom in 957, meant that the English court was ill-placed to intervene actively to support the aspirations of Hywel's son to regain his father's kingships across north-western and northern Wales, even had that been the ultimate intention.

It is in this context that we should read the Arthurian entries in a work apparently written at the height of dynastic conflict in western Wales and before Eadred's imposition of peace. The Arthur of the entry for 516 is clearly in many respects the same figure as constructed in the *Historia Brittonum*, albeit he is accommodated into a chronicle framework and the Joshua connections have been shed, although the Arthurian claim to Badon, as first developed in the *Historia*, remains. Again, one must suspect that this author had not read Gildas for himself, where that claim is absent. However, the differences of detail between the Arthurian material in the *Historia* and the *Annales* are fundamental to our understanding since they allow us to distinguish the later author's particular and different purpose. So, for example, an obvious omission from the *Annales* is any reference to the Saxons as Arthur's opponents, as is made explicit repeatedly in the *Historia*: instead Arthur is without named enemies and not even obviously a warrior, and his audience's understanding of a battle of Badon in which the *Brittones victores fuerunt* depends on their having knowledge independent of the text – ultimately of the battle as named by Gildas. Given the fame of this particular conflict, and its textualization in the *Historia*, that was probably not problematic. Badon was, perhaps, the one battle of early post-Roman Britain which could not reasonably be omitted from a British history of the period, which perhaps accounts for its inclusion, but the anti-English message is very carefully veiled.

The Arthur of the *Annales* is still beloved of Christ, but (as has long been recognized) the author has conflated his characterization in the *Historia*'s eighth battle, with the arguably more famous *Bellum Badonis*, which the *Historia* placed twelfth and last in the battle-list. The remaining detail derives from the New Testament and is apparently included so as to reinforce connections between Arthur and Christ, to make this Arthur figure primarily a Christ-helper rather than a warrior of the type of Joshua fighting the unbelieving 'Others'. So the *Historia*'s vision of Arthur bearing an image of Mary becomes the *Annales*'s Arthur carrying the cross, which connects him more particularly with the crucifixion. In Luke xxiii, 26, Simon, a Cyrenian, famously carried the cross for Jesus (*crucem portare post Iesum*), and this was presumably the inspiration for this phrase in the *Annales*. The 'three days and nights' are plainly both typical of Welsh poetic idiom and sacral. They were used in the *Historia* in the account of the siege of Lindisfarne, and this may well have been the immediate source used by the author of the *Annales*. However, the list of metaphorical meanings is virtually endless. Here the context presumably connects with the crucifixion, so perhaps Christ's rebuilding of the Temple in three days (Matthew xxvii, 40) is relevant. More particularly, however, this reference recalls the days and nights spent in the tomb by Christ and 'the third day [when] he shall rise again' (Mark x, 34).

The case for this account of Badon being independent of the *Historia* is therefore unsustainable. It is a mixture of elements and phraseology from at least two sources. The dominant strand derives from chapter 56 of the *Historia*, but there are additions from elsewhere in this text. However, the whole is reconfigured to carry a rather different message. The author has added some details of his own from the Bible, apparently designed to position Arthur as a figure close to Christ and as the representative of a chosen people of the Lord – more as a *servus Dei* than as the Saxon-slaughtering *miles* and Joshua-figure of the *Historia*. This very different image was conditioned by the contemporary need to accommodate English power and authority, and has no retrospective historical validity.

The *Annales* also includes a second Battle of Badon in 665, but this time presented without elaboration. Despite much comment on it and efforts to historicize it at Bath (Alcock 1971), it is far from clear what the author was seeking to achieve in this second reference, or where (if anywhere) he found it. A late sixth-century king of Ulster, Fiachra, was the son of one *Baedán*, but there seems little to connect this Irish personal name otherwise with the *Annales* entry and the battle does not occur in Irish texts. The *Anglo-Saxon Chronicle* reference to the English capture of Bath is similarly a century too early to have been a likely source, even supposing that the author made this connection. This entry falls within that problematic early part of the middle section of the *Annales*, which was developed from an earlier chronicle written at St David's from the late eighth century, in combination with other materials. The author apparently identified this battle with the locality of that fought by Arthur 149 years previously, but that may simply mean that he had his own understanding of where the original battle was fought.

Camlann is similarly presented as a battle in which one of the protagonists is anonymous, although the reason is unlikely to be the same. *Gueith Camlann* does not occur in the *Historia*. That said, it is included in the *Annales* in a sentence which has debts to both the Irish chronicle (regarding the 'great mortality') and the *Historia*, so was arguably the author's own construct. The term *Gueith* occurs five times for 'battle' in the *Annales* (and in a personal name in the entry for 862), the others being in the extended entry for 722 (*Gueith Gartmailauc*), in 876 (*Gueith Din Sol*), in 906 (*Gueith Dinmeir*) and in 921 (*Gueith Dinas Neguid*). Whether or not it was used in the late eighth-century original of the chronicle, it was certainly part of the language of the tenth-century author. In all instances it is linked with a vernacular descriptor or place-name, but *Bellum* also occurs in this context (as in 573: *Bellum Armterid*; 631: *Bellum Cantscaul*) so it seems likely that the author was using these two words for battle as alternatives (there are additionally occasional 'sieges' and 'slaughters'), as had the author of the *Historia*. That said, the entry for 722 is reminiscent of a Triad (see Bromwich 1961), and is an unusual 'Welsh' entry at this point, so it may be that some '*Gueith*' entries reflect vernacular sources.

The entry for 537 may, but need not, therefore, derive from a Welsh written source, such as an elegy or eulogy. *Camlann* is perhaps a lost place-name. Traditional attempts to interpret it by reference to Cornwall have been discarded by etymologists keen to sever the later development of connections between *Camlann* and the River Camel (e.g. Jackson 1959a). That said, the two syllables are sufficiently separate in the Harleian text as to suggest two words, *cam* and *lann*, which might translate as 'crooked church', 'crooked cemetery', 'irregular enclosure' or perhaps 'crooked bank' (A. H. Smith 1956: i, 79; ii, 16; Padel 1985: 36, 142–4, 249, 275–7). There is a possibility, therefore, that this is a description in the vernacular, rather than a place-name, comparable to *Gueith Din Sol* ('Battle [on] Sunday'). The alternative view, that it represents Roman *Camboglanna* (Birdoswald: as suggested by Crawford 1935), should probably be set aside as coincidental in a text which seeks to re-envisage Arthur in a south-western Welsh context.

There is, however, no good reason to suppose that whatever sources lay behind the *Annales* notice of *Camlann* were of any great antiquity in the mid-tenth century (Koch 1996). Given the heavy textual debts to the Irish Chronicle and the *Historia* and the apparent lack of early British material, as already established, the author had apparently not taken this entry verbatim from an earlier text. The entire story is best set aside as unverifiable, and potentially, at least, entirely unhistorical.

*Medraut* is equally obscure. The name derives from the Welsh *Medrawd* (Modern Welsh *Meddrawd*), meaning 'a revel rout', from *medd*, 'mead'. The Old Cornish and Old Breton *Modrot* produced the *Modret* of the Domesday Survey (123b) estate of *Tremodret* in Cornwall. The name is generally absent from very early medieval poetry: both he and Arthur displayed excessively bad manners as guests in Triad 54 and 'the three-fold dividing by Arthur of his men with Medrawd at Camlann' was considered one of the 'three unfortunate counsels of the Island of Britain' in Triad 59 (Bromwich 1961: 147, 159). Rowland (1990: 255–6) suggested that Medraut may have been the speaker of a late saga-type *englynion* about Arthur, and is certainly mentioned in the last line of the next: '*Medrawd* is dead. I myself almost', spoken by Arthur, but this was clearly post-Galfridian and its Arthur a late construct. Generally, *Medraut* was characterized as a virtuous and valorous figure in his earlier appearances and seems to have been envisaged as fighting on the same side as Arthur. He did not begin the long slide into villainy until Geoffrey of Monmouth identified him as Arthur's nephew and the cause of his ruin and he was ultimately reconstructed as Arthur's incestuous son and the archetypal figure of evil within the Arthurian narrative. This is, however, far in the future in the mid-tenth century. Where the author of the *Annales Cambriae* found this figure is entirely obscure, but it is a conventional Welsh form of the period and highly unlikely to represent any particularly early tradition or record, particularly given the artificiality of the Arthurian material with which it is associated.

The author's means of dating his Arthurian entries has been a matter of some discussion. The earliest conceivable date of composition lies in the late eighth century (Dumville 1977a: 176). However, the reliance of this early part of the chronicle on an early tenth-century Irish text strongly implies that the Arthurian entries were not written until composition of the full, surviving version of the *Annales* in the mid-tenth century. At that date the notion of British material derived from the sixth century capable of providing an authoritative date seems remote.

The author's dating of his Arthurian entries was presumably governed in part by the obituary notice of St Patrick, whose death he took from his Irish source for the year 457, whom Arthur follows in the *Historia Brittonum*. There is a substantial gap, however, between 457 and the first appearance of Arthur in 516, which suggests that the author was not guided in detail by this account in his chronological strategy. Wiseman (2000) has argued that the author may have used Bede's *Chronica Majora* (written *c.* 725), which locates Gildas's British victory under the leadership of Ambrosius Aurelianus in the period 474–91, then added the 44 years which are attached to the battle by both Gildas and Bede, giving a time-frame of 518–35. At *c.* 516 and 537, the Arthurian entries in the *Annales* certainly make this schema seem attractive, since they are arguably identical within the boundaries of the processes of estimation which underpin all these dates. Wiseman's thesis is, therefore, strengthened when *both* Arthurian entries are considered, as opposed to just one (as he postulated). Although we should not be beguiled too far by the symmetry of this correspondence, which could be coincidental, it is possible that the author had access to the *Chronica Majora*, albeit this solution requires that the author substituted the *Historia Brittonum*'s Arthur for Bede's Ambrosius in a way which is not obviously explicable. This solution is attractive, therefore, but it must remain in the realm of hypothesis.

To approach this issue from an alternative direction, the early golden age in the *Annales* was characterized by a string of saints and the Christ-helper Arthur, and seems to have ended with the successive deaths of two great figures of the *Historia Brittonum*, Arthur (*HB* 56) and Maelgwn (*HB* 62: note the textual similarities once more). The *Historia* mentioned the deaths of neither but this is an annalistic work, the author of which was presumably encouraged by his stock of existing chronicle material to provide death dates. These two were followed by the famous author and prophet-like figure of Gildas, who is not named by the *Historia* but was nevertheless heavily influential in its construction, and would certainly be considered a contemporary of Arthur in southern Wales by the mid-twelfth century.

The *Annales* associates the deaths of both Arthur and Maelgwn with plagues in the Christian insular world. The earliest outbreaks in the Irish chronicles are two 'great mortalities' in the *Annals of Clonmacnoise* in 546 and 550 (*Annals of Ulster* has 545 and 549). While Maelgwn's *obit* (547) approximates to the earlier of these dates, Arthur's predates both. There is, of course, the outside chance that some such plague year was recorded in the now-lost Irish Chronicle which our author used, which has been omitted from later, surviving versions. That is unverifiable, however, and must be considered improbable, so will here be set aside.

The date chosen for Arthur's *obit* was not, therefore, in deference to the first mention of plague in his Irish chronology, but the positioning of Maelgwn's death was. The author could surmise from his reading of the *Historia Brittonum* (*HB* 62) that Maelgwn was an approximate contemporary of Ida of Bernicia. He probably also knew from the *Historia Ecclesiastica*, or from his northern British materials based on that work, that Ida's reign dated *c.* 547–59. The adoption of a date at the very beginning of this range enabled him to connect Maelgwn with his earliest record of plague in the Irish Annals, and explain his death in this way. To this we will return.

This end date meant that the author of the *Annales* had a time-frame for Arthur's career beginning with Patrick's death in 457 and Maelgwn's in 547. Where he was to place Arthur in this ninety-year period was perhaps up to him, but it must be significant that the Arthurian story available in the *Historia Brittonum* placed Badon at the end of a long sequence of victories. These started, at least, against the son of the first Saxon leader, Hengist. This would tend to encourage the positioning of Badon comparatively late in this time-frame. Furthermore, little separates the appearance in the *Historia Brittonum* of Arthur's victories from reference to Ida, who first occurs at the close of chapter 56. This may help contextualize the author's poitioning of his two Arthurian events, in 516 and 537 respectively, only shortly before Maelgwn's death date in 547.

There are a number of possible mechanisms, therefore, which might have encouraged the author to come to this general positioning of Arthur. We have already seen that the author might have used Bede's *Chronica Majora* to narrow down the chronology, albeit only by conflating Ambrosius Aurelianus with Arthur. He may have drawn his conclusions primarily from the *Historia Brittonum*, with some assistance from northern material. Additionally, it may be significant that, within the cycle of years adopted by the author, Camlann was fought in year 93, which is a suspiciously sacral number ($3 \times 3 \times 10 + 3$). However, whichever of these mechanisms be preferred (if any), there seems no good reason to suppose that the author had any near contemporary evidence to connect Badon with the year 516.

To return to the issue of plague, it might be argued that this be considered a suitable means of disposing of the great Maelgwn of the *Historia*. However, this is perhaps to take too simplistic a view since he could simply have been omitted altogether, rather than a death invented. This monastic author, like others throughout the Christian world, had a providential vision of history, in which, on biblical authority, plague and illness were normally interpreted as manifestations of divine displeasure. One need only note Adamnan's unquestioning assumption that the great plagues of the 680s were sent by God, and that only divine dispensation kept him and his companions from being stricken 'although we walked in the midst of this danger of plague' (Anderson and Anderson 1961: 103B, 462–3). The 'great mortalities' in the *Annales* would therefore have been conceived as punishments sent by the Lord, and the deaths of individuals from plague viewed as divine punishment visited upon them, or at least as a lack of special favour.

It is, therefore, a matter of some significance that the deaths of Arthur and Maelgwn were located by this author within plague years. So too was Cadwaladr's, following the record of Cadwaladr's death in the *Historia Brittonum* (*HB* 64): '*Venit mortalitas hominum, Catgualart regnante apud Brittones post patrum sum, et in ea periit.*' Contrast the *Annales* entry for 682 (roman reflecting identical words): '*Mortalitas magna fuit in Brittania in qua*

Catgualart, *filius Catguolaum, obiit*', which is arguably a paraphrase. That said, the *Annales* entry regarding Oswiu's death in 669 suggests that the author was 'correcting' the *Historia's* positioning of Cadwaldr's *obit* as falling within Oswiu's reign.

Following through the logic appropriate to a providential text, their respective deaths from plague would suggest that the author was presenting both Maelgwn and Cadwaladr as having lost divine protection or even having incurred the wrath of God. To a monk at St David's both were, of course, figures specifically associated with the powerful first dynasty of Gwynedd, and we may well be seeing here further evidence of his south-western perspective, which was naturally unfriendly towards political icons peculiar to Gwynedd. That said, both were paternal ancestors of King Owain, as well as his opponents, the sons of Idwal, and their appearance here in this guise had considerable meaning in a current, political context. With regard to the dates, however, in the absence of evidence of nearer contemporary source materials there is no clear basis for seeing either *obit* as authoritative (as Dumville 1984b concluded of Maelgwn).

In contrast, the deaths of Arthur and *Medraut* were in battle, to which the author referred immediately before, and in the same year that, a 'great pestilence' struck both Britain and Ireland. The *Annales Cambriae* generally follows closely the record of Irish 'mortalities', eclipses and other astronomical and natural phenomena, right through to the 'hot summer' of 721, but no plague years occur any earlier than 546. This earlier plague was, therefore, arguably as much a construct as Arthur's death and the whole was presumably developed for rhetorical effect. Gildas had made repeated use of plagues of various kinds to denote God's anger, as Bede had noted. The author perhaps intended that his references in the same entry to the death of the hero Arthus and the first great plague to strike down the the Britons be read as cause and effect, thus as divine punishment of His people incurred by the death of a man portrayed in such laudatory terms in the entry for 516. The Lord rarely intervened directly in events in this text, but, in 880, Owain's great-grandfather was 'avenged' (in Welsh) by God on unnamed enemies. The same idea seems implicit here. The entry dealing with *Camlann* has, therefore, apparently been constructed in this text so as to bring together Arthur's death and the inception of divine punishment of the Britons, as if this catastrophe were the original sin which led to the expulsion of Adam and Eve from the Garden of Eden. *Camlann* therefore marks the eclipse of the golden age of the saints, references to whom had hitherto dominated the text. The author's purpose was apparently to imply that Arthur's death in battle had caused divine punishment to be visited upon the Britons and the Irish.

*Camlann* was not, therefore, offered as a battle between Britons and Saxons, but between rival Britons and/or Irish, since it was the British and Irish nations jointly that were being punished. Indeed, it has always since been interpreted in terms of an inter-British conflict. Like Christ, therefore, the Christ-helper Arthur of the *Annales* was represented as having been slain by his own people, on whom the wrath of the Lord was then visited.

Arthur is, in this construct, a God-beloved, Christ-like, British leader in war, fighting against unnamed opponents in two engagements. Badon was arguably known by the audience to be a battle against the Saxons, but at *Camlann*, these are implicitly British opponents. Arthur was constructed as a symbol of the golden age of divine protection and sanctity, and his death at the hands of his own people brought the vengeance of God down upon them. In biblical terms, the Old Testament positioning of Arthur as Joshua, which the author found in the *Historia Brittonum*, was replaced by a mix of Old Testament Genesis (as first suggested in the context of Bishop Ebur) and New Testament typology. With regard to the latter, Arthur was envisioned variously as Christ or Simon the Cyrenian who carried the Lord's cross. Around this entry were others relating to the conversion of the Irish and the lives of its saints, thus the place of the Britons in salvation history alongside the apostles, whose acts were described in the later books of the Bible.

How, though, did the author arrive at this particular vision of Arthur? The final piece of the jigsaw lies in the second of the Harleian genealogies, which traces the putative ancestry of King Owain, the author's patron one must presume, in the female line back to the ancient rulers of Dyfed and beyond (Figure 32). Owain's maternal ancestor thirteen generations removed was *Arthur map Petr* ('Arthur son of Peter'). We should be in no doubt that this lineage was familiar to the author of the *Annales*, and to the court under whose patronage he wrote. Indeed, it was probably at this point that a clerical scribe was extending the genealogy which was the immediate source of the Harleian text, and the author of the *Annales* is likely to have been aware of this process. Arthur was arguably not added at this point, since we can be reasonably sure that the name was already there in this genealogy in the late eighth century (Miller 1975–6, 1977–8). It gave the author, however, the opportunity when writing a chronicle in support of King Owain to capture the hitherto unrelated Arthur type of Joshua, whom he found in the *Historia*, and conflate this national icon implicitly for local consumption with his patron's obscure ancestor. The result is a very different Arthur, whose meaning would have lain, for an élite audience at the court of Deheubarth, within the ancient dynasty of Dyfed. This understanding of Arthur would have reinforced the sense of a Dyfed-centred golden age in the past by establishing an ancestral figure as its secular protector. The Arthur of the *Historia* was, therefore, being recruited by the author of the *Annales* to support the political agenda of King Owain in the mid-tenth century.

There are further connections to be drawn out of Owain's ancestry. The Irish material, which has been accepted as an authentic eighth-century version, ends with its earliest entry as *Tryffin* (= *Triphun*), five generations before Arthur. The Harleian manuscript constructs the lineage back a further fourteen generations via Magnus Maximus and *Protector* (perhaps on the basis of the inscription on the Vortepor stone: Nash-Williams 1950: no. 138) to Constantine the Great and Helen, who 'left Britain to seek the cross of Christ even to Jerusalem and then bore it even to Constantinople and it is there even now today'. This additional reference to the *crucem Christi* connects with the Arthur figure of the *Annales*, who had (metaphorically one must presume) 'carried the cross of our Lord Jesus Christ' at Badon. More distantly, such ideas connect also with Hywel Dda's pilgrimage to Rome and the author's wider interest in Welsh conformity with Roman practices, including the dating of Easter.

The first Harleian genealogy is equally significant (Figure 33). Owain's paternal descent was taken back to one *Aballac*, the son of a certain *Amalech*, 'who was the son of *Beli* [or *Belus*] *Magnus*, and Anna his mother, whom they say was cousin of the Virgin Mary, mother of our Lord Jesus Christ'. *Beli* occurs later as the great-grandfather of Cadwallon and in other British contexts. *Aballac* is a biblical form, perhaps from Adbeel, a son of Ishmael and grandson of Abraham (Genesis xxv, 13). Amalek was a descendant of Esau and ancestor of the Amalekites, who were bitter enemies of the Israelites, God's chosen people (Genesis xxxvi, 12; I Chronicles i, 36). This conflation of sacred history and royal genealogy positioned Owain's paternal lineage as descended from the very family of Christ, but via individuals whose names connect them with the dispossessed among the early Hebrews. It is important to remember that Owain's cousins shared this lineage, but not Owain's maternal line, and thus were tainted by this sense of 'Otherness', which was perhaps the intention.

Owain was, therefore, being presented as an exceptionally well connected king. He was the immediate product of two glittering lineages, one including Arthur, Magnus Maximus, Constantine and Helen, the other taken back via the first dynasty of Gwynedd to the family of Christ himself, but via several figures whose names signify dispossession and 'Otherness'. All of this helps us to appreciate the intellectual context surrounding the representation of Arthur in the *Annales* and explains the author's particular positioning of his Arthur in partial contradiction to that offered by the *Historia*. This new, tenth-century version of Arthur was implicitly intended to be read as a Demetian ancestor figure, thus as an ancestor of Owain whom he did *not* share with Idwal's sons. Hence Arthur's linkages with Christ were developed, even while he is removed from explicit conflict with the English. His death, at British hands, was avenged by God, much as Owain wished to suggest that his own might be, should he be slain by Idwal's sons. So, too, had God turned away his face from the Jews for their responsibility for the death of Christ. The entirety of this development of Arthur away from the figure offered by the *Historia* was in accord with the very pressing, contemporary political needs of Owain himself, for whom this work had apparently been written. It is Owain alone, not his cousins and enemies, who represents the fusion of these two lines, so the opportunity for reparation of the flawed patrilineal descent.

Ovein
map Elen, merc
  Ioumarc, map
  Himeyt.
map Tancoystl, merc
  Ovein
map Margetiud
map Teudos
map Regin
map Catgocaun
map Cathen
map Cloten
map Nougoy
map Arthur
map Petr
map Cincar
map Guortepir
map Aircol
map Triphun
map Clotri
map Gloitguin
map Nimet
map Dimet
map Maxim Guletic
map Protec
map Protector
map Ebiud
map Eliud
map Stater
map Pincr misser
map Constans
map Constantini Magni
map Constantii et Helen Luic-
  dauc, quae de Britannia
  exivit ad crucem Christi
  quaerendam usque ad Je-
  rusalem et inde attulit
  secum usque ad Constan-
  tinopolin et est ibi usque
  in hodiernum diem.

Oven
map Iguel
map Catell
map Rotri
map Mermin
map Etthil
  merch Cinnan
map Rotri
map Iutgaul
map Catgualart
map Catgollaun
map Catman
map Iacob
map Beli
map Run
map Mailcun
map Catgolaun Lauhir
map Eniaun Girt
map Cuneda
map Aetern
map Patern Pesrut
map Tacit
map Cein
map Guorcein
map Doli
map Guordoli
map Dumn
map Gurdumn
map Amguoloyt
map Anguerit
map Oumun
map Dubun
map Brithguein
map Eugein
map Aballac
map Amalech, qui fuit Beli
  Magni filius, et Anna ma-
  ter ejus, quam dicunt esse
  consobrinam Mariae virgi-
  nis, matris Domini nos-
  tri Jhesu Christi.

**Figure 32** The maternal lineage of Owain: Harleian genealogies, ii (taken from Faral 1929: 51)

**Figure 33** The paternal lineage of Owain: Harleian genealogies, i (taken from Faral 1929: 50–1)

This accounts for Arthur's reconstruction more as a Christ-figure, and less as a Joshua-figure than in the *Historia*, within a New Testament typology.

## CONCLUSIONS

Arthur is only an occasional figure, therefore, in British literature in the period between *c.* 850 and *c.*1000, having been omitted from the bulk of the saga poetry which survives. A single, fleeting reference in the *Gododdin*, which may have been inserted within this time-frame, is best interpreted as a witty allusion to the *Historia Brittonum*. Otherwise the vernacular literature notably lacks any reference to an 'historical' Arthur even in circumstances where such might have been appropriate, and the only figure we come across belongs in the world of magic and mythology (Padel 1994; T. Green 1998).

The two Arthurian entries in the *Annales Cambriae* are far from independent of the *Historia*, but are both included and developed for rhetorical purposes specific to the world picture of St David's and the political agenda of Owain ap Hywel in the mid-950s. While the nationalist warrior-figure of the *Historia* can still be identified in the entry for 516 in the *Annales*, the accommodation of English political power, which is such a feature of that text and the world in which it was written, necessarily required a shift in the characterization and role of Arthur. The new representation veers towards a Christ/Christ-helper figure and away from the British nationalistic and unconquerable *miles* type of Joshua written up for Merfyn's court in the early ninth century.

The Arthur-figure of the *Annales* is further developed, apparently on the understanding that this Arthur was a maternal ancestor of King Owain. The author implicitly took advantage of the coincidence that the same name occurred quite independently in both the royal genealogy of Dyfed and the *Historia Brittonum*. So his Arthur became a hero of Dyfed, who was presented as a Christ-like British leader who was peculiarly under divine protection, and whose death in battle, implicitly against other Britons or the Irish whom they had converted, was avenged by a wrathful God upon the British and Irish nations via the first plague of the post-Roman period. From this providential catastrophe or original sin – not Vortigern's activities, which are unmentioned in this text – stems, implicitly at least, all the later problems of the Britons. One can usefully contrast the relationship between God and Arthur, and those between the Lord and both Maelgwn and Cadwaladr, Owain's putative ancestors in the male line, whom he shared of course with the current rulers of Gwynedd.

Complex messages of contemporary relevance can be read into this. The age of the saints in western Britain and Ireland was symbolized by the leadership in war of a member of Owain's maternal kin. In Owain's veins flowed the blood of the northern Welsh heroes, Maelgwn and Cadwaladr, but their undoubted achievements were tarnished morally and brought down upon them the wrath of God. The combination of the holy Arthur's blood with that of Maelgwn in Owain himself offered the opportunity in the present to renew the British people as a chosen race. This is, therefore, a political tract promoting Owain's claim to Gwynedd and Powys, as had been held by his father (942–50), constructed against Iago and Ieuaf, the sons of Idwal, who were currently in possession. This war was fought out between 952 and 954, the last date in the *Annales*. Both Iago and Owain attended the court of King Eadred shortly before his death in 955, and that seems to have concluded their active hostilities. The text was, therefore, as suggested earlier, arguably written in 954–5, in Owain's first regnal year.

It is this Demetian Arthur of the *Annales* whom we meet again in Triad 1, the author of which perhaps grasped the typological messages implicit in this text (Bromwich 1961: 1):

> Three Tribal Thrones of the Island of Britain:
> Arthur as Chief Prince in Mynyw [St David's]
> And Dewi [St David] as Chief Bishop, and Maelgwn
> Gwynedd as Chief Elder.

There follow two other localities, *Celliwig* in Cornwall and *Pen Rhionydd* in the North, but the Arthur of Wales is herein identified very specifically with Dyfed. This reflects the influence of the St David's community on Arthur's historicization for later generations, alongside their twelfth-century struggle for archiepiscopal status for their bishopric, but its roots lie in the Arthurian material in the *Annales* and genealogies.

The *Annales* entries were developed, therefore, primarily from a known, ninth-century source to conform with a particular dynastic and political agenda in 954–5. Material was added from the New Testament and from at least one now unidentified source (hence references to *Camlann* and *Medraut*), the historical validity of which is unknowable but unlikely. These entries were constructed primarily for contemporary rhetorical purposes and have considerable meaning in the context of the mid-tenth century. They are, however, without any independent historical meaning in a sixth-century context. The *Annales* is valueless, therefore, as to modern constructions of an historical Arthur, but these brief entries had a considerable impact on the later development of the legend. The genealogies are no more capable of sustaining historicity as far back as the sixth century. In a masterpiece of understatement, Molly Miller (1975–6) remarked that they are 'too official to be fully trust-worthy' as evidence for the Dark Ages. They are clearly dynastic propaganda at this remove (Dumville 1977a, 1977b). They are, however, a powerful indicator of the thought-world shared between St David's and Owain's court at the opening of his reign and were developed alongside the *Annales* for immediate political purposes.

# CHAPTER V

# THE RISE AND FALL OF THE 'HISTORICAL' ARTHUR

—— ·◆· ——

> No character, eminent in ancient history, has ever been treated with more extravagance, mendacity and injustice, than the renowned Arthur, the illustrious monarch and valiant commander of the Britons.
>
> (Ritson 1825: i)

## THE ARTHURIAN LEGEND TO *c.* 1100

In the previous chapters, we have explored the ways in which different authors in the early and central Middle Ages positioned the Britons. The character of Arthur was developed by two British writers to establish particular perceptions of their own people within insular history, for specific and contemporary purposes. The *Historia Brittonum* is a post-colonial text, in regard to the aftermath of Roman colonialism. It is also a text developed so as to contest colonialism, written against the threat of renewed Mercian colonization of Wales. In contrast, the *Annales* is far more concerned to contest colonialism from Gwynedd, and its author and his audience were relatively sanguine regarding English political power at the date of composition.

Both these works are highly politicized and their messages essentially contemporary, therefore, each betraying different circumstances and agendas. Of course, one rhetorical package leads from another but each is distinct and contests pre-existing visions of the past. Each sought to use the past for particular present purposes and it is this concept of an author grasping at power via the reconfiguration of history in a particular contemporary context that emerges as paramount for the particular style and type of history being offered.

It is when this sense of immediacy and particularity is lost and these texts are read in parallel, as if composed in some apolitical and timeless space, that reconciliation of their several messages outside the context of their individual authorship seems to be an attractive proposition. A composite or synthetic vision of insular history – and Arthur – then emerges, which combines the

Arthurs of both the *Historia* and the *Annales* as if different but mutually reconcilable facets of the same, historical individual.

To a later medieval reader uninterested in the immediate context of authorship in each case, most of the characterization of the medieval (King) Arthur was at least implicit in one or other of the *Historia Brittonum* or *Annales Cambriae*, or naturally developed therefrom, particularly given periodic cross-fertilization with British folkloric traditions which were still circulating, and developing further, in the eleventh century and beyond.

The *Historia* constructed Arthur as a great warrior and a universally successful, national war-leader. Leadership in war was perceived as a fundamental part of the role of kings in the central Middle Ages, so it is unsurprising that Arthur was rapidly enthroned. Nor were such glorious victories of such number as he was said to have won the norm among petty kings. The *Historia*'s claim that Arthur invariably led the kings of the Britons in battle was naturally read by later audiences as indicative of a great king ruling over other kings. Arthur necessarily emerged, therefore, as an 'overking' and as an emperor – and the role was in a sense pre-ordained by reference to British emperors within the Roman period in the *Historia*. Thus did the twelfth-century *Life of Gildas* written by Caradoc of Llancarfan term Arthur both *rex totius maioris Britanniae* and *rex universalis Britainniae*, clearly developing the logic of the *Historia* within the political understandings of his own day.

It was in part the resulting mirage of a long past, British imperial court among a latterly status-shorn people which sucked in other stories and other heroes. The process is already visible in *Culhwch ac Olwen* in its earliest surviving version *c.* 1100, which was developed in the context of extensive Norman encroachment into Wales (see Edel 1983; Bromwich and Simon Evans 1992; and Diverres 1994 for further comment).

If Arthur was an imperial figure ruling over British kings, then his warfare had presumably, in part at least, to be envisaged somewhere else than in Britain – unless it was all to be construed as petty wars against the Saxons. From this reading of the *Historia*, and the ongoing development of Arthurian folklore in Brittany, there developed the idea of Arthur's conquests on the continent, which are first met with in passing in the pre-Galfridian Breton *Life of St. Goueznovius* and *Culhwch ac Olwen*. These campaigns were developed on the grand scale in Geoffrey's *Historia Regum Britanniae*, which has his empire stretching from Iceland and Scandinavia to the Alps, and contesting even the power of Rome. Arthur's imperial pretensions were developed (as Auguselus, King of Albany, argued therein: *HRB* ix, 18): to 'avenge our ancestors, safeguard our liberty and exalt our king'. They offered a rhetorical and morale-boosting counterbalance to the successive occupations of Britain in the distant past, by Rome and ultimately the Anglo-Saxons. This was a narrative about power and self-esteem, therefore, which was naturally taken up at a later date by others with similar agendas.

Arthur's depiction as the beloved of Christ and the Virgin Mother, and as a Christ-helper, encouraged his reign to be envisaged as a peculiarly golden age, characterized not only by glorious victory and extensive rule but also by high moral standing. There are implicit parallels here with the Old Testament Garden of Eden, the occupation of Canaan and the reign of David. The *Annales* reference to his death, implicitly at British hands, sowed the seeds from which developed the idea of a great treachery which brought about his tragic downfall in Geoffrey's *Historia Regum Britanniae* and pretty well all subsequent Arthurian literature. To flesh out this story of treachery for dramatic effect, the obscure figure of *Medraut* of the *Annales* became Arthur's nephew and adulterous nemesis, Mordred (the name now embraces the Cornish idiom) who treacherously seized the crown. As was necessitated by his new role as the national villain, he then entered into league with the various hateful ravagers of Britain as depicted by Gildas – the Scots, Picts and Irish, but most of all the Saxons, whom Geoffrey had arriving in some 800 ships. This reformulation of *Medraut* is Geoffrey's development. It may well have been inspired by an ironic twist given the story by the author: Old English *Medren* means 'mother's kin', and this may have given him the idea. The notion was given further nuance in the later Middle Ages, when *Medraut* was reinvented as the product of incest committed by the unwitting Arthur and his scheming sister.

As the *Stanzas of the Graves* was later to note, no burial place was known for Arthur – unsurprising, of course, if his origins lay in the fusion of folklore and political utility. This aspect may, of course, owe something to the treatment of Patrick in the *Historia Brittonum* (as suggested on p. 140). However, this fact had a new significance once Arthur had become historicized. Combined with the Christ-like qualities in which he was variously clothed by the *Historia* and *Annales*, this peculiarity provided the kernel from which developed the idea of a real and historical king who did not die but who, like Christ, had been healed of his wounds. Geoffrey manages the obvious contradictions with his accustomed nonchalance (*HRB* xi, 2): 'Arthur himself, our renowned king, was mortally wounded and was carried off to the Isle of Avalon, so that his wounds might be attended to'. One day such a rested hero, undead, might return to defend his people –as Christ too succours his people *post mortem*. This notion of the undead king who could be invoked as a national saviour naturally combined with the folkloric Arthur, who was conceived as being both ageless and deathless, hence outside mortal time-frames. The result was arguably a reinforcement of belief in a folk Arthur as a protective force, as met with by the canons of Laon in Cornwall and Devon early in the twelfth century, who was considered by members of the local community to be still living. William of Newburgh, almost a century later, similarly noted (*The History of English Affairs* I, 9): 'the Britons . . . are considered to be so barbaric that they are said to be still awaiting the future coming of Arthur, being unwilling to entertain the fact of his death'. A messianic figure was the result, who is first encountered in the context of Welsh rebellion under Owain Gwynedd and Rhys ap

Gruffydd against Henry II (Bullock-Davies 1981a). So, too, was the court of Christ's helper and the beloved of the Virgin Mary naturally envisaged as the appropriate space for the contextualization of the Grail and its quest. While neither 'historical' text had even hinted at such a connection, the logic is inherent in their rhetoric when read out of the immediate political contexts in which they were written, and ultimately proved irresistible.

## ARTHUR AS CULTURAL ICON

We have, therefore, by the eleventh century an historicized Arthur developed from the brief entries in the *Historia Brittonum* and *Annales Cambriae*, initially within the Brittonic-speaking lands of western Britain and Brittany but escaping into the mainstream of European culture during the eleventh and twelfth centuries. Two factors particularly affected this wider dissemination, the one cultural, the other political. To establish the cultural dimension, the Arthur figures which were constructed successively in the *Historia* and the *Annales*, despite their brevity, when combined provide a powerfully magnetic literary character. The warrior who dispatched 960 opponents necessarily equates with the biblical champion as well as the dashing hero-type, and his leadership over other kings implies high status, assurance, imperial authority and bearing. Taken together with the conventional Christian virtues of obedience to Christ and the Virgin, which these Arthurs had in abundance, and the figure of a leader avenged by God, we have, either explicitly or implicitly, all the qualities of the classic medieval knightly and crusading hero – virtue, piety, humility, comeliness, bravery and magnificence. Furthermore, the key texts were Latin, hence immediately accessible to the literate classes of western Europe in the eleventh and twelfth centuries, and the name was comprehensible within a Latin and classical milieu. Interest in such a magnetic and virile character across the dominant literary cultures of medieval Europe is entirely understandable once the mechanisms for his escape from the Brittonic-speaking world were in place.

Those mechanisms were ultimately political. The twelfth-century Arthur emerged very largely as a consequence of the Norman conquests of all of Brittany, England and (less securely) Wales. Breton story-telling perhaps provided the source materials from which Chrétien de Troyes developed the earliest surviving continental Arthurian literature (McKenna 1984), under the patronage of Countess Marie of Blois, but it has been argued that Chrétien was also associated closely with the Angevin court (Diverres 1994). Further development of the Arthurian stories is particularly associated with the borderlands between Brittany and France, whence Lancelot, for example, derived (Warren 2000: 171 ff.).

Welsh vernacular literature reflects the deep sense of shock in Wales at the rapid Norman encroachment of the late eleventh century, and this disaster was interpreted internally as yet another consequence of Welsh sins and failures within the national character, as in the lament of *Rhigyfarch* (McCann 1991), a text which was quite intentionally archaic and made connections between the loss of Britain to the English and current losses to the Normans. The colonial process also stimulated a series of hagiographical responses, by which Welsh cult sites stressed the sanctity of pre-existing saints and so defended local traditions and practices against incoming, Anglo-Norman personnel. In some instances, Arthur was utilized therein. Alongside these new texts, copies of the *Historia* and *Annales* were becoming accessible and the Arthur-figure which they offered rapidly passed into the mainstream of Anglo-Norman culture. This was largely through the genius of one Oxford cleric, probably an Austin canon of St George's, who was himself of mixed Celtic-Norman birth and had grown up within the cross-cultural world of south-east Wales, where he had developed a deep fascination with the idea of an ancient British history stretching, as in the *Historia Brittonum*, from Brutus to King Arthur and beyond. This cleric was, of course, Geoffrey of Monmouth, whose *Historia* burst onto the literary scene in the late 1130s.

To place Geoffrey in context, the new generation of Anglo-Norman monks who set about rewriting insular history in the early twelfth century generally found their starting point in Bede's *Historia*, which they considered both prestigious and authoritative. Scholars such as Florence of Worcester, William of Malmesbury and Henry of Huntingdon set about bringing his historical *magnum opus* up to the present, using in large part versions of the *Anglo-Saxon Chronicle* as framework documents around which to work. The latter two did, however, also have access to the *Historia Brittonum* and on occasion sought to reconcile these two traditions. So, for example, Henry included the latter's Trojan origin story in his history and William included Vortimer's and Arthur's victories over the Saxons and Hengist's murder of Vortigern's council (*Gesta Regum Anglorum* i, 8, 1–4). The Anglo-Norman William wrote under the patronage of senior members of the insular political establishment during the second half of the reign of Henry I (1100–35), and probably died in the mid- to late 1140s (Thomson 1999), but his work was fundamentally Anglo-centric, reflecting the nature of his pre-Conquest sources.

However, Anglo-Saxon history was ill-suited to legitimizing the new Norman regime in Britain. For all the Conqueror's claims to be the Confessor's intended successor, William and his sons were too obviously usurpers at a time when Cerdic's blood was still believed to course through the veins of several prominent figures (particularly Edgar the Ætheling who was still alive in the 1120s, thereafter his Scottish nephews). Not until the reign of Henry II was a Norman king able to claim descent from the pre-Conquest English royal house, by which date the matter had become increasingly irrelevant. Nor was English history of any value in regard to the novel interests of its post-Conquest kings in extensive continental territories and the rivalries which those brought, most particularly with the Capetian kings of France.

It was in this context that Geoffrey of Monmouth developed an alternative history of Britain – the *Historia Regum Britannie* – completed at Oxford *c.* 1138. Geoffrey's method is in general terms well understood:

> Geoffrey gathered disparate strands from previous historians, Gildas, Bede and the author of the pseudo-Nennian *Historia Brittonum*, from genealogical material, from Welsh (and probably Breton) legends, from toponymic lore and from Latin literature, and transformed them into a largely unified and seemingly authoritative history of the British people from their origins to the seventh century A.D.
>
> (N. Wright 1985: xviii)

The result was a moralizing text which reads like a history, but one which was highly imaginative as a reconstruction of the past. Admittedly, that fact was concealed to an extent by a veneer of historical style and rhetoric, and Geoffrey was careful to stay sufficiently close to his sources in many areas for his narrative to be acceptable to a reader conversant with a limited range of pre-existing material. However, his great story suited the immediate needs of Anglo-Norman society remarkably well in various respects. In particular, it provided the new Anglo-Norman kings with a predecessor of heroic size, a great pan-British king in a long line of monarchs capable of countering contemporary pressures for decentralization, as had occurred in France, and reinforcing claims of political superiority over the Celtic lands. Existing claims that the Normans were descended from the Trojans gelled easily with the descent of the Britons from the same stock, which Geoffrey excavated from the *Historia Brittonum*, and could ignore the fact that the English had never made any such claim. At the same time, Arthur offered an Anglo-Norman counterbalance to the Capetian development of Charlemagne as an historical icon (e.g. Gerould 1927; but see more recently Gillingham 1991). In a society in which tenure of great estates by particular families was generally no more than two or three generations old, Geoffrey's grand sweep of history carried back an indicative sample of contemporary titles into a distant and authoritative past. The developing use of primogeniture as a means of defending family land required a myth of royal descent from an ancient and prestigious stock, and a rehearsal of the social contracts – and particular gender roles – capable of defending property (Shichtman and Finke 1993). It has reasonably been suggested that this political and dynastic utility was always Geoffrey's intention (e.g. Tatlock 1950: 426), given that he was competing with other writers of history for élite patronage. His was in addition an extraordinarily good story, and the nearest thing to Virgil's *Aeneid* available in an insular setting. As history, it seemed to fill a great gap left by Bede, who had very little to say about the Britons or Britain and its rulers before the seventh century, and particularly before the Roman conquest. Geoffrey was, of course, quite prepared to contest Bede's version of events where necessary to his own rhetorical development (N. Wright 1986), but his narrative did much to fill the substantial space in history which he had identified.

These discrepancies worried some contemporaries: Alfred of Beverley attempted a reconciliation of Bede and Geoffrey *c.* 1143; Gerald of Wales was openly sceptical of the historicity of Geoffrey's work, even while he also quarried it for information on occasion; and William of Newburgh later launched a blistering attack on Geoffrey's credibility, dismissing his *magnum opus* in his introduction as (*The History of English Affairs* I, 5) 'the most laughable web of fiction' which amounted to 'wanton and shamelss lying virtually throughout his book', which should be 'instantly rejected by everyone'. However, the breadth, brilliance and lucidity of this pseudo-history, allied with its developing political and cultural utility, ensured that Geoffrey's version of the past dominated insular history writing from the late twelfth century to the fifteenth and even beyond (MacDougall 1982: 13).

Despite considerable differences, Geoffrey shared several objectives with the author of the *Historia Brittonum*, although he was oblivious to the immediate political context of that work in the early ninth century. In particular, Geoffrey was as keen to defend the reputation of the Britons for bravery in battle and effective military action, against the Gildasian and Bedan vision of an incompetent and degenerate race. So too was he careful to develop a vision of the Britons as an ancient people, derivative of the most authoritative pseudo-history of the day and of a status equivalent or even superior to the ancient Romans. The Trojan origins which he found sketched-out in the *Historia* were therefore developed into a rich chronological narrative of great endeavours and proud achievements attributable to a noble and ancient lineage. The damaging effects of the Roman conquest were mitigated by the development of an entirely spurious pair of victories over Rome. One was achieved by Arthur in the post-Roman period and one in distant antiquity by Brennius and Belinus – the former 'recovered' from the legendary figure of Brennus the Gaul, who putatively attacked Rome itself, as narrated by Livy (*Historia* v, 38). Once again, the touchstone was the issue of tribute paid to Rome (*HRB* ix, 13). Geoffrey developed the *Historia Brittonum*'s narrative of mitigation to the point where British leaders could be depicted as conquerors and tribute-takers on a European scale. Lastly, Geoffrey's vision was of the Britons as the new Israel, a latter-day people of God. In support of this positioning he stressed the paganism, trickery and barbarity of the Saxons and developed the sanctity of British clergy contemporary with Arthur, in particular, alongside putative acclaimed and God-given victories vouchsafed to British armies.

Geoffrey pillaged earlier texts in pursuit of his objectives, with wit and enormous enthusiasm (Hammer 1946). Thus, for example, we find the Arthurian sections making extensive use of the *Historia Brittonum*'s *mirabilia* (*HRB* ix, 6) and the battle-list. At Badon (*HRB* ix, 4), Arthur is depicted as killing just 470 Saxons – rushing into battle with a visage of the Virgin Mary on his shield, which was slung across his shoulders (one might almost imagine that he anticipated the twentieth-century debate on this subject). In the aftermath of Badon, he has some of the Saxons fleeing to the mountains and seeking mountain caves as refuges (*HRB* ix, 5: *fugientes aliquando montes et cavernas montium petebant*: N. Wright 1985 [ch. 148]), which wittily reminds us of the hiding places of the Britons in fear of barbarian attack as depicted by Gildas (*DEB* xx, 2; xxv, 1). The state of York following Saxon occupation (*HRB* ix, 8) similarly mirrors Gildas's description (*DEB* xxvi, 2) of the towns of Britain following the 'war of the Saxon federates'. So too does Geoffrey's work utilize political prophesy – even discounting the prophesies of Merlin which began life as a separate work, and particularly the prophetic clash of two animals (*HRB* x, 2), following the style already established in the *Historia Brittonum* (*HB* 42). The dragon now symbolizes Arthur and the Britons against the bear of Rome – despite Arthur's own name, which reflects perhaps Geoffrey's assumption that his intended audience would have no grounding in Welsh. While the *Historia Brittonum* had depicted his sexual partners as instrumental in Vortigern's downfall, so was Guinevere now caught up, and even to an extent instrumental, in the fall of Geoffrey's Arthur, which was an aspect of the work which would later be massively redeveloped.

The list of Geoffrey's borrowings and adaptations is virtually endless, and is certainly too extensive to detain us at this point, provided his general debts be recognized, and his narrative be construed as a developed example of Cambro-Latin pseudo-history. That said, although Geoffrey was clearly an Arthurian enthusiast (he even abrogated the name to himself) he was not writing just a piece of Arthurian literature. Rather, his was a work of biblical proportions, running across millennia, from a Trojan origin story to Cadwaladr and ultimately Æthelstan, and conceived at a moment when the Welsh were beginning to contest Norman conquest (see Crouch 2000 for the contemporary political circumstances). Arthur was just a part of that narrative, albeit his Arthurian passages are extensive and clearly captured the imagination of his audience. Geoffrey's work provides the foundations of most later treatments.

Geoffrey's Arthur was, therefore, an influential construct. His king was of royal birth but conceived out of wedlock – and Geoffrey may well have developed his hero's family in part as an extended metaphor. Arthur's background had similarities with the family circumstances of the similarly royal but illegitimate Robert, earl of Gloucester, eldest surviving son of Henry I, who was prominent among those to whom he dedicated the work. The young Arthur was depicted as a man others wanted to aid and he developed in stature as he won victories over the enemies of God. He emerged ultimately as a great leader of men, an extraordinarily generous patron who gave lands to his supporters in legendary quantities, but a man too who was feared. In counsel he was judicious and statesmanlike, and his under-kings competed to both praise him and give the advice that they believed he wanted to hear. This Arthur was, therefore, the quintessential twelfth-century ruler writ improbably large, and a highly desirable role model for any insular king with extensive ambitions to overlordship in Britain and territory in France. Geoffrey wrote against a backdrop of political insecurity, as the crisis of succession following Henry I's death in 1135 moved inexorably towards a reign-long civil war. His Arthur offered an icon of strong royal government sustained by a cohort of loyal aristocrats and clergy, but his several dedications demonstrate his personal need to find patronage where he could.

Geoffrey's Arthur was, therefore, a fundamentally twelfth-century figure, operating within a contemporary political context, which had been only marginally adapted to his vision of the past. Like Arthur (*HRB* ix, 11), William the Bastard and Henry I both employed many French soldiers in their service, even against French enemies. The prosperous borough of Totnes (Figures 34 and 35) recurs repeatedly as the main port of entry from Brittany – a function which it may well have served in the early twelfth century (it had a total of 110 burgesses inside and outside in 1086, when it had a lord with a Breton name), but which has no known historicity in the sixth. Geoffrey recognized the significance of current centres, such as London, York and Winchester. However, he added to them, presumably for sentimental reasons to do with his own local upbringing, the Roman fortress at Caerleon-on-Usk (Figure 36), where he positioned Arthur's principal palace, and which he raised too to the status of an archdiocese. His knowledge of Cornwall seems well researched (Ditmas 1972–3; Padel 1984), but it is arguably contemporary Cornwall which he had in mind, with its legends gathered around sites such as Tintagel. One might go on almost indefinitely.

## ARTHUR AS ROYAL CULT

Arthur was taken up in many different parts of Europe, in many instances in contested or border situations (Warren 2000). However, Geoffrey's *Historia* offered the twelfth-century monarchy in England both a foreshortened Anglo-Saxon domination in Britain (Leckie 1981), which barely begins therein before Æthelstan's reign in the tenth century, and powerful precedents for a British *imperium* capable of exploitation in both an insular or a continental context. Geoffrey clearly intended his narrative for élite, court consumption: his texts were variously dedicated to Henry I's eldest illegitimate son, Robert, to the wealthy and erudite courtier Count Waleran of Meulan and (in one instance) to King Stephen himself. Arthur rapidly became an historical fact within these circles, even despite their fission by civil war. When Gaimar wrote a French version of English history, soon after Geoffrey had completed his work, he contextualized King Edgar's imperial status by reference to Arthur's (*L'Estoire des Engleis* lines 3562–7). From Henry II onwards until at least Henry VIII, English kings, their courtiers and their apologists took the existence of Geoffrey's Arthur as a matter of fact which was beyond doubt. Many, most obviously Edward I, made extensive use of his reign as a

**Figure 34** Totnes: the shell keep of the twelfth-century castle

**Figure 35** Totnes: the harbour, to which Geoffrey of Monmouth imagined his British heroes sailing

**Figure 36** Caerleon-on-Usk, the Roman walls

source of political precedent and propaganda to be reformulated for present purposes of political status and aggrandizement. Those English kings who had territorial or political ambitions in France found in Geoffrey's work a valuable retort to the Capetian development of political legends based on Charlemagne, and his vision of the great battle against the Romans and their eastern tributary kings had resonances too for any ruler interested in crusading.

Even without the crusade – on which he failed ultimately to depart, Henry II's territorial interests from 1154 onwards extended from Northumberland to the Pyrenees, and he was additionally minded on occasion to exercise power across all of Wales, Ireland and Scotland. On the continent he contracted marriages for his daughters with the kings of Castille and Sicily and dukes of Saxony and Toulouse. In such circumstances, Arthur's career provided appropriate political precedents for Henry's position and an interest in his story was almost obligatory by the late 1150s. Henry duly patronized the Norman cleric, Wace, who had translated Geoffrey's work into French octosyllabic couplets, the *Roman de Brut*, in the early 1150s, and commissioned him to do something similar for the Norman Rollo. Marie de France wrote at his court: she may even have been the king's half-sister. A copy of the *Roman*, which was, incidentally, the first text to incorporate a round table at Arthur's court, was presented to Eleanor of Aquitaine very soon after her arrival. Arthurianism was active elsewhere as well, with Laȝamon, the parish-priest of Areley-Kings in the Severn valley, rewriting Wace in alliterative English vernacular (the *Brut*: Barron 1989, Barron and Weinberg 1995).

Arthur had, of course, to be laid to rest, and so disabled as a symbol of Welsh resistance to Anglo-Norman domination, and this was achieved spectacularly at Glastonbury, where his remains (alongside those of Guinevere) were 'discovered' in 1191 (Figure 37). Arthur had already been connected with Glastonbury by Caradoc of Llancarfen early in the century, but the new enterprise was envisaged on an entirely different level. The 'discovery' followed a great fire, which gutted the buildings in 1184, and the monks clearly expected their find to generate publicity and tourism capable of aiding their rebuilding, as had worked so well in recent years at Canterbury (Rahtz 1993). However, there was also a political dimension. Henry II (died 1189) had himself allegedly instructed their excavations, having putatively been advised of the whereabouts of Arthur's body by a Welsh bard, and the highly secretive excavations were undertaken with King Richard's support. In somewhat variant forms the story was told by Gerald of Wales, Ralph of Coggeshall (J. Stevenson 1875) and Adam of Domerham (Hearne 1727: ii, 341–3). The whole event seems to have been entirely fraudulent, as was the inscription allegedly establishing the identity of the remains, of which Gerald's version reads in translation:

HERE IN THE ISLE OF AVALON LIES BURIED THE RENOWNED
KING ARTHUR, WITH GUINEVERE, HIS SECOND WIFE

**Figure 37** Glastonbury, the site of Arthur's shrine

A seventeenth-century edition of William Camden's *Britannia* offered a drawing of the cross, and the first edition recorded its inscription as *HIC IACET SEPULTUS INCLITUS REX ARTURIUS IN INSULA AVALONIA*. The style was not out of place in the tenth–twelfth centuries and it assuredly was not sixth century. We must assume a forgery. Further we cannot say, since it has been missing since the late seventeenth century, other than to note that it was good enough to be accepted as genuine at the time. When the 'excavation' of 1191 was opened up, slab-lined graves dating to the seventh century were discovered beneath material dumped on the area in the tenth century.

The Glastonbury 'recovery' was part of an appropriation of the idea of Arthur from its Welsh origins by the Anglo-Norman élite who now held power across most of Britain and parts of Ireland and the Continent. It opened the door to a political cult to rival that of Charlemagne, which Richard much needed in his dealings with his rival, brother-in-law and fellow crusader, Philip Augustus. Note Richard's gift of a sword, which he passed off as Excalibur, to his ally Tancred of Sicily, while on crusade. Henry II's first grandson had by this date already been christened Arthur (1187–1203), although this may say more about Breton politics than Henry's, and was acknowledged by the childless King Richard as his intended heir. He later came close to becoming ruler of all the Plantagenet territories on the continent before his capture and murder by King John.

Even following Prince Arthur's brutal death, the political cult of Arthur continued, under the active encouragement and exploitation of English kings. Ralph of Coggeshall, writing under John, summarized Geoffrey's British saviour, who 'expelled the Saxons and restored the churches' and recorded the results of the excavations at Glastonbury (J. Stevenson 1875: 36, 435).

Both Edward I and his grandson, Edward III, were avid Arthurians, visiting and further endowing the cult site at Glastonbury and patronizing the development of Arthurian court culture. Edward I liked to think of himself as Arthur reborn and he and Eleanor presided over a grand reopening of the Glastonbury tomb just after Easter in 1278, by which he orchestrated the connection (Loomis 1953). Thereafter he patronized a shrine of Arthur in the church, which seems to have survived up to the Dissolution, the base of which was discovered by excavation in 1963. Similarly, Edward promoted the cult of Joseph of Arimathea, also at Glastonbury (Carley 1985), depicting this insular church as apostolic, therefore less dependent on Roman jurisdiction (which accorded well with Edward's wider policies towards the papacy), and his representatives mined Geoffrey's history for evidence in support of a court case at Rome in 1301 regarding suzerainty over Scotland (Stubbs 1882: I, 113–14). He could well have been responsible additionally for the Winchester Round Table, which is first known to have been used as the centrepiece of a great feast at Winchester in 1290 and was probably commissioned for the purpose (Biddle 2000). However, the idea of a round table apparently even predates Wace and seems to have Breton roots (McKenna 1984). Arthur continued, of course, to be remoulded to current cultural needs.

The female and romantic interests in the story came more to the foreground from the twelfth century onwards, reflecting the nature of medieval court life and the rise of *courtoisie*. Such interests also reflect the concern of predominately male authors with the dangers to the well-being of dynasties posed by such evil women as Geoffrey's Saxon Renwein, who ensnared Vortigern and so ruined a people. Arthur's preoccupations, however, tended to mirror those of the current monarch. So, for example, Peter of Langtoft's French verse chronicle, written in the reign of Edward I, adapts what is an essentially Galfridian vision of Arthur to accord with Edward's attempts to impose his authority on the Scots (T. Wright 1866: I):

> en Morreve s'en vait,
> Sur les Escoz e Pyctes segnurer volayt.

> he proceeds into Murray,
> He wished to be lord over the Scots and Picts.

John of London's tribute to Edward I would later compare him favourably with Alexander, Brutus, Arthur, Edgar and Richard I (Stubbs 1882: II, 15), enabling us to see the early stages of his inclusion in lists of worthies. The young Edward III, who ascended the throne at 14, was similarly compared favourably by a contemporary with Arthur, who was putatively 15 when he became king (Stubbs 1882: II, 95). Under Edward, English writers continued to envisage Arthur as historical, even despite the recognition, by such scholars as Ranulph Higden at Chester, that he was unknown in continental chronicles, as well as to Gildas and Bede (Babington 1865: 334). However, the well connected Ranulph concluded, 'the custom of every nation is to extol some of their blood in great excess', and that, as far as he was concerned, explained the differences between Galfridian and other versions of history. He therefore took his vision of Arthur from Geoffrey and the *Brut*, but he annotated the story for local, north-western consumption, equating Douglas, for example, with the Lancashire river of that name. Thereafter, he sought to reconcile the Galfridian tradition with that of the *Anglo-Saxon Chronicle* by concluding that Arthur had got tired of fighting the Saxons and ultimately settled Cerdic in Hampshire and Dorset.

Edward III was later to capitalize on his Arthurian connections: he announced a plan to 'revive' the Order of the Round Table at a great tournament at Windsor in 1344, apparently so as to project and glorify his own reign via this association. His inspiration was clearly the literary model going back to Geoffrey, but Alfonso XI of Castille's new Order of the Band may also have influenced his thinking. However, the project was abandoned in November of the same year, apparently owing to its anticipated cost at a moment when the French war was reviving. Edward adopted the Garter badge and motto for his new expedition to France and established the Order of that name in far more modest fashion after his triumphant return from Crécy, in August 1348, in part inspired by the chivalric fraternity recently established by Duke Jean of Normandy. The new institution was an 'Arthurian' type of secular order, albeit under a new name, established at Windsor, which was popularly believed to have been founded by Arthur. However, it was now under the aegis of St George, whose sanctity and crusading connections apparently gave him the edge over Arthur (Vale 1982; Boulton 1987; Collins 2000). That said, Arthur remained an invaluable icon: Geoffrey's narrative provided justification for Edward's French engagements and probably both encouraged and popularized them (for wider discussion, see Ormrod 1990).

A century later, Edward IV sought to capitalize on his own Welsh forebears (he was descended from the Welsh kings via the Mortimers), in an attempt to shore up his otherwise contestable claim to the English throne by claiming descent from Geoffrey's kings of Britain (Anglo 1961–2). This politically astute obfuscation portrayed him, therefore, as the British messiah and the Red Dragon, whose recovery of power over Britain had been prophesied to Cadwaladr in Geoffrey's *Historia*. Contemporary English history fully acknowledged Arthur's role in the history of Britain and focused on his glorious successes in France, and on Welsh belief in his continuing existence. So, for example, John Capgrave, who dedicated his *Chronicle of England* to Edward, wrote (Hingeston 1858: 87, quoting a near-contemporary translation):

> In these dayes was Arthure Kyng of Bretayn, that with his manhod conqwered Flaunderes, Frauns, Norwey, and Denmark; and, aftir he was gretely wounded, he went into a ylde cloped Avallone, and there deyed. The olde Britones suppose that he is o lyve.

During Edward's reign Malory completed his *Morte d'Arthur*, the production of which coincided with the development of printing in England, and William Caxton guaranteed this work immortality by printing it in 1485. Caxton, who had already printed *The Chronicles of England* – a compilation of Geoffrey's work and the *Chronicle of the Brut* – was a keen Arthurian whose histories had a moral purpose, as his preface attests:

> I, according to my copy, have set in imprint, to the intent that noble men may see and learn the noble acts of chivalry, the gentle and virtuous deeds that some knights used in those days. . . . Do after the good and leave the evil, and it shall bring you to good fame and renown.

In this same year, Henry Tudor returned from exile and, marching through Wales under the banner of the Arthurian Red Dragon, defeated and killed

Richard III at Bosworth Field to take the English crown. Henry's accession let loose a brief storm of Arthurianism, but one which had relatively few long-term resonances outside Wales itself, where he was just one of a long line of messianic figures to be hailed by Welsh bards throughout the fifteenth century. Henry's central claim was to unite in his own person the rival dynasties of Lancaster and York (the latter rapidly reinforced by marriage to Elizabeth of York), but he was also popularly perceived as rightful king by descent from Cadwaladr and Arthur (Gairdner 1858: 9–11), and some of the numerous royal genealogies constructed during his reign, particularly in the early years, record this putative descent (Anglo 1961–2). The centrality of the Arthurian cult to Henry's position at the very beginning of his reign is attested by his naming of his first-born son Arthur, significantly at Arthurian Winchester where he was also born, in 1486. Arthurianism rapidly lost its central place at Henry's court, however. For example, in the detailed description of the great tournament staged to celebrate the dubbing of Prince Henry knight and his investiture as Duke of York in 1494, King Arthur receives no mention. Few pageants of the reign of Henry VII used the motif and Henry VIII's ministers failed to include it in the English contribution to the pageantry of the Field of the Cloth of Gold in 1520, although it did occur in the entertainment of Charles V at Calais later that year. Both Geoffrey's work and the Winchester Round Table were called back into play in the development of Henry VIII's imperial pretensions as the divorce crisis unfolded, but neither assumed a particularly central role in the dynasty's positioning of itself.

## ARTHUR IN QUESTION

Even while Arthur retained both popularity and a degree of political utility under the early Tudors, the more critical historical writing which characterized the continental Renaissance had already found Arthur and the entire *Brut* tradition less than persuasive. This reaction reached England initially in the second half of the fifteenth century, with such figures as John Whethamstede, abbot of St Albans, voicing mild doubts. William Caxton felt himself bound to contradict (in his preface to Malory) the view that 'divers men hold opinion that there was no such Arthur, and that all such books as been made of him, be but feigned and fables, because that some chronicles make of him no mention, nor remember him nothing, nor of his knights'. John Rastell's *Pastyme of People* (1529) was highly critical of the historical Arthur, and there was growing scepticism by the mid-century about the legendary British ancestors claimed for the Tudor monarchs. Henry VIII's genealogies generally focused on his claims of descent from both York and Lancaster and quietly forgot his paternal grandfather, Owen Tudor, whose descent from Cadwaladr had previously been given considerable prominence.

But it was the Italian humanist Polydore Vergil, whose *Anglica Historia* was commissioned by Henry VII to advertise the legitimacy of his jejune dynasty in Europe, who first subjected Geoffrey's *Historia* and the *Brut* tradition of insular history to detailed scholarly criticism. Apparently completed in 1513, it was not published until 1534, arguably because it dismissed the entirety of Geoffrey's narrative as unproven, ejected Arthur from history to the realm of legend and romance and ridiculed the Arthurian cult site of Glastonbury (Hay 1950, 1952). Polydore's method was to have recourse to as near contemporary writers as possible, and he used the works of Caesar, Tacitus, Gildas, Bede, William of Newburgh and Henry of Huntingdon as a counter-balance to the *Brut* and Ranulph Higden's *Polychronicon*. His historical analysis was devestating (Hay 1950: xxix).

However, by 1533 Henry VIII had other concerns. He was apparently prepared to sacrifice Arthur and back publication of Polydore's work in Basle in order to profit from its portrayal of his English kingship as an empire. This was now a pressing need, since the Act in Restraint of Appeals passed through Parliament in the same year (Koebner 1953). The *Anglica Historia* was both a work of high politics, therefore, and history of a revolutionary kind by contemporary standards, but it proved highly contentious. Insular critics were particularly incensed by its 'foreign' attacks on many of the basic tenets of English nationalism as then understood, for, as Caxton had previously averred, 'he [Arthur] was a man born within this realm [i.e. England and Wales], and king and emperor of the same'. Popular perceptions of national identity were at stake, and to question the Arthurian narrative was considered by many to be tantamount to treason.

As the Reformation gathered pace, Polydore's Catholic, Italian background rendered his historical vision particularly vulnerable to Protestant as well as nationalist criticism in England, and chroniclers such as Raphael Holinshed and Richard Robinson, the antiquarians John Leland and Humphrey Lhuyd, Bishop John Bale and the Welsh lawyer Sir John Price all protested the historicity of Arthur, whose imperial status remained of considerable utility to the Tudors in their dealings with both Scotland and Ireland. Leland was among the best connected of Geoffrey's apologists. In his *Itinerary*, written as rough notes of his travels in the 1540s, Arthur plays a comparatively minor role. The author was content to acknowledge Arthur as historical and as a significant feature of England's past, to be documented as such wherever appropriate. So he reported Arthur's epitaph on the Edwardian shrine at Glastonbury (Leyland, ed. Smith 1964: i, 288), wherein he was described as the *flos regum*, *gloria regni* ('the flower of kings, glory of the kingdom'), and also his place in the landscape around (*ibid.* p. 148): 'Or ever this river [Bruton] cum to Glessenbyri by a mile it cummith to a bridge of stone of a 4. Arches communely caullid Pont-perlus, wher men fable that Arture cast in his swerd.' In Cornwall, he reported the story of Camlann (*ibid.* p. 316): 'By this ryver Arture fowght his last feld, yn token wherof the people fynd there yn plowyng bones and harneys.' Polydore's work was, however, considered dangerous by Leyland, who produced a pamphlet in response in 1536 and then the impassioned *Assertio Inclytissimi Arturii* (published in London in 1544), which exhibited outright xenophobia in its patriotic defence of the historicity of both Brutus and Arthur. Bale similarly argued that Polydore 'hath in this point deformed his writings greatly, polluting our English Chronicles most shamefully with his Romish lies and other Italian beggarys' (quoted by Hay 1950: xxxv).

Hostility to Polydore's debunking of Arthur coincided with the beginning of a full-scale reconstruction of national, political theory to accommodate the revolutionary consequences of the Henrician Reformation. New readings of the past were designed to differentiate the English people from the remainder of Latin Christendom and focus it instead on obedience to the monarch, and so develop the special nature of the English *vis-à-vis* their continental neighbours (E. Jones 1998). Faced with the dissolution of the monastic libraries, Leland sought to persuade Henry VIII to found a national collection to preserve the ancient records of the realm for the 'greater glory of Britain' (Flower 1935). Despite further efforts at persuasion, none of Henry, Edward VI, Mary or Elizabeth took up the challenge to particular effect, but their subjects did: Archbishop Parker and Sir Robert Cotton created their own libraries, Holinshed wrote histories and Laurence Nowell began what was essentially the modern study of the Anglo-Saxon past (Warwicke 1979). After about 1570, interest in ancient British history was particularly widespread, providing the context, for example, for the imaginative development of the story that a Welsh princeling, Madoc, had discovered America long before Columbus (Roberts 1991). This notion was, of course, politically motivated, providing as it did the necessary precedent through which to claim all of North America for Queen Elizabeth. Such intent well illustrates both the value and the vitality of British pseudo-history at this date. Despite the doubts of the intelligentsia, therefore, to contest the historicity of Arthur was generally perceived as both unpatriotic and papist.

The widespread reaction to Polydore Vergil in England enabled the court cult of Arthur to be retained under Elizabeth, with Arthurian pageantry, tournaments and the newly conceived 'Society of Archers' (or 'Prince Arthur's Round Table'). Thomas Hughes wrote *The Misfortunes of Arthur* (1587), a serious play intended to evoke horror at civil war, which was performed before the Queen in 1588, the year of the Spanish Armada (Cunliffe 1912: 220–96). Spenser's *Faerie Queen* (produced in 1590), served once again to connect Elizabeth with the putative Arthurian golden age. Spenser (J. C. Smith 1909) used Britain's antique past to provide the setting for allegorical romance in the present, with Prince Arthur recruited to sustain the current, Tudor myth of legitimacy by excluding potentially embarrassing difficulties around primogeniture within the current royal family. In this context, the utility of political mystification and Arthur's role as a model patron and sovereign were valuable means of holding back the tides of scepticism (Finke 1994).

This was, however, the last real flowering of court Arthurianism: a growing number of English antiquarians were finding it ever more difficult to defend the historicity of the *Brut* tradition, even despite the foreignness of its principal critic. Elizabethan parliamentarians were already exploring the origins of contemporary institutions and the English legal system, looking back to a more consensual, medieval past than was implicit in Arthurianism. The developing tension between intellectual history and political correctness was magisterially dealt with by William Camden, in his *Britannia* (first published 1586). Camden circumnavigated the potential political embarrassment by damning the Arthurian tradition with faint praise and the criticisms – which he but feebly protested – of other men. Arthur was entirely omitted from his brief historical summary but does appear, for example, in his treatment of the tomb at Glastonbury (pp. 103–4) and of the Welsh Marches, where (p. 356) 'the name is allotted by the vulgar to the great King Arthur of the Britons'.

As Elizabeth aged without heirs of her own body, James VI of Scotland developed his own claim to the British crown, not only by descent from the Tudors but also, more imaginatively, via the Stuarts from Llewelyn the Last, and so back to the royal line of the *Brut* and Arthur, and his genealogy was developed accordingly. Scotland was no stranger to the Arthurian tradition and its political utility. References were adopted wholesale into official poetry addressed in the fifteenth and sixteenth centuries to the Campbells of Argyll, to reinforce their claims to British descent and contest the Gaelic basis of rival political and territorial claims made on behalf of Clan Donald (Gillies 1982). From the 1540s through to about 1615, reappraisals of Arthur were conducted by successive Scottish writers of the pro-Reformation and unionist political persuasion. Their works prepared the ground for the Jacobean reassertion of pan-British imperialism, which was to be a feature of government policy under James I (Allan 1997). James was hailed in a pageant staged at the beginning of his reign as 'a second Brute sent to redeem political sin committed when the first king divided Britain' (Axton 1977: 132) but the Commons successfully resisted his attempts to formalize union (J. Wormald 1992). This struggle is the context for the first performance of *King Lear* before the King in 1606, which was the first of two plays which Shakespeare based loosely on the *Brut* tradition (the second, *Cymbeline*, was written c. 1609–10: Hieatt 1988). Thomas Heywood's *Troia Britanica*, first produced in 1609, adopted the same theme, and was perhaps the last work of the age to portray Arthur as a magnificent, historical monarch (Bush 1945).

James's eldest son, Prince Henry, showed considerable interest in the Arthurian royal cult, but he died young and enthusiasm at court subsided with his death. Thenceforth, English court ideology was to provide little protection for Arthur's historicity, parliamentarians were increasingly hostile to its implications and the growing concerns of antiquarians variously with Geoffrey's reliability and with an Anglo-Saxon past were allowed increasingly free rein.

To sum up, therefore, intellectuals in Renaissance England experienced considerable difficulty in accepting Arthur as historical, but élite patronage had, to an extent, worked in his favour throughout the fifteenth and sixteenth centuries. Arthur was too useful, for a variety of interlocking political and cultural purposes, for the early modern court circle readily to let go. Although it is quite easy to over-emphasize Arthur's importance, he was successively used for political and cultural purposes by Edward IV, Henry VII, Henry VIII and Elizabeth, then James VI and I, variously as a source of dynastic legitimacy and imperial status, as a Protestant icon, as a touchstone of nationalism and the new identity of the realm with the monarch's own person, and as a source of courtly ideals and pageantry.

## THE FALL OF KING ARTHUR

The balance between historical scepticism and politico-cultural utility was to shift dramatically during the seventeenth century. The change of dynasty ultimately marginalized Arthur by the end of the second decade and, as a political idea and cultural icon, he was too closely identified with absolutist kingship and royalist political circles not to be damaged mortally by the Civil War and Protectorate. Arthur and republicanism made improbable bedfellows, to say the least. The Restoration brought a more consensual and oligarchical system of royal government into existence, with the power of the monarchy circumscribed in ways utterly at odds with Arthur as a political icon. Then, again, Jacobean ideology was seriously compromised by the 'Glorious Revolution' of 1688, to which later generations looked back as a cusp event in British history. In consequence, Arthur's legend began to be displaced within insular culture by others of greater cultural and political utility. It is no surprise that the marginalization of the historical Arthur coincided with an irruption of interest in the origins and antiquity of political institutions and liberties, such as were believed from the seventeenth century onwards to form the principal defence against royal tyranny. Arthur was eventually superseded by the adoption of King Alfred as a founding father for the Anglo-centric British state, a process which reached its apogee with the work of Sharon Turner and his Anglo-Saxonist successors during the nineteenth and twentieth centuries.

Two very different authors of the seventeenth century effectively illustrate the decline of Arthur, John Milton and John Dryden. Milton wrote his historical essay *Britain under Trojan, Roman, Saxon Rule* in 1639, but it was ultimately printed only under heavy censorship in 1670, with the suppressed passages then reappearing from 1681 onwards (quotations here are from the 1870 edition). Milton combined a Gildasian vision of terrified Britons alongside a Bedan picture of valorous Saxons. He followed the *Historia Brittonum* in reconstructing Vortigern, Vortimer, Ambrosius and Arthur, albeit he had

239

some reservations about the latter (p. 81): 'Arthur, as being then chief general for the British Kings, made great war; but more renown'd in songs and romances, than in true stories'. His was, however, a work interested primarily in a moral vision of history, written against (p. 192) 'sottishness' and tippling, 'with other vices, which effeminate men's minds', and for Milton it was the weakness induced by immorality that had caused the downfall of the Britons.

John Dryden's handling of Arthur marks the next stage in these processes. The playwright and satirist was in origin a Puritan and an admirer of Cromwell but adjusted his output to the Restoration and enjoyed a successful career under royal patronage. There followed a string of stage extravaganzas beginning with *The Indian Queen* (1664), efforts at popular comedy and heroic tragedy. He achieved high favour and the offices of laureate and historiographer royal at the royal court from 1670. On James II's succession in 1685, Dryden converted to Catholicism. His last work for the king was the poem *Britannia rediviva* in 1688, to celebrate the birth of a royal heir. Arthur was a late choice of subject, however, which in itself reflects his marginalization within the political culture of the day. The opera, *King Arthur, The British Worthy*, for which Purcell memorably wrote the music, was begun in 1684. It was intended as an allegorical representation of King Charles's struggle, as Arthur, against the Whigs (C. A. Price 1984), represented by the Saxon Oswald, here portrayed somewhat improbably as a pagan 'valiant dog'. It was, however, laid aside, presumably on account of Charles's death in 1685 and the subsequent rebellion and execution of Monmouth. When it was finally completed, in 1691, it was in a totally different political environment, in which, as a Catholic, Dryden had lost his place at court following William's seizure of power, and he had had to alter it considerably (Summers 1931–2: vol. 6).

Arthurianism was a further casualty of the new intellectual environment of the 'long eighteenth century', which is perhaps best exemplified in its earliest manifestation by the works of John Locke (1632–1704), who placed his pen at the disposal of William of Orange within months of his arrival in England. William's position was far from secure. The vision of a popular uprising in his favour is very largely retrospective and he was all too dependent on Dutch troops, a small clique of political activists, his own consummate skills as a propagandist and politician and the self-interest and personal commitment of John Churchill. Although William's own preferences were far more conservative on this issue, Locke's political vision was at odds with the ideals of hereditary and absolute kingship which had accumulated around King Arthur, and the political philosophy which he represented.

William's coup was problematic on many levels, but his supporters used history as one of several weapons in his defence. Sir William Temple was a successful career diplomat and long-time supporter, who had been instrumental in arranging his marriage and had admired him for two decades (see, for example, Temple 1672). His *An Introduction to the History of England* (1695) provided a sketch of Anglo-Saxon history and the Norman Conquest, but dwelt at length only on the career of William I. Temple's purpose was clearly to provide an historical parallel capable of flattering the new, foreign king, whose position had been significantly weakened by the death of Mary in the previous year (Woodbridge 1940; Steensma 1970). Temple's treatment of earlier history has been criticized as sketchy and amateurish, but this is to ignore the currency of its political purposes, wherein Arthur could not be reconciled. His reworking of the past in support of the Revolution of 1688 was ably supported by other writers, who likewise sought the origins of much-vaunted 'present liberties' in 'an inherited Gothic genius for creating and maintaining free institutions' (MacDougall 1982: 75), hence in Anglo-Saxon England rather than the *Brut* and Arthurian past (R. J. Smith 1987). Such liberties were then envisaged to have passed, via William I in the strange role of conservator of the Anglo-Saxon constitution and people, into 'constitutional' documentation of the Middle Ages, such as Magna Carta, and so into the defence of parliamentary liberties in the sixteenth and seventeenth centuries.

There continued from the sixteenth century, however, an eclectic and antiquarian approach to the British past, epitomized perhaps most famously at this date by the observations of William Stukeley (1724), which remained prepared to accommodate King Arthur in a minor and local role, as a figure of legend. A new, updated edition of Camden's *Britannia* appeared in 1695, and rapidly spread among the libraries of the gentry. Daniel Defoe used it extensively in writing his *Tour through the Whole Island* of Great Britain (1724–6), not least in his description of Glastonbury (letter 4), where he noted both the twelfth-century excavation of King Arthur's grave and the thorn tree reputed to derive from the staff of Joseph of Arimathea. His central endeavour was, of course, a present one, in 'praise of the British: their commerce, their industry, their history' (Rogers 1971: 34), and such antique figures were included primarily as ornaments to add depth to a text more interested in local economies and stately homes in the present.

Defoe repeatedly used local legends as a vehicle to demonstrate his own, superior critical faculties by refuting them as unhistorical, and this was his approach at Winchester (letter 3), where he noted:

> the tale of King Arthur's round table ... which table hangs up still, as a piece of antiquity, to the tune of 1200 years, and has, as they pretend, the names of the said knights in Saxon characters, and yet such as no man can read. All this story I see so little ground to give the least credit to, that I look upon it, and't shall please you, to be no better than a FIB.

The painting itself dated only from Henry VIII's reign, when the table was hurriedly 'improved' to impress the representatives of the Hapsburgs, so we must sympathize with Defoe on this issue. With Arthurian Britain deeply devalued within this intellectual environment, the details which had formerly seemed collectively to have sustained the entire corpus of legends were become individually vulnerable to specific criticism as unhistorical and manufactured.

The nonconformist Defoe distinguished very little between the English, the Welsh and the Scots, although he was quite capable of condemning particular places, as Bangor-is-y-coed for example, which he detested as the putative birthplace of the arch-heretic Pelagius (letter 7). His was not, however, primarily a racial vision of history. Rather, Defoe contested that tendency in an ironic poem published in 1701, arguing that the English were a peculiarly hybrid people, and that the increasingly strident claims being made at the time by members of the aristocracy to Anglo-Saxon ancestry were both irrational and incapable of providing distinction in the present.

Defoe and like-minded writers (Voltaire included) were contesting more racially constructed histories, which found new strength in the arrival of the Hanoverians from what was increasingly being viewed as the ancestral, Germanic homeland of the English. This new monarchy was, therefore, perceived as complementing the Germanic people already in control of Britain, and now progressively colonizing the New World. As the majority, the richest and the focal community within Britain, the English prioritized their own particular origin stories and came to insist that contemporary liberties and institutions descended quite specifically from their own particular past, hence from the Teutonic tribes. This vision was encouraged by the shared Protestantism of Germany and England and the development of a distinctive political ideology, based on Teutonic roots. It was not racially exclusive in the present, in that non-Teutons could equally attach themselves to these political precepts and uphold the institutions which were central to them. However, this vision was racially exclusive when projected into the past, to which the non-English Arthur as an icon of any value in insular history was necessarily anathema.

This new emphasis on the Germanic barbarians eventually achieved near-consensual status in eighteenth-century histories. The earliest comparatively successful and substantive attempt at an inclusive English history was that of the Scottish philosopher and writer, David Hume (1754–62), who has been interpreted as having set himself to write (J. V. Price 1968: 106) 'a readable and intelligent history of England, free of factious partisanship, impartial where possible, judicious even where unnecessary'. Hume's approach to history was laid out in an essay on the subject, which he had already published in 1741, in which he took a comparatively pragmatic approach to the central epistemological problems of the relationship between evidence and fact. These were obviously at their most difficult when dealing with the earlier periods, and here Hume took a comparatively liberal view of what constituted acceptable evidence.

Hume's narrative was framed in both moral and racial terms. The first of his six volumes, as reordered for the 1848 edition, began with Caesar and ended with 1688. His treatment of the sub-Roman period was highly derivative of Gildas and the *Historia Brittonum*, with a Vortigern, for example, 'stained with every vice', and he had a very patriotic and idealized vision of the Saxons, well suited to his anticipated audience, who (p. 13):

> seem to have been the most distinguished [of the German peoples] both by their manners and political institutions, and to have carried to the highest pitch the virtues of valour and love of liberty; the only virtues which can have place among an uncivilized people.

From his reading of later annals, Hume reconstructed an imaginatively detailed account of the battles of the sixth century (p. 20):

> Cerdic . . . laid siege to Mount Badon or Banesdowne near Bath, whither the most obstinate of the discomfited Britons had retreated. The southern Britons, in this extremity, applied for assistance to Arthur, Prince of the Silures, whose heroic valour now sustained the declining fate of his country. This is that Arthur so much celebrated in the songs of Thaliessin, and the other British bards, and whose military achievements have been blended with so many fables, as even to give occasion for entertaining a doubt of his real existence. But poets, though they disfigure the most certain history by their fictions, and use strange liberties with truth where they are the sole historians, as among the Britons, have commonly some foundation for their wildest exaggerations.

Hume's Arthur has become, therefore, a minor local figure, heroic still and valorous, historical even, but little more than a footnote in the triumphant story of Anglo-Saxon settlement. The Galfridian Arthur and the entire *Brut* tradition has been otherwise discarded.

Edward Gibbon (1737–94) was perhaps the most brilliant English historian of the eighteenth century, ranging far more widely in both space and time than his contemporaries. He chose to focus in his multi-volumed *magnum opus*, *The Decline and Fall of the Roman Empire*, published over the period 1776–88, on the later Roman Empire and its collapse in the face of civil war, poor government, religious change and barbarian onslaughts. His central themes were the decline of the Roman world from its early excellence to a morally bankrupt world tyranny, coupled with a central role for the rise of Christianity, which was complicit in its fall, by inculcating 'the duty of passive obedience to a lawful and orthodox sovereign'. So, for example, 'the sacred indolence of the monks was devoutly embraced by a servile and effeminate age'. This was, in part, intended as a metaphor for the present polities of Britain and her continental neighbours, and Gibbon looked askance at the consequences of political systems which stifled liberty, which had left the Roman population as mere 'pigmies', hence vulnerable to the incoming Gothic 'giants'. He was an enthusiast in the present for republican Switzerland, and considered a fatal weakness of Roman civilization to be the dependence of the body politic on the personal virtues of its absolutist rulers: 'The happiness of an hundred millions depended on the personal merit of one or two men, perhaps children, whose minds were corrupted by education, luxury and despotic power.' Like other English writers, therefore, he sought the origins of contemporary liberties among the Germanic barbarians of early post-Roman history. These 'Goths' were considered to have triumphed over the morally bankrupt and illiberal totalitarianism of the late Roman Empire, in large part because of the political and social liberties enshrined within their free, tribal societies. Gibbon was not, however, otherwise enamoured of these tribes, thinking them barbaric, ruthless, faithless and destructive, and this was nowhere more true than in Britain, where his own emotional commitment was to the sub-Roman Britons, and against the Saxons. Like Hume, Gibbon championed an historical Arthur against the rising tide of outright scepticism, and there are obvious comparisons to be made between their two presentations:

> every British name is effaced by the illustrious name of Arthur, the hereditary prince of the Silures, in South Wales, and the elective King or general of the nation. According to the most rational account [he is referring to the *Historia Brittonum*], he defeated, in twelve successive battles, the Angles of the North and the Saxons of the West; but the declining age of the hero was embittered by popular ingratitude and domestic misfortunes. The events of his life are less interesting than the singular revolutions of his fame . . .
>
> At length the light of science and reason was rekindled; the talisman was broken; the visionary fabric melted into air; and by a natural, though unjust, reverse of the public opinion, the severity of the present age is inclined to question the *existence* of Arthur.
>
> (Gibbon, 1901 edn: vol. 4, pp. 150–2)

The English finally conquered, 'and conquest has never appeared more dreadful and destructive than in the hands of the Saxons, who hated the valour of their enemies, disdained the faith of treaties, and violated, without remorse, the most sacred objects of the Christian worship'. However, Gibbon opposed the theory that the Britons were totally exterminated, if only because he felt that the Saxons would have preserved the peasantry from self-interest. Wales was no more secure than England from his moral censure, despite its freedom from barbarian intruders, falling away into Druidism, rude schism and licentious barbarism. Thus, in Gibbon's view, did insular civilization collapse from its Roman excellence of the past, in what he termed (p. 155) the 'revolution of Britain'. Its fall suggested to him, as others (p. 153), 'a probable suspicion that the arts of Rome were less deeply rooted in Britain than in Gaul or Spain'.

Gibbon's defence of Arthur did not persuade every patriotic, English contemporary, although his inclusive vision of different races making up the English in the present remained the dominant view over the next century. The connection between current political liberties and Germanic racial origins was spelled out by Catherine Macaulay in her popular historical treatise (1763), which cemented present claims on the Anglo-Saxon past and placed English history and the English constitution firmly within the fullness of divine providence. In this reconstruction, English liberties stretched back to the days of King Alfred and beyond, despite successive attempts to subvert them by Norman and Angevin tyrants and the Stuart monarchs, all of which had had to be fought off by patriotic Englishmen.

If present liberties derived from Germanic immigrants to England, the value attached to other peoples within Britain, who were considered to have been ancestral to the Scots (thus the Irish), the Welsh and the Cornish, was seriously threatened. An understanding of the Anglo-Saxon, thus the English, past was becoming the most powerful historical project of the modern era within Britain. This project had at its core a race-centric discourse. King Arthur was necessarily marginalized by this powerful new focus on early English history and Anglo-centric and Germanist historical values. Historians were now free to share their long-running concerns at the inadequacy of the source materials for his career. Even where his activities were considered to be potentially factual, they were widely perceived as regressive and opposed to the ever-upward march of history and the progress of mankind. If it was a part of divine providence that Anglo-Saxon England and the institutions that it nurtured should be triumphantly secured over and against its opponents, then Arthur's putative efforts to hold back that enterprise were necessarily as misguided as they were an irrelevance. His story lost, therefore, for Whig historians, that powerful mixture of heroic tragedy, of a Christian king made by God struggling nobly against great odds and ultimate betrayal. Arthur was reduced in scale and significance to an only quarter-credible walk-on part in insular history. He had become a minor hindrance to the great narrative of a patriotic, English past. He was, consequently, increasingly disowned by the dominant historical voices of the day and his part disallowed as a dispensable irrelevance to the inevitable, and divinely ordained, rise of England.

Sharon Turner's great *History of the Anglo-Saxons* (1799–1805) provided a new beginning for the scholarly enterprise of exploring the sources for Anglo-Saxon England. Indeed, the editor of the third edition claimed that the Anglo-Saxon past 'had been nearly forgotten by the British public' hitherto (see Mandler 2000 for the depth of this disinterest). Turner followed (bk. 2, ch. 8) Gildas's description of sub-Roman Britain, complete with his denunciations of the leaders of his own people, their military ineptitude and their crass disunity. These tyrants, and 'Nennius's' Arthur, he saw as obscure figures, 'like the distant wood at the last refractions of the departed sun: we behold only a dark mass of gloom, in which we can trace no shapes, and distinguish no individuals'. Taking the moral high ground for his own Anglo-Saxons, he was caustic in his judgement on the Britons: 'no country could be more worthless in its legal chieftains and religious directors, or in its general population'. Into this sink of iniquity came the Anglo-Saxons, whom he envisaged as 'fearless, active and successful pirates', whose ferocity was matched by a splendid hereditary physique, and free tribal institutions. Noble savages, then, equipped with a free society, were conceived as an appropriate starting point to England's history, displacing physically, institutionally and morally the sinful race already in occupation.

The historical process of Anglo-Saxon conquest was reconstructed synthetically from the available literary sources. These included Arthur's battles (bk. 3, ch. 3), but Turner was unusually, at this date, prepared to seek historical material in early Welsh poetry, thus providing himself with a far larger body of material evidence than others had employed. Arthur clearly impressed him, even despite his Anglo-centric enterprise, although he struggled to obtain rhetorical advantage for the 'Anglo-Saxon' Cerdic – putative ancestor of the late Anglo-Saxon royal house – from the Briton's putative successes:

> Arthur was the British chieftain who so long resisted the progress of Cerdic. The unparalleled celebrity which this Briton has attained, in his own country and elsewhere, both in history and romance, might be allowed to exalt our estimation of the Saxon chief, who maintained his invasion, though an Arthur opposed him, if the British hero had not himself been unduly magnified into an incredible and inconsistent conqueror.
>
> The authentic actions of Arthur have been so disfigured by the additions of the minstrels, and of Jeffry, that many writers have denied that he ever lived: but this is an extreme, as objectionable as the romances which occasioned it . . .
>
> He was a chieftain in some part of Britain near its southern coasts. As a Mouric, king of Glamorganshire, had a son named Arthur at this period, and many of Arthur's actions are placed about that district, it has been thought probable that the celebrated Arthur was the son of Mouric: but this seems to have been too petty a personage, and too obscure for his greater namesake.

Turner's vision, then, was of an heroic Arthur, his career filled out by use of medieval Welsh poetry, standing against the rising tide which was leading inexorably to the construction of England, and the passage of Anglo-Saxon virtues and institutions to the present people of Britain. If Arthur was great, then his opponent was necessarily greater, but the figure of Arthur was more probably inflated far beyond historical reality by later acclaim, leaving the historical Arthur devalued as well as fighting for the losing side. Cerdic's greatness in opposing Arthur reflected on his lineal descendant King Alfred, who was Turner's real hero and founding figure. The whole of his book 5, in six chapters and 106 pages, was given over to a eulogistic account of Alfred's character, his reign and his significance in English history. All that had gone before did little more than lead up to this triumphant, Anglo-Saxonist cusp of national development.

This latter vision was contested, but not very effectively. In Wales, efforts were being made to construct a new platform on which scholarly treatment of the past could be established (e.g. E. Jones 1784; O. Jones, Williams and Pughe 1801–7; Owen 1803), and the collecting and editing of medieval texts was begun by such figures as William Owen Pughe (Carr 1983). More directly, the Reverend T. Price (1829) offered the view that Celtic survival had been considerable even despite Saxon attempts at extermination, and that 'our [i.e. national] boasted privileges' in the present derived primarily from the ancient British, rather than the Germanic immigrants. In Price's reconstruction, Asser's role at Alfred's court was the key in facilitating a transfer of British political ideals to the English, and it may be significant that Geoffrey of Monmouth had already argued that Alfred's laws had British origins. In Germany, the historian Lappenberg, who had, of course, no personal investment in Anglo-Saxonism, could afford the luxury of portraying Arthur as an heroic Christian warrior (1845: 101–2): 'the able champion who defended the liberty, usages and language of the ancient country from destruction by savage enemies; who protected the cross against the pagans'. It is difficult, however, to imagine an English writer adhering to such sentiments. Ritson's was arguably the ablest insular defence of Arthur at this date, achieved in conjunction with a vigorous rejection of Geoffrey (Ritson 1825: xxv: 'HOW PETULANTLY AND HOW IMPUDENTLY HE LIES'). Ritson's is the Arthur therefore of the *Historia Brittonum*, the historicity of which he accepted, with the addition of a Cornish locale and the status of king but with post-eleventh-century accretions otherwise stripped away, and it was the refutation of the later romances which chiefly interested him, hence sentiments such as that in the quotation which begins this chapter.

However, alternative and in various respects less than palatable visions of the past could be ignored by a readership which was predominantly English and which urgently wanted a historical continuum between an Anglo-Saxon past and the present political regime. It was essentially Hume's and Turner's visions of the early Middle Ages which were taken up by the scholarly community thereafter. Perhaps the most influential of all nineteenth-century English historians was Thomas Babington Macaulay, who was born on 25 October 1800. Educated at Trinity College, Cambridge, he was called to the Bar in 1826 but rapidly made a name for himself as an essayist and critic, as well as an orator, and the young Whig entered Parliament in 1830. He is today best known as the author of the massively influential *The History of England* (1848) but he had already published extensively, including the *Lays of Ancient Rome* (1842). Like Hume's, Macaulay's *History* begins in earnest only with the reign of James I, but he also offered a brief introduction and explanation of that fact. Macaulay was himself the son of an ex-governor of Sierra Leone who later played a leading, if not particularly successful, role in the commercial life of the colony, and he wrote when the British Empire straddled the world. He was an ardent opponent of slavery, and highly paternalistic in his approach to colonial peoples, much in tune with the Aborigines' Protection Society, for example, founded in 1838. However, for all his concerns for the 'native' peoples of the Empire, Macaulay's position was founded on an absolute belief in the right of his own community to rule, but not to abuse, other peoples. The British imperial enterprise seemed (to him and to his peers) the very apogee of civilized achievement, and in this achievement and his sense of an unstoppable progress of mankind the author revelled:

> the general effect of this chequered narrative will be to excite thankfulness in all religious minds, and hope in the breast of all patriots. For the history of our country during the last hundred and sixty years is eminently the history of physical, of moral, and of intellectual improvement. Those who compare the age on which their lot has fallen with a golden age which exists only in their imagination may talk of degeneracy and decay: but no man who is correctly informed as to the past will be disposed to take a morose or desponding view of the present.

His brief survey at the start of the work acknowledged that insular history had not always held within itself – visibly at least – these seeds of future greatness. Rather, the indigenous population of Britain in late prehistory was to be compared with the 'native of the Sandwich Islands' of the present, who had, since Captain Cook's reports in the 1770s, been adopted in Britain as a veritable exemplar of primitive savagery. Proper homage was paid by Macaulay to the greatness of Rome, whose furthest outpost Britain was, but (reflecting Gibbon's concerns) sub-Roman British history was not safely Roman, and did not, therefore, warrant being valued alongside classical culture. Gentlemen of his generation belonged to a world which much admired the great ruins of Italy and the remains of Aix-en-Provence or Pont de l'Arche, alongside the works of Virgil or Catullus with which they were familiar from school and university. Macaulay was unimpressed by the provinciality of Britain's Roman remains and the apparently total lack of great ruins, such as aqueducts or monumental arches. Nor could he point to any insular contribution to Rome's literary or cultural triumphs. Consequently he assumed (with Gibbon) that the Britons were never as Romanized as their continental neighbours, deriving from the Romans just a 'scanty and superficial civilization', which easily collapsed under the joint pressures of barbarian invasion and indigenous, Celtic, cultural revival in the fifth century. The sub-Roman Britons were, therefore, in Macaulay's work, demoted from the high cultural value accorded by the nineteenth-century élite to Rome, to the low value traditionally accorded by the English to illiterate barbarians, whose stories were deemed neither comprehensible nor significant. In this incomprehensibility, Britain, he proposed, differed from her European neighbours (vol. 1, p. 3):

> It is only in Britain that an age of fable completely separates the two ages of truth. Odoacer and Totila, Euric and Thrasimund, Clovis, Fredegunda, and Brunechild, are historical men and women. But Hengist and Horsa, Vortigern and Rowena, Arthur and Mordred, are mythical persons, whose very existence may be questioned, and whose adventures must be classed with those of Hercules and Romulus.

Macaulay had commented in similar vein in his *Lays of Ancient Rome*, suggesting that an earlier, oral literature underlay Roman civilization, to be compared with verses which since had been composed in an oral environment to celebrate such leaders as Attila the Hun and the English King Æthelstan. The parallel was clearly one which attracted him. Similarly: 'The chants of the Welsh harpers preserved, through ages of darkness, a faint and doubtful memory of Arthur.' For Macaulay, therefore, Arthur was historically inconsequential, if historical at all, and the entire period not one which attracted him, lying far too distant from the historical certainties and values of the two great ages of civilization, the Roman past and the English (or British) present.

Increasing numbers of Anglo-Saxonists adopted a less haughty approach to the early Middle Ages than Macaulay, and had less need to place the Anglo-centric present in a universal context which had necessarily to rest on a classical past. Rather, Anglo-Saxon scholarship was generally narrowly English and patriotic in its development of historical narrative. Sir Francis Palgrave was prepared to allow far more of these legendary figures of the fifth and sixth centuries into his *History of the Anglo-Saxons* (1837) than was Macaulay. However, he omitted Arthur from any role in his discussion of the English settlement, perhaps because he could find no reference to him in contemporary English texts or the *Anglo-Saxon Chronicle*, which he and many others treated as the definitive (and patriotic) guide to the period.

John Mitchell Kemble was arguably the most erudite Anglo-Saxonist of the second quarter of the century, and it is significant that he was profoundly influenced by contemporary German scholarship. He visited Jacob Grimm at Gottingen in 1834, where he met and eventually married a daughter of the Professor of Philosophy (Dickens 1939). Like many other Anglo-Saxonists, he was in part motivated by a commitment to political liberty in the present, both at home and also abroad, having lent his support to constitutionalists in

Spain in 1830–1, in a movement which, however, proved to be a fiasco. A keen internationalist, Kemble's principal connections thereafter were with Germany and his English history reflects this stance; he had a keen interest in contemporary German thought concerning a Teutonic past.

Kemble emerged as by far the most sceptical scholar of this period regarding early literary sources (1849), setting aside the accounts of both Bede and the *Anglo-Saxon Chronicle* as unreliable as a basis for the writing history, and preferring to focus quite exclusively on the evidence for social and constitutional history from the late Anglo-Saxon period. He was, therefore, far from prepared to allow any historicity to Arthur on the basis of non-contemporary, British or Welsh sources:

> at a later period, the vanquished Britons found a melancholy satisfaction in adding details which might brand the career of their conquerors with the stain of disloyalty … the spells of Merlin and the prowess of Arthur, or the victorious career of Aurelius Ambrosius, although they delayed and in part avenged, yet could not prevent the downfall of their people.
>
> (Kemble 1849: 2–3)

Rather, the stories coming down to him were 'a confused mass of traditions borrowed from the most heterogeneous sources, compacted rudely and with little ingenuity, and in which the smallest possible amount of historical truth is involved in a great deal of fable'.

To Kemble, Arthur was best explained, therefore, as unhistorical and belonging rather to the realm of later political and cultural mythology. His comments do suggest that he held the (remarkably current) view that Arthur was constructed retrospectively by the British élite for their own ideological purposes. So his Arthur was part of a moral counter-attack long after the process of English settlement had been consolidated, launched by British intellectuals against their Anglo-Saxon conquerors, their purpose being to invalidate that conquest in moral terms via accusations of infamy of various sorts.

Both Macaulay and Kemble imagined that the two great periods of civilization – that of ancient Rome and that of the British present – were separated by a vast Dark Age which was impenetrable to the historian, due to the poverty of reliable evidence, and thus of little historical value and best passed over rapidly. However, few nineteenth-century scholars approached history from as consciously a philosophical perspective as Macaulay, or as critically as Kemble, and the desire to explore the roots of the current 'genius' of the English encouraged more accepting approaches to at least the Anglo-Saxon part of the Dark Age equation. Kemble's assumption that there was a large Celtic survival into Anglo-Saxon England was a fair outcome of his researches but at odds with the perceptions of much of his audience, who preferred a much cleaner slate for the inception of a thoroughly different, English national history.

In a much more homely context, this issue is very visible in Dickens's widely read *A Child's History of England* (serialized in *Household Words*, 1851–3), which reflects the dominant interpretation of the day. Dickens's Saxons 'came pouring into Britain', driving the poor Britons, whom he had hitherto imagined quite stout-hearted against their foes (the Scots and Irish, of course), into Wales and the south-west, or Dumnonian peninsula. In this simple, migrationist reconstruction, Germanic settlement expelled and thereby entirely marginalized the previous inhabitants, at least as far as the dominant, English, strand of history was concerned. Such a construct usefully divided the Romano-British world and its classics-derived value system from Anglo-Saxon England, which could thereafter be positioned on centre stage. The logic was compelling, since Cornwall and Wales were still perceived in the nineteenth century as being 'Celtic', as opposed to 'English', with their own local, minority languages or dialects, and ideas about group identity.

Dickens could not quite decide whether or not he wanted Arthur as an historical figure, but he used him to symbolize this cusp moment, in all its historical haze, remarking:

> Among the histories of which they sang or talked, there was a famous one, concerning the bravery and virtues of KING ARTHUR, supposed to have been a British Prince in those old times. But, whether such a person really lived, or whether there were several persons whose histories came to be confused together under that one name, or whether all about him was invention, no one knows.

For Dickens, Arthur was located, if anywhere, in Cornwall, where there were 'very ancient ruins, which people call the ruins of King Arthur's castle' – Tintagel one must assume (Figures 38 and 39, and Figure 20 earlier). Dickens's interest in, and concern to enrol, a wider sub-set of historical sources contrasts with the more scrupulous approach of Macaulay or Kemble, but his interpretation reflected contemporary views of both history and racial descent across a wide spectrum. The vision of a Germanic exclusivity came to permeate contemporary perceptions of the foundations of England, shared by scholars and the burgeoning middle classes alike.

Arthur remained of great interest, however, to other, non-historical writers. The following quotation provides a taste of this:

> To me, methought, who waited with a crowd,
> There came a bark that, blowing forward, bore
> King Arthur, like a modern gentleman
> Of stateliest port; and all the people cried,
> 'Arthur is come again: he cannot die.'

**Figure 38** Mound in the cemetery of St Materiana's parish church, Tintagel. Excavation of one of these mounds revealed a Dark Age slab-formed grave

**Figure 39** Tintagel, the peninsula from the south

Then those that stood upon the hills behind
Repeated – 'Come again, and thrice as fair;'
And, further inland, voices echoed – 'Come
With all good things, and war shall be no more.'
At this a hundred bells began to peal,
That with the sound I woke, and heard indeed
The clear church-bells ring in the Christmas morn.
(Alfred Lord Tennyson, *Morte D'Arthur*)

The great establishment figure and poet laureate Lord Tennyson (1809–92) mined Arthurian literature for subject matter and captured the public imagination with his *Morte D'Arthur* (initially privately printed in 1842) and the best-selling *Idylls of the Kings* (1859 onwards). Through this medium, the well connected Tennyson offered the middle classes of the day a satisfying mixture of romanticism and tragedy in a pseudo-historical setting, which was heroic and remote from reality, yet local enough, and sufficiently well known in outline to feel relevant. It also provided him with an opportunity to comment on numerous issues current at the time, such as sexuality and prostitution (e.g. Umland 1994; Mancoff 1998), and his Arthur is in many respects a highly contemporary figure, a veritable 'modern gentleman' indeed.

Tennyson's treatment was not, of course, in any sense isolated from other areas of intellectual endeavour. He was himself a friend of Kemble. The 'Young England Movement' was founded by Disraeli and his political allies in 1842, to promote both themselves and a revival of neo-Gothic and pseudo-feudal social values. The third quarter of the century additionally saw growing interest in Arthurian subjects among artists such as Edward Burne-Jones and Frederick Sandys (Mancoff 1990), as well as a new enthusiasm for Gothic architecture, to which we owe numerous stately homes. In 1847, Prince Albert commissioned William Dyce to decorate the Queen's Robing Room at Westminster. The principal theme adopted was Arthurian, although the project was incomplete when Dyce died. As a romanticized symbol of the Middle Ages and its contemporary cultural value, therefore, Arthur enjoyed something of a renaissance in the Victorian era, even while becoming increasingly excluded from the dominant historical enterprise of the day.

Coming back to the world of explicitly historical writing, there are in these the closing lines of the first of Tennyson's Arthurian poems, a resonance of issues about legitimacy and authority which would increasingly engage historians over the decades to come. Tennyson followed closely the story as told in Sir Thomas Malory's *Le Morte D'Arthur* (XXI, 4–6), but retold it in verse for his own generation. He conjured up the image of an ageing, but virtuous and heroic, King Arthur, who had been mortally wounded in a great battle, the circumstances of which were barely revealed. Conscious of his own imminent passing (and I use this euphemism advisedly), we see him divesting himself of Excalibur, the symbol of his earthly kingship and the legitimacy of his authority. This he purposed not to pass on to an heir but to restore to the Lady of the Lake and the magical waters in which it had been forged. As an aside, this scene was later reflected in the immortal line: 'Strange women lying in ponds distributing swords is no basis for a system of government' (the movie *Monty Python and the Holy Grail*, 1975). Thereafter the king himself was to be borne away by barge, to a place of healing and renewal, the Isle of 'Avilion', where we are left to presume that he would escape death. He left behind just one of his knights to pray for him in the ruined world which he was vacating, and within which his kingdom was now over. Sir Bedevere, of course, has something of the role of St Peter in this story, who thrice denied his Saviour ere cockcrow, while the 'once and future king' was depicted as a Christ-figure. With his kingdom ceremoniously renounced and handed symbolically to the elementals, the stricken Arthur spoke from the barge: 'The old order changeth, yielding place to new, Lest one good custom should corrupt the world.'

In this conception, a brand new order, with its own separate values and legitimacy, had indeed, and very properly, replaced a Roman and then (quite briefly), a deeply flawed British *regnum* in the Dark Ages. The figure of King Arthur is left hovering on the edge of history and the edge of that great divide, but definitely on the further side, and it may well be that one can detect Kemble's influence in this.

This concept of a rather shorter, but profoundly deep, historical and moral chasm between sub-Roman Britain, on the one hand, and subsequent Anglo-Germanic civilization, on the other, was a significant development away from the vision of two separate civilizations offered by Macaulay, in which the gulf was nearer a millennium in length. It had its historiographical roots in the closure of Roman, Latin historical authorship within the fifth century, and in Bede's influential *Historia Ecclesiastica*, which reflects that closure. In Book I (15–22), Bede offered a narrative based on Gildas and continental Latin sources, plus his own deductions backed up apparently by foundation legends of the Anglo-Saxons. At the close of chapter 22, he continued beyond these texts, and reverted to a Canterbury and Rome-derived, Anglo-centric story of Augustine's mission, which provided the moral opening of his history and legitimized, albeit retrospectively, the Germanic ancestral peoples – whose arrival in Britain he had just described – as a people of the Lord. Similarly, the widely respected *Parker Chronicle* reached back to trace the history of the Anglo-Saxons in Britain from the arrival of Cerdic in 494. Since he was considered the ancestor of Alfred and all other late Anglo-Saxon kings, Cerdic's appearance and activities legitimized nineteenth-century reference to this early period of Anglo-Saxon construction of England, as historically linked via a political, institutional and racial continuum with the present. Whether or not Bede or the author of the late ninth-century *Chronicle* had ever heard of Arthur is unknowable – the latter at least may have done so via Asser – but neither gave the fact away if they had. What they did provide was narrative, or at least the raw materials for narrative, capable of offering the political community of the second half of the nineteenth century a satisfying and validating continuum by which a Teutonic past of high moral status could be claimed as the originator of institutions prized in the present as the defining features of English civilization.

Growing interest in Anglo-Saxon England, and a willingness to accept its early 'records' as a sound basis on which to write history, was fuelled in large part by the increasing identification of the English social and intellectual élite with Germany and recent German thinking on a wide variety of philosophical issues. English historiography was influenced by Immanuel Kant's proposition that a universal, moral history could, and should, be envisaged, focused on the European-centric progress of mankind towards an ever more advanced condition. Kant (1724–1804) lived out his life in Koenigsberg, then the capital of East Prussia, and his visions of the past and its role in the present were necessarily German-centric. His universal, German-centric vision contrasted, of course, with the political fragmentation of the Germany he knew, within which a legendary focus had considerable value as the foundation of national identity. Kant's vision was developed by the Hegelian conception of a 'German Spirit', constructed as the defining, mystical spirit of the new industrial age in Europe, and was to have considerable value to the new state of Germany as constructed by Bismarck in 1871.

Against this backdrop, insular historians were encouraged to engage with the notion of their English forebears positioned within a morally and racially superior Teutonic race. It was that race which had constructed England by colonial settlement in the Dark Ages, bringing its ancient liberties, its freedoms and its political ideals out of the dark forests of Tacitus's Germany. A deep divide between the existing British inhabitants and the Germanic settlers was, therefore, of increasing symbolic importance. The story of steep Celtic moral decline and degeneracy, followed by Germanic revival and renewal, was brought to the fore, and became increasingly strident in both racial and moral terms. A clean slate for a new and virtuous polity was provided by a full-scale replacement of the few 'enervated and demoralized' British inhabitants by a virtuous and vigorous 'new race . . . sharing the primaeval German pride of purity of extraction' (Stubbs 1870).

There was, of course, some rationale for this position in Gildas's well known indictment of the moral condition of his British countrymen, written in the late fifth or sixth century. However, Stubbs's vision should be seen primarily as one in tune with the world in which he lived. His Anglican and imperialist world-picture in the present was one which he needed to replicate, and so validate, in the distant past, and he sought in the writing of Bede and the *Chronicle* the necessary vision of his ancestors as already endowed with superior institutions, vigorous and beloved of God.

Under these influences, most mid- to late-Victorian historians wanted to envisage an Anglo-Saxon settlement writ large as a full-scale folk movement, with little if any reference to opposition, pre-existing populations or interracial hybridization. Indeed, this last concept was increasingly considered to be anathema, both in the past and the present, with the very idea of hybridization being expressed in terms of dilution, contamination and mongrelization, particularly in a current colonial context. Again, this had roots in German thought. So, for example, Lappenberg (1845: 99–100) considered that the diverse origins of the Germanic races in Britain, which then accommodated an existing Celtic population, led directly to weakness when attacked by the Vikings. Scholars were increasingly inclined to accept the notion of a long, if episodic, war of extermination, won by the Anglo-Saxons, so as to avoid such moral dangers. The influx of Germanic people had to be kept pure and untarnished. Otherwise, how could it have borne along with it a special racial genius, inherent in which were the seeds of the unique 'English Constitution' of recent times, and English greatness within a world setting, which were compelling themes within Victorian academic circles? In such a climate, Arthur was again pushed towards, and even beyond, the margins.

Victorian attitudes towards race as a social construct would eventually be influenced both by the new science of geology, which revolutionized the whole concept of time, and by the work of Charles Darwin. Modern palaeontology has its roots in the work of seventeenth-century figures such as the Danish intellectual, Bishop Nicholas Steno (1631–87), who first theorized stratigraphy. However, it was figures such as William Smith (1789–1839) and Sir Charles Lyell (1797–1875), who developed in Britain the dating of geological deposits by reference to their fossil remains. The identification of human bones within the fossil record gradually eroded the creationist historical time-frame. In line with the natural laws proposed by Newtonian science, Lyell initially considered his fossil species to be each a permanent type, but his interactions with Darwin led to his adoption of the notion of evolution. Darwin's theories of progressive divergence within biology were first circulating in the 1840s, even prior to his *On the Origins of Species* (1859). Hitherto, the comparatively brief time-scale of Christian history virtually required that the several races of mankind were created as distinct by God. With the irruption of alternative time-scales and theories of evolution, the Christian time-frame and creation myth came under huge pressure, as exemplified by the verbal duel fought out between T. H. Huxley and Bishop Wilberforce of Oxford on these issues in 1860.

Faced by Darwin's challenge to the contemporary vision of a naturally ordered world of unique species, scholars in many disciplines had necessarily to begin considering the implications of common ancestry, which threatened a host of theories about social and cultural issues. Among these was the inherent separateness of one human race from another, which enabled some dramatic contrasts to be made which were unbounded in time. So, for example, the London physician Robert Knox asserted (1850: 325):

As a race, the Celt has no literature, nor any printed books in his original language. Celtic Wales, Ireland and Scotland are profoundly ignorant. There never was any Celtic literature, nor science, nor arts.

Darwin's *The Descent of Man and Selection in relation to Sex* was published in 1871 and applied his theories, which had been developed in the animal kingdom, to mankind (B. Campbell 1972), providing a direct intellectual challenge to current constructs of English history. Even so, Darwin was not of the opinion that either climate or lifestyle had the capacity to massively affect racial characteristics in human populations, as he argued they had the evolution of animal species. The debate between monogenists, who favoured a single origin for all races, and polygenists, who preferred multiple origins for man- and woman-kind, was to continue over the next two generations, and it is only via modern genetics that the victory of the monogenists seems now to be virtually complete.

With these issues fiercely debated across the second half of the nineteenth century, it is not surprising that they began to surface in early insular history. Nicholas's popular study, first published in 1868, specifically acknowledged their impact (p. v): 'The liberalizing influence of science has relaxed many sturdy prejudices, and its light has so far dispelled historic superstitions'. His vision of the origins of the present population lay in a process of 'race-amalgamation which has issued in the compound people called English', from a stock which included the ancient Britons, and he dismissed the idea of a unique English blood as (p. 19) 'impossible'. Nicholas was inclined to accept Arthur as an historical figure behind 'the abundance of mythological fiction' which had been constructed around him by such as Geoffrey of Monmouth, but his part was small in this conception of history.

This vision of a hybrid past was taken up by Beddoe (1885), who was originally a medical doctor by profession but who rose to eminence in anthropological circles. Beddoe used measurements of early skeletal remains as well as observations of contemporaries' cranial shape, hair-type and eye colour to develop a racially constructed vision of Anglo-Saxon England, in which putative Celtic survival was mapped on the basis of 'nigrescence' within the current population, region by region. The resulting regionalized picture of Germanic settlement was to retain a degree of credibility right up to the Second World War, despite the idiosyncratic nature of the data and its collection.

Other writers were less prepared to engage with such issues and preferred to ignore the implications of Darwinian theory. Anglo-Saxon history remained very largely in the hands of career Anglicans, like Edward Freeman and Bishop William Stubbs himself, who had every reason to contest the intellectual revolution going on around them. Writers of early English history were, therefore, disinclined for a further generation to accept the historical implications of Darwinian theory and remained committed to a racially constructed vision of the origin of prized modern institutions. In this they reflected a public mood which continued to seek reassurance in theories capable of accounting for the unique achievements of the English, thus underpinning their world power, colonial exploitation and empire.

Hostility to the concept of racial contamination was widespread in England, as in Germany. Anti-Semitism was popular already in the 1830s, as evidenced in songs, for example, and was never far from the surface thereafter. That said, it was in Germany that anti-Semitism developed as the more powerful political force from the 1870s, when Jews were scapegoated for the economic ruin suffered by many victims of the financial crisis of 1873, initially by the Hamburg journalist Wilhelm Marr. Thereafter, notions of a Judeo-Masonic world conspiracy, first developed in early nineteenth-century France, began to be circulated by such figures as Herman Goedsche (Cohn 1967). Few of his fellow countrymen went to the extremes of Houston Stewart Chamberlain, who adopted German citizenship and found his spiritual home and personal mission among the Wagnerites of Bayreuth. Chamberlain lent his talents to the task of justifying the new pan-Germanic imperialism of the period by reference to racial history, constructing an inherent superiority for the Teutonic peoples by denigrating the Jews (Chamberlain 1899; G. G. Field 1981). In England, anti-Semitism remained a significant thread, but English visions of racial superiority related primarily to a belief in the inherent superiority of particular institutions (Anglicanism included), which were accessible to all mankind, albeit they had been developed by a particular and uniquely progressive and civilized people (Mandler 2000). Additionally, English attitudes were constructed on a far broader plinth of interactions and comparisons, if only because a long colonial experience had brought the British into unequal contact with large numbers of different indigenous communities around the globe. This experience had been translated into a broader vision of superiority, characterized by a belief in the inherent and universal advantage of the white man and woman – particularly the Englishman/woman – over all others. That belief was sustained by contemporary ethnology as much as history, some at least of the theories emanating from craniometry (such as Beddoe developed), anthropometry, and a host of pseudo-sciences (including psephology). It was deeply embedded in the very language of everyday discourse, via a string of pejorative or low-value terms used of conquered peoples within the Empire. Not only were other languages, religions and material cultures considered comparatively inferior but, as evolutionary theory spread to mankind, other peoples were considered in some texts either to have attained only a lower level of a single tree of development, or to have derived from very different origins. Macnamara's *Origin and Character of the British People* (1900) was based on heredity and imposed a powerful value system on the peoples of Britain (p. 160, my emphasis):

the progenitors of the Iberian race consisted of *an extremely low* type of human beings, who inhabited Western Europe, Northern Africa, and other parts of the world during the early quaternary period.

Such were considered to have survived in western Britain. There followed, in ascending order of status and modernity, the 'Celtic Aryans' of the Neolithic, and subsequent Germanic Aryans, and (p. 162): 'these Teutons came to play an all-important part in the origin of the racial character of Englishmen'. Despite their extermination of previous populations, however (p. 170), 'in isolated parts . . . a remnant of the ancient occupiers of the land continued to exist . . . though by far the greater number were destroyed and supplanted by Teutons'. By this line of argument, the ancestry of the 'Celtic' regions of the British Isles was particularly suspect and the inhabitants were considered descendants of earlier (thus inferior) types of mankind.

When translated into the historical perspective, this culture of racial distinctiveness and superiority made it undesirable to give weight to other histories and other values, and least of all to give credence to the great hero-figure of the despised losers in the struggle for control of Britain. Charles Kingsley's forays into history were among the most racist of any English writer, portraying Teutonic warriors, for example, as of (1867: 152): 'a truly noble race, the old Nobility of the Continent; a race which ruled simply because, without them, there would have been naught but anarchy and barbarism'.

Elton's *Origins of English History* (1882) focused closely on blood and descent. While he was prepared to use, for example, the *Historia Brittonum* as a source for the Saxon seizure of Kent (pp. 376–7), he wrote off Arthur as unhistorical (p. 389). Elton further extolled Anglo-Saxon virtues by comparison. He made frequent, damning reference to the 'barbarous usages' of the Irish and Scottish Highlanders in the early modern period, and the soothsayers and dark skin which characterized the 'Silurians' of south-east Wales (p. 180).

Wright's substantial *opus*, *The Celt, The Roman and The Saxon*, unusually for the time sought to overview the whole period from ancient to medieval in an insular context. He chose (T. Wright 1875: 393–9) to manage the interface between Roman Britain and Anglo-Saxon England by favouring the second 'British' entry in the 'Gallic Chronicle of 452', which records Saxon conquest of much of 'the Britains' (thus the British diocese) in 441. This obviated any need to discuss a struggle for Britain thereafter, hence minimized the entire problem of sub-Roman Britain. Of the relatively brief period between the end of Roman rule (*c.* 410) and 441, he wrote 'The period which intervened, left a blank by contemporary annalists, was at a later period filled up by fable'. Elton paraphrased Gildas's account from 383 onwards, but considered this writer extremely ignorant when compared with 'Saxon Chroniclers'. This was, in part at least, because the *De Excidio* was interpreted as a forgery perpetrated by an English priest in the late seventh century, hence at a considerable distance from the events he purposed to describe (though not so distanced as either Bede or the *Chronicle*).

Most English historians identified with Anglo-Saxon authors – most particularly Bede and the *Anglo-Saxon Chronicle* – and adopted their value systems, content to be complicit with the way that 'our' Anglo-Saxon histories had been constructed against the indigenous Britons, homogenizing their various identities and their diverse pasts. As already noted, Bede avoided reference to specific British kingships or kingdoms, preferring to construct an overriding, and pejorative 'Britishness' to encompass such diverse kingships as Strathclyde, Gwynedd and Elmet. Both his *Historia* and the *Anglo-Saxon Chronicle* offered what were essentially 'transition narratives', which sought to explain the passage of Britain from a highly valued Roman past to an equally valuable, English present. The latter, in particular, offered an 'unashamed celebration of the imperialist capacity for violence and conquest' (paraphrasing, with apologies, from Chakrabarty 1994: 347, whose subject was India's colonial histories). Their nineteenth-century admirers followed suit. Non-English insular sources were victims of this attitude, and consequently neglected or dismissed by such distinguished writers as Edward Freeman (1869) and his friend, the more populist John Richard Green (1883), both of whom treated the *Anglo-Saxon Chronicle* as the fundamental framework for early English history.

Many twenty-first-century historians might sympathize with Freeman's scepticism concerning the historicity of the Arthur presented in Welsh literature. However, few are likely to be attracted by his value-system and partisanship, or his poor referencing and comparatively uncritical use of English monastic sources:

> Most likely there was such a man [as Arthur], but we can tell nothing about him for certain. Some of the Welsh Kings are spoken of in *our* Chronicle, but there is nothing there about Arthur, and the Welsh writers who speak of him did not write till long after. It is said that he won a great battle over the English at Badbury in Dorsetshire in 520, and that he was buried at Glastonbury. This is not unlikely, as there can be no doubt that Glastonbury was a great church in the Welsh times before the English came. And it is quite certain that the West-Saxon King did not conquer any part of Somersetshire till after the time when Arthur is said to have lived.
>
> (Freeman 1869: 35–6, my emphasis)

Freeman's vision of the Anglo-Saxon past played an important part in the construction of a Germanic identity in the present for the English élite. Both he and Charles Kingsley, for example, celebrated Germany's victory in the Franco-Prussian War (1870), interpreting it as symptomatic of the rise of the Teutonic spirit of the age, with which he believed the English should engage themselves (Oergel 1998). It was in that spirit that Freeman asserted a close connection between the age of the English settlement and Victorian England, referring to (1860):

> The Teutonic Kingdom of England, rich in her barbaric greatness and barbaric freedom, with the germs, but as yet only the germs, of every institution which we most dearly prize.

The English Settlement, as described by Bede and in the *Chronicle*, was the starting point of this great enterprise (Freeman 1869: 31, my emphasis): 'Thus it was that *our* fathers came into the land where *we* now dwell; and, like the men whom we read of in old times, they called the land after their own name.' Legendary figures such as Arthur were discarded in favour of Alfred, whose attributes could be fashioned into a package which was far better suited to high Victorian England. The king who putatively burnt the cakes, although Freeman actually doubted this tradition, was developed as the quintessential king of Anglo-Saxon England and as a prototype for modern British leadership: he was a warrior-king who had defeated the (Viking) pagan hoards; he was a founding figure for England, itself, and its great maritime tradition and fleet, thus its empire; he could be promoted as an educationalist and a proto-Anglican, thus as the originator of the public schools system, the English episcopacy and missionary efforts in the colonies. More than all else, there was more evidence for Alfred than for any other figure of insular history prior to 1066. In many respects, therefore, Alfred lent himself as an appropriate exemplar for the Victorian officer, gentleman or cleric, fit for imperial service (see Frantzen and Niles 1997). In such a vision of the past, there was no room for an aberrant warrior figure, however heroic, who might detract from the carefully balanced attributes of Alfred, the quintessential Victorian man of letters and of the sword, translated into the remoteness of pre-Conquest England. As Walter Sellar and Robert Yeatman were later to remark (1930): 'Alfred ought never to be confused with King Arthur, equally memorable but probably non-existent and therefore perhaps the less important historically (unless he did exist).'

Green's vision, expressed in the *History of the English People* (1877), was much like that of Freeman, although he, like others, accepted the *Historia Brittonum* as a source for the English conquest of Kent. Like Freeman, he adopted a low-key Arthur (pp. 24–5):

> the Britons rallied [around 520] under a new leader, Arthur, and threw back the invaders as they pressed westward through the Dorsetshire woodlands in a great overthrow at Badbury or Mount Badon.

There followed a long pause in the conquest of the south, until the West Saxons renewed their advances in the 550s in a series of campaigns which led inexorably to the great victory at Dyrham in the 570s. For Green, therefore, Arthur's intervention was a mere blip on the historical record, of no ultimate significance since it only delayed the inevitable. His *The Making of England* (1881) was a briefer and far more populist work, the stance of which was more uncompromisingly racial. He was happy to equate the ancient Britons with the Zulu or Maori of the present colonial era, and to envisage the Romans as having (p. 14) 'crushed all local vigour by crushing local independence'. However, he envisaged a stubborn resistance by the sub-Roman British population, contesting 'with courage and tenacity' the English advance (pp. 132–7):

> Field by field, town by town, forest by forest, the land was won; and as each bit of ground was torn away from its defenders the beaten men sullenly drew back from it to fight as stubbornly for the next.
> . . . almost to the end of the sixth century, the English conquest of Britain was a sheer dispossession of the conquered people; and, so far as the English sword in these earlier days reached, Britain became England, a land that is, not of Britons, but of Englishmen.

By the late sixth century 'they know themselves only as Englishmen, and in the history or law of these English inhabitants we find as yet not a trace of the existence of a single Briton among them'.

Green had disposed of the dangers of racial hybridity and dilution, therefore, by the most complete extermination of the indigenous population ever proposed. Despite the stubbornness which he apportioned to the British, who clearly preferred death to dishonour to a man, woman and child, he treated the entire process as anonymous, pointedly avoiding a second mention of Arthur, while proclaiming the historicity of a legion of legendary English leaders of the same period.

This vision of ancient liberties secured by a racially distinct Anglo-Saxon people was the dominant mantra of late-Victorian historiography, therefore. Although the collective vision was of an inheritance which was now open to all England's population, whatever its origins, its exclusion of the Britons in the sub-Roman period necessarily gave it a racial tone. Such arguments also had their adherents in the New World, where figures such as Hosmer (1890) and Del Mar (1900) saw American political and constitutional liberties as inherited from an 'ancient Anglo-Saxon freedom'.

Over against Freeman, Stubbs and Green, few indeed were the authors who cared to argue that English medieval society owed significant debts in any sphere (beyond her roads, that is) to the Romano-British world. Seebohm (1883) was that rare commodity, suggesting that medieval villainage might be traceable back to the Roman-British villa system. Little support was offered by the historical community until 1905, when Henry Munro Chadwick concluded from his study of Anglo-Saxon laws that there had been a sizeable

British or Welsh underclass in Anglo-Saxon England – just as Kemble had suggested half a century earlier and Gibbon before him.

Late in the 1890s, however, the literary scholar and critic John MacKinnon Robertson offered a compelling critique of the mainstream interpretations of English and Germanic racial history (J. McK. Robertson 1897), particularly exposing (p. 222) Green's 'unreasoned Teutonic bias', sending up his almost religious fervour for Germanic ancestry and the mythology of settlement, revealed in such infamous lines as 'no spot in Britain can be so sacred to Englishmen as that which first felt the tread of English feet' (which occurs in J. R. Green 1881: 29). To Robertson, the entire case for racial purity was an absurdity and he imagined a high proportion of the populations of particularly Mercia and Northumbria to be of British descent. However, while Robertson's criticisms now seem in all respects unanswerable, it took two further generations for many even of the least convincing aspects of this racially conceived vision of the past to lose widespread support even among academics. Once again, the utility of racial perspectives on early medieval history to contemporary conceptions of the world outweighed all other factors in the construction of national history. The late Victorian and Edwardian vision of the world had at its core such narratives as Kipling's *Plain Tales from the Hills* (1887) and *Kim* (1901), so it is little wonder that its origins were envisioned in similarly racial terms (as the same author's *Puck of Pook's Hill* would imply).

The more critical and self-consciously 'scientific', historical writing which was coming to the fore (largely under German influence) in the 1890s was naturally suspicious of the materials for Dark Age Britain, and focused instead on later, more robust texts. Domesday Book was considered both a more reliable and a more weighty object of research, from which excursions might be possible into Anglo-Saxon England, but not beyond (Maitland 1897, part of whose *magnum opus* was a critique of Seebohm; see also Round 1895). In these circumstances, King Arthur was seen primarily as a literary character peculiar to a distant and only quasi-historical heroic age or discussed within the arena of mythology and folklore, far away from the increasingly critical craft of the historian.

Dickens's supposition that the Britons had fled *en masse* from what would later become England had become the popular view among scholars and the public alike, with only the number slaughtered as they fled at issue. These unfortunates had taken refuge in the far west (and so become the ancestors exclusively of the Welsh, the Cornish and the Bretons of the 'Celtic fringe'), far from the political and cultural epicentre of Victorian Britain. The necessary near-clean slate for England's origins was constructed of many layers. Accompanying this vision of depopulation was that of a densely wooded England, which the in-comers cleared for themselves by hand, wielding great axes, and in which they built nucleated villages and laid out open fields. Thus was the fabric of primitive Germanic society envisaged as having been transposed *in toto* into their new world (Stubbs 1870; Vinogradoff 1892; Gray 1915).

It was with this understanding of Arthur primarily as a figure of myth and legend, far away and long ago, unhistorical but fit for the world of literature and art, that Mark Twain adapted Malory's vision of Arthur's court. His own historical fantasy (written 1884/5–9, published in 1889) is ostensibly about a brash, young, American mechanic inadvertently dropped through a window in time into the Dark Ages. The novel is also, of course, a satire about power, cruelty and ignorance in Twain's own world, but its sheer sense of fun required the elasticity of a relatively unbounded context capable of almost endless manipulation, and the lack of contemporary historicity invested in the Arthurian legend provided just that.

## CONCLUSION

In slightly less than a millennium, therefore, we have seen Arthur developed as a dominant figure of early British history, primarily by Geoffrey of Monmouth, but then marginalized and ultimately discredited in the sixteenth and seventeenth centuries as an historical character and ultimately excluded from past reality. At the very least, Arthur was viewed in the later nineteenth century as an irrelevance within the dominant, English historical paradigm. To the late Victorians, Arthur was, therefore, very largely a mythical figure whom historians of the early Middle Ages could virtually ignore even while he was taken up as a valuable icon in the worlds of art and literature. At the close of the nineteenth century, in a new national history, Charles Oman summarized the English conquest in terms which owed much both to Green's vision of unstoppable English conquests and the growing assumption of a mythological Arthur:

> Gradually pushing onwards along the ridges of the downs, successive generations of the kings of Wessex drove the Britons out of Dorsetshire and Wiltshire till the line of conquest stopped at the forest-belt which lay east of Bath. Here the advance stood still for a time, for the British kings of the Damnonians, the tribes of Devon and Cornwall, made an obstinate defence. So gallant was it that the Celts of a later generation believed that the legendary hero of their race, the great King Arthur, had headed the hosts of Damnonia in person, and placed his city of Camelot and his grave at Avilion within the compass of the western realm.
>
> (Oman 1895: 16)

What prevails throughout, however, is the potency of contemporary political and cultural values and the ways in which different histories were constructed to serve those values. Arthur had considerable utility to the leaders of insular society over a long period stretching from the twelfth to the sixteenth centuries, if only because the Norman Conquest had undermined the value-system hitherto underpinned by Anglo-centric histories. Despite the several learned criticisms which were available, the logic of which was unanswerable, Geoffrey of Monmouth's historicization of Arthur in the 1130s was adopted enthusiastically at the English court and throughout the Anglo-Norman establishment, both because it provided a magnificent model of an earlier insular kingship which had prevailed across all western Europe, and because it was embedded within an historical tradition redolent with ancient and prestigious British, as opposed to Anglo-Saxon, origins to which they could attach themselves. Geoffrey's Arthur was attuned to the political needs of the political establishment so successfully that he became the object of a court cult, the evolution of which can be traced from the reign of Henry II to that of James I. Put simply, the Anglo-Norman, medieval and Renaissance rulers of England had every reason to own Arthur and the small matter of historical fragility was not going to stop them.

Criticism of the historicity of the Arthurian and *Brut* historical enterprise was, therefore, largely ignored until its utility began to wane during the sixteenth and seventeenth centuries. It was the development of new historical enterprises thereafter, at least as much as improving standards of textual criticism, that enabled pre-existing scepticism to be heard. The loss of élite patronage empowered the critics and their voices combined with new ideological imperatives to effectively marginalize King Arthur within insular history and validate his exclusion.

The dominant historical activity within Britain from the later seventeenth century onwards to the two World Wars was the contextualization and validation of a new set of fast-changing élite constructs, the particular concerns of which were with the balance of power within English, then British, society, and issues surrounding 'liberty', free institutions, religious authority, race and the colonial process. As new visions of identity developed, so did this enterprise require the replacement of the entire *Brut* tradition of insular history – Arthur included – with a new, Anglo-Saxon-centred historical endeavour, within which current concerns could be explored more effectively. Within this project, King Alfred was adopted as the quintessential English hero-type, first primarily by Sharon Turner and then more widely within both historical authorship and popular culture. Alfred's rise was necessarily at Arthur's expense and reinforced his committal, on the basis of a poverty of evidence, to the realms of myth and legends.

Not only do these two pre-Conquest heroes share an initial letter (a fact which on occasion still confuses undergraduates). They also share the peculiarity of having become historical icons, albeit within very different, and mutually incompatible, historical traditions, yet within different strands of insular history which have on occasion become hopelessly entwined. It was these several circumstances to which Sellar and Yeatman so wittily drew attention, to close with the most comic confusion of the two ever to have appeared in print:

> King Arthur invented Conferences because he was secretly a Weak King and liked to know what his memorable thousand and one Knights wanted to do next. As they were all parfitly jealous Knights he had to have the Memorable round Table made to have the Conferences at, so that it was impossible to say which was top knight. He had a miraculous sword called Exgalahad with which he defeated the Danes in numerous battles. In this he was also much assisted by his marine inventions, including the water-clock and the British Navy. The latter invention occurred as follows.
>
> Alfred noticed that the Danes had very long ships, so he built a great many more much longer ones, thus cleverly founding the British Navy. From that time onwards foreigners, who, unlike the English, do not prefer to fight against long odds, seldom attacked the British Navy. Hence the important International Law called the Rule Britannia, technically known as the Freedom of the Seas.
>
> (Sellar and Yeatman 1930: Chapter VI)

Did Sellers and Yeatman recall that 'Rule, Brittania' had been composed by Thomas Arne (in 1740) for a semi-opera titled *Alfred*? One must, surely, assume so.

# CHAPTER VI

# POSTSCRIPT
## The Rhetorical Arthur

—— ·◆· ——

> with their sins they [the Britons] angered God so excessively that
> finally he allowed the army of the English to conquer their land and
> to destroy the host of the Britons entirely.
>
> ('Sermon of the Wolf to the English': Archbishop Wulfstan,
> 1014; Whitelock 1955: 933)

In Chapters II, III and IV, we explored the formation of images of the Britons
over a period of some 500 years, and in particular ninth- and tenth-century
portrayals by British writers of their own race as a martial people of the Lord.
To recap very briefly, the process begins with Gildas's perception of himself
as a Jeremiah-like figure berating the Britons (Israelites) in captivity among
the Saxons (Babylonians), whose return to obedience alone will bring
redemption through God. The Britons are depicted as not only so wicked as
to be in danger of losing their status among the elect (albeit they have not yet
done so), but also as inveterate cowards and military incompetents. The
Saxons, however, were the 'Other' – violent animals to be associated with all
the enemies of God and man in the Old Testament, devils and a scourge of
God's own people, whom biblical parallels imply would be swept away like
leaves by an angry God when His protection of His own people was rekindled
through their repentance.

Bede adapted Gildas's vision, developing the Britons' wickedness and
disobedience to God further through time to the point where he could finally
expel them from the providential framework of history on account of their
refusal to proselytize among the English and their rejection of the authority
of Augustine. Thereafter he positioned them in turn as the 'Other' – heretics
and a powerless, inept people hated by God and men alike, thus akin to the
status of the Jews, whose persons and lands had been handed over by the Lord
to the English. There is evidence that Anglo-Saxon clerical contemporaries
shared this view of a redemptive past for their own people. The fall of the
Britons from grace was later used as an object lesson of immediate relevance
by Archbishop Wulfstan in his 'Sermon of the Wolf to the English', at the
height of the Viking crisis in the latter days of King Æthelræd (see epigraph

to this chapter). In contrast to the British passage into moral darkness, for Bede the *adventus Saxonum* was part of the divine plan. The English were a chosen people of the Lord, to whom He had granted rule in Britain, whose conversion He foreknew and oversaw and whom He protected via His saints and duly appointed kings. Their conquests were God-given, therefore, and their great destiny secure.

A century later the author of the *Historia Brittonum* contested that positioning in his own 'transition narrative', constructing the Britons as a people of the highest moral status and great antiquity, whom he meshed into biblical, Roman and providential history from an early date. This was another piece of rhetorical writing which sought to both validate and legitimize a particular community in the present by use of the past. For this author, the English were unscrupulous descendants of pagan gods – cunning and duplicitous rather than brave – and the Mercian kingship derived from, and was tainted by, the satanic Penda. The early land-seizures of the Saxons were interpreted as God's punishment of a single figure, Vortigern, who alone had sinned against the Lord, under the influence of the guileful Hengist and his wicked and manipulative daughter. With Vortigern dead, the author developed the vision of a golden age among the Britons. St Patrick was constructed as a British type of Moses and the writer developed an Arthur figure as a type of Joshua and Christ, thus as an undefeated, British Christian hero leading his people under God's protection and with His guidance against the pagan Saxons for possession of the Promised Land. These characters were developed for rhetorical purposes to symbolize that God and His people were as one in the aftermath of Vortigern's career, like the Israelites passing out of Egypt through the desert to Canaan. Arthur's role as *dux bellorum* is derivative of the Old Testament positioning of Joshua, the *dux bellum* of the Israelites. His twelve battles likewise invoke important connections with the conquest of the Promised Land. The author made up their number from a wide variety of sources, including battles hitherto associated with other British heroes (Badon arguably included) and a rag-bag of other places, both real and imaginary. Once the biblical connections are understood, it is clear that no pre-existing and coherent British legend concerning an historical figure was necessary to the genesis of this Arthur, who derives from the author's own contemporary purposes in the context of salvation history. Arthur's development illustrates cogently the centrality of myth and the construction of memory and traditional symbols to the issue of national identity. Internal evidence suggests that the author derived his Arthur figure directly from folkloric stories, but the name itself would seem to have entered British legend and folktales from the Roman period, fixed presumably by reference to the distant memory of some such figure as Lucius Artorius Castus.

The tone of the *Historia* is defiant towards Mercia but more conciliatory towards Northumbria and several of Mercia's erstwhile satellites, with which the northern Welsh of the present (829/30) may well have thought to make common cause. It invokes the past to justify positioning Merfyn of Gwynedd in the present as the rightful leader of a united British reaction to recent English encroachments, which had been prophesied ultimate victory long ago in the dark days of Vortigern. One can argue that this author's Arthur is one of several rhetorically constructed and value-laden metaphors within this text for Merfyn Frych, which include also Cunedda, Vortimer, Patrick, Urien and even the red worm or dragon itself. Whether or not that be accepted, the principal message of chapter 56 concerns the status of the Britons as a martial people of the Lord and is immediate, empowering and highly political at the time of composition. This positioning confronts the history of English supremacy and encroachments upon Wales of the recent past, forestalls its reoccurrence in the future, and pre-empts any further English writings on the subject of God's intentions for Britain. Bede had constructed a vision of an English people of the Lord taking over Britain from an indigenous race who had sinned so badly that they had fallen out of salvation history. The *Historia Brittonum* is a rebuttal, written by a man who owned and valued the idea of 'Britishness', and who saw a need to reinvigorate this identity over against 'Englishness'. The central meaning of his narrative lay not in such details as Arthur and his battles but in the greater myth of an honourable, righteous and courageous nation, of which Arthur was symbolic.

The *Annales Cambriae* then took this set of images and reformulated this golden age of British achievement under divine protection in the distant past for rather different current purposes. As behoved a writer at St David's working under the patronage of the more Irish-accommodating court of Dyfed, his was far more a joint Cambro-Irish golden age than that of the *Historia Brittonum* (although Irish texts were of course utilized effectively therein). This author was far less keen to contest the distant past with unwelcome incomers: the Irish are unnoticed in early Wales and the English do not surface before their conversion. Once converted, all peoples are implicitly acknowledged as of God in the past and the present. Arthur appears as the Christ-helper hero of Badon, who was killed implicitly by the Britons themselves at Camlann but whose death God avenged, again by implication, through the scourge of plague.

Owain, now king of *Demetia*/Dyfed/Deheubarth, could trace his maternal descent back to an obscure Arthur in his maternal ancestry, and this chronicler arguably (but not explicitly) conflated the Demetian ancestral figure with the Arthur extracted from the *Historia Brittonum*. Owain, like Arthur in this construct, was also locked in a life and death struggle with Welsh opponents. The Arthur of the *Annales* is therefore arguably a metaphor for Owain of Deheubarth in the present, developed to deliver a specific political message of immediate relevance only in the mid-950s, when he was in danger of losing control of south- and central-western Wales, and indeed his very life, to his cousins in Gwynedd. Again, this interpretation supposes the construction of history to legitimate and validate a political regime in the present. The *Annales* therefore adds a new layer of politically motivated development to the pre-existing rhetorical construct of Arthur found in the *Historia*. It is a necessary conclusion that its Arthur has no better claim to historicity than the one who had already been conceived over a century earlier.

As is established in Chapters IV and V, all other Arthurian texts arguably derive ultimately either from these two or from the folkloric perceptions of Arthur which were circulating concurrently with them. One should probably interpret the Arthur of the *Gododdin* as a witty aside to the description of Arthur's personal prowess at Badon as constructed in the *Historia Brittonum*. The Arthur figures to be found in other early vernacular poems are best interpreted as folkloric or mythological, and it is worth noting that Welsh saga poetry rarely makes mention of Arthur until a comparatively late date. The Welsh and Breton saints' lives derive their figures of Arthur from the same sources. Geoffrey's borrowings from both Latin texts are transparent, and it is even possible to pursue something of the logic which led him to construct the grandiose figure of Arthur as a European emperor on this slight foundation. It is Geoffrey's Arthur – or the Arthur of the *Brut* tradition of history which emerged from his work – that then dominates English visions of the British past throughout the Middle Ages, and led to the inauguration of a royal and national cult of Arthur at Glastonbury, initially in the late twelfth century.

Thereafter, the Arthurian past was virtually unchallenged in popular esteem, although it was on occasion treated with some scepticism, until the fragility of its foundations was exposed by Polydore Vergil and other writers under the early Tudors. From that point onwards Arthur's historicity was increasingly contested, as even patriotic English writers found the medieval construct progressively more difficult to accept. Some limited political utility kept the cult alive at the Tudor courts, and it retained a degree of popularity at large. With the Stuarts, however, and more particularly with the political upheavals of the mid- to late seventeenth century, the dominant English historical enterprise changed dramatically, Arthur's political utility dissipated and he became both discredited historically and a marginalized figure in English history. Even the most basic historicity of Arthur was disputed during the eighteenth and nineteenth centuries, and he was ultimately overshadowed by the adoption of Alfred as the iconic founding figure for the English state and, by extension, the British Empire. The rising tide of Germanism and Anglo-Saxon racial history during the nineteenth century not only swept Arthur to the very edge of history but the entirety of his countrymen and their historical traditions along with him.

The twentieth-century resurrection of the historical Arthur coincided with the first serious challenges to Germanism and Anglo-Saxonism, following several decades during which he was perceived primarily as mythological. This process was begun by Chambers and then Collingwood in the aftermath of the 'Great War', and Collingwood's vision of Arthur as the last great figure of Roman Britain achieved considerable influence. However, it was the final collapse of Germanism and the dismantling of empire in the decades following the Second World War which provided both the better opportunity and stronger need to salvage a British contribution to insular history. This search for a new and non-Germanic starting point for the British past found its most grandiose expressions in the works of Leslie Alcock and John Morris, but these have subsequently had numerous imitators.

Even while these national 'metahistories' were being constructed, the texts on which they were loosely based were beginning to be scrutinized anew to establish their several histories and intertextual relationships. The detailed exploration of the key ninth- and tenth-century texts, in particular by David Dumville and Kathleen Hughes, has enabled new and far more critical assessments of Arthur's role within them, albeit largely as a by-product of numerous other developments in our understanding. Alongside that enterprise has come renewed discussion (largely by Oliver Padel) of the folkloric sources which lie behind the adoption of Arthur as a British hero by the author of the *Historia Brittonum*.

What becomes most apparent from an overview of the entire period discussed, from the fifth and sixth centuries right through to the end of the twentieth, is the sense in which Arthur's historicity has depended primarily on the contemporary political and cultural positioning of particular authors and their audiences, leaving his role in historical narratives at all periods subject to the ever-changing purposes of historians and the predilections of their audiences. In an Arthurian context, recognition of this phenomenon has not hitherto been consistent across time. In particular, there has been a common insistence that the pre-Galfridian texts be separated out to be treated as 'historical sources', capable of shedding light on actual events in the fifth and sixth centuries. This is as opposed to the Galfridian and post-Galfridian works on Arthur, which have generally been assumed, since the sixteenth century at least, to be devoid of original insights of historical merit. What I hope that this exploration has achieved is the recognition that neither the *Historia Brittonum* nor the *Annales Cambriae* should be treated very differently from, for example, Geoffrey's *Historia*, or other later texts. All are highly imaginative works, none of whose authors saw their prime task as the reconstruction of what actually happened in the distant past. Rather, in all cases, then as now, the past was pressed into the service of the present and was subject to the immediate, and highly variable, purposes of political theology. It is only through an understanding of those purposes and the several contexts within which those authors wrote that we can develop a better understanding of the portrayal of Arthur in each one of these highly ideological, historical discourses (for a theoretical discussion, see Berkhofer 1995: 203ff.). All three are equally appropriate subjects, therefore, for the processes of historical deconstruction, but this process has no obvious potential to further our knowledge of the sub-Roman period – only our understanding of the world-visions and particular perspectives lying behind the narratives which each author constructed.

At this point in the open-ended, partial and relative process of understanding these works, we come again up against that nagging question which has been so often asked, and with which this work began: 'Did King Arthur really exist?' The answer merits a considered response, which should be framed somewhat as follows:

Arthur seems to derive ultimately from a Roman-period Artorius, legendization of whom fixed the name in this form. By the early ninth century, a folkloric tradition had developed, with stories attached to particular places invoked as folk etymologies which imply that he had become identified with a huntsman-hero. There is a certain consistency in their occurrence and in the circumstances in which Arthur was pressed into use as a place-naming and explaining element. The temptation cannot be entirely resisted to suppose that the name was by this date associated with the Old Welsh *arth* ('bear') and perhaps even conflated with some lost pagan deity. The widespread utility of this folkloric package of ideas in the countryside of the central Middle Ages is arguably, therefore, on its own sufficient explanation of its origins, and explanation too of the survival of the name as symbolic of power.

In the late 820s, however, this warrior/hero-type Arthur-figure was adopted into his Latin text by a Welsh cleric writing in Gwynedd, who was already demonstrably familiar with the folkloric persona in the south-central marches of Wales. This author transplanted Arthur as a martial exemplar into an historically organized, political polemic which he was sketching out for very specific and immediate ideological purposes at (or at least for) the court of Merfyn Frych. This work was completed, seemingly, in 829/30. Arthur was used therein symbolically to serve as a British Joshua figure and constructed as the second half of a pairing of virtuous Britons, alongside St Patrick. So Patrick was presented as a British type of the Old Testament Moses and Arthur as his younger contemporary and successor as leader, the *dux bellum* Joshua. Combined, their function in this text was to sustain the author's vision of the Britons post-Vortigern as a people of the Lord, by identifying them metaphorically at a cusp point in insular history as the Israelites of the Old Testament passing through the desert and entering the Promised Land under divine protection. This construct contested the Old Testament positioning adopted by Gildas. Arthur's inclusion was excitingly novel – although the historicization of Fionn in Ireland provides an apt parallel which might have influenced our author (if he was aware of it), and his construct conforms to ideas current in the late eighth century about the typological use of the Bible in Carolingian texts. It was also well executed and the text shows signs of both considerable wit and competence in its efforts to shore up the implicit identification with Joshua and Christ. Arthur's characterization was a key part of the ideological rebuttal of Bede's portrayal of the Britons in his earlier, and widely accessible, *Historia Ecclesiastica*, which was a major factor influencing this author's approach to his subject. It must be stressed, however, that this Arthur was a rhetorical device used by the author in pursuit of contemporary political purposes, and would presumably have been recognized as such by his immediate audience. It is only when this text is read away from its immediate context and outside its intended audience that its portrayal of Arthur begins to read as if it were constructing an historical figure of the insular past.

Nor does the *Annales Cambriae* provide original information on Arthur of any obvious historical merit. The brief entries therein are not statements of fact derived from pre-existing but now-lost texts. They are primarily a pastiche of phrases and vocabulary from the Arthurian and other passages in the *Historia Brittonum*, to which a few further details of unknown origin have been added, the whole reconfigured with allusions to the New Testament for rhetorical effect. Both Arthurian entries were inserted into a chronological framework based on an Irish exemplar as best suited the author, and there is little evidence that he had any textual materials capable of governing with any precision at what dates these entries should be placed. Arthur's inclusion is a rare addition of 'Welsh' material into the Irish narrative entries which characterize the early part of the work. The principal purpose of Arthur in this text was arguably to serve as a legendary metaphor for Owain of Deheubarth, at a moment of considerable insecurity consequent on his brother and predecessor's recent death and the vigorous efforts currently being made by his cousins in Gwynedd to kill him or drive him out. Arthur's existing status as an ancestral figure of the kingship of Dyfed combined with his symbolic role within the *Historia Brittonum* to suggest his use in this text for very particular, local and political purposes, but this reading is never made explicit.

In neither case was this a *King* Arthur that was being constructed. The Arthur of the *Historia* was positioned as a non-royal leader of his people, a Joshua-like leader of the Britons in war, thus a *dux bellorum*, in deliberate contrast to the British kings against whom Gildas had previously and famously fulminated. The Arthur of the *Annales* is not explicitly a king, although it is understandable that he might later have been read as such therein. However, Arthur's kingship is primarily a later medieval gloss on the ninth-century character, constructed in compliance with contemporary perceptions of what leadership of other kings in war necessarily implied. *King* Arthur is a highly retrospective construct, therefore, but a logical development of the figure as presented by both early texts. So a figure originally developed by a Welsh writer in the ninth century as a symbol of national identity, martial prowess and God-given victory was subsequently taken up by Celto-Norman and Anglo-Norman writers in fulfilment of other agendas, becoming ultimately the centre of one of the most vigorous 'cultural-ideological' myths of the Middle Ages. To that fast-changing cycle of myth a plethora of élite communities, scattered through both space and time, looked to find a golden age of heroism and virtue

# BIBLIOGRAPHY

———— •◆• ————

Adams, J. du Q. (1993) 'Sidonius and Riothamus: a glimpse of the historical Arthur', *Arthurian Literature* 12: 157–64.

Alcock, L. (1971) *Arthur's Britain: History and Archaeology AD367–634*, Harmondsworth: Penguin.

Alcock, L. (1972) *By South Cadbury is that Camelot: Excavations at Cadbury Castle 1966–70*, London: Thames & Hudson.

Alcock, L. (1982) 'Cadbury-Camelot: a fifteen year perspective', *Proceedings of the British Academy* 68: 355–88.

Allan, D. (1997) '"*Arthur Redivivus*": politics and patriotism in Reformation Scotland", *Arthurian Literature* 15: 185–204.

Anderson, A. O. and Anderson, M. O. (1961) *Adamnan's Life of St Columba*, London and Edinburgh: Thomas Nelson & Sons.

Anglo, S. (1961–2) 'The British history in early Tudor propaganda', *Bulletin of the John Rylands Library* 44: 17–48.

Arnold, C. J. (1984) *Roman Britain to Saxon England*, London: Croom Helm.

Ashe, G. (1957) *King Arthur's Avalon*, London: Collins.

Ashe, G. (1960) *From Caesar to Arthur*, London: Collins.

Ashe, G. (1968) *The Quest for Arthur's Britain*, London: Pall Mall Press.

Ashe, G. (1981) '"A certain very ancient book": traces of an Arthurian source in Geoffrey of Monmouth's History", *Speculum* 56: 301–23.

Ashe, G. (1991) 'Annales Cambriae', in N. J. Lacy (ed.) *The New Arthurian Encyclopedia*, New York and London: Garland Publishing, 8–9.

Ashe, G. (1995) 'The origins of the Arthurian Legend', *Arthuriana* 5.3: 1–24.

Axton, M. (1977) *The Queen's Two Bodies: Drama and the Elizabethan Succession*, London: Royal Historical Society.

Babington, C. (ed.) (1865) *Polychronicon Ranulphi Higden Monachi Cestrensis*, London: Longman (Rolls Series).

Bachrach, B. S. (1991) 'The question of King Arthur's existence and of Romano-British naval operations', *The Haskins Society Journal* 2: 13–28.

Baillie, M. (1999) *Exodus to Arthur: Catastrophic Encounters with Comets*, London: Batsford.

Barber, R. (1972) *The Figure of Arthur*, Harlow: Longman.

Barber, R. (1985) 'Was Mordred buried at Glastonbury? An Arthurian tradition at Glastonbury in the Middle Ages', *Arthurian Literature* 4: 37–64.

Barber, R. (2001) *Legends of Arthur*, Woodbridge: Boydell & Brewer.

Barron, W. R. J. ed. and trans. (1989) *Layamon. Layamon's Arthur*, Harlow: Longman.

Barron, W. R. J. (ed.) (1999) *The Arthur of the English*, Cardiff: University of Wales Press.

Barron, W. R. J. and Weinberg, S. C. (1995) *Le Roman de Brut de Wace*, Harlow: Longman.

Bartrum, P. C. (ed.) (1966) *Early Welsh Geneaological Tracts*, Cardiff: University of Wales Press.

Bartrum, P. C. (1983) *Welsh Genealogies: A.D. 300–1400*, Aberystwyth: National Library of Wales.

Bassett, S. (1992) 'Medieval ecclesiastical organisation in the vicinity of Wroxeter, Shropshire and its British antecedents', *Journal of the British Archaeological Association* 145: 1–28.

Bassett, S. (2000) 'How the west was won: the Anglo-Saxon takeover of the West Midlands', *Anglo-Saxon Studies in Archaeology and History* 11: 107–18.

Beddoe, J. (1885) *The Races of Britain*, republished 1971, London: Hutchinson.

Bede (n.d.) *De Temporum Ratione*, in *Corpus Christianorum Series Latina* CXXIIIB, Turnholt: Brepols, 461–544.

Beresford, M. and Hurst, J. G. (1971) *Deserted Medieval Villages*, London: Lutterworth.

Berkhofer, R. F. (1995) *Beyond the great story: history as text and discourse*, Cambridge, Mass.: Belknap Press of Harvard University Press.

Beverley Smith, J. (1986) 'Dynastic succession in Medieval Wales', *Bulletin of the Board of Celtic Studies* 33: 199–232.

Biddick, K. (1998) *The Shock of Medievalism*, Durham and London: Duke University Press.

Biddle, M. (ed.) (2000) *King Arthur's Round Table*, Woodbridge: Boydell Press.

Bieler, L. (1979), with a contribution from Kelly, F., *The Patrician Texts in the Book of Armagh*, Dublin: The Dublin Institute for Advanced Studies.

Birch, W. de G. (1887) *Cartularium Saxonicum* II, London: Whiting & Co.

Birley, A. R. (2001) 'The *Anavionenses*', in N. J. Higham (ed.) *Archaeology of the Roman Empire: A tribute to the life and works of Professor Barri Jones*, Oxford: British Archaeological Reports International Series 940, 15–24.

Bord, J. and Bord, C. (1976) *The Secret Country*, London: Paul Elek.

Boulton, D'A. J. D. (1987) *The Knights of the Crown: The Monarchical Orders of Knighthood in Later Medieval Europe 1325–1520*, Woodbridge: Boydell & Brewer.

Bowman, A. (1996) 'Post-Roman imports in Britain and Ireland: a maritime perspective', in K. R. Dark (ed.) *External Contacts and the Economy of Late Roman and Post-Roman Britain*, Woodbridge: Boydell & Brewer, 97–108.

Bowman, A. K. and Thomas, J. D. (1994) *The Vindolanda Writing Tablets (Tabulae Vindolandenses* II), London: British Museum Press.

Breeze, A. (1997a) *Medieval Welsh Literature*, Dublin: Four Courts Press.

Breeze, A. (1997b) '*Armes Prydein*, Hywel Dda, and the reign of Edmund of Wessex', *Études Celtiques* 33: 209–22.

Breeze, A. (2001) 'Seventh-century Northumbria and a poem to Cadwallon', *Northern History* 38(1): 145–52.

Brodeur, A. G. (1939) 'Arthur *Dux Bellorum*', *University of California Publications in English* 3: 237–84.

Bromwich, R. (1959) 'The Welsh Triads', in R. S. Loomis (ed.) *Arthurian Literature in the Middle Ages*, Oxford: Clarendon Press, 44–51.

Bromwich, R. (1961) *Trioedd Ynys Prydein: The Welsh Triads*, Cardiff: University of Wales Press.

Bromwich, R. (1975–6) 'Concepts of Arthur', *Studia Celtica* 10–11: 163–81.

Bromwich, R. and Simon Evans, D. (1992) *Culhwch and Olwen: An Edition and study of the oldest Arthurian text*, Cardiff: University of Wales Press.

Bromwich, R., Jarman, A. O. H. and Roberts, B. F. (eds) (1991) *The Arthur of the Welsh*, Cardiff: University of Wales Press.

Brooks, D. A. (1983–4) 'Gildas' *De Excidio*: Its revolutionary meaning and purpose', *Studia Celtica* 18–19: 1–10.

Brooks, N. (1984) *The Early History of the Church at Canterbury*, Leicester: Leicester University Press.

Brooks, N. (1989) 'The formation of the Mercian Kingdom', in S. Bassett (ed.) *The Origins of the Anglo-Saxon Kingdoms*, Leicester: Leicester University Press, 159–70.

Brown, T. and Foard, G. (1998) 'The Saxon landscape: a regional perspective', in P. Everson and T. Williamson (eds) *The Archaeology of Landscape*, Manchester: Manchester University Press.

Bruce, J. D. (1923) *Evolution of Arthurian Romance from the Beginnings down to the Year 1300*, Göttingen and Baltimore: Vandenhoeck & Ruprecht/The Johns Hopkins University Press.

Bullock-Davies, C. (1981a) '"*Exspectare Arturum*": Arthur and the Messianic hope', *Bulletin of the Board of Celtic Studies* 29: 432–40.

Bullock-Davies, C. (1981b) 'Chrétien de Troyes and England', *Arthurian Literature* 1: 1–61.

Burton, J. H. (1873, 2nd edn) *The History of Scotland*, Edinburgh and London: W. Blackwood & Sons.

Bush, D. (1945) *English Literature in the Earlier Seventeenth Century, 1600–1660*, London.

Calhoun, C. (1997) *Nationalism*, Buckingham: Open University Press.

Camden, W. (1586) *Britannia sive Florentissimorum regnorum, Angliae, Scotiae, Hiberniae*, London: Radulphus Newbury.

Cameron, K. (1968) 'Eccles in English place names', in M. W. Barley and R. P. C. Hanson (eds) *Christianity in Britain, 300–700*, Leicester: Leicester University Press.

Campbell, B. (ed.) (1972) *Sexual Selection and the Descent of Man, 1871–1971*, London: Heinemann.

Campbell, E. (1996) 'The archaeological evidence for external contacts: imports, trade and economy in Celtic Britain', in K. R. Dark (ed.) *External Contacts and the Economy of Late Roman and Post-Roman Britain*, Woodbridge: Boydell & Brewer, 83–96.

Campbell, J. (1975) 'The Age of Arthur', *Studia Hibernica* 15: 177–85.

Campbell, J. (ed.) (1982) *The Anglo-Saxons*, London: Phaidon.

Campbell, J. (1986) 'Asser's Life of Alfred', in C. Holdsworth and T. P. Wiseman (eds) *The Inheritance of Historiography 350–900*, Exeter: Exeter Studies in History 12, 115–35.

Campbell, J. (2000) *The Anglo-Saxon State*, London and New York: Hambledown & London.

Carley, J. (1985) 'Appendix: The discovery of the Holy Cross of Waltham at Montacute, the excavation of Arthur's grave at Glastonbury and Joseph of Arimathea's burial', in R. Barber, 'Was Mordred buried at Glastonbury? An Arthurian tradition at Glastonbury in the Middle Ages', *Arthurian Literature* 4: 37–69 (at 64–9).

Carley, J. (1994) *The Irish National Origin-Legend. Synthetic Pseudohistory*, Cambridge: Cambridge University, Dept. of Anglo-Saxon, Norse and Celtic.

Carr, G. (1983) *William Owen Pughe*, Caerdydd: Gwasg Prifysgol Cymru ar run Bwrdd Gwybodau Cetaidd Prifysgol Cy.

Castleden, R. (2000) *King Arthur: the truth behind the legend*, London: Routledge.

Cavalli-Sforza, L. L. (2000) *Genes, Peoples and Languages*, London: Allen Lane.

Cessford, C. (1997) 'Northern England and the Gododdin Poem', *Northern History* 33: 218–22.

Chadwick, H. M. (1905) *Studies on Anglo-Saxon Institutions*, Cambridge: Cambridge University Press.

Chadwick, H. M. and Chadwick, N. K. (1932) *The Growth of Literature*, I, Cambridge: Cambridge University Press.

Chadwick, N. (ed.) (1958) *Studies in the Early British Church*, Cambridge: Cambridge University Press.

Chadwick, N. K. (1963) *Angles and Britons*, Cardiff: University of Wales Press.

Chakrabarty, D. (1994) 'Postcoloniality and the artifice of history: who speaks for "Indian" pasts?', in H. A. Veeser (ed.) *The New Historicism*, New York and London: Routledge, 342–69.

Chamberlain, H. S. (1899) *Die Grundlagen des Neunzehnten Jahrhunderts*, Munich: Bruckmann.

Chambers, E. K. (1927) *Arthur of Britain*, London: Sidgwick & Jackson.

Chapman, J. and Hamerow, H. (eds) (1997) *Migrations and Invasions in Archaeological Explanation*, Oxford: British Archaeological Reports, International Series 664.

Chapman, M. (1992) *The Celts: The Construction of a Myth*, London: Macmillan.

Charles-Edwards, T. M. (1976) 'Boundaries in Irish law', in P. H. Sawyer (ed.) *Medieval Settlement*, Chichester: Phillimore, 83–7.

Charles-Edwards, T. (1978) 'The authenticity of the Gododdin: an historian's view', in R. Bromwich and R. B. Jones (eds), *Astudiaethau ar yr Hengerdd*, Cardiff: University of Wales Press, 44–71.

Charles-Edwards, T. M. (1991) 'The Arthur of history', in R. Bromwich *et al.* (eds) *The Arthur of the Welsh*, Cardiff: University of Wales Press, 15–32.

Charles-Edwards, T. (1993) 'Palladius, Prosper, and Leo the Great: mission and primatial authority', in D. N. Dumville ed., *Saint Patrick AD493–1993*, Woodbridge: Boydell Press, 1–12.

Churchill, Sir W. (1956–8) *A History of the English Speaking Peoples*, London.

Coates, R. and Breeze, A. (2000) *Celtic Voices English Places: Studies of the Celtic Impact on Place-Names in England*, Stamford: Shaun Tyas.

Coe, J. B. and Young, S. (1995) *The Celtic Sources for the Arthurian Legend*, Llanerch: Felinfach.

Cohn, N. (1967) *Warrant for Genocide: The Myth of the Jewish World Conspiracy and the Protocols of the Elders of Zion*, London: Eyre & Spottiswoode.

Colgrave, B. (ed.) (1956) *Felix's Life of St. Guthlac*, Cambridge: Cambridge University Press.

Collingwood, R. G. and Myres, J. N. L. (1936) *Roman Britain and the English Settlements*, Oxford: Clarendon Press.

Collingwood, R. G. and Wright, R. P. (1995) *Roman Inscriptions of Britain*, I, *Inscriptions on Stone*, 2nd edn, Stroud: Allan Sutton.

Collingwood, W. G. (1929) 'Arthur's battles', *Antiquity* 3: 292–8.

Collins, H. E. (2000) *The Order of the Garter 1348–1461. Chivalry and Politics in Late Medieval England*, Oxford: Clarendon Press.

Confino, A. (1997) *The Nation as a Local Metaphor*, Chapel Hill and London: University of North Carolina Press.

Constantius, *Vita Germani*, in B. Krusch and W. Levison (eds) (1920) *Passiones Vitaeque Sanctorum Aevi Merovingici: Monumenta Germaniae Historica, Scriptorum Rerum Merovingicarum*, VII, Hanover and Leipzig: Impensis Bibliopolii Hahniani: 225–83.

Crawford, O. G. S. (1935) 'Arthur and his battles', *Antiquity* 9: 277–91.

Crouch, D. (2000) *The Reign of King Stephen 1135–1154*, Harlow: Pearson Education.

Cunliffe, J. W. (ed.) (1912) *Early English Classical Tragedies*, Oxford: Clarendon Press.

Dahlman, C. (1980) *The Open Fields and Beyond*, Cambridge: Cambridge University Press.

Dark, K. R. (1985) 'The plan and interpretation of Tintagel', *Cambridge Medieval Celtic Studies* 9: 1–18.

Dark, K. R. (1994) *From Civitas to Kingdom: British Political Continuity 300–800*, London: Leicester University Press.

Dark, K. R. (2000) *Britain and the End of the Roman Empire*, Stroud: Tempus Publishing.

Dark, S. P. (1996) 'Palaeoecological evidence for landscape continuity and change in Britain ca A.D. 400–800', in K. R. Dark (ed.) *External Contacts and the Economy of Late Roman and Post-Roman Britain*, Woodbridge: Boydell Press, 23–52.

Dark, S. P. (2000) *The Environment of Britain in the First Millennium A.D.*, London: Duckworth.

Davies, E. (1929) *Prehistoric and Roman Remains in Denbighshire*, Cardiff: University of Wales Press.

Davies, N. (1999) *The Isles: A History*, London: Macmillan.

Davies, R. R. (1987) *Conquest, Coexistence and Change: Wales 1063–1415*, Oxford: Oxford University Press.

Davies, R. R. (1994) 'The peoples of Britain and Ireland 1100–1400. I. Identities', *Transactions of the Royal Historical Society* (6) 4: 1–20.

Davies, W. (1979) *The Llandaff Charters*, Aberystwyth: The National Library of Wales.

Davies, W. (1982) *Wales in the Early Middle Ages*, Leicester: Leicester University Press.

Davies, W. (1990) *Patterns of Power in Early Wales*. Oxford: Clarendon Press.

Dean, C. (1987) *Arthur of England: English Attitudes to King Arthur and the Knights of the Round Table in the Middle Ages and the Renaissance*, Toronto: University of Toronto Press.

Deary, T. (2000) *The Smashing Saxons*, London: Scholastic Children's Books.

Defoe, D. (1724–6) *Tour through the Whole Island of Great Britain*, ed. and abridged P. Rogers, Harmondsworth: Penguin, 1971.

Del Mar, A. (1900) *Ancient Britain*, New York: Cambridge Encyclopedia Co.

Dickens, B. (1939) 'John Mitchell Kemble and Old English scholarship', republished in E. G. Stanley (ed.) (1990) *British Academy Papers on Anglo-Saxon England*, Oxford: Oxford University Press for the British Academy, 57–90.

Dickinson, W. H. (1900) *King Arthur in Cornwall*, London: Longmans, Green & Co.

Ditmas, E. M. R. (1972–3) 'Geoffrey of Monmouth and the Breton families in Cornwall', *Welsh History Review* 6: 451–61.

Diverres, A. (1994) 'Arthur in *Culhwch and Olwen* and in the Romances of Chrétien de Troyes', in M. B. Shichtman and J. P. Carley (eds) *Culture and the King*, Albany: State University of New York Press, 54–69.

Dodgshon, R. A. (1980) *The Origin of the British Field Systems: An Interpretation*, London: Academic Press.

Doel, F., Doel, G. and Lloyd, T. (1998) *Worlds of Arthur: King Arthur in History, Legend & Culture*, Stroud: Tempus.

Dorson, R. M. (1968) *The British Folklorists. A History*, London: Routledge & Kegan Paul.

Duchesne, L. (1894) '*Nennius retractus*', *Revue Celtique* 15: 174–97.

Dumville, D. N. (1972–4a) 'Some aspects of the chronology of the *Historia Brittonum*', *Bulletin of the Board of Celtic Studies* 25: 439–45.

Dumville, D. N. (1972–4b) 'The Corpus Christi "Nennius"', *Bulletin of the Board of Celtic Studies* 25: 369–80.

Dumville, D. N. (1974–6) 'The *Liber Floridus* of Lambert of Saint-Omer and the *Historia Brittonum*', Bulletin of the Board of Celtic Studies 26: 103–22.

Dumville, D. N. (1975–6) '"Nennius" and the *Historia Brittonum*', *Studia Celtica* 10–11: 78–95.

Dumville, D. N. (1976) 'The Anglian collection of royal genealogies and regnal lists', *Anglo-Saxon England* 5: 23–50.

Dumville, D. N. (1976–7) 'On the north British section of the *Historia Brittonum*', *Welsh History Review* 8: 345–54.

Dumville, D. N. (1977a) 'Sub-Roman Britain: history and legend', *History* 62: 173–92.

Dumville, D. N. (1977b) 'Kingship, genealogies and regnal lists', in P. H. Saywer and I. N. Wood (eds) *Early Medieval Kingship*, Leeds: the editors, 72–104.

Dumville, D. N. (1977c) 'Celtic-Latin texts in Northern England c. 1150–c. 1259', *Celtica* 12: 19–49.

Dumville, D. N. (1977d) 'Palaeographical considerations in the dating of early Welsh verse', *Bulletin of the Board of Celtic Studies* 27 (2): 246–51.

Dumville, D. N. (1977–8) 'The Welsh Latin Annals', *Studia Celtica* 12–13: 461–7.

Dumville, D. N. (1984a) 'The chronology of *De Excidio Brittaniae*, Book I', in M. Lapidge and D. N. Dumville (eds) *Gildas: New Approaches*, Woodbridge: Boydell & Brewer, 61–84.

Dumville, D. N. (1984b) 'Gildas and Maelgwyn: problems of dating', in M. Lapidge and D. N. Dumville (eds) *Gildas: New Approaches*, Woodbridge: Boydell & Brewer, 51–9.

Dumville, D.N. (1985) *The Historia Brittonum: The Vatican Recension*, Cambridge: Brewer.

Dumville, D. N. (1986) 'The historical value of the *Historia Brittonum*', *Arthurian Literature* 6: 1–26.

Dumville, D. N. (1988) 'Early Welsh poetry: problems of historicity', in B. F. Roberts (ed.) *Early Welsh Poetry*, Aberystwyth: National Library of Wales.

Dumville, D. N. (1993) *Saint Patrick: A.D.493–1993*, Woodbridge: Boydell & Brewer.

Dumville, D. N. (1994) '*Historia Brittonum*: an insular history from the Carolingian Age', in A. Scharer and G. Scheibelreiter (eds) *Historiographie im frühen Mittelalter*, Vienna and Munich: R. Oldenbourg.

Dunning, R. W. (1988) *Arthur: The King in the West*, Stroud: Alan Sutton.

Edel, D. (1983) 'The Arthur of "Culhwch and Olwen" as a figure of epic-heroic tradition', *Reading Medieval Studies* 9: 3–15.

Edel, D. (1984–5) 'Geoffrey's so-called animal symbolism and insular Celtic tradition', *Studia Celtica*, 18–19: 96–109.

Edwards, N. and Lane, A. (1988) *Early Medieval Settlements in Wales: AD 400–1100*, Cardiff: University of Wales Press.

Edwards, N. and Lane, A. (eds) (1992) *The Early Church in Wales and the West*, Oxford: Oxbow Monograph 16.

Elton, C. (1882) *Origins of English History*, London: Bernard Quaritch.

Faral, E. (1929) *La légende arthurienne: Études et documents, les plus anciens textes*, 3 vols, Paris: Librairie Ancienne Honoré Champion.

Faull, M. (1977) 'British survival in Anglo-Saxon Northumbria', in L. Laing (ed.) *Celtic Survival*, Oxford, *British Archaeological Reports* British Series 37, 1–56.

Faull, M. L. and Stinson, M. (eds) (1986) *Domesday Book Yorkshire*, Vol. 2, Chichester: Phillimore.

Femia, J. V. (1981) *Gramsci's Political Thought. Hegemony, Consciousness and the Revolutionary Process*, Oxford: Clarendon Press.

Field, G. G. (1981) *Evangelist of a Race: The Germanic Vision of Houston Stewart Chamberlain*, New York: Columbia University Press.

Field, P. J. C. (1996) 'Nennius and his History', *Studia Celtica* 30: 159–65.

Finke, L. A. (1994) 'Spenser for hire: Arthurian history as cultural capital in *The Faerie Queen*', in M. B. Shichtman and J. P. Carley (eds) *Culture and the King*, Albany: State University of New York Press, 211–33.

Fletcher, R. H. (1906) *Arthurian Material in the Chronicles*, Boston: Modern Languages Departments of Harvard University.

Flower, R. (1935) 'Laurence Nowell and the discovery of England in Tudor times', reprinted in E. G. Stanley (ed.) (1990) *British Academy Papers on Anglo-Saxon England*, Oxford: Oxford University Press for the British Academy, 1–27.

Foot, S. (1996) 'The making of Angelcynn: English identity before the Norman Conquest', *Transactions of the Royal Historical Society* (6) 6: 25–50.

Foot, S. (1999) 'Remembering, forgetting and inventing: attitudes to the past in England at the end of the first Viking age', *Transactions of the Royal Historical Society* (6) 9: 185–200.

Ford, P. (1970) 'Llywarch, ancestor of Welsh princes', *Speculum* 45: 442–50.

Ford, P. K. (1977) *The Mabinogi and Other Medieval Welsh Tales*, London and Los Angeles: University of California Press.

Foster, I. L. (1959) 'Culhwch and Olwen and Rhonabwy's Dream', in R. S. Loomis (ed.) *Arthurian Literature in the Middle Ages*, Oxford: Clarendon Press, 31–43.

Foucault, M. (1977) *Language, Counter-Memory, Practice: Selected Essays and Interviews*, with an introduction by D. F. Bouchard, Oxford: Blackwell.

Fox, Sir C. (1955) *Offa's Dyke: a field survery of the western frontier works of Mercia in the seventh and eighth centuries*, Oxford: Oxford University Press.

Frantzen, A. J. (1990) *Desire for Origins. New Language, Old English and teaching the tradition*, New Brunswick: Rutgers University Press.

Frantzen, A. J. and Niles, J. D. (1997) *Anglo-Saxonism and the Construction of Social Identity*, Gainesville: University Press of Florida.

Freeman, E. A. (1860) 'The continuity of English history', *Edinburgh Review*, reprinted in E. A. Freeman (1872) *Historical Essays*, London: Macmillan.

Freeman, E. A. (1869) *Old English History for Children*, London: Macmillan.

Frere, S. S. (1967) *Britannia*, Cambridge, Mass.: Harvard University Press; 3rd edn, Routledge and Kegan Paul, 1987.

Fulford, M., Handley, M. and Clark, A. (2000) 'An early date for Ogham: the Silchester Ogham Stone rehabilitated', *Medieval Archaeology* 44: 1–24.

Gairdner, J. (ed.) (1858) *Memorials of King Henry VII*, London.

Gardner, R. (1995) 'Gildas's New Testament models', *Cambrian Medieval Celtic Studies* 30: 1–12.

Garrison, M. (2000) 'The Franks as the New Israel', in Y. Hen and M. Innes (eds) *The Uses of the Past in the Early Middle Ages*, Cambridge: Cambridge University Press, 114–61.

Geary, P. (1983) 'Ethnic identity as a situational construct in the early middle ages', *Mitteilungen der Anthropologischen Gesellschaft in Wien* 113: 15–26.

Geary, P. (1988) *Before France and Germany: The Creation and Transformation of the Merovingi*, Oxford: Oxford University Press.

Geary, P. (1994) *Phantoms of Remembrance*, Princeton, N.J.: Princeton University Press.

Gelling, M. (1988) *Signposts to the Past: Place-names and the history of England*, 2nd edn, London: J. M. Dent & Sons Ltd.

Gelling, M. (1992) *The West Midlands in the Early Middle Ages*, London: Leicester University Press.

Gerould, G. H. (1927) 'King Arthur and politics', *Speculum* 2: 33–51.

Gibbon, E. (1776–88) *The Decline and Fall of the Roman Empire*, ed. J. B. Bury (1901), 8 vols, London: Methuen.

Gilbert, A. with Wilson, A. and Blackett, B. (1998) *The Holy Kingdom: The Quest for the Real King Arthur*, London: Bantam Press.

Gillies, W. (1981) 'Arthur in Gaelic tradition. Part I: folktales and ballads', *Cambridge Medieval Celtic Studies* 2: 47–72.

Gillies, W. (1982) 'Arthur in Gaelic tradition. Part II: romances and learned lore', *Cambridge Medieval Celtic Studies* 3: 41–75.

Gillingham, J. (1991) 'The context and purposes of Geoffrey of Monmouth's *History of the Kings of England*', *Anglo-Norman Studies* 13: 99–118.

Goffart, W. (1983) 'The supposedly "Frankish" Table of Nations: an edition and study', *Frühmittelalterliche Studien* 17: 98–130.

Goffart, W. (1988) *The Narrators of Barbarian History (AD 550–800)*, Princeton, N.J. and Guildford: Princeton University Press.

Goffart, W. (1990) 'The *Historia Ecclesiastica*: Bede's agenda and ours', *Haskins Society Journal* 2: 29–46.

Grabowski, K. and Dumville, D. (1984) *Chronicles and annals of medieval Ireland and Wales: the Clonmacnoise-group*, Woodbridge: Boydell Press.

Gray, H. L. (1915) *English Field Systems*, Cambridge, Mass.: Harvard University Press.

Green, J. R. (1877) *The History of the English People*, London: Macmillan.

Green, J. R. (1881) *The Making of England*, London: Macmillan.

Green, J. R. (1883) *The Conquest of England*, London: Macmillan.

Green, T. (1998) 'The historicity and historicisation of Arthur', <http://www.users.globalnet.co.uk/~tomgreen/arthur.html>.

Griscom, A. (1929) *The Historia Regum Britanniae of Geoffrey of Monmouth*, London: Longman, Green & Co.

Gruffydd, R. C. (1989–90) 'From Gododdin to Gwynedd: reflections on the story of Cunedda', *Studia Celtica* 24–5: 1–14.

Hamerow, H. (1994) 'Migration theory and the migration period', in B. Vyner (ed.) *Building on the Past: Papers Celebrating 150 Years of the Royal Archaeological Institute*, London: Royal Archaeological Institute, 163–77.

Hamerow, H. (1997) 'Migration theory and the Anglo-Saxon "identity crisis"', in J. Chapman and H. Hamerow (eds) *Migrations in Archaeological Explanations*, Oxford, *British Archaeological Reports* International Series 664, 33–44.

Hammer, J. (1946) *Les Sources de Geoffrey de Monmouth Historia Regum*, Brussels.

Handley, M. A. (2001) 'The origins of Christian commemoration in late antique Britain', *Early Medieval Europe* 10.2: 177–200.

Hanning, R. W. (1966) *The Vision of History in Early Britain*, New York and London: Columbia University Press.

Hargie, O., Saunders, C. and Dickinson, D. (1994) *Social Skills in Interpersonal Communication*, 3rd edn, London: Routledge.

Härke, H. (1997) 'Material culture as myth: weapons in Anglo-Saxon graves', in C. K. Jensen and K. H. Nielsen (eds) *Burial and Society: The Chronological and Social Analysis of Archaeological Data*, Oakhouse, Connecticut: Aarhus University Press.

Härke, H. (1998) 'Archaeologists and migrations. A problem of attitude?', *Current Anthropology* 39, 1: 19–45.

Haverfield, F. (1912) *The Romanization of Roman Britain*, 2nd edn, Oxford: Oxford University Press.

Hawkes, S. C. (1989) 'The South-East after the Romans: the Saxon settlement', in

V. A. Maxfield (ed.) *The Saxon Shore: a handbook*, Exeter: Exeter University Press Studies in History 25, 78–95.

Hay, D. (1950) *The Anglica historia of Polydore Vergil*, London: Camden Society 3rd Series, 74.

Hay, D. (1952) *Polydore Vergil: Renaissance Historian and Man of Letters*, Oxford: Clarendon Press.

Hearne, T. (ed.) (1727) *Adam de Domerham Historia de rebus gestis Glastoniensibus*, 2 vols, Oxford: Theatre Sheldon.

Hehir, B. O. (1988) 'What is the Gododdin?', in B. F. Roberts (ed.) *Early Welsh Poetry*, Aberystwyth: National Library of Wales.

Hen, Y. and Innes, M. (eds) (2000) *The Uses of the Past in the Early Middle Ages*, Cambridge: Cambridge University Press.

Henken, E. R. (1987) *Traditions of the Welsh Saints*, Cambridge: D. S. Brewer.

Hieatt, A. K. (1988) 'The passing of Arthur in Malory, Spenser and Shakespeare: the avoidance of closure', in C. Baswell and W. Sharpe (eds) *The Passing of Arthur: New Essays in Arthurian Tradition*, New York and London: Garland, 173–92.

Higham, N. J. (1986) *The Northern Counties to A.D. 1000*, Harlow: Longman.

Higham, N. J. (1991) 'Old light on the Dark Age landscape: the description of Britain in the *De Excidio Britanniae* of Gildas', *Journal of Historical Geography* 17: 363–72.

Higham, N. J. (1992a) *Rome, Britain and the Anglo-Saxons*, London: Seaby.

Higham, N. J (1992b) 'Medieval "overkingship" in Wales: the earliest evidence', *Welsh History Review* 16, 2: 145–59.

Higham, N. J. (1993a) *The Kingdom of Northumbria, AD350–1100*, Stroud: Alan Sutton.

Higham, N. J. (1993b) *The Origins of Cheshire*, Manchester: Manchester University Press.

Higham, N. J (1994) *The English Conquest: Gildas and Britain in the Fifth Century*, Manchester: Manchester University Press.

Higham, N. J. (1995) *An English Empire: Bede and the early Anglo-Saxon Kings*, Manchester: Manchester University Press.

Higham, N. J. (1997) *The Convert Kings: Power and religious affiliation in early Anglo-Saxon England*, Manchester: Manchester University Press.

Higham, N. J. (1998) 'The Saxon Conquests in Britain: literary evidence and the case for acculturation in the formation of Anglo-Saxon England', *Sonderdruck aus Studien zur Sachsenforschung* 11: 135–44.

Higham, N. J. (2001a) 'Britons in Northern England in the Early Middle Ages: through a thick glass darkly', *Northern History* 38.1: 5–25.

Higham, N. J. (2001b) 'Bancornaburg: Bangor-is-y-coed revisited', in N. J. Higham (ed) *Archaeology of the Roman Empire: A tribute to the life and works of Professor Barri Jones*, Oxford, *British Archaeological Reports* International Series 940, 311–18.

Hill, D. (1985) 'The construction of Offa's Dyke', *Antiquaries Journal* 65: 140–2.

Hill, D. (2000) 'Offa's Dyke: Pattern and Purpose', *Antiquaries Journal* 80: 195–206.

Hill, D. and Worthington, M. (eds) (forthcoming) *Æthelbald and Offa*.

Hines, J. (1984) *The Scandinavian Character of Anglian England in the pre-Viking Period*, Oxford: British Archaeological Reports, British Series 124.

Hines, J. (1990) 'Philology, archaeology and the *adventus Saxonum vel Anglorum*', in A. Bammesberger and A. Wollman (eds) *Britain 400–600: Language and History*, Heidelberg: Carl Winter, 17–36.

Hingeston, F. C. (ed.) (1858) *The Chronicle of England by John Capgrave*, London: Longman (Rolls Series).

Hobsbawm, E. and Ranger, T. (1983) *The Invention of Tradition*, Cambridge: Cambridge University Press.

Hodges, R. (1989) *The Anglo-Saxon Achievement*, London: Duckworth.

Hodgkin, R. H. (1935) *A History of the Anglo-Saxons*, 2 vols, Oxford: Oxford University Press.

Hogg, A. H. A. and King, D. J. C. (1963) 'Early castles in Wales and the Marches', *Archaeologia Cambrensis* 112: 77–124.

Hood, A. B. E. (ed.) (1978) *St Patrick, His Writings and Muirchu's Life*, London and Chichester: Phillimore.

Hopper, V. F. (1939) *Medieval Number Symbolism. Its Sources, Meaning and Influence on Thought and Expresson*, New York: Cooper Square Publishers.

Hosmer, J. K. (1890) *A Short History of Anglo-Saxon Freedom*, London.

Houwen, L. A. J. R. and MacDonald, A. A. (eds) (1996) *Bede Venerabilis: Historian, Monk and Northumbrian*, Groningen: E. Forsten.

Howlett, D. (1992) '*Orationes Moucani*: early Cambro-Latin prayers', *Cambridge Medieval Celtic Studies* 24: 55–74.

Howlett, D. (1998) *Cambro-Latin Compositions: Their Competence and Craftsmanship*, Dublin: Four Courts Press.

Hughes, K. (1973) 'The Welsh Latin chronicles; *Annales Cambriae* and related texts', *Proceedings of the British Academy* 59: 233–58.

Hughes, K. (1980) *Celtic Britain in the Early Middle Ages in Scottish and Welsh Sources*, Woodbridge: Boydell & Brewer.

Hughes, K. (1981) 'The Celtic Church: is this a valid concept', *Cambridge Medieval Celtic Studies* 1: 1–20.

Hume, D. (1754–62) *The History of England*. 6 vols, London: Longman, new edn 1848.

Hutchinson, J. and Smith, A. D. (eds) (1996) *Ethnicity*, Oxford: Oxford University Press.

Isaac, G. R. (1998) 'Gweith Gwen Ystrat and the northern heroic age of the sixth century', *Cambrian Medieval Celtic Studies* 36: 61–70.

Isaac, G. R. (1999) 'Readings in the history and transmission of the Gododdin', *Cambrian Medieval Celtic Studies* 37: 55–78.

Jackson, K. H. (1938) 'Nennius and the twenty-eight cities of Britain', *Antiquity* 12: 44–55.

Jackson, K. H. (1945) 'Once again Arthur's battles', *Modern Philology* 43: 44–57.

Jackson, K. H. (1949) 'Arthur's Battle of Breguoin', *Antiquity* 23: 48–9.

Jackson, K. H. (1953) *Language and History in Early Britain*, Edinburgh: Edinburgh University Press.

Jackson, K. H. (1959a) 'The Arthur of history', in R. S. Loomis (ed.) *Arthurian Literature in the Middle Ages*, Oxford: Clarendon Press, 1–11.

Jackson, K. H. (1959b) 'Arthur in early Welsh verse', in R. S. Loomis (ed.) *Arthurian Literature in the Middle Ages*, Oxford: Clarendon Press, 12–19.

Jackson, K. H. (1969) *The Gododdin: The Oldest Scottish Poem*, Edinburgh: Edinburgh University Press.

Jackson, K. H. (1982) 'Varia: II. Gildas and the names of the British princes', *Cambridge Medieval Celtic Studies* 3: 30–40.

James, E. (2001) *Britain in the First Millennium*, London: Arnold.

Jarman, A. O. H. (1960) *The Legend of Merlin*, Cardiff: University of Wales Press.

Jarman, A. O. H. (1978) 'Early stages in the development of the Myrddin legend', in R. Bromwich and R. Brinley Jones (eds) *Astudiaethau ar yr Hengerdd*, Cardiff: University of Wales Press, 326–49.

Jarman, A. O. H. (ed. and trans.) (1988) *Aneirin. Y Gododdin*, Llandysul: Gomer Press.

Jarman, A. O. H. (1989–90) 'The Arthurian allusions in the Book of Aneirin', *Studia Celtica* 24–5: 15–25.

Jarrett, M. G. (1983) 'Magnus Maximus and the end of Roman Britain', *Honourable Society of Cymmrodorion Transactions*, 22–35.

Jenkins, R. (1996) *Social Identity*, London: Routledge.

Jenkins, R. (1997) *Rethinking Ethnicity*, London: Sage Publications.

Jones, E. (1784) *Musical and Poetical Relicts of the Welsh Bards*, Llundain.

Jones, E. (1998) *The English Nation. The Great Myth*, Stroud: Sutton Publishing.

Jones, G. D. B. and Mattingly, D. (1990) *An Atlas of Roman Britain*, Oxford: Basil Blackwell.

Jones, M. (1986) *England Before Domesday*, London: Batsford.

Jones, M. E. (1996) *The End of Roman Britain*, Ithaca and London: Cornell University Press.

Jones, M. J. (1994) 'St Paul-in-the-Bail, Lincoln: Britain in Europe?', in K. Painter (ed.) *'Churches Built in Ancient Times': Recent Studies in Early Christian Archaeology*, London: Society of Antiquaries of London, 325–47.

Jones, M. J. (2001) 'Early Christian archaeology in Europe: some recent research', in N. J. Higham (ed.) *Archaeology of the Roman Empire. A tribute to the life and works of Professor Barri Jones*, Oxford, *British Archeological Reports* International Series 940, 319–34.

Jones, O., Williams, E. and Pughe, W. D. (eds) (1801–7) *Myvyrian Archaiology of Wales*, Denbigh: Thomas Gee.

Jones, S. (1997) *The Archaeology of Ethnicity*, London: Routledge.

Jones, T. (ed. and trans.) (1952) *Brut Y Tywysogyon or the Chronicle of the Princes*, Cardiff: University of Wales Press.

Jones, T. (1964) 'The early evolution of the legend of Arthur', *Nottingham Medieval Studies* 8: 3–21.

Jones, T. (ed. and trans.) (1971) *Brenhinedd Y Saesson or the Kings of the Saxons*, Cardiff: University of Wales Press.

Kay, S. (1997) 'Who was Chrétien de Troyes?', *Arthurian Literature* 15: 1–35.

Kemble, J. M. (1849) *The Saxons in England*, 2 vols, London: Longman, Brown, Green and Longmans.

Kendrick, T. D. (1950) *British Antiquity*, London: Methuen.

Keynes, S. (1990) 'Changing faces: Offa, King of Mercia', *History Today* 40.11: 14–19.

Keynes, S. (1995) 'England, 700–900', in R. McKitterick (ed.) *The New Cambridge Medieval History, II, 700–900*, Cambridge: Cambridge University Press, 18–42.

Keynes, S. and Lapidge, M. (eds and trans.) (1983) *Alfred the Great, Asser's Life of King Alfred and Other Contemporary Sources*, Harmondsworth: Penguin.

Kingsley, C. (1867) 'The Ancien Regime', in *The Works of Charles Kingsley. Vol. 17, Historical Lectures and Essays*, London: Macmillan, 1880, 135–234.

Kirby, D. P. (1966) 'Bede's native sources for the *Historia Ecclesiastica*', *Bulletin of the John Rylands Library* 48: 341–71.

Kirby, D. P. (1976) 'British dynastic history in the pre-Viking period', *Bulletin of the Board of Celtic Studies* 27: 81–114.

Kirby, D. P. (1976–7) 'Hywel Dda: Anglophil?', *Welsh History Review* 8: 1–13.

Kirby, D. P. (1977) 'Welsh bards and the border', in A. Dornier (ed.) *Mercian Studies*, Leicester: Leicester University Press, 31–42.

Kirby, D. P. (1979–80) 'King Ceolwulf of Northumbria and the *Historia Ecclesiastica*', *Studia Celtica* 14–15: 168–73.

Kirby, D. P. (1991) *The Earliest English Kings*, London: Unwin Hyman.

Kirby, D. P. and Williams, J. E. C. (1975–6) 'Review of *The Age of Arthur*, J. Morris', *Studia Celtica* 10–11: 454–86.

Knight, J. (1992) 'The early Christian Latin inscriptions in Britain and Gaul', in N. Edwards and A. Lane (eds), *The Early Church in Wales and the West*, Oxford: Oxbow, 45–50.

Knight, J. K. (1995) 'Penmachno revisited: the Consular Inscription and its context', *Cambrian Medieval Celtic Studies* 29: 1–10.

Knight, J. K. (1996) 'Seasoned in salt: Insular-Gaelic contacts in the early memorial stones and cross slabs', in K. R. Dark (ed.) *External Contacts and the Economy of Late Roman and Post-Roman Britain*, Woodbridge: Boydell Press, 109–20.

Knight, J. K. (1999) *The End of Antiquity*, Stroud: Tempus Publishing.

Knox, R. (1850) *The Races of Man, a Fragment*, London: H. Renshaw.

Koch, J. T. (1985–6) 'When was Welsh literature first written down?', *Studia Celtica* 20–1: 43–66.

Koch, J. T. (1996) 'The Celtic lands', in N. J. Lacy (ed.) *Medieval Arthurian Literature: A Guide to Recent Research*, New York: Garland Publishing, 239–322.

Koch, J. T. (1997) *The Gododdin of Aneirin. Text and Context from Dark-Age Northern Britain*, Cardiff: University of Wales Press.

Koebner, R. (1953) ' "The Imperial Crown of the Realm": Henry VIII, Constantine the Great and Polydore Vergil', *Bulletin of the Institute of Historical Research* 26: 29–53.

Lacy, N. J. *et al.* (1996) *The Arthurian Encyclopedia*, New York, Garland Publishing.

Lapidge, M. (1984) 'Gildas's education and the Latin culture of sub-Roman Britain', in M. Lapidge and D. Dumville (eds) *Gildas: New Approaches*, Woodbridge: Boydell & Brewer, 27–50.

Lapidge, M. and Dumville, D. (eds) (1984) *Gildas: New Approaches*, Woodbridge: Boydell & Brewer.

Lappenberg, J. M. (1845) *History of England under the Anglo-Saxon Kings*, trans. B. Thorpe, 2 vols, London: John Murray.

Leckie, R. W. (1981) *The Passage of Dominion: Geoffrey of Monmouth and the Periodization of Insular History in the Twelfth Century*, Toronto: University of Toronto Press.

Leeds, E. T. (1945) 'The distribution of the Angles and Saxons archaeologically considered', *Archaeologia* 19: 1–106.

Lewis, C., Mitchell-Fox, P. and Dyer, C. C. (1997) *Village, Hamlet and Field: Changing Medieval Settlements in Central England*, Manchester: Manchester University Press.

Leyland, J. (1535–43) *The Itinerary*, ed. L. T. Smith, 1964, 5 vols, London: Centaur Press.

Lindahl, C. (1998) 'Three ways of coming back: folklore perspectives on Arthur's return', in D. N. Mancoff (ed.) *King Arthur's Modern Return*, New York and London: Garland Publishing, 13–29.

Littleton, C. S. and Malcor, L. A. (1994) *From Scythia to Camelot: A Radical Reassessment of the Legends of King Arthur, the Knights of the Round Table and the Holy Grail*, New York, Garland Publishing.

Lloyd, J. E. (1911) *A History of Wales*, 2 vols, London: Longmans.

Loomis, C. G. (1933) 'King Arthur and the Saints', *Speculum* 8: 478–82.

Loomis, R. S. (1953) 'Edward I, Arthurian enthusiast', *Speculum* 28: 114–27.

Loomis, R. S. (ed.) (1959) *Arthurian Literature in the Middle Ages*, Oxford: Clarendon Press.

Lot, F. (1934) *Nennius et L'Histoire Brittonum, Étude Critique*, Paris: Librairie Ancienne Honoré Champion.

Loth, J. (1930) 'L'"*Historia Brittonum*" dite "de Nennius"', *Revue Celtique* 51: 1–31.

Loyon, A. (1960–70) *Sidonius Apollinaris Poèmes – Lettres*, 3 vols, Paris.

Mac Airt, S. and Mac Niocaill, G. (eds) (1983) *The Annals of Ulster to AD 1131: Part I: Text and Translation*, Dublin: Institute for Advanced Studies.

Macalister, R. A. S. (1922) 'Notes on some of the early Welsh inscriptions', *Archaeologia Cambrensis* 7.2: 198–219.

Macalister, R. A. S. (1928) 'The ancient inscriptions of Wales', *Archaeologia Cambrensis* 7.8: 285–315.

Macalister, R. A. S. (1935) contribution to 'Excursion Report', *Archaeologia Cambrensis* 90: 330–3.

Macalister, R. A. S. (1945) *Corpus Inscriptionum Insularum Celticarum*, Dublin: The Stationery Office.

Macaulay, C. (1763) *The History of England from the Accession of James I to that of the Brunswick Line*, 5 vols, London: J. Nourse.

Macaulay, T. B. (1848) *The History of England*, 4 vols, London.

MacCullough, J. A. (1911) *The Religion of the Ancient Celts*, Edinburgh: T. & T. Clark.

MacDougall, H. A. (1982) *Racial Myth in English History*, Montreal, Hanover New England and London: Harvest House.

Macnamara, N. C. (1900) *Origin and Character of the British People*, London: Smith, Elder & Co.

MacQueen, J. (1990) *St. Nynia*, Edinburgh: Polygon.

Maitland, F. W. (1897) *Domesday Book and Beyond: Three Essays in the Early History of England*, Cambridge: Cambridge University Press.

Malone, K. (1924) 'The historicity of Arthur', *The Journal of English and Germanic Philology* 23: 463–91.

Malone, K. (1925) 'Artorius', *Modern Philology* 22: 367–74.

Mancoff, D. N. (1990) *The Arthurian Revival in Victorian Art*, New York: Garland Publishing.

Mancoff, D. N. (ed.) (1998) *King Arthur's Modern Return*, New York and London: Garland Publishing.

Mandler, P. (2000) '"Race" and "nation" in mid-Victorian thought', in S. Collini, R. Whatmore and B. Young (eds) *History, Religion and Culture: British Intellectual History 1750–1950*, Cambridge: Cambridge University Press.

Martin, J. (1998) *Gramsci's Political Analysis: A critical introduction*, New York: St Martin's Press.

Marwick, A. (1998) *The Sixties: Cultural Revolution in Britain, France, Italy and the United States*, Oxford: Oxford Unversity Press.

Masefield, J. (1947) *Badon Parchments*, London: Heinemann.

Mattingly, D. (ed.) (1997) *Dialogues in Imperialism: Power, discourse and discrepant experience in the Roman Empire*, Portsmouth: *Journal of Roman Archaeology* Suppl. Vol. 23.

Maund, K. L. (1998) 'Dynastic segmentation and Gwynedd *c.* 950–*c.* 1000', *Studia Celtica* 32: 155–68.

Maund, K. L. (2000) *The Welsh Kings: The Medieval Rulers of Wales*, Stroud: Tempus.

Mawer, C. F. (1995) *Evidence for Christianity in Roman Britain. The Small Finds*, Oxford: *British Archaeological Reports* British Series 243.

McCann, W. J. (1991) 'The Welsh view of the Normans in the eleventh and twelfth centuries', *Honourable Society of Cymmroddorian Transactions*, 39–67.

McKee, H. (2000) 'Scribes and glosses from Dark Age Wales: the Cambridge Juvencus manuscript', *Cambrian Medieval Celtic Studies* 39: 1–22.

McKenna, M. (1984) 'The Breton literary tradition', *Celtica* 16: 35–51.

McKitterick, R. (1997) 'Constructing the past in the Early Middle Ages: the case of the Royal Frankish Annals', *Transactions of the Royal Historical Society* (6) 7: 101–30.

Megaw, R. and Megaw, V. (1997) 'Do the ancient Celts still exist? An essay on identity and contextuality', *Studia Celtica* 31: 107–23.

Metcalf, D. M. (ed.) (1987) *Coinage in Ninth-Century Northumbria*, Oxford, British Archaeological Reports British Series 180.

Miller, M. (1975a) 'Bede's use of Gildas', *English Historical Review* 90: 241–61.

Miller, M. (1975b) 'Historicity and the pedigree of the North Countrymen', *Bulletin of the Board of Celtic Studies* 26: 255–80.

Miller, M. (1975c) 'The commanders at Arthuret', *Cumberland and Westmorland Antiquarian and Archaeological Society Transactions* NS 75: 96–118.

Miller, M. (1975–6) 'Date-guessing and pedigrees', *Studia Celtica* 10–11: 96–109.

Miller, M. (1976–7) 'Starting to write history: Gildas, Bede and "Nennius"', *Welsh History Review* 8: 456–65.

Miller, M. (1977–8) 'Date-guessing and Dyfed', *Studia Celtica* 12–13: 33–61.

Miller, M. (1980) 'Consular years in the *Historia Brittonum*', *Bulletin of the Board of Celtic Studies* 29: 17–34.

Millett, M. (1990) *The Romanization of Britain*, Cambridge: Cambridge University Press.

Milton, J. (1639) *Britain under Trojan, Roman, Saxon Rule*, printed in *Kennet's England* (1719), reprinted 1870, London: Alex. Murray & Son.

Moffat, A. (1999) *Arthur and the Lost Kingdoms*, London: Weidenfeld & Nicholson.

Moisl, H. (1980–2) 'A sixth century reference to the British Bardd', *Bulletin of the Board of Celtic Studies* 29: 269–73.

Mommsen, T. (ed.) (1891–8) *Chronica Minora saec IV, V, VI, VII*, 3 vols, III, 111–222, Berlin: Weidmann.

Mommsen, T. (ed.) (1894) *Monumenta Germaniae Historica, Auctorum Antiquissimorum, xii, 1, De Excidio et Conquestu Brittaniae*. Berlin: Weidmann.

Morris, C. D. and Harry, R. (1997) 'Excavations on the Lower Terrace, Site C Tintagel Island 1990–94', *Antiquaries Journal* 77: 1–144.

Morris, J. (1973) *The Age of Arthur*, London, Weidenfeld & Nicolson.

Morris, J. (ed.) (1980) *Nennius, The British History and the Welsh Annals*, London and Chichester: Phillimore.

Murphy, G. (1953) *Duanaire Finn, III*, London: Irish Texts Society, 43.

Murphy, P. (1994) 'The Anglo-Saxon Landscape and rural economy: some results from sites in East Anglia and Essex', in J. Rackham (ed.) *Environment and Economy in Anglo-Saxon England*, York: Council for British Archaeology Research Report 89.

Mynors, R. A. B., Thomson, R. M. and Winterbottom, M. (eds) (1998) *William of Malmesbury Gesta Regum Anglorum*, Vol 1, Oxford: Clarendon Press.

Myres, J. N. L. (1969) *Anglo-Saxon Pottery and the Settlement of England*, Oxford: Clarendon Press.

Myres, J. N. L. (1986) *The English Settlements*, Oxford: Clarendon Press.

Mytum, H. (1992) *The Origins of Early Christian Ireland*, London: Routledge.

Nash-Williams, V. E. (1938) 'Some dated monuments of the "Dark Ages" in Wales', *Archaeologia Cambrensis* 93: 31–56.

Nash-Williams, V. E. (1950) *The Early Christian Monuments of Wales*, Cardiff: University of Wales Press.

Nastali, D. (1999) 'Arthur without fantasy: Dark Age Britain in recent historical fiction', *Arthuriana* 9: 5–22.

Nicholas, T. (1868) *The Pedigree of the English People*, London: C. Kegan Paul & Co.

Nickel, H. (1975) 'The dawn of chivalry', *Metropolitan Museum of Art Bulletin* 32: 150–2.

Noble, F. (1983) *Offa's Dyke Reviewed*, Oxford, *British Archaeological Reports* British Series 114.

Nowakowski, J. A. and Thomas, C. (1990) *Excavations at Tintagel Parish Churchyard, Cornwall, Spring 1990*, Truro: Cornwall Archaeological Unit.

Oergel, M. (1998) 'The redeeming Teuton: nineteenth-century notions of the "Germanic" in England and Wales', in G. Cubitt (ed.) *Imagining Nations*, Manchester: Manchester University Press, 75–91.

Ó hÓgáin, D. (1988) *Fionn mac Cumhaill: Images of the Gaelic Hero*, Dublin: Gill & Macmillan.

Ó hÓgáin, D. (1999) *The Sacred Isle: Belief and Religion in Pre-Christian Ireland*, Woodbridge and Cork: Boydell Press/Collins Press.

Oman, C. (1895) *History of England*, London: Edward Arnold.

O'Reilly, R. (1995) 'Introduction', in S. Connolly (ed. and trans.) *Bede: On the Temple*, Liverpool: Liverpool University Press, xvii–lv.

Ormrod, W. M. (1990) *The Reign of Edward III. Crown and Political Society in England 1327–1377*, New Haven and London: Yale University Press.

Orosius: *Orose Histoires (Contre Les Païens)*, ed. M.-P. Arnaud-Lindet (1990–1), Paris: Les Belles Lettres.

O'Sullivan, T. D. (1978) *The De Excidio of Gildas, its Authenticity and Date*, Leiden: E. J. Brill.

Owen, W. (1803) *A Dictionary of the Welsh Language*, Rhagymadrodd.

Padel, O. (1984) 'Geoffrey of Monmouth and Cornwall', *Cambridge Medieval Celtic Studies* 8: 1–28.

Padel, O. (1985) *Cornish Place Name Elements*, Nottingham: English Place Name Society.

Padel, O. (1994) 'The nature of Arthur', *Cambrian Medieval Celtic Studies* 27: 1–31.

Padel, O. (1995) 'Recent work on the origins of the Arthurian legend: a comment', *Arthuriana* 5.3: 103–14.

Padel, O. J. (1998) 'A new study of the *Gododdin*', *Cambrian Medieval Celtic Studies* 35: 45–55.

Padel, O. (2000) *Arthur in Medieval Welsh Literature*, Cardiff: University of Wales Press.

Parrins, M. J. (1996) 'Modern Arthurian scholarship', in N. J. Lacy (ed.) *The New Arthurian Encyclopedia*, New York and London: Garland Publishing, 402–11.

Parsons, D. (1997) 'British \*Caraticos, Old English Cerdic', *Cambrian Medieval Celtic Studies* 33: 1–8.

Palgrave, Sir F. (1837) *History of the Anglo-Saxons*, London: John Murray.

Patterson, L. (1987) *Negotiating the Past: The Historical Understanding of Medieval Literature*, Madison, Wisconsin: University of Wisconsin Press.

Peters, E. (ed.) (1974) *Paul the Deacon: History of the Lombards*, trans. W. D. Foulke, Philadelphia: University of Pennsylvania Press.

Phillips, G. and Keatman, M. (1993) *King Arthur: The True Story*, London: Arrow Edition.

Phythian-Adams, C. (1996) *Land of the Cumbrians. A study in British provinical origins A.D.400–1120*, Aldershot: Scolar Press.

Plummer, C. (1896) *Venerabilis Bedae opera Historica*, 2 vols, Oxford: Clarendon Press for Oxford University Press.

Pohl, W. (1998) 'Ethnicity in Early Medieval studies', in L. K. Little and B. H. Rosenwein (eds) *Debating the Middle Ages*, Oxford: Blackwell, 15–24.

Pohl, W. with Reimitz, H. (eds) (1998) *Strategies of Distinction: The Construction of Ethnic Communities, 300–800*, Leiden: Brill.

Price, C. A. (1984) *Henry Purcell and the London Stage*, Cambridge: Cambridge University Press.

Price, J. V. (1968) *David Hume*, New York: Twayne Publishers.

Price, Rev. T. (1829) *An Essay on the Physiognomy and Physiology of the Present Inhabitants of Britain with Reference to their Origin as Goths and Celts*, London: J. Rodwell.

Rahtz, P. (1993) *English Heritage Book of Glastonbury*, London: Batsford.

Ralegh Radford, C. A. (1952–3) 'Locus Maponi', *Transactions of the Dumfriesshire and Galloway Natural History and Antiquarian Society* 3rd Series, 31: 35–8.

Ralegh Radford, C. A. and Hemp, W. J. (1957) 'The Cross-Slab at Llanrhaiadr-ym-Mochnant', *Archaeologia Cambrensis* 56: 109–16.

Reid, H. (2001) *Arthur the Dragon King: The Barbarian Roots of Britain's Greatest Legends*, London: Headline.

Rhŷs, Sir J. (1891) *Studies in the Arthurian Legend*, Oxford: Clarendon Press.

Richards, M. (1969) *Welsh Administrative and Territorial Units*, Cardiff: University of Wales Press.

Ritson, J. (1825) *The Life of King Arthur*, London: Payne & Foss.

Rivet, A. L. F. and Smith, C. (1979) *The Place-Names of Roman Britain*, London: Batsford.

Roberts, R. J. (1991) 'John Dee and the matter of Britain', *Honourable Society of Cymmroddorion Transactions*: 129–44.

Robertson, A. J. (ed.) (1939) *Anglo-Saxon Charters*, Cambridge: Cambridge University Press.

Robertson, E. W. (1862) *Scotland under her Early Kings*, Edinburgh: Edmonston & Douglas.

Robertson, J. McK. (1897) *The Saxon and the Celt: A Study in Sociology*, 8 vols, London: University Press.

Rogers, P. (1971) 'Introduction', in P. Rogers (ed.) *Daniel Defoe, A Tour through the Whole Island of Great Britain*, Harmondsworth: Penguin, 9–34.

Ross, A. (1967) *Pagan Celtic Britain*, London: Routledge & Kegan Paul.

Round, J. H. (1895) *Feudal England. Historical Studies on the Eleventh and Twelfth Centuries*, London: S. Sonnenschein.

Rowland, J. (1983–4) 'The manuscript tradition of the Red Book *Englynion*', *Studia Celtica* 18–19: 79–95.

Rowland, J. (1990) *Early Welsh Saga Poetry: A Study and Edition of the Englynion*, Cambridge: Cambridge University Press.

Rowley, T. (ed.) (1981) *The Origins of Open Field Agriculture*, London: Croom Helm.

Rumble, A. R. (2001) 'Edward the Elder and the churches of Winchester and Wessex', in N. J. Higham and D. H. Hill (eds) *Edward the Elder, 899–924*, London: Routledge, 230–47.

Rutherford Davis, K. (1982) *Britons and Saxons: The Chiltern Region 400–700*, Chichester: Phillimore.

Salway, P. (1981) *Roman Britain*, Oxford: Oxford University Press.

Sawyer, P. H. (1968) *Anglo-Saxon Charters: An Annotated List and Bibliography*, London: Royal Historical Society.

Scharer, A. (1982) *Die angelsächsische Königsurkunde im 7. und 8. Jahrhundert*, Wien–Köln–Graz: Veröffentlichungen Des Instituts für Österreichische Geschichtsforschung Band XXVI, Herman Böhlaus Nachf.

Scharer, A. (1996) 'The writing of history at King Alfred's Court', *Early Medieval Europe* 5, 2: 177–206.

Scragg, D. and Weinberg, C. (eds) (2000) *Literary Appropriations of the Ango-Saxons from the Thirteenth to the Twentieth Century*, Cambridge: Cambridge University Press, Cambridge Studies in Anglo-Saxon England 29.

Scull, C. (1995) 'Approaches to material culture and social dynamics of the Migration Period in eastern England', in H. Hamerow and J. Bintliff (eds) *Europe Between Late Antiquity and the Middle Ages*, Oxford: British Archaeological Reports, International Series 617.

Seymour, M. with Couture, J. and Nielsen, K. (1998) 'Introduction: questioning the ethnic/civic dichotomy', in J. Couture, K. Nielsen and M. Seymour (eds) *Rethinking Nationalism*, Calgary, Alberta: University of Calgary Press, 1–61.

Seebohm, F. (1883) *The English Village Community*, London: Longmore, Green & Co.

Sellar, W. C. and Yeatman, R. J. (1930) *1066 and all that*, London: Methuen.

Shichtman, M. B. and Finke, L. A. (1993) 'Profiting from the past: history as symbolic capital in the *Historia Regum Britanniae*', *Arthurian Literature* 12: 1–36.

Shichtman, M. B. and Carley, J. P. (1994) 'Introduction: the social implications of the Arthurian legend', in M. B. Shichtman and J. P. Carley (eds) *Culture and the King: The Social Implications of the Arthurian Legends*, Albany: State University of New York Press, 4–12.

Shippey, T. A. (2000) 'The undeveloped image: Anglo-Saxon in popular consciousness from Turner to Tolkien', in D. Scragg and C. Weinberg (eds) *Literary Appropriations of the Anglo-Saxons from the Thirteenth to the Twentieth Century*, Cambridge: Cambridge University Press, Cambridge Studies in Anglo-Saxon England 29, 215–36.

Sims-Williams, P. (1983) 'Gildas and the Anglo-Saxons', *Cambridge Medieval Celtic Studies* 6: 1–30.

Sims-Williams, P. (1984) 'Gildas and vernacular poetry', in M. Lapidge and D. Dumville (eds) *Gildas: New Approaches*, Woodbridge: Boydell and Brewer.

Sims-Williams, P. (1990) *Religion and Literature in Western England 600–800*, Cambridge: Cambridge University Press.

Sims-Williams, P. (1991) 'The emergence of Old Welsh, Cornish and Breton orthography, 600–800: the evidence of Archaic Old Welsh', *Bulletin of the Board of Celtic Studies* 38: 20–86.

Sims-Williams, P. (1993) 'The provenance of the Llywarch Hen Poems: a case for Llan-gors, Brycheiniog', *Cambridge Medieval Celtic Studies* 26: 27–64.

Sims-Williams, P. (1994) 'Historical need and literary narrative: a caveat from ninth-century Wales', *Welsh History Review* 17: 1–40.

Sims-Williams, P. (1996) 'The Death of Urien', *Cambrian Medieval Celtic Studies* 32: 25–56.

Sims-Williams, P. (1998) 'The uses of writing in early medieval Wales', in H. Pryce (ed.) *Literacy in Medieval Celtic Societies*, Cambridge, Cambridge University Press.

Skene, W. (1868) *The Four Ancient Books of Wales*, Edinburgh: Edmonston & Douglas.

Skene, W. F. (1876) *Celtic Scotland: A History of Ancient Alban*, Edinburgh: Edmonston & Douglas.

Smith, A. D. (1999) *Myths and Memories of the Nation*, Oxford: Oxford University Press.

Smith, A. H. (1956) *English Place-Name Elements*, 2 parts, Cambridge: Cambridge University Press.

Smith, A. H. W. (1990) 'Gildas the poet', *Arthurian Literature* 10: 1–11.

Smith, J. C. (1909) *The Poetical Works of Edmund Spenser*, 3 vols, Oxford: Clarendon Press.

Smith, R. J. (1987) *The Gothic Bequest: Medieval Institutions in British Thought, 1688–1863*, Cambridge: Cambridge University Press.

Smyth, A. P. (1998) 'The emergence of English identity, 700–1000', in A. P. Smyth (ed.) *Medieval Europeans*, Basingstoke: Macmillan, 24–52.

Snyder, C. (1998) *An Age of Tyrants: Britain and the Britons A.D. 400–600*, Pennsylvania: Pennsylvania State University Press.

Snyder, C. (2000) *Exploring the World of King Arthur*, London: Thames & Hudson.

Spiegel, G. (1997) *The Past as Text: The Theory and Practice of Medieval Historiography*, Baltimore and London: Johns Hopkins University Press.

Stancliffe, C. (1999) 'The British Church and the mission of Augustine', in R. Gameson (ed.) *St. Augustine and the Conversion of England*, Stroud: Sutton Publishing, 107–51.

Steensma, R. C. (1970) *Sir William Temple*, New York: Twayne Publishers.

Stenton, F. M. (1943) *Anglo-Saxon England*, Oxford: Oxford University Press.

Stevenson, J. (ed.) (1838) *Nennii Historia Brittonum*, London.

Stevenson, J. (ed.) (1875) *Radulphi de Coggeshall Chronicon Anglicanum*, London: Longman (Rolls Series).

Stevenson, W. H. (1904) *Asser's Life of King Alfred*, Oxford: Oxford University Press.

Stuart-Glennie, J. S. (1869) *Arthurian Localities: Their historical origin, chief country, and Fingalian Relations: with a map of Arthurian Scotland*, Edinburgh: Edmonston & Douglas.

Stubbs, W. (1870) *Select Charters and other illustrations of English Constitutional History*, Oxford: Clarendon Press.

Stubbs, W. (1882) *Chronicles of the Reigns of Edward I and Edward II*, 2 vols, London: Longmans (Rolls Series).

Stukeley, W. (1724) *Itinerarium Curiosum*, London.

Summers, M. (ed.) (1931–2) *John Dryden: The Dramatic Works*, Vol. 6, London: Nonesuch.

Suzuki, S. (2000) *The Quoit Brooch Style and Anglo-Saxon Settlement*, Woodbridge: Boydell Press.

Tatlock, J. S. P. (1933) 'The English journey of the Laon Canons', *Speculum* 8: 454–65.

Tatlock, J. S. P. (1939) 'The dates of the Arthurian Saints' Legends', *Speculum* 14.3: 345–65.

Tatlock, J. S. P. (1950) *The Legendary History of Britain*, New York: Gordian Press.

Taylor, C. C. (1983) *Village and Farmstead*, London: George Philip.

Temple, Sir W. (1672) *An Essay upon the Origin and Nature of Government*, reprinted by the Augustan Reprint Society 109 (1964).

Thacker, A. (1985) 'Kings, saints and monasteries in pre-Viking Mercia', *Midland History* 10: 1–25.

Thacker, A. (2000) '*Peculiaris Patronus Nostrem*: the saint as patron of the state in the Early Middle Ages', in J. Maddicott and D. Palliser (eds) *The Medieval State: Essays Presented to James Campbell*, London: Hambledown Press, 1–24.

Thirsk, J. (1964) 'The commonfields', *Past and Present* 29: 1–25.

Thomas, A. C. (1971) *The Early Christian Archaeology of North Britain*, Oxford: Oxford University Press.

Thomas, A. C. (1981) *Christianity in Roman Britain*, London: Batsford.

Thomas, C. (ed.) (1988) *Tintagel Papers*, Cornish Studies Special Issue 16, Redruth.

Thomas, C. (1991–2) 'The Early Christian inscriptions of southern Scotland', *Glasgow Archaeological Journal* 17: 1–10.

Thomas, C. (1994) *And Shall These Mute Stones Speak? Post-Roman Inscriptions in Western Britain*, Cardiff: University of Wales Press.

Thomas, C. (1998) *Christian Celts: Messages and Images*, Stroud: Tempus Publishing Limited.

Thomas, G. C. G. (1968–70) 'Dryll o Hen Lyfr Ysgrifen', *Bulletin of the Board of Celtic Studies* 23: 309–16.

Thompson, E. A. (1979) 'Gildas and the history of Britain', *Britannia* 10: 203–26.

Thompson, E. A. (1984) *Saint Germanus of Auxerre and the End of Roman Britain*, Woodbridge: Boydell Press.

Thomson, R. M. (1999) *William of Malmesbury Gesta Regum Anglorum II General Introduction and Commentary*, Oxford: Clarendon Press.

Thorpe, L. (ed. and trans.) (1966) *The History of the Kings of Britain*, Harmondsworth: Penguin.

Thorpe, L. (ed. and trans.) (1978) *Gerald of Wales: Description of Wales*, Harmondsworth: Penguin.

Tolkien, J. R. R. (1954–5) *The Lord of the Rings*, 3 vols, London: George Allen and Unwin.

Trevelyan, G. M. (1926) *History of England*, London: Longmans, Green & Co.

Tristram, H. L. C. (1999) 'Bedas *Historia ecclesiastica gentis anglorum* im Altenglischen und Altirischen', in E. Poppe and H. L. C. Tristram (eds) *Übersetzung, Adaptation und Akkulturation im insularen Mittelalter*, Münster: Nodus Publikationen, 51–72.

Trompf, G. W. (2000) *Early Christian Historiography: Narratives of Retribution*, London: Continuum.

Turner, S. (1799–1805) *History of the Anglo-Saxons*, 3 vols, London.

Twain, M. (1889) *A Connecticut Yankee at the Court of King Arthur*, New York: Webster.

Umland, R. (1994) 'The snake in the woodpile: Tennyson's Vivien as Victorian prostitute', in M. B. Shichtman and J. P. Carley (eds) *Culture and the King*, Albany: State University of New York Press, 274–87.

Vale, J. (1982) *Edward III and Chivalry*, Woodbridge: Boydell & Brewer.

Van Hamel, A. G. (1934) 'Aspects of Celtic mythology', *Proceedings of the British Academy* 20: 207–48.

Vernon, J. (1998) 'Border crossings: Cornwall and the English (imagi)nation', in G. Cubitt (ed.) *Imagining Nations*, Manchester: Manchester University Press, 153–72.

Vinogradoff, P. (1892) *Villainage in England*, Oxford: Clarendon Press.

Wade-Evans, A. W. (1944) *Vitae Sanctorum Britanniae et Genealogiae*, Cardiff: University of Wales Press Board.

Wade-Evans, A. W. (1956) *The Emergence of England and Wales*, Wetteren: De Meester.

Waitz, G. and Kehr, K. A. (eds) (1904) *Widukindi Monachi Corbeiensis Rerum Gestarum Saxonicarum Libri Tres*, Hannover and Leipzig: Impensis Bibliopoli Hahniani.

Walker, I. W. (2000) *Mercia and the Making of England*, Stroud: Sutton.

Warren, M. R. (2000) *History on the Edge: Excalibur and the Borders of Britain, 1100–1300*, Minneapolis and London: University of Minnesota Press.

Warwicke, R. M. (1979) 'The Laurence Nowell Manuscripts in the British Library', *British Library Journal* 5: 201–12.

White, H, (1973) *Metahistory*, Baltimore: Johns Hopkins University Press.

White, H. (1978) *Tropics of Discourse*, Baltimore: Johns Hopkins University Press.

White, R. (1978) 'New light on the origins of the Kingdom of Gwynedd', in R. Bromwich and R. B. Jones (eds) *Astudiaethau ar yr Hengerdd*, Cardiff: University of Wales Press, 350–5.

White, R. (1997) *King Arthur in Legend and History*, London: J. M. Dent.

Whitelock, D. (1952) *The Beginnings of English Society*, Harmondsworth: Penguin.

Whitelock, D. (ed.) (1955) *English Historical Documents c. 500–1042*, Vol. 1, London: Eyre & Spottiswoode.

Whittaker, C. R. (1994) *Frontiers of the Roman Empire: A Social and Economic Study*, Baltimore and London: Johns Hopkins University Press.

William of Newburgh (c. 1197) *The History of English Affairs*, ed. and trans. P. G. Walsh and M. J. Kennedy, Warminster: Aris & Phillips Ltd, 1988.

Williams, H. (1899) *The Ruin of Britain together with the Lorica of Gildas*, London: D. Nutt for the Honourable Society of Cymmroddorion.

Williams, I. (1932) 'The Poems of Llywarch Hen', *Proceedings of the British Academy* 18: 269–302.

Williams, I. (1935) 'Hengerdd', *Bulletin of the Board of Celtic Studies* 7: 23–32.

Williams, I. (1938) *Canu Aneirin*, Caedydd: Gwasg Prifysgol Cymru.

Williams, I. (1972a) *The Beginnings of Welsh Poetry*, ed. R. Bromwich, Cardiff: University of Wales Press.

Williams, I. (ed.) (1972b) *Armes Prydein. The Prophecy of Britain* with a translation by R. Bromwich, Dublin: Dublin Institute for Advanced Studies.

Williams, N. J. A. (1978) '*Canu Llywarch Hen* and the Finn Cycle', in R. Bromwich and R. B. Jones (eds), *Astudiaethau ar yr Hengerdd*, Cardiff: University of Wales Press, 234–65.

Wilson, D. (1987) 'Bateman, Carrington and the Anglians in the Peak District', in P. Morgan (ed.) *Staffordshire Studies: Essays Presented to Denis Stuart*, Keele: University of Keele Department of Adult & Continuing Education.

Winterbottom, M. (ed.) (1978) *Gildas: The Ruin of Britain and other documents*, London: Phillimore.

Wiseman, H. (2000) 'The derivation of the date of the Badon entry in the *Annales Cambriae* from Bede and Gildas', *Parergon* NS 17.2: 1–10.

Wood, I. (1987) 'The fall of the Western Empire and the end of Roman Britain', *Britannia* 18: 251–62.

Wood, M. (1999) *In Search of England*, London: Viking.

Woodbridge, H. E. (1940) *Sir William Temple: The man and his work*, New York and London: Modern Language Association and Oxford University Press.

Wooding, J. M. (1996) 'Cargoes in trade along the Western seaboard', in K. R. Dark (ed.) *External Contacts and the Economy of Late Roman and Post-Roman Britain*, Woodbridge: Boydell Press, 67–82.

Wormald, J. (1992) 'The creation of Britain: multiple kingdoms or core and colonies?', *Transactions of the Royal Historical Society* (6) 2: 175–94.

Wormald, P. (1978) 'Bede, Beowulf and the conversion of the Anglo-Saxon aristocracy', in R. J. Farrell (ed.) *Bede and Anglo-Saxon England*, Oxford: *British Archeolgoical Reports* British Series 46, 32–95.

Wormald, P. (1982) 'The age of Bede and Æthelbald', in J. Campbell (ed.), *The Anglo-Saxons*, Oxford: Phaidon Press, 70–100.

Wormald, P. (1983) 'Bede, the *Bretwaldas* and the origins of the *gens Anglorum*', in P. Wormald *et al.* (eds) *Ideal and Reality in Frankish and Anglo-Saxon Society*, Oxford: Oxford University Press, 99–129.

Wormald, P. (1995) 'The making of England', *History Today* 45.2: 26–32.

Wright, N. (ed.) (1985–) *The Historia Regum Britanniae of Geoffrey of Monmouth*, Cambridge: D. S. Brewer.

Wright, N. (1985) 'Did Gildas read Orosius', *Cambridge Medieval Celtic Studies* 9: 31–42.

Wright, N. (1986) 'Geoffrey of Monmouth and Bede', *Arthurian Literature* 6: 27–59.

Wright, R. P. and Jackson, K. (1968) 'A late inscription from Wroxeter', *Antiquaries Journal* 48: 269–300.

Wright, T. (ed.) (1866) *The Chronicle of Pierre de Langtoft*, 2 vols, London: Longmans (Rolls Series).

Wright, T. (1875) *The Celt, the Roman and the Saxon: a history of the early inhabitants of Britain*, 3rd edn, London: Trübner.

Yalden, D. (1999) *The History of British Mammals*, London: Academic Press.

Yorke, B. (1993) 'Fact or fiction? The written evidence for the fifth and sixth centuries A.D.', *Anglo-Saxon Studies in Archaeology and History* 6: 45–50.

Zimmer, U. (1896) *Nennius Vindicatus*, Berlin.

# INDEX

—— ◆ ——